ARCHITECTURAL
DRAWING
AND
PLANNING

WILLIAM T. GOODBAN

JACK J. HAYSLETT
American Institute of Architects

ARCHITECTURAL DRAWING AND PLANNING

Second Edition

McGRAW-HILL BOOK COMPANY

*New York   San Francisco   St. Louis   Düsseldorf   Johannesburg
Kuala Lumpur   London   Mexico   Montreal   New Delhi
Panama   Rio de Janeiro   Singapore   Sydney   Toronto*

The book was set in Fototronic Bulmer by York Graphic Services, Inc., and printed and bound by Levison McNally Company. The designer was Janet Bollow. The editors were Cary F. Baker, Jr. and Charles A. Goehring. Charles A. Goehring also supervised production.

ARCHITECTURAL DRAWING AND PLANNING

Printed in the United States of America.

Library of Congress catalog card number: 79-179883

8 9 10 11 12 13 14 HDHD 7 8 3 2 1 0 9 8

CONTENTS

PREFACE

A knowledge of drafting techniques and their relation to the process of architectural design is required by all architects and draftsmen. Most architects spend time at the drawing board, and all competent draftsmen understand the importance of their jobs in the overall function of architecture. At the beginning of their training, the needs and interests of both types of students are similar. This book is designed to orient the beginner to the art, science, and business of architecture, and to develop communication, the primary purpose and skill of drafting. Our aim is to demonstrate the logical processes that occur between the conception and the realization of a structure. The book will be equally useful to both the future architect and draftsman. Members of other trades and occupations will also profit greatly from the use of the book: carpenters and other building tradesmen, building supply salesmen and clerks, city and county building department employees, realtors, and others who must know about structures.

The functional objective of the book is to develop, by the following means, the student's ability to communicate, through the use of pictorial and verbal concepts, with all parties concerned in the building of a structure:

1. Definition and demonstration of the vocabulary, symbols, and conventions of architectural drafting.
2. Explanation of the functions and relationships

of all parties involved in a building project—client, lender, designer, draftsman, building inspector, and builder.

3. Presentation of a logical procedure for developing a set of working drawings from design through drafting.

4. Emphasis on the relationships between drawings to demonstrate that the student is working on a "set" of drawings.

5. Use of short chapters, each concerned with a logical step in the process or with a certain drawing; for quick, easy reference.

6. Display of two complete sets of working drawings, one residential and one commercial, each keyed to the text in all chapters. Each drawing is complete; each residential drawing includes at least one full-sized extract to demonstrate the character of professional drafting.

7. Emphasis on the use of freehand sketching and perspective at all stages of planning and drafting.

8. Presentation of three sets of student problems, varying only in degree of difficulty at the planning stage.

9. Encouragement of the student to investigate his own community for resources related to the work of architectural drafting and building.

10. Use of a residence to demonstrate the procedures of the book. Even though residential work is not representative of most architectural practice, it provides problems familiar and interesting to the beginning student.

11. Reproduction of illustrations from actual penciled drawings on vellum to represent accurately the appearance of professional drafting.

There are many things this book is not intended to be or do. They are listed below, with our reasons for them:

1. Neither this book nor any other can be a complete drafting program. A complete course entails more semester units of course work, volumes of references, and several instructors. We have resisted the suggestions of reviewers whose recommendations, had all been taken, would have resulted in an encyclopedia.

2. This book is not an engineering treatise. The work of structural, electrical, and other engineering consultants is shown in context with the process of architectural design. Tabular data provided are adequate for the design of simple structures. Of course, the mere use of tabular data does not constitute engineering and would be risky in a real situation. The tables do, however, provide the data needed by the draftsman for sizes and notations.

3. The book is not a complete work on perspective drawing or rendering. Because the results achieved by all methods of perspective projection are almost indistinguishable, we chose the simplest method, since any geometrical object can be constructed in perspective, point by point, by this means. Rendering techniques are so personal that we have presented only one style and have discussed only general methods of achieving realism and depth. The techniques develop from individual talent and the knowledge and appreciations acquired in art courses.

Every effort has been made to minimize a regional bias. Such a bias is difficult to avoid; any knowledgeable person can look at the structures in the illustrations and make an accurate guess as to their location. Unfortunately, it is impossible to illustrate every type of regional building and architecture. It is the instructor's responsibility to explain to his students how their drawings *must* differ from those in the book.

We recommend that each student seek an adult client for whom to design and draft a house. This device will be useful to most students, as it provides a reservoir of adult experience and presents a lifelike problem. For those unable to find a client, or in situations where the instructor does not wish to use that device; provision is made in the planning stage of the student problems either to provide a client or to eliminate him altogether in order to concentrate solely on drafting technique. In any case, the student can proceed with his project at his own level. After the planning is completed, the student problems are all the same—namely, the production of working drawings.

Architectural design as defined in this book refers to the functional planning of space and structure, not to architectural styles, periods, or appearance. The principal reason for this emphasis is that simplicity and function alone often constitute good structural design. In addition, such factors as the student's background, local practices, the great scope of the subject, and the principal objectives of the book argue against the addition of a section on architectural styles. Such decisions must be based on the student's or instructor's judgment.

Because architectural drafting is highly specialized and because the book is intended for use at the technical institute or junior-college level, it is assumed that the student who uses the book will already have completed a basic course in drafting. This seems to be a reasonable prerequisite, since all technically trained students are required to take a course in beginning drafting.

Our aim of writing a nationally usable book accounts for the liberal use of the words *generally, usually, commonly, local practice, see local building codes,* and *and so on.* While this gives the teacher the responsibility for defining the meanings of these terms, it also gives him the opportunity to acquaint the student with local problems, regulations, and practices.

We feel that any student using the book should have access to the following references or their equivalent:

1. "Architectural Graphic Standards" (Wiley) or "Time-Saver Standards" (McGraw-Hill)
2. A local building code
3. Sweet's Architectural File or a personal collection of manufacturers' literature

William T. Goodban
Jack J. Hayslett

NOTE TO THE USER

"Architectural Drawing and Planning" is a basic text to be supplemented by additional references and classroom instruction. Depending upon his background and methods, each instructor will use the book in a slightly different manner. Even if you plan to study the book outside of school, we feel that you can gain from it a good understanding of architectural-drafting methods and standards. Many of the references cited are available in most libraries, and others in print are equally good. In place of the teacher, we offer some advice for using the book which will help it serve you better.

First read the Contents and Preface, skim through the text, and look at the illustrations to get an idea of what is in store for you. This is a good first step with any text. When you're ready to start drawing, start at the beginning of the book with pencil and paper in hand. Sketch as you read; it will clear up many important points. When you encounter references to subjects which are more fully covered later in the book, mark your place and skip ahead to the chapters indicated. Before starting any drawing, study the vocabulary and symbols which apply; you will go faster this way. When working on any particular drawing, first make freehand sketches of what you intend to do. This will eliminate much erasing and redrawing. Use the Review Questions and Study Suggestions at the ends of the chapters. They should extend your knowledge and help you apply the material you have studied.

NOTES ON
THE SECOND EDITION

After five years' use of the book we have found several areas which could be improved; and other people; whose opinions we value, agreed. In view of our experience with the first edition, we have made several additions, changes, and a few deletions, which we know will make the book more useful. These are the most important:

1. In the area of basic skills we have added a section on mechanical perspective and a small amount of material on lettering.
2. There is a short section on the relationship of a draftsman in a small office to his employers.
3. A different and more complete set of drawings is used in this edition to demonstrate commercial buildings.
4. A student problem has been added to most chapters. These are intended to keep the student's efforts in line with the book's objective—a complete, integrated set of sketches and working drawings of his concept.
5. We have added more detailed information on methods and devices for manipulating floor plans to fit varying conditions. This practice is hardly architecture, but it is widely practiced and very useful to draftsmen.
6. We have included information on building materials designed to introduce the student to the general criteria for choosing materials.

7. A discussion of sources and references useful to the draftsman has been added.

8. We have included a chapter on building codes and restrictions.

9. More explicit instruction is given in many small areas, particularly in the methods of developing the planes and intersections of the common types of roofs.

10. More emphasis is placed on the necessity of filing and retrieving detailed information at all stages of planning and drafting.

11. We have added information concerning the problems of designing split-level structures.

12. The method of taking earth sections to design sections and foundation details has been described.

13. We have given examples of drafting done in other areas of the country to illustrate the effects of local conditions and techniques on the drawings.

14. We have arranged the chapters in a more logical manner:

   a. Basic skills
   b. Planning
   c. Architectural drawings
   d. Structural drawings
   e. Mechanical drawings
   f. Specifications

CHAPTER 1
BASIC SKILLS
AND TERMINOLOGY

REQUIREMENTS

The student interested in architectural drawing must have a certain background of knowledge and skills. He should have a fair degree of artistic ability; he must understand orthographic projection thoroughly; he should have good study habits and the ability to use simple research procedures. These few factors are essential. Skill in freehand perspective drawing, in addition, is an asset.

MATERIALS

Freehand sketching is the best means of capturing and developing ideas in the planning stage of an architec-

tural project. The principles are simple, and only a few basic tools and materials are needed. In fact, paper, a soft pencil, and an eraser are enough equipment for the beginner.

Any inexpensive paper is suitable for practice sketching. Some students like unlined binder paper; all the sheets are the same size, and it is easy to organize and keep track of information in a binder. It is best to use fairly transparent paper; the best parts of previous sketches can be traced and improved upon without the need of tedious measuring. Architects and draftsmen use large rolls of cheap transparent paper and tear it off as needed. Use a soft 2B to 6B pencil. A soft pencil encourages freedom of line, and the marks are easy to erase. Use a big, soft eraser; the first idea is usually not the best one.

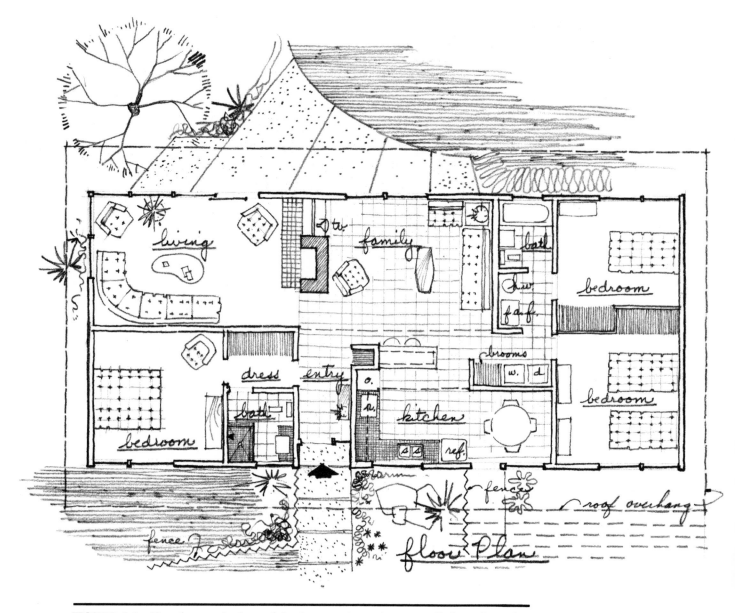

FIGURE 1-1   Use of trees, shrubs, and furniture to give scale to a preliminary floor plan

METHODS

Good freehand sketching looks freehand. Do not try to duplicate mechanical drawing in sketches. At the start, too much precision in drawing wastes time. More accurate measurement and more careful drawing can be used after a general scheme has been decided on. A few suggestions follow:

1. Use a free arm motion with the pencil, not a cramped finger stroke.

2. Do not try to make all corners and line intersections precise; let them cross occasionally.

3. Sketchy, multiple lines are sometimes more effective than a single line.

4. Make the sketches fairly large; small drawings are hard to read. As a guide, no more than two rough floor plans should be drawn on one side of a sheet of 8½- by 11-in. binder paper.

5. Be careful of proportions, but do not worry about actual measurements. If the drawing is in proportion, size is unimportant at this stage.

6. Label everything! A week-old drawing without notes will mean very little, even to the person who drew it.

7. Avoid small detail in rough sketches. The overall effect is most important, particularly in pictorial drawings. Use plan views of trees, shrubs, furniture, automobiles on floor plans and plot plans to give an effect of scale (see Fig. 1-1).

8. Use simplified human figures, trees, shrubs, and automobiles on elevations and pictorial drawings to give scale, depth, and a natural effect (see Fig. 1-2).

9. Try to copy the sketching style of some professional delineator. Few students can develop a distinctive style in a short time (see Bibliography).

10. Learn the standard symbols required for each type of drawing before starting on it.

11. Avoid paints, colored pencils, and crayons at first. They are unsatisfactory unless you have a good background in their use.

12. Practice sketching in any spare time you have. "Practice makes perfect" may sound trite, but it is true.

When more accuracy in a sketch is required, two easy means of achieving it are available. First, the use of a grid placed behind transparent sketch paper provides accurate guides. Second, prints can be made on blue-lined grid tracing paper, and the grid lines will not show. This tracing paper is especially useful for working out floor plans at scale size. The grids are made for orthographic and pictorial drawings.

APPROXIMATE PERSPECTIVE

A working knowledge of perspective drawing is necessary to show what a proposed building might look like when finished. Approximate perspective is accurate enough for preliminary studies even when done by an amateur, and in the hands of an expert it may be used for presentation drawings. The best way to learn is to read the following text and look at the illustrations with a pencil and paper in hand and to follow the instructions by sketching while reading.

Two-point perspective is most often used. One- and three-point perspectives will not be described (see Fig. 1-3). The method of drawing two-point perspective described here is not the only method, but it is simple. The finished drawings will be very similar to those drawn by other methods.

Learn to use approximate perspective well before attempting mechanical perspective. Once you get the "feel" of using approximate perspective, all that remains to be learned in the mechanical method is the relatively simple process of finding vanishing points and determining perspective distances.

DEFINITIONS

Definitions of perspective terms (see Fig. 1-4):

1. *Horizon:* The eye level of the person viewing the drawing. Place it below the ground line for a worm's-eye view; place it above for a bird's-eye

FIGURE 1-2 Use of trees, cars, and people to lend realism and scale to a preliminary elevation

3

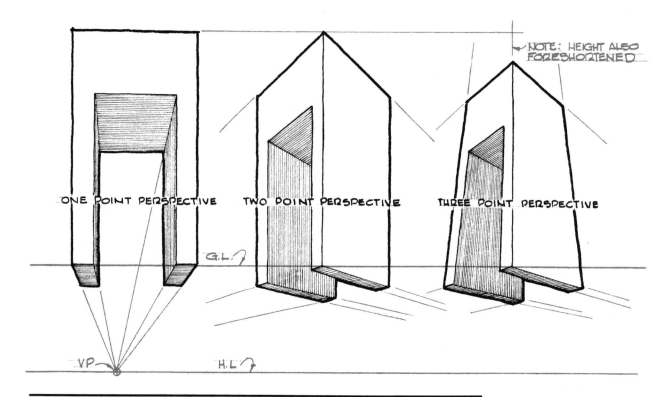

FIGURE 1-3 Appearance of an object drawn in one-, two-, and three-point perspective

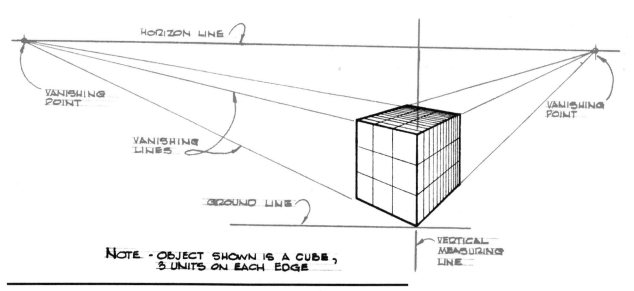

FIGURE 1-4 Definitions of terms as used in approximate perspective drawing

view; place it near the ground line for a normal view.

2. *Ground line:* The bottom of the object being drawn. Place it below the horizon for a bird's-eye view; place it near the horizon for a normal view; place it above for a worm's-eye view.

3. *Vertical measuring line:* The part of the object closest to the person viewing the object. It is also the line on which heights are measured. Place it to the left to see more of the right side of the object, to the right to see more of the left side. Vertical distances may be measured or estimated by a uniform scale.

4. *Vanishing points:* The points on the horizon where parallel horizontal lines converge. Place them far apart for a distant perspective; place them close together for a closer view.

5. *Vanishing lines:* Horizontal lines of the object which converge on the vanishing points. The nearest foot (starting at the vertical measuring line) is longer than the next foot behind it, and so on. When the vanishing points are far apart, the distances diminish slowly as they approach the vanishing points; when they are close together, distances diminish rapidly (Fig. 1-5).

PROCEDURE

A bird's-eye view is easiest when you are learning to draw a perspective. The procedure follows (Fig. 1-6):

1. Establish the horizon line as desired. A straightedge may be used for drawing long lines.
2. Mark the vanishing points.
3. Establish the ground line of the object.
4. Establish the vertical measuring line.
5. Lay off on the vertical measuring line the estimated total height of the object.
6. Lay off on the vanishing lines the estimated total width and depth of the object. Remember that if the vertical measuring line is off-center to the right, a given distance on the right of the object will be apparently shorter than the same distance on the left, and vice versa. In any case, a given distance in a horizontal direction will always appear smaller than the same distance on the vertical measuring line. To estimate horizontal distances in

either direction, lay off the estimated total length of that side between the vanishing lines. Draw lines from opposite corners of this four-sided figure. The intersection will always be in the perspective center of the area. Draw a vertical line through the intersection. This process may be repeated as often as desired, and the space will always be divided in half. These points may then be used as a basis for estimating any desired distance (Fig. 1-7).

7. Steps 5 and 6 will form a box exactly large enough to contain the whole object. From this point on, "cut out" the shape of the object, using the methods in step 6 for estimating distance. Cut out only large masses; estimate most detail by eye. After a little practice it will be easy to estimate practically every dimension (Fig. 1-8).

8. When the shape of the object, in this case a house, is finished, erase unnecessary lines, sketch in trees, shrubbery, people, and so on, and strengthen the essential lines (Fig. 1-9). Letter in desired notes and title to finish sketch.

SHORTCUTS

Two simple methods which will speed up the construction of perspective sketches follow. First is the *rubber-band perspective board.* Simply drive a short nail in at each vanishing point on the drawing board and tie a piece of strong rubber band between them. To draw a vanishing line, pull the band tight; it will act as a rigid straightedge. Pull it in the other direction for a line to the opposite vanishing point. All other instructions regarding perspective drawing should be followed. Second, *perspective grid forms,* based on several distances and angles of view, are available. These grids, when used properly, enable one to produce mechanically correct drawings.

TO INCREASE EFFECT OF DEPTH

Some visual devices which will strengthen the feeling of perspective are (Fig. 1-10):

1. The use of overlapping planes, such as fences and trees. Any object or plane, regardless of size, which overlaps another object or plane is naturally the closest to the viewer.

5

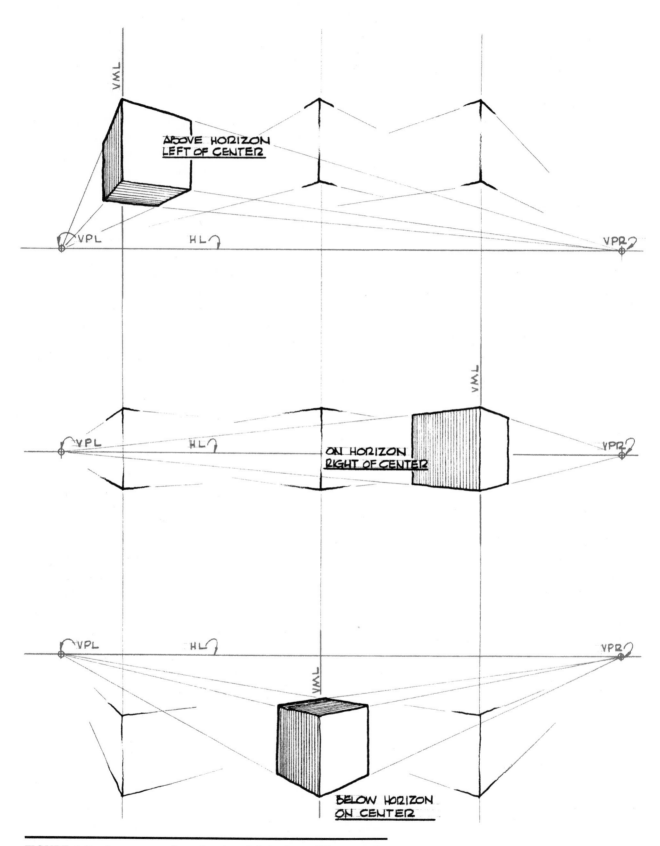

FIGURE 1-5 Appearance of a cube viewed from three different angles

6

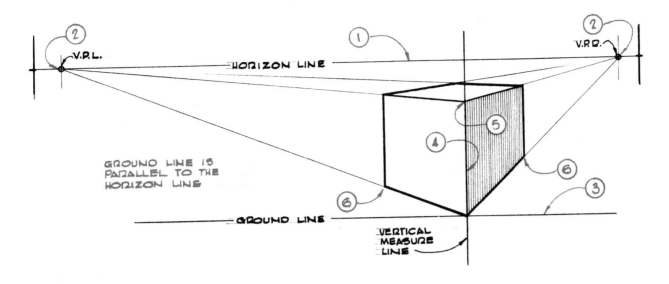

FIGURE 1-6 Procedure in drawing a perspective block (circled numbers agree with outline in text)

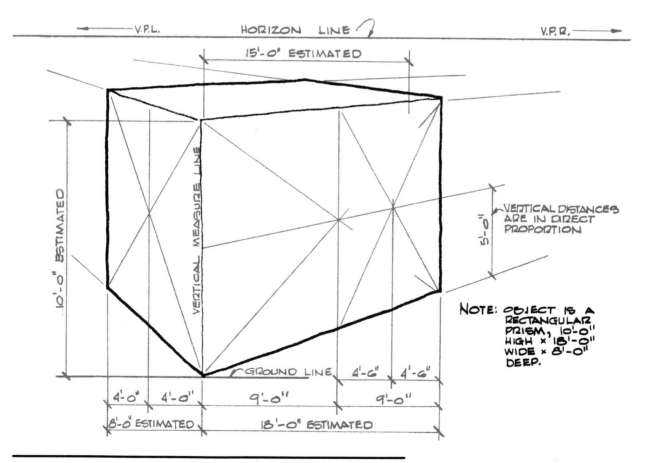

FIGURE 1-7 Method of dividing perspective spaces by the use of diagonals

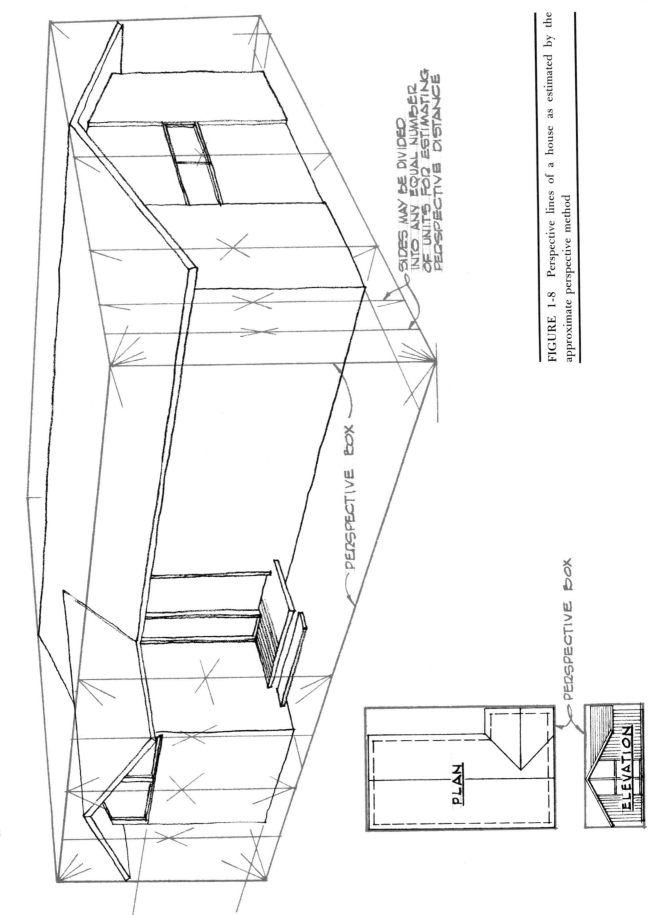

SIDES MAY BE DIVIDED INTO ANY EQUAL NUMBER OF UNITS FOR ESTIMATING PERSPECTIVE DISTANCE

PERSPECTIVE BOX

PERSPECTIVE BOX

PLAN

ELEVATION

PERSPECTIVE BOX

FIGURE 1-8 Perspective lines of a house as estimated by the approximate perspective method

8

FIGURE 1-9 Finished sketch derived from Fig. 1-8
FIGURE 1-9 Finished sketch derived from Fig. 1-8

9

A THE USE OF OVER-LAPPING PLANES

B THE USE OF RELATIVE SIZES OF FAMILIAR OBJECTS

C THE USE OF DETAIL TO INDICATE DEPTH

COMBINATION OF METHODS A-B-C TO INCREASE THE PERSPECTIVE DEPTH AND INDICATE RELATIVE SCALE

FIGURE 1-10   Devices used to create a feeling of depth in a drawing

2. The use of objects of known size, such as people, at varying distances from the observer. A person near the observer appears larger than one farther away.

3. The use of aerial perspective. Objects near the observer are drawn in more detail than those farther away.

MECHANICAL PERSPECTIVE

It is recommended that the beginning student skip the following discussion and return to it later. It is included here simply because that is the logical order.

There are several variations of the methods of drawing mechanical perspective, all based on the same geometrical principles. The method described here is considered the simplest, and it relates in all respects to the method of approximate perspective previously discussed. There is no change in the vocabulary already learned, but there are a few additions. The principal difference lies in the locating of vanishing points, the use of two views of the object for projection purposes, and the use of a *station point* for the establishment of vanishing points and perspective distances.

ADDITIONAL DEFINITIONS

1. *Station point:* The plan view of the location of the observer's eye in relation to the picture plane and the top view of the object.
2. *Picture plane:* The plan view of the "transparent" plane on which the object is to be drawn (the paper). Think of it as a pane of glass when constructing perspective distances.
3. *Visual rays:* Rays of light from selected points on the object which pierce the picture plane on their way to the station point (observer's eye).
4. *Central visual ray:* The visual ray from the corner of the "box" which touches the picture plane.

PROCEDURE

Draw the object below the observer's eye in the first drawing you attempt (Fig. 1-11).

1. Draw the picture plane near the top of the paper.
2. Establish the central visual ray at right angles to the picture plane. It is possible to use any angle, but this way the same visual effect can be obtained by rotating the plan view of the object.
3. Locate the station point on the central visual ray at the desired distance. A short distance in relation to object size will give a distorted picture because of the wide visual angle. This device may sometimes be used for dramatic effect, however.
4. Place the plan view of the object on the picture plane so that the corner of the "box" touches the intersection of the picture plane and the central visual ray.
5. Place the horizon below the picture plane wherever desired. (The horizon is not part of the plan view; it is used for constructing the actual perspective.)
6. Place the ground line where desired; in this case below the horizon for a bird's-eye view.
7. Draw construction lines from the station point to the picture plane parallel to each side of the plan view of the object. (The included angle between these lines is always 90°.) From the points where they intersect the picture plane, draw lines parallel to the central visual ray and extend these to the horizon. The points where they intersect the horizon are the vanishing points.
8. Place the side view of the object on the ground line.
9. Draw a construction line from the top of the side view to the central visual ray. From these intersections at the top and bottom of the object, draw lines to the vanishing points. These pairs of converging lines represent the height of the object projected to infinity.
10. Draw visual rays from the right and left corners of the top view of the object to the station point. Their intersections with the picture plane represent the right and left perspective dimensions of the box. Draw construction lines from these points to the converging lines of the sides of the figure. The resulting "solid" figure represents the perspective box which exactly contains the object.
11. To cut out the box or to find a point within it, always work in the above order. First, establish the height from the side view and draw the two lines to the vanishing points. These lines represent the edges of a plane within the box which contains the desired point or the height of the cut. Second, find the projections of the point or cut

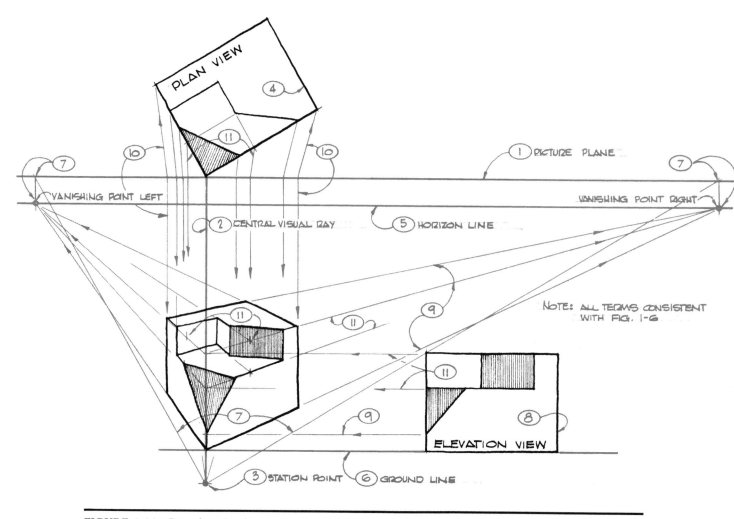

FIGURE 1-11   Procedure for drawing mechanical perspective (circled numbers correspond to outline in text)

in the plan view and bring them to the near edges of the plan view. Project these to the picture plane and then to the two lines just drawn on the perspective object. From these intersections project them to the appropriate vanishing points; their intersection represents the end of the cut or the point desired.

It can be seen that the construction of a mechanical perspective breaks down to simply finding and connecting many salient points on an object.

CIRCLES AND IRREGULAR OBJECTS

Any circle or irregular outline can be drawn by the process of *craticulation,* or the method of squares (Fig.

1-12). This process involves drawing the desired outline over a uniform grid in orthographic projection and then drawing the perspective of the grid. Points of the outline which intersect the lines of the grid are then located proportionately on the perspective. The points are then connected with a straightedge or template, or freehand.

DELINEATION

In architectural practice, delineation is the process of drawing pictures for display, as opposed to the drafting of working drawings. These pictures may include preliminary idea sketches, presentation drawings, or embellished working drawings. Their purpose is mainly to suggest the reality of the designer's ideas rather than to provide exact instructions for the building of the project. Such drawings vary greatly in appearance depending on their purpose and the ability of the person doing the drawing.

Whether the drawings are perspectives or orthographic drawings, many degrees of complexity are possible.

1. *Line only.* The line may be black or any other color and may be drawn with any desired instrument (Fig. 1-13).

2. *Dark and white.* No middle tones are used, and the dark areas are usually chosen to emphasize important features (Fig. 1-14).

3. *Gray scale of three or more tones.* The use of several consistent tones will give a more realistic appearance to the finished drawing. The tones may represent color or shade on the object (Fig. 1-15).

4. *Photographic realism.* By using many graded tones, color, and extreme detail, an artist can closely represent the actual appearance of any object. Because of the purposes of the usual rendered drawing

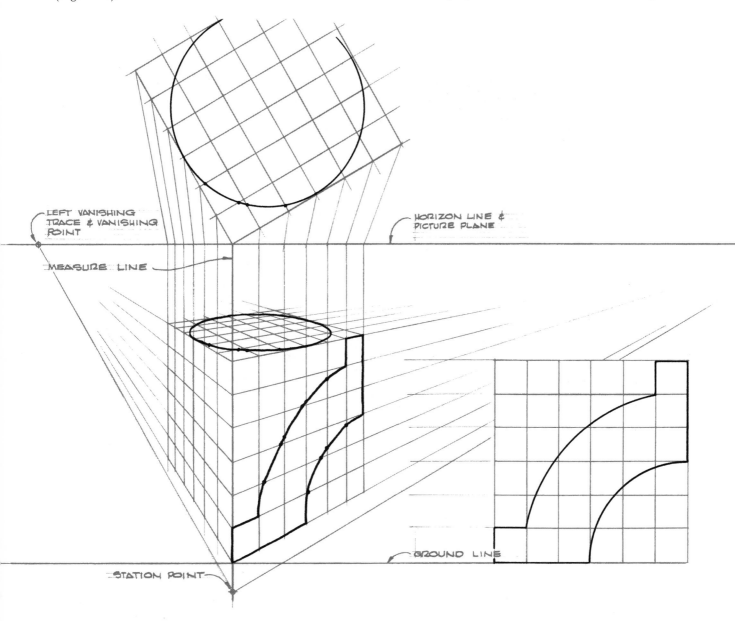

FIGURE 1-12 Procedure for drawing curved or irregular shapes in perspective by craticulation (the method of squares)

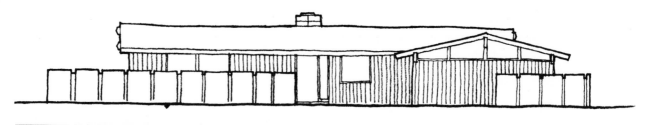

FIGURE 1-13   Rendering by line only

FIGURE 1-14   Rendering in black and white

FIGURE 1-15   Rendering in tone

and the high cost of labor, such extremely realistic drawings as these are seldom done in the office. Some firms employ commercial artists who produce accurately detailed renderings to the specifications of the architect.

THE ENTOURAGE

Since buildings of any type are always viewed in relation to people, trees, clouds, automobiles, airplanes, other buildings, and so on, the student should learn to draw these objects. Because the building is the most important thing in the picture, the emphasis should be on the building itself. Therefore other objects in the picture—the entourage—are not usually drawn in great detail. Proportion, scale, and placement on the paper are the most important considerations regarding the entourage. Automobiles should not be identifiable by brand, small details of clothing should be omitted, and trees and shrubs should be stylized. The use of these devices will create a natural appearance but not distract attention from the building itself.

14

FIGURE 1-16 Procedure for rendering an elevation

RENDERED ELEVATIONS

A rendered elevation will, in most cases, give an effect similar to that of a distant one-point perspective drawn from a viewpoint five or six feet above the ground line. Since an elevation is easier to develop than a perspective, and because elevations are usually available early in the planning stage, they are often rendered by draftsmen and architects (see Fig. 1-2).

PROCEDURE

The simplified procedure for rendering an elevation or a perspective follows (Fig. 1-16):

1. Tape a piece of inexpensive tracing paper over a completed elevation or perspective.
2. Sketch in people, cars, trees, shrubs, and other structures in their correct relationships to the building (see Plot Plan). Avoid placing the curb line too low on the drawing; this will necessitate drawing paths, drives, and so on in perspective.
3. Tape the tracing paper for the finished drawing over these two sheets. At this point all the overlapping lines will be visible. Starting with the object nearest the viewer and proceeding backward, trace the objects on the first copy. Omit lines which are hidden by foreground objects. This procedure completely eliminates erasing on the final copy.
4. Draw all shading, tones, and textures.

Once a student has the basic tools—the ability to sketch and make perspectives—he is ready to start the actual planning of a residence or commercial building. At the start remember that the first attempt at planning will be slow, since all the factors in planning must be learned one at a time. The second project attempted will go much faster, because the student learns to anticipate more of the problems. An architect has the advantage over the student of knowing all the factors at the start, and he is able to avoid many conflicts.

STUDY SUGGESTIONS

1. Make several perspective sketches of simple objects; label the principal construction lines. Try several angles and distances from the observer. Try normal, bird's-eye, and worm's-eye positions.
2. Practice rendering trees, people, automobiles, and so on, on your perspective drawings.
3. Mount a photograph of a building on a large sheet of paper. Using a straightedge, extend pairs of lines in each plane until they intersect at the vanishing points. Various drawings will demonstrate one-, two-, or three-point perspective.

CHAPTER 2
LETTERING

USE OF LETTERING

Much of the information found in a set of architectural working drawings is in verbal form. It would be practically impossible to build a house from pictures alone. It would be even more difficult to build it from a purely verbal description. Drawings, notes, dimensions, specifications—all of these are needed in a complete set of working drawings. It is important that the quality of the lettering equal the quality of the drawings.

REQUIREMENTS

The first requirement of good lettering is that it be legible. This means that the shapes of the letters must be uniform, easily recognized, of proper size, and dark enough to print every time. The second requirement is that it be well proportioned and in good taste. Architectural lettering usually differs from machine lettering in that more differences in letter shapes are permitted from one office to another. The artistic effect of the lettering is important to most architects. Though ordinary Gothic lettering is frequently used, only specifically architectural lettering styles will be discussed here (Fig. 2-1).

In all cases, legibility is considered far more important than artistic effect. Therefore, do not try to invent an architectural alphabet; very few people have this ability. It is best for the student to copy a style that has been proved through use.

Titles and headings should be larger than notes,

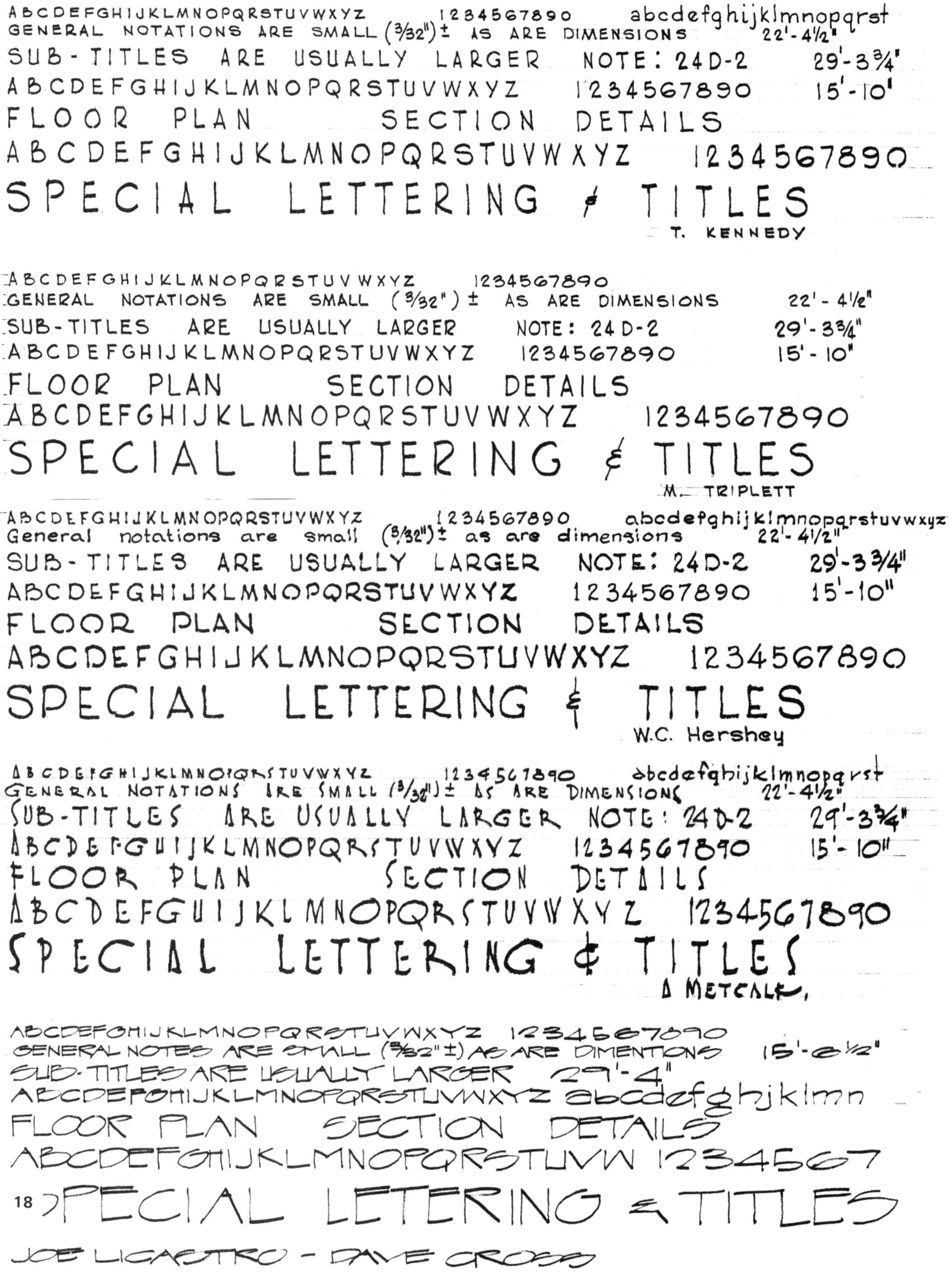

ABCDEFGHIJKLMNOPQRSTUVWXYZ   1234567890   abcdefghijklmnopqrst
GENERAL NOTATIONS ARE SMALL (3/32")± AS ARE DIMENSIONS   22'-4½"
SUB-TITLES ARE USUALLY LARGER   NOTE: 24D-2   29'-3¾"
ABCDEFGHIJKLMNOPQRSTUVWXYZ   1234567890   15'-10"
FLOOR   PLAN   SECTION   DETAILS
ABCDEFGHIJKLMNOPQRSTUVWXYZ   1234567890
SPECIAL   LETTERING ≠ TITLES
                                        T. KENNEDY

ABCDEFGHIJKLMNOPQRSTUVWXYZ   1234567890
GENERAL NOTATIONS ARE SMALL (3/32")± AS ARE DIMENSIONS   22'-4½"
SUB-TITLES   ARE USUALLY LARGER   NOTE: 24D-2   29'-3¾"
ABCDEFGHIJKLMNOPQRSTUVWXYZ   1234567890   15'-10"
FLOOR   PLAN   SECTION   DETAILS
ABCDEFGHIJKLMNOPQRSTUVWXYZ   1234567890
SPECIAL   LETTERING ≠ TITLES
                                        M. TRIPLETT

ABCDEFGHIJKLMNOPQRSTUVWXYZ   1234567890   abcdefghijklmnopqrstuvwxyz
General notations are small (3/32")± as are dimensions   22'-4½"
SUB-TITLES ARE USUALLY LARGER   NOTE: 24D-2   29'-3¾"
ABCDEFGHIJKLMNOPQRSTUVWXYZ   1234567890   15'-10"
FLOOR   PLAN   SECTION   DETAILS
ABCDEFGHIJKLMNOPQRSTUVWXYZ   1234567890
SPECIAL   LETTERING ≠ TITLES
                                        W.C. Hershey

ABCDEFGHIJKLMNOPQRSTUVWXYZ   1234567890   abcdefghijklmnopqrst
GENERAL NOTATIONS ARE SMALL (3/32")± AS ARE DIMENSIONS   22'-4½"
SUB-TITLES ARE USUALLY LARGER NOTE: 24D-2   29'-3¾"
ABCDEFGHIJKLMNOPQRSTUVWXYZ   1234567890   15'-10"
FLOOR   PLAN   SECTION   DETAILS
ABCDEFGHIJKLMNOPQRSTUVWXYZ   1234567890
SPECIAL LETTERING & TITLES
                                        A. METCALF,

ABCDEFGHIJKLMNOPQRSTUVWXYZ   1234567890
GENERAL NOTES ARE SMALL (3/32"±) AS ARE DIMENTIONS   15'-2½"
SUB-TITLES ARE USUALLY LARGER   29'-4"
ABCDEFGHIJKLMNOPQRSTUVWXYZ abcdefghjklmn
FLOOR   PLAN   SECTION   DETAILS
ABCDEFGHIJKLMNOPQRSTUVW 1234567
18 SPECIAL   LETERING & TITLES
JOE LICASTRO - DAVE CROSS

FIGURE 2-1 Examples of lettering by practicing architects and draftsmen

and all entries of equal importance should be the same size. Variations in size will spoil the total effect of the drawing.

METHODS

The ability to letter well comes from practice. Some helpful rules follow:

1. Experiment to find the pencil that works best. It may be a different grade from the one used for linework.
2. Always use guidelines.
3. Try for accuracy at the start; develop speed later.
4. Practice whenever possible.

Even though the draftsman may always use the same lettering case, he should know several others. There are two types of letters: uppercase, or capital, and lowercase. The shapes of individual letters may vary in upper and lowercase, and they may be vertical or slant. Special lettering types are used for presentation drawings, large titles, and displays; experiment with these also.

LETTERING AIDS

There are several types of lettering devices that use guides, templates, or dry-transfer letters. By using such aids, it is possible to have absolute uniformity in lettering. These devices have certain advantages and disadvantages compared with freehand lettering. They afford uniformity of shape in letters, even with a drawing on which several people have worked, but they are slower and make the lettering look mechanical. They are particularly useful, though, for titles, record strips, and display lettering.

Dry-transfer letters are available in sheets containing several "transfers" of each letter and number (Fig. 2-2). A dry adhesive on the back of each character bonds to the drawing surface when the top of the letter is rubbed firmly. These letters are available in a great variety of type faces and sizes. Caution: because the adhesive on the letters is wax based, do not try to reproduce a drawing containing transfer letters in any machine which develops heat.

GENERAL NOTES

General notes on the drawing are the ones that call attention to some condition or requirement which applies to the entire drawing or set of drawings, for example, "Contractor shall verify all dimensions and report any discrepancies to the architect." These notes should be located prominently, usually under the heading "Notes" (Fig. 2-3).

SPECIFIC NOTES

Specific notes are directed to specific points on the drawing by the use of leaders, or call-outs, for example, "G.E. #145A Surface Unit." Wherever possible, the note should be close to the object, the call-out should slant or curve to call attention to itself, and the lettering should be so placed as to avoid other lines or lettering (Fig. 2-4). The object of any drawing or note is to communicate, and if part of it is unclear or unreadable it will not communicate fully. Avoid lettering on or very close to lines of the drawing which are parallel to the lettering. Lines which pass through notes at an angle, however, do not conflict with many letters. Notes are usually lettered horizontally. Group the notes so that they do not run into other notes; the vertical spaces between separate notes should be greater than the vertical spaces between notes of more than one line (Fig. 14-1).

FORM OF NOTES

Notes should be consistent, complete, and as short as possible. Avoid using sentences, for example, "This is a stove, 1756, G.E." Avoid functional descriptions like "This 2 × 4 brace holds up the roof." Notes describing manufactured parts to be installed in a building should be arranged in this order: catalog number, manufacturer, name of object; for example, "#1431 Westinghouse wall oven." Notes concerning structural parts should be listed in this order: size of member, material, name of member, and spacing if any; for example, "2 × 6 D.F. ceiling joists, 16″ O.C.," or "4 × 12 redwood beam." The student should observe notes on professional drawings and copy their form, style, and usage. Use standardized abbreviations at all times.

LEGEND
- ***** Caps, lower case and numerals
- **C** Caps only
- **L** Lower case only
- **N** Numerals only

All type faces shown actual size.
Most PRESTYPE sheets contain numerals.
All alphabet sheets and numeral sheets are printed in black, white, blue, red and gold.

TYPE FACE	IDENTIFYING SYMBOL	8 POINT	10 POINT	12 POINT	14 POINT	18 POINT	24 POINT	30 POINT	36 POINT	42 POINT	48 POINT	54 POINT	60 POINT	72 POINT	84 POINT	96 POINT	120 POINT	144 POINT	160 POINT
Bodoni Bold	BB		N	N		*N	*N		*N		*N		*N	C N					
Cartoon	N						*			*			*		C				
Caslon 540	N-540						*	*			*		C	C		C			
Century Schoolbook	SK					*	*	*	*		*		C						
Clarendon Bold (20 POINT)	H						*		*		C L		C						
Craw Clarendon Cond.	CL-C							*	*		*		*	C		C			
Commercial Script	LS					*	*		*		*		*						
Cooper Black	CB						*		*		*		C	C					
Fortune Bold	ED					*	*		*		C *		C	C		C		ON 3 SHEETS	ON SHE
Franklin Gothic Extra Cond.	NC-AD		*N	*N		*N	*N		*CN		*N	*	*CN	*CN		CN	CN	3" C	CLN 1 SHE
FREELY GOTHIC	YC		3 SIZES ON 1 SHEET								C		C		C				
Futura Medium	FM	*	*NNN	*	*	*	※		*		C L		C L	C N	C	C	C	C	
Futura Demibold	TD	*	*CN	*CN		*CN	*CN	*C	*CN	*C	*CN		CN	CN	CN	CN	CN		
Futura Demibold Italic	TD ital		3 SIZES ON 1 SHEET	*		2 SIZES ON 1 SHEET *	*		*		*		C	C					
Futura Bold	NK	*	*NNN C	*CN	*C NN	*C	*		*C		*CLN		CLN	CLN		C	CN	CN	
Futura Bold Italic	NK ital						*		*				C						
Grotesque No. 7	CS						*	*	*		*		*	CL					
Grotesque No. 9	G					*	*		*	*	CL		C	CLN					
Grotesque No. 9 Italic	G ital					*	*		*		CL			CL					
Grotesque No. 216	GR	*	*	*	*	*	*		*		*		CLN						
Inserat Grotesk	GK		*	*		*	*		*		*		*	*	*	*			
MICROGRAMMA (THIS IS 14 POINT MICROGRAMMA BOLD EXTENDED)	KB		C			C	C	C	C										
Murray Hill Bold	ML-B						*	*	*	*	*		*						
News Gothic	SC					*	*		*		*		*	*					
Old English	DE						*	*	*		*								
Venus Bold Ext. (THIS IS 18 POINT VENUS BOLD EXTENDED)	S-DD					*C	*C	*C		*C			C	C		C			

FIGURE 2-2 Examples of dry-transfer letters

* Caps, lower case and numerals / **C** Caps only / **L** Lower case only / **N** Numerals only

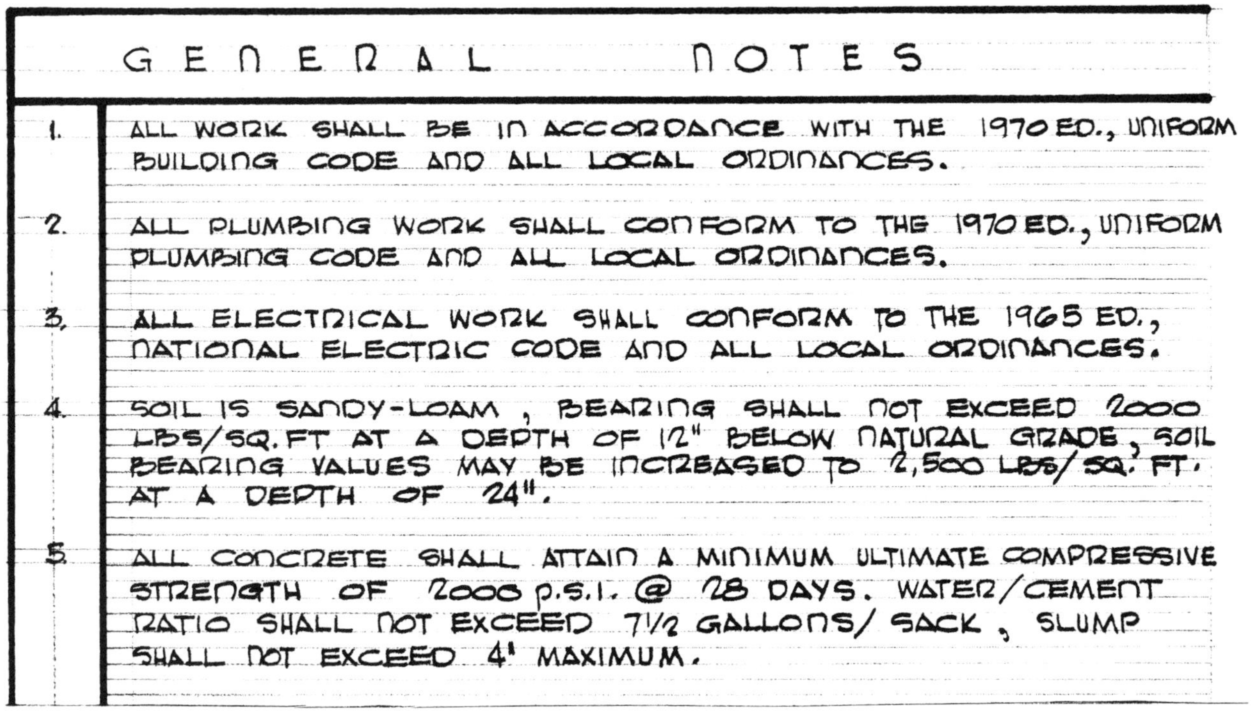

GENERAL NOTES

1. ALL WORK SHALL BE IN ACCORDANCE WITH THE 1970 ED., UNIFORM BUILDING CODE AND ALL LOCAL ORDINANCES.

2. ALL PLUMBING WORK SHALL CONFORM TO THE 1970 ED., UNIFORM PLUMBING CODE AND ALL LOCAL ORDINANCES.

3. ALL ELECTRICAL WORK SHALL CONFORM TO THE 1965 ED., NATIONAL ELECTRIC CODE AND ALL LOCAL ORDINANCES.

4. SOIL IS SANDY-LOAM, BEARING SHALL NOT EXCEED 2000 LBS/SQ. FT AT A DEPTH OF 12" BELOW NATURAL GRADE, SOIL BEARING VALUES MAY BE INCREASED TO 2,500 LBS/SQ. FT. AT A DEPTH OF 24".

5. ALL CONCRETE SHALL ATTAIN A MINIMUM ULTIMATE COMPRESSIVE STRENGTH OF 2000 P.S.I. @ 28 DAYS. WATER/CEMENT RATIO SHALL NOT EXCEED 7½ GALLONS/SACK, SLUMP SHALL NOT EXCEED 4' MAXIMUM.

FIGURE 2-3 Example of general notes on a working drawing

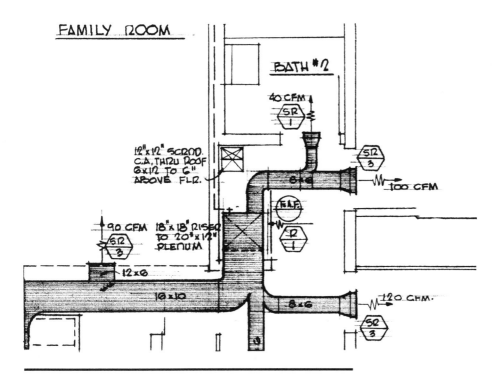

FIGURE 2-4 Examples of specific notes on a working drawing

When you place the notes on a finished drawing, it is a good idea to sketch in lightly their location to see how they will look on the drawing. This will avoid crowding and interference. Notes do not have to be in the same open space as the object they describe. Call-outs may cross object lines.

STUDY SUGGESTIONS

1. Study working drawings from several architectural offices and evaluate the effect of the lettering on the total drawing.
2. Practice lettering whenever you have spare time.

CHAPTER 3
RESIDENTIAL PLANNING

SPECULATIVE BUILDING

Most residences built for a large building development are designed to suit an "average" family. The main trouble is that there is no such thing as an average family. Families differ in size, distribution of sexes, interests, desires, habits, income, and so on. The sites for residences vary in size, climate, relation to other buildings, trees and shrubbery, zoning restrictions, cost. It is possible to design a house to be built for a mass market that will, in many ways, suit many people and many sites. However, people who live in this house will have to make a number of adjustments and get along without many things they desire. To design a house for a particular family, it is first neces-

sary to investigate the client and his family, as well as the building site.

THE CLIENT AND THE SITE

The client and the site together determine the house. Do not try to design a house for someone until all the information regarding the site has been assembled. A house that works well when faced north might be unsatisfactory when faced west. At all stages of planning, the relationships of the three basic areas of the house (working, living, and sleeping) to the site must be kept in mind.

The student should plan a house for someone he

knows, not for himself. This will create a more realistic problem, since architects plan many more houses for others than they plan for themselves. The largest part of the problem in architectural planning lies in executing the half-formed plans of other people. They usually know approximately what they want, but not how to develop, refine, or express their ideas. For the student, relatives and neighbors are all good prospective clients. Another good project might be to design a new house that will suit the needs of a family better than the house they now live in.

Because of the beginning student's limited background, a good first project would be based on a one-line floor plan and checklist devised by an instructor. Such a plan is included in the Student Problems (see Fig. 3-4).

RESEARCH

A checklist is provided in the Appendix, on which the client can indicate what he desires in his house. Use it. It will help to avoid changes, extra visits to the client, and unnecessary work. It will also force the client to organize his thoughts, and in the end, he will likely be happier with the job.

A student will not be required to do as much research on his client or to consider as many problems as an architect would. The factors mentioned here are generally felt to be most important; however, any others encountered should also be considered.

THE CLIENT

The client's needs and desires must be the starting point in planning, as the house will be for him. Some of the factors involved are simple and need no explanation, while others are more complex and will be discussed.

Some obvious points are:

1. The size of the family determines the size of the house.
2. The distribution by age and sex determines the number of bedrooms.

3. The number of automobiles determines the size of the garage or carport.
4. The amount of money available for building will affect the quality and size of the entire project. (Cost estimating is a field in itself; the student should consider costs in general terms only.)

OTHER FACTORS TO CONSIDER

1. *Social habits.* Some families live very formally and have no use for a family, rumpus, or game room. Others will need such a special-purpose room to suit their informal way of life. Durable, easily cleaned walls and floors are necessary if the family likes to entertain and give parties often. An open plan, in which the living and working areas flow together, lends itself to informal entertaining. A more rigid plan, in which these areas are closed off from each other, works better for formal living. Extra bedrooms and baths will be needed if the family often entertains overnight guests.
2. *Furniture and appliances already owned by the family.* Standard-size furniture will not cause much trouble, but oversize pieces can create problems. Be sure they will fit into the house.
3. *Special interests and hobbies.* Books, collections, and hobbies all require space. Often, special storage or rooms must be added for them. For instance, hobbies like woodworking and photography require special rooms; stamp collecting generally does not.
4. *The client's ideas.* His ideas for the number of bathrooms, architectural style, colors, and so on should be worked into the house as far as possible. If they cannot be used, show him why not.

HUMAN SCALE

Houses are built for people. Therefore, all parts of a house should be built to the scale of the owners and the things they use. A 5-ft ceiling, a 5-ft-square bedroom, a 5-ft-high table—all of these are obviously ridiculous and would not work; however, other errors are not so easy to see. For instance, a 30-in.-high built-in food bar is just right, while 24 in. would be too low to use with the average chair. Before starting, check "Architectural Graphic Standards" for the sizes of furniture, appliances, standard working heights, and so forth.

THE THREE BASIC AREAS

The first step in the development of the floor plan is to determine the approximate area requirements of the client, and to separate them into the three basic areas of a house: sleeping area, living area, and working area. The requirements for these areas can be taken from the client's checklist. The sleeping area includes the bedrooms, den, bath, storage, and halls in that part of the house. The living area includes the living room, family room, and dining room. The working area includes the kitchen, utility room, pantry, and possibly bath. Where rooms serve two purposes, such as working and living, be sure to keep the areas close together. Room for the furnace or air-conditioning unit must be provided in the area in which it is to be placed.

Most manufacturers produce unit air conditioners for roof mounting which contain a furnace, cooling coils, motor, and condenser. Such a unit completely eliminates the need for a furnace room. However, the units are fairly large and might be unacceptable to some people because of their appearance.

THE FIRST SKETCHES

The sleeping, living, and working areas are represented by "balloons" in the first sketches (see Chap. 5, "Mechanical Steps in Planning"). The first sketches should be drawn on the site plan, usually a plan of the lot. In this way the basic areas of the house can be properly placed to take advantage of the weather, the view, and access to the property. The garage, walks and driveways, service areas, outdoor living, and major landscaping can be planned before any detailed floor planning is attempted. This procedure will avoid many problems in the final planning of the individual working drawings (see Fig. 5-1).

There are many general arrangements of the rooms in a house which will satisfy different people. Try to plan for efficient use of space and ease of traffic flow.

A particular client may want changes made from the most efficient arrangement and may resist all logical argument. Remember, part of the designer's job is to satisfy the client.

TRAFFIC

The problem of traffic flow should be considered first—that is, the most-used areas of the house should be kept fairly close together to avoid unnecessary steps (Fig. 3-1). As the housewife is in the house much more than the rest of the family and is responsible for its upkeep, it stands to reason that "traffic" refers mainly to her traffic.

SPECIFIC ROOMS

The basic requirements of the main rooms of the house, starting in a logical order from the front door, are listed here:

1. *Entry.* An entry is a great convenience. Though not required in all houses, the use of an entry is generally considered preferable to the alternative of having the front door open directly into the living area. The entry should, when possible, provide access to the living, working, and sleeping areas of the house. It has no required size or shape as long as it works. It may be completely walled or set off by room dividers, or it may be an extension of the living, family, or dining room.
2. *Living room.* The living room should be fairly close to the front door but should not be a passageway to other parts of the house. It should be near the kitchen or dining room for ease of entertaining and hospitality. Isolate it from the bedrooms for quiet and privacy in the bedrooms. An average size for a living room is 300 sq ft.
3. *Kitchen.* This is the most important room in the house from the standpoint of the housewife. It should be near the front door for admitting front-door visitors; adjacent to the utility room for washing, storage, and so on; and near the back door for facilitating traffic to the service yard and garage. An average size for a kitchen is 120 sq ft.

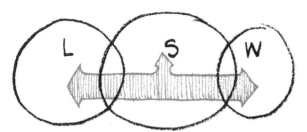

INADVISABLE, TRAFFIC LANES
TOO LONG, LACK OF PRIVACY.

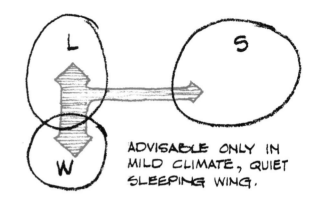

ADVISABLE ONLY IN
MILD CLIMATE, QUIET
SLEEPING WING.

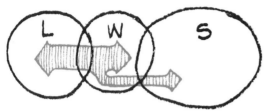

RAMBLING, INADVISABLE IN
COLD, WINDY CLIMATE.

ENTRANCE
SYMBOL

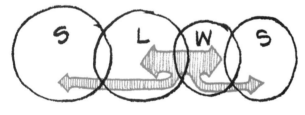

RAMBLING, VARIATION OF ABOVE

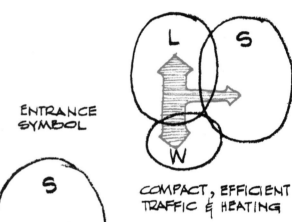

COMPACT, EFFICIENT
TRAFFIC & HEATING

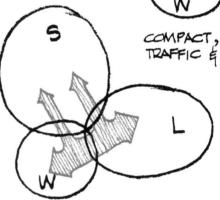

VARIATION OF ABOVE, SEPARATE
SLEEPING WING FOR GUESTS,
RENTAL, ETC..

"ELL" OR "TEE" SHAPED, EFFICIENT
TRAFFIC, CAN PROVIDE PROTECTED
PATIO

NOTES:
1 S=SLEEPING, L=LIVING, W=WORKING AREA
2. WIDTH OF ARROWS INDICATE RELATIVE AMOUNT OF TRAFFIC
3. ANY SCHEME MAY BE VARIED BY PLACING ANY OF THE
   AREAS ON ANOTHER LEVEL,

FIGURE 3-1 Simplified residential traffic flow diagrams

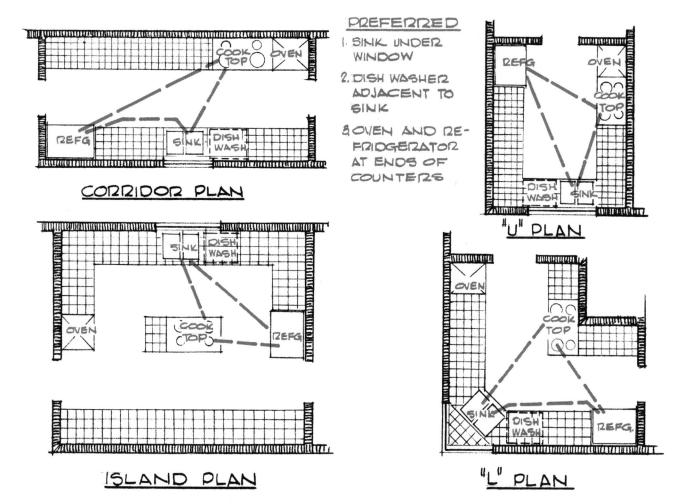

PREFERRED

1. SINK UNDER WINDOW

2. DISH WASHER ADJACENT TO SINK

3. OVEN AND RE- FRIGERATOR AT ENDS OF COUNTERS

CORRIDOR PLAN

"U" PLAN

ISLAND PLAN

"L" PLAN

FIGURE 3-2 Four basic kitchen plans

The draftsman must have definite information about the desired type of kitchen before he starts the preliminary floor plan. Many shapes and sizes of kitchen are possible, and housewives have firm ideas about what type they want. The location of major fixtures and appliances is of first importance. The sink, stove, oven, refrigerator, and freezer must be so located as to eliminate extra steps. A short triangular path between sink, stove, and refrigerator, the most-used fixtures, is considered desirable. The freezer and oven are not used as often, and therefore may be placed out of the mainstream. The location and type of doors greatly affect the efficiency of the kitchen. The width of the aisle between counters is also important; for instance, too wide an aisle in a corridor kitchen would eliminate the principal advantage of this arrangement. Several basic kitchen types are shown in Fig. 3-2; the notes explain some of the advantages and restrictions of each. A student interested in kitchen planning can find a great deal of information in manufacturers' brochures, textbooks, and magazines.

4. *Dining room.* A dining room is not always needed when a dinette, family room, or similar room is included in the plan. But when it is required, it should be adjacent to the kitchen and close to the living room for serving and hospitality. An average size for a dining room is 120 sq ft.

5. *Family room, all-purpose room, den, rumpus room, and so on.* Many contemporary homes have such rooms. Some of them are used mainly for dining

27

and may be extensions of the kitchen. Others are entirely separate and are used for television viewing, hobbies, entertaining, and sometimes sleeping. In any case a room of this type should be near the kitchen and patio or terrace. Depending on its main use, it could be near the living room or the sleeping area of the house. An average size for an all-purpose room is 240 sq ft.

6. *Utility room.* It should be adjacent to the kitchen and back door and should provide easy access to the service yard and garage. An average size for a utility room is 60 sq ft.

   When a separate utility room is not included in the plan, the washer, dryer, ironing board, and soiled-clothes hamper must be located elsewhere. Some women feel that the washer and dryer are more convenient in the bedroom hall, or even in a large bathroom. Some washers and dryers are designed to fit under the counter in a large kitchen. When space is limited, they can be placed in the garage or in the basement.

7. *Bedrooms.* Bedrooms should be isolated from the noisy areas of the house, adjacent to the bathroom, and preferably arranged around a storage hall with a bathroom. An average size for a bedroom is 130 sq ft.

8. *Bathroom.* At least one bathroom should be in the bedroom wing of the house. If there is more than one bath, the other could be near the back door and utility area, or adjoining the master bedroom. An average size for a bathroom is 50 sq ft.

9. *Halls.* When space and expense must be considered, halls should be kept small. One hall should be in the bedroom wing and have access to the bathroom and linen closets. Do not try to omit halls entirely to save space; they are necessary in an efficiently planned house. The recommended minimum width for a hall is $3\frac{1}{2}$ ft.

10. *Basement.* When a basement is included, it can be placed under any desired part of the house. The entrance may be either outside or inside. Avoid a basement entrance from the bedroom wing or living room. Place heating and ventilation equipment, water heaters, and water softeners in the basement. A large basement is useful as a rumpus room or storage area. A basement may be any desired size.

11. *Heater room.* When no basement is provided and a central heating and/or cooling plant is called for, the equipment may be put in the garage or in a special heater room. The room should be designed around the particular pieces of equipment desired. Access must be provided for installation and maintenance of the equipment. It must be located at a point where it can easily be hooked up to ducts and pipes serving the building. An average size for a heater room housing a gas-fired unit is 15 sq ft.

12. *Storage space.* Space must be provided in each of the three main areas of the house for the things that people own. Generally, too much storage is better than too little. In the living area of the house, provide a coat closet and space for books, hi-fi equipment, television, games, extra tables and chairs, and so on. The linen closets in the sleeping area of the house must be large enough for linens, extra blankets, and bathroom supplies. The closets should be about 18 in. deep. Bedrooms and dens should have adequate wardrobe or closet space for clothing. The largest amount of storage space is needed in the working area. Various types of storage must be allowed for: dry, canned, frozen, and fresh foods; dishes; silverware; food utensils; linens; cleaning equipment; and staple items. For more complete information, check "Time-Saver Standards," or "Architectural Graphic Standards." The designer should remember that storage requirements will vary greatly with clients. Be sure to get the client's ideas about storage.

13. *Mud room.* In cold or wet climates, such a room is placed near the building entrance to take care of the problems of changing and storing wet clothes. Floor and wall surfaces should be durable and easily cleaned.

14. *Garage or carport.* Requirements for car storage vary considerably from place to place. In all cases it is necessary to consider size, location, access, and other uses for the space.

15. *Miscellaneous.* Many other considerations concerning the functioning of the entire project affect the site and floor plans. Provision must be made for installation, access, and maintenance of coal chutes, fuel oil tanks, LPG tanks, utility meters, wells, swimming pools, septic tanks, hot water heaters, and so on.

If the house has more than one level, draw the proper stair sections to check for clearance in stairwells, access to rooms, and space required for stairs and halls. When the relationships between the rooms become definitely established, check the plan for unnecessary "jogs" and setbacks in the wall lines. Unless needed for functional reasons, corners cost money but contribute little to the livability of the house.

Proper orientation of the building to the sun and weather must be considered at all times as the floor plan is developed. Read Chap. 8 before attempting the floor plan. Chapter 7 and other specific chapters must also be used in conjunction with this chapter to furnish needed planning information.

REVIEW QUESTIONS

1. In your own words, explain the importance of having full information regarding the client and the site before starting the preliminary sketches. Use a hypothetical case to prove your points.
2. Do the three basic functions of a house (living, working, sleeping) sometimes overlap in one room of the house? Explain.
3. On the basis of convenience and efficiency, point out the advantages and disadvantages of placing a washing machine and dryer in the utility room, in the bathroom, in the bedroom hall.
4. Discuss the use of a patio, lanai, terrace, or breezeway in your own locality. Would your answers be different if you lived 500 miles north or south?

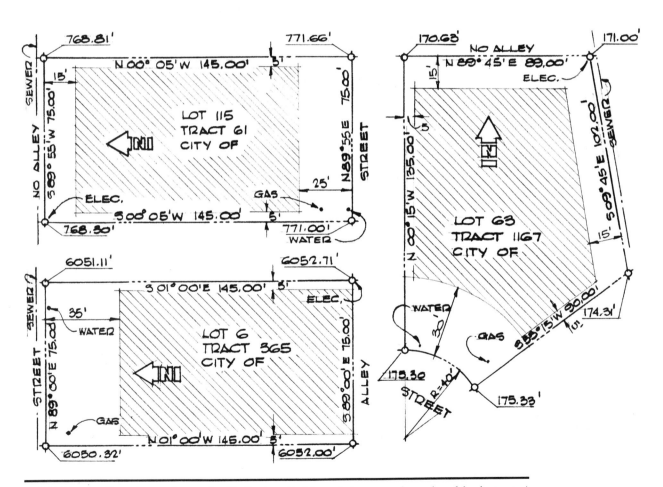

FIGURE 3-3 Three lots to be used with Student Problems (others may be assigned by instructor)

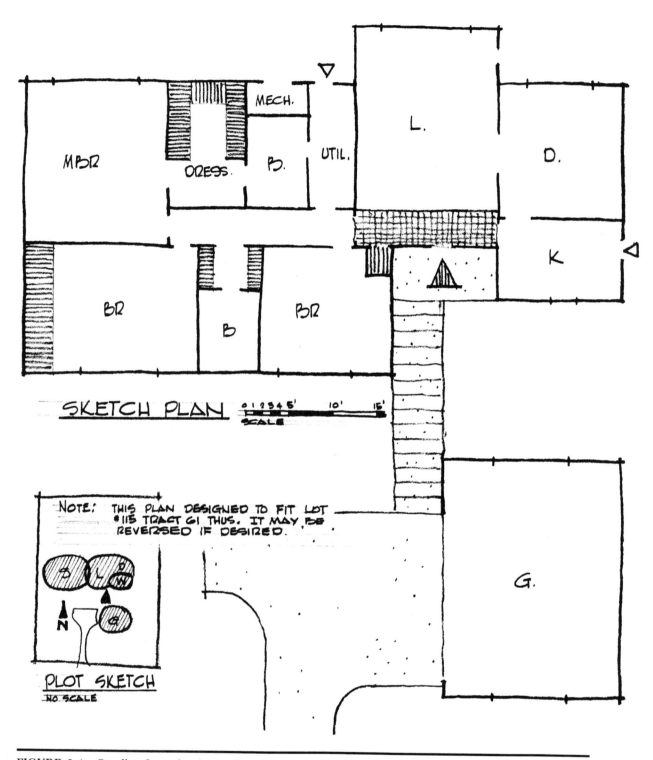

SKETCH PLAN

0 1 2 3 4 5'   10'   15'
SCALE

MBR

DRESS.   B.

MECH.

UTIL.

L.

D.

K.

BR

B

BR

G.

NOTE: THIS PLAN DESIGNED TO FIT LOT
#115 TRACT 61 THUS. IT MAY BE
REVERSED IF DESIRED.

PLOT SKETCH
NO SCALE

N

FIGURE 3-4   One-line floor plan for Student Problem Two (to be used by student unable to develop his own)

Three thousand feet higher or lower in elevation?

5. What are the main reasons for using or not using basements in your area?

6. Are most of the residences in your area of single or multistory construction? Why?

STUDY SUGGESTIONS

1. Sketch a rough plan of your own house and divide it into the three basic areas. Try to improve the plan from the standpoint of traffic and your family's needs.

2. Compare the floor plans of two houses from different parts of the country. Try to explain why they best suit their own areas and why they probably would not work as well if built elsewhere.

3. Many texts and magazines contain home planning information and descriptions of new developments in materials and equipment. Study them.

STUDENT PROBLEMS

Depending on course objectives, your instructor will assign one of the following problems. Problem One requires research and planning in filling out the checklist (A-1) with your client and in developing the rough floor plan and structure. For Problem Two, the checklist has already been completed, and one-line plans that satisfy the checklist have been developed. Problem Three will be created by your instructor.

PROBLEM ONE

1. Go through the checklist (A-1) with your client; use one of the lots provided (Fig. 3-3) or have your client provide a drawing of an actual lot. Ignore the information written in the blanks of the checklist; this is for Student Problem Two. Do not "invent" the lot, as this will not provide a realistic problem. When you encounter items in the checklist which are not clear, look for your answers elsewhere in the text or discuss them with your client.

2. Experiment with particular rooms of the house, such as the kitchen, living room, or bedroom. Have your client demonstrate his ideas regarding size; orientation; furniture placement; location of stove, sink, or refrigerator; and so on within the rooms. Use graph paper to simplify the problem of scale. Check these arrangements for accessibility, window and door arrangements, traffic flow.

3. Discuss the advantages and problems of the site with your client. Have him explain his preferences regarding orientation of rooms, location of outdoor areas, types of landscape materials, construction materials, flat versus sloping ceilings, windows and door types, and so on.

4. Sketch the three basic areas (in relative size and close to the scale of the lot), the garage, fences, drives, walks, and major landscaping on the lot chosen. Try more than one scheme.

5. Check the best sketch against the client checklist to be sure that it satisfies the conditions stated.

6. No basement is required, but if basements are usually used locally, include one. Be careful in designing the basement stairs, as to both location and clearance.

7. It is necessary to read Chaps. 4 and 5 together, as the factors in planning here are so closely related that it is extremely difficult to classify and separate them.

PROBLEM TWO

The requirements for this project are based on the information written into the client checklist (A-1) and on any one of the three lots provided (Fig. 3-3). It is very possible that different students may develop slightly different plans and that all of them will satisfy the conditions of this hypothetical client and site. The student unable to devise a suitable site and floor plan may use Fig. 3-4, which satisfies the requirements of the client checklist.

PROBLEM THREE

If the instructor feels that neither Problem One nor Two is suitable for your locality, he may set up a problem consisting of a lot, site plan, one-line floor plan, and client checklist, as was done in Problem Two.

The research, planning, and sketching done to this point will be the basis for student problems in later chapters. Save all your sketches! 31

CHAPTER 4
PLANNING
LIGHT-COMMERCIAL
BUILDINGS

RESIDENTIAL VERSUS
COMMERCIAL PLANNING

Many factors affect the design of a light-commercial building. The main difference in planning lies in the many different functions of commercial occupants compared with the relatively limited functions of residential occupants. Though the average commercial building may be simpler to design than the average residence, the problem of instruction in planning becomes more difficult merely because of the wide range of businesses encountered. Obviously, it would be impractical to attempt a detailed analysis of every type of business likely to be encountered by an architect. Because of this problem, our method will be to list

the important considerations encountered in the design of any commercial building. Use this list only as a guide in any particular problem. For instance, the category "merchandising areas" generally does not apply to a storage warehouse. Some projects will demand much more independent research on the part of the designer than others. It is better to start with a fairly simple problem.

GENERAL-USE CATEGORIES

Rules of thumb for relative areas and traffic flow which will apply to all businesses are impossible to state. Determination of these factors is the responsibility of the client and the designer. Following is the list of general-use categories to be considered in the design of a commercial building:

1. Merchandising areas
   a. Sales
   b. Display and advertising
   c. Demonstration
2. Areas provided for the comfort of employees and/or customers
   a. Living
   b. Sanitation, rest rooms, and so on
   c. Rest and recreation
   d. Waiting rooms
3. Working areas
   a. Preparation
   b. Receiving
   c. Shipping
   d. Administration and records areas
   e. Customer services—tellers' windows, cash registers, booths, and so on
4. Storage areas
   a. Warehousing, stock rooms
   b. Special storage, lockers, safes, vaults
   c. Refrigerated storage
5. Outdoor areas
   a. Parking and access for automobiles
   b. Transport facilities, spur tracks, and so forth
   c. Landscaping
   Note: Any of the other categories may be entirely or in part out-of-doors. In some cases, such as a horticultural nursery in a hot climate, most of the business is in the open.
6. Provision for future expansion
   a. More land for horizontal expansion
   b. Proper design of footings and walls for vertical expansion
7. Utilities
   a. Lighting and electrical services
   b. Ventilating and air conditioning
   c. Plumbing, sewage, water, gas, steam, and so on
8. Miscellaneous
   a. Stairs, elevators, ramps
   b. Overhead facilities, cranes, tracks
   c. Provision for mobile equipment

Though these last facilities are difficult to classify elsewhere, they do take up space and volume and in

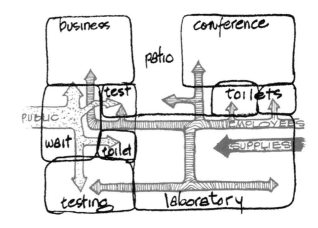

FIGURE 4-1   Traffic pattern for laboratory-clinic

all cases affect the structure as well as the floor plan of the building.

PROCEDURE

To use this list to advantage, it is best first to determine the categories into which all the areas of a project will fall. Determine the floor space required by each area. Check the sizes of all equipment which will be installed or used in each area. Establish the relationship of each area with all the others, and determine the most efficient traffic pattern between areas (Fig. 4-1). This information, when compiled, will correspond to the client's checklist used in the design of a residence. Use the methods of Chap. 5 from here on.

SOURCES OF INFORMATION

It is the student's responsibility at this stage to do some independent research for his client. As with any other job, the quality of the result will depend on the effort expended. Fortunately, many sources of research material are at hand to aid in the solution of these problems. Here are a few:

1. *The client.* He is usually the one who knows most about his type of business. It is necessary to spend much time with him at all stages of planning and development. Record all of his ideas, and try to work them into the building.

33

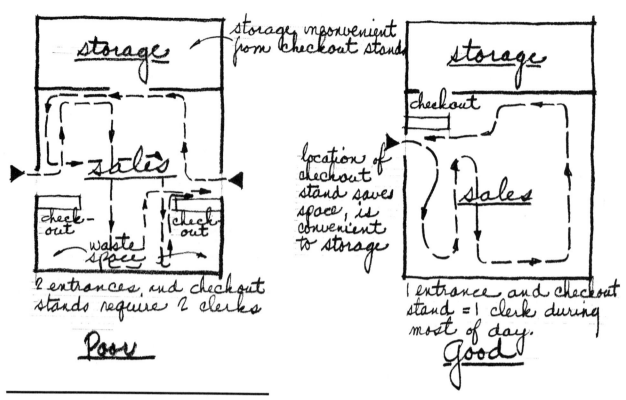

FIGURE 4-2   Two traffic patterns for a small store

2. *Existing businesses of similar kind.* A lot can be learned, both good and bad, from the client's competitors. Investigate them and consider their plants in the light of the problem.

3. *Trade papers.* Most businesses subscribe to papers which report on the overall problems and progress of the trade. Though each man is in competition with his neighbor, it is to the advantage of both to keep up with the trade as a whole. The trade paper keeps its subscribers abreast of new trends and developments as well as new products, processes, and equipment of interest to the businessman.

4. *Architectural magazines.* In recent years, most of the important architectural magazines have made it a practice to devote several issues each year to particular types of buildings. Certain issues will feature schools, department stores, service stations, small retail buildings, warehouses, and so on. These articles contain many examples of good work in each category and are well illustrated and documented.

5. *Books.* Any library has references which will be of use in solving many aspects of problems.

6. *Time and motion study.* This is a particularly useful subject to the architect. A person aware of the possibilities in this field may be able to do a client a great service. Sometimes the location of a checkout stand at a certain spot may eliminate the need for an extra employee (Fig. 4-2), and sometimes eliminating the salary of that one employee may mean the difference between a profit or a loss in a small business.

The fresh viewpoint of the architect or designer, though not exactly a research source, may be extremely valuable to the client. The client may be so close to his problems that he is unable to see them in proper perspective. In other words, his awareness of small detail may prevent him from seeing the overall problem clearly. It is possible that the designer's ignorance of the client's small troubles may allow him to change a conventional design and actually increase the efficiency of the business as a whole.

34

PROBLEMS OF COMMERCIAL PLANNING

Here are some of the problems which are peculiar to commercial planning and which must be considered carefully:

1. *Traffic flow and access to the public.* Most commercial occupancies must be more carefully planned than the average residence to handle large numbers of people. In a residence, the housewife is the one to be considered; in a retail store, the employees and customers should have plenty of room and access to various areas but should not get in each other's way (Fig. 4-2). Exits must be provided according to code requirements.

2. *Large equipment.* Many businesses require such equipment as display cases, grease racks, check-out counters, and forklift trucks, and they must go into place or have adequate space in which to operate when the building is finished. Get all the information about required equipment (Fig. 4-3).

3. *Site conditions.* Often a commercial building may have to be placed in a very restricted spot. For instance, a frontage 20 ft wide in a row of buildings may be the only site available for the business. This will limit the solution of the problem in many ways, for example, orientation and architectural treatment. When placing the building on an open lot, other problems will be encountered, such as parking spaces, access to truck or train services, and space for advertising displays.

4. *Orientation.* Many factors in orientation are common to both types of occupancy, residential or business, but there are several which are peculiar to business buildings. These factors often affect the storage or display of merchandise. Fabrics, wallpaper, cigars, candies, and rubber goods are damaged by sunlight; sugar, salt, fertilizers, furniture, and paper goods are damaged by water; cameras, fine machinery, and foods are damaged by windborne dust. Provide protected display and storage areas for such items.

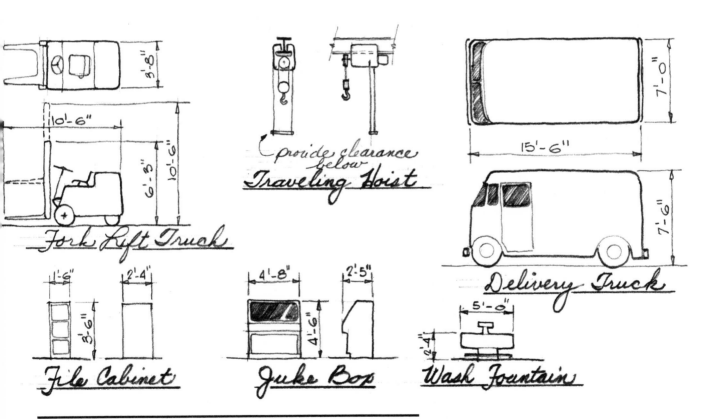

FIGURE 4-3 Space requirements of several common pieces of equipment

5. *Zoning, building, and architectural-design restrictions.* These requirements are generally more detailed and technical than the ones applied to a typical residence. Because of zoning restrictions it may be possible to build a service station on one lot, but not on the one adjacent to that lot. Building codes vary from place to place and cover every type of construction work. Architectural restrictions are sometimes very strict. In an area of great historical interest, a certain style of architectural treatment may be required, like Early American or Cape Cod. In many cases the only restriction may be on the heights of awnings and canopies.

6. *Surface materials.* Because of the hard use that commercial buildings receive, it is more economical from the standpoint of maintenance and depreciation to use high-quality materials. Plastic counter tops, plastic or tile wainscoting, terrazzo or high-quality tile floors, and stainless steel or ceramic-surfaced storefronts are examples of wise choices for a commercial building.

7. *Provision for advertising or display.* In some businesses, the choice of advertising and display areas is of first importance and will have a tremendous effect on the success of the venture. Two good examples of this would be a drive-in restaurant and a new-car salesroom.

This chapter should be used in conjunction with Chap. 5.

REVIEW QUESTIONS

1. Define the merchandising areas in a small variety store; an automotive repair garage.

2. Define the areas provided for the comfort of the customer in a doctor's office; a motel.

3. Define the working areas in a small electronics assembly plant; a grocery store.

4. What use areas overlap at the check-out stand in a grocery store?

5. Compare any two businesses on the basis of relative areas devoted to all of the use categories listed.

6. In a small restaurant, what types and lines of traffic must be kept separate?

7. What effect would provision for the use of a large forklift truck have on a small warehouse?

8. Which would demand the more careful orientation to the sun, a warehouse or a candy store?

9. On the basis of your answers to the above questions, can you devise a formula for assigning area requirements, traffic flow, or special provisions for *all* types of businesses? Why?

STUDY SUGGESTIONS

1. Visit two similar businesses of the same size and try to evaluate their differences in terms of use and traffic flow.

2. Is the grocery store nearest your home laid out as well as it could be? If not, try to sketch your ideas for improvement, and state your reasons for changes.

3. Get a book on time and motion study, and try to apply some of the principles to some small aspect of your drawing project.

4. Study the special issues on building types of the *Architectural Record.* The articles are valuable to the student because they explain, in many cases, the controlling factors which have affected the design of the project that is under discussion.

CHAPTER 5
MECHANICAL STEPS
IN PLANNING

PURPOSE OF PRELIMINARIES

When a structure is designed for a certain family or business, the first drawings are called preliminary studies. They may be pictorials or three-view drawings or both. The purpose of this type of drawing is to experiment with possible solutions to the problem. These solutions do not usually come to mind in finished form. They develop through knowledge of the client and much research into space requirements, building site, structure, orientation to the weather, and other factors.

At the beginning of the design phase of a project, an organized system of work must be developed. It must be brief but inclusive, covering all requirements of the project which control or influence design. At this stage, much small detail can be omitted in the interest of developing the overall scheme. Following are factors which must be considered in developing a logical scheme:

1. *Basic function of the project:* Shoe store, cannery, steel mill, residence, and so on.
2. *Occupancy of the project:* The number and activities of the people and processes involved—people, white mice, forklift trucks, assembly lines, and so forth.
3. *Internal and external circulation of the people and processes to be housed:* Flow diagrams, traffic patterns.

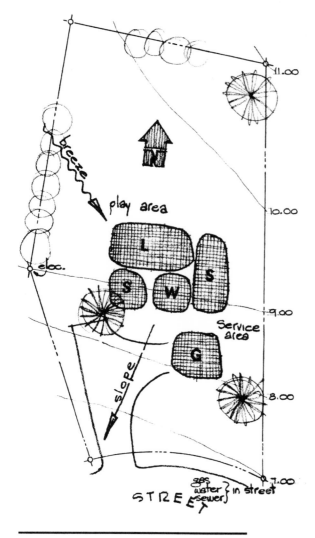

play area

L

S
W

S

G

breeze

elec.

N

slope

Service area

STREET

gas
water
sewer } in street

11.00

10.00

9.00

8.00

7.00

FIGURE 5-1   Site-to-plan relationship study

4. *Influence of the site:* Geography, weather, relationship to roads, nearby structures.
5. *Space requirements of furnishings and equipment to be used in the structure:* Counters, shelves, checkout stands, and so on.
6. *Level of comfort required by the inhabitants:* Temperature, light, humidity, and the like.
7. *Budget:* The establishment of priorities based on funds available.
8. *Details:* Small space requirements, amenities, mechanical devices required by the client.

All of the foregoing are considered as input supplied by the client or consultants, as opposed to specific

solutions and details evolved by the designer. The next step would be the designer's solution of the problem. It is important that all the foregoing data be accurate and complete, as the entire project will be based on them.

USE OF THIS BOOK

Though the floor plan is usually the first drawing started, it is a good idea for the student to read ahead to see how the many factors in planning are interrelated. This chapter deals only with the mechanical processes and procedures of planning; it has nothing to do with planning considerations such as family size, orientation, and structure. This chapter must be used in conjunction with the chapters on residential planning or light-commercial planning regarding floor plans, or the chapters on orientation, structure, elevations, and so on, when working out the other preliminaries.

METHOD OF SKETCHING

The following method of sketching rough floor and site plans works very well. Draw the desired area as a "balloon" or oval of the approximate size (Fig. 5-1). Avoid straight lines and exact measurement at the start, but be very careful of proportion. Straight lines and square corners tend to discourage experiment and make it difficult to change existing sketches. On the other hand, balloons flow into and around each other and are easier to manipulate. The relative areas of the balloons can be established from the checklist or the client's estimates. Use a light sketchy line that can be easily erased or drawn over.

RESIDENTIAL PLANNING

The first sketches of a residence should show the general relationships of the three main use areas—living, working, and sleeping—to the site, which is usually a lot (Fig. 5-1). These sketches are based on the detailed information derived from the client's checklist and from further conversations with the client. Often it is possible to develop more than one

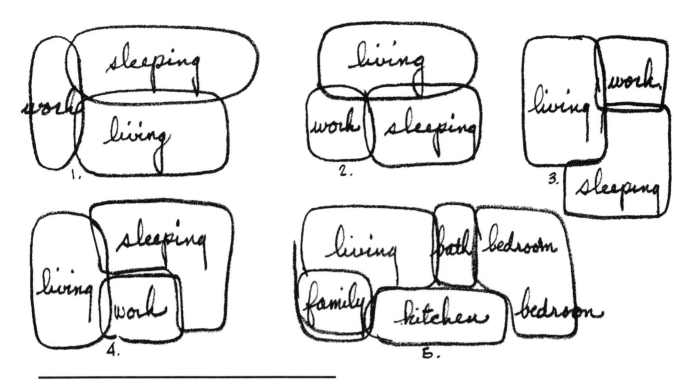

FIGURE 5-2 Five preliminary area studies of a residence

basic scheme. Every possibility should be explored at this stage, since changes can be made easily here which would involve a much greater loss of time and money later (Fig. 5-2).

The next step should be a complete room-by-room traffic diagram. The locations of and access routes between all rooms of the house in relation to the garage, entry, service, and other outdoor areas should be shown. For clarity in demonstrating traffic patterns, it is a good idea to draw the paths of cars, residents, visitors, and service people with different types of lines (Figs. 5-3 and 5-7). Once the plan reaches this stage, have the client choose the scheme he likes best (Figs. 5-4 and 5-8).

Before trying to draw the plan to scale, check the Appendix for the space requirements of certain important items in the building, for instance, fireplace, inside planters, linen closets, showcases, large equipment, halls, and plumbing fixtures. If these are not drawn fairly close to scale on the sketches, trouble will develop later when drawing to exact size.

The traffic diagram, when approved, will become the basis for the first rough scale floor plan. Very few major changes may be made once the client approves the traffic diagram.

Take the approved solution and draw a one-line floor plan, at small scale, in which the thickness of walls is not shown (Figs. 5-5 and 5-9). When used as an outside wall or wall break, the single line must represent the outside of the wall; as an inside wall, the single line must represent the center line of the wall. This rule should be followed, or the dimensioning when placed later will not be consistent. Finally, trace a plan from this copy showing wall thicknesses. Further refinements of small detail and exact measurement can now be made. The finished floor plan can be drawn from this rough copy after it has been approved by the client (Figs. 5-6 and 5-10). Use $\frac{1}{8}$ or $\frac{1}{4}$ in. to the foot scale for the finished drawing.

BASIC RESIDENTIAL FLOOR PLANS

Fortunately for the student, there are relatively few possible arrangements of use areas in a residence. Of the three in-line arrangements of a single-story resi-

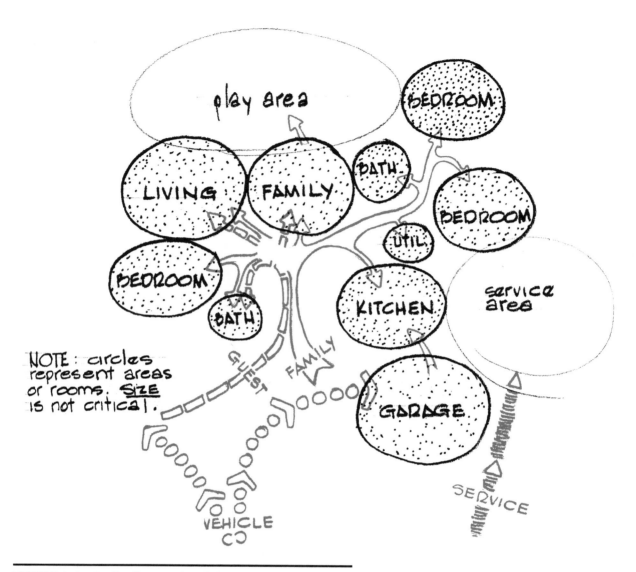

FIGURE 5-3 Traffic diagram of preliminary sketch of a residence

dence, the one in which the sleeping area lies between the living and working areas is seldom used. Such a scheme would create serious problems of traffic, noise, and privacy for any family. The addition of another sleeping or living area to one end of a house does not really create a new basic arrangement. House plans can be turned or reversed in many ways; this does not change the basic arrangement, either, though turning might make the arrangement work better on the site or solve other problems. Therefore, there are only a few basic single-story floor plans to consider.

Split-level or multistory schemes complicate the problem slightly. However, because the working and living areas must be close to each other, in most houses the principal sleeping area is usually isolated from the noisy part of the house. This fact limits the number of possible split-level and multistory plans (Fig. 5-11).

COPYING FLOOR PLANS

It is certainly not unethical for a student to copy a floor plan from a magazine or a book. However, if the copying is done line for line and without thought, the copied project will be wasted effort. To gain useful experience the student should manipulate the plan in

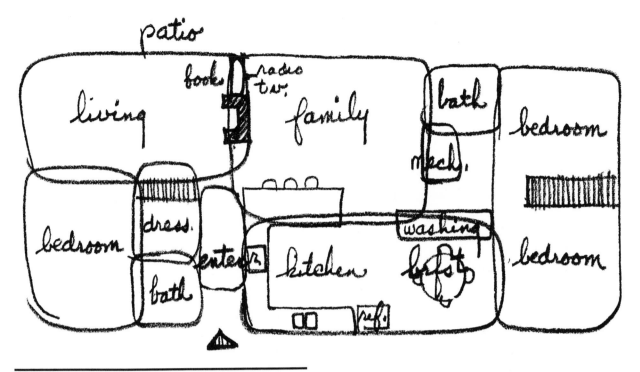

FIGURE 5-4 Further development of preliminary sketch

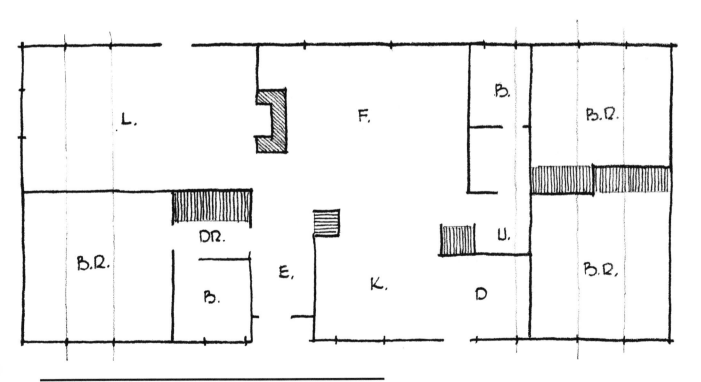

FIGURE 5-5 One-line floor plan developed to scale from Fig. 5-4

41

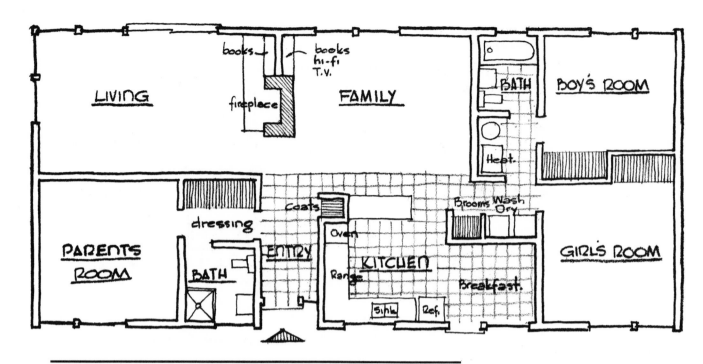

FIGURE 5-6   Floor plan showing wall thickness, traced or copied from Fig. 5-5

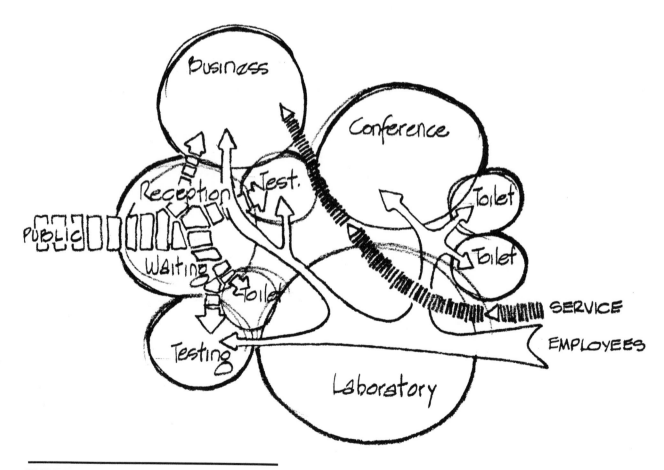

FIGURE 5-7   Traffic pattern for laboratory-clinic

some way, revolve it, change the size or function of certain rooms, add more storage, or enlarge the entry. This is the only way to gain an appreciation of the difficulties which can arise during the development of a floor plan. Of course, the arrangement of the copied plan must be consistent with the approved site–floor plan sketch.

MANIPULATING FLOOR PLANS

Once a likely floor plan has been developed or copied intact, it is possible to adjust it to satisfy most conditions. Possible adjustments include revolving it, tracing it from the back, or any combination of the two. It is usually possible by these means to satisfy any requirement of orientation, shape of lot, direction of view, and so on without a basic change in the plan (Fig. 5-12).

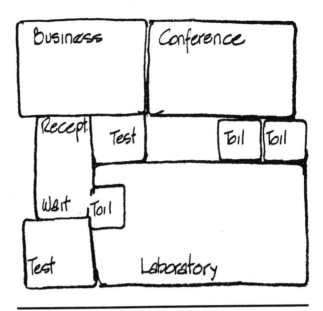

FIGURE 5-8 Further development of preliminary sketch

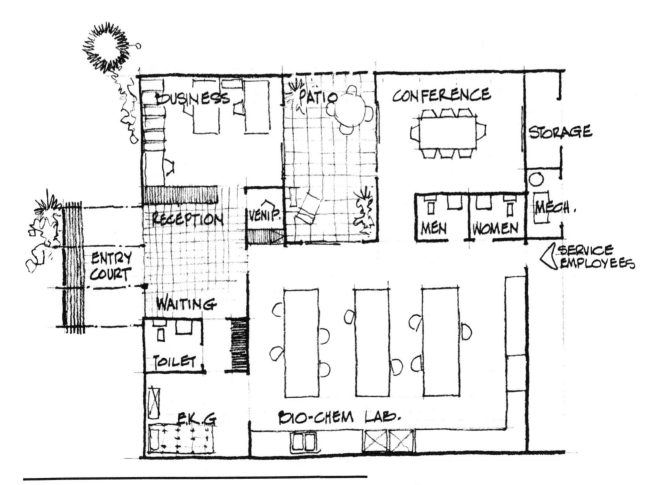

43

FIGURE 5-9 One-line floor plan developed to scale from Fig. 5-8

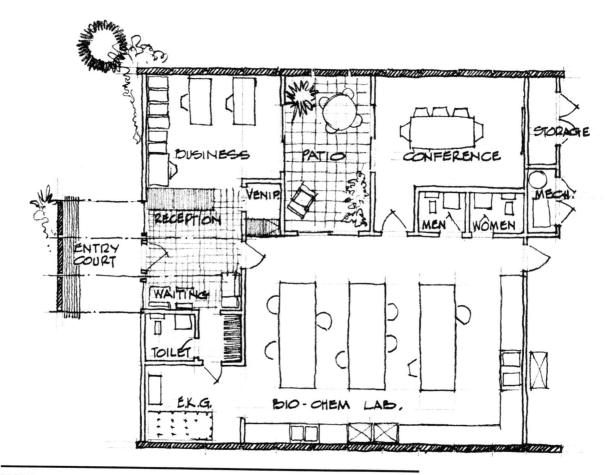

FIGURE 5-10   Floor plan showing wall thickness, traced or copied from Fig. 5-9

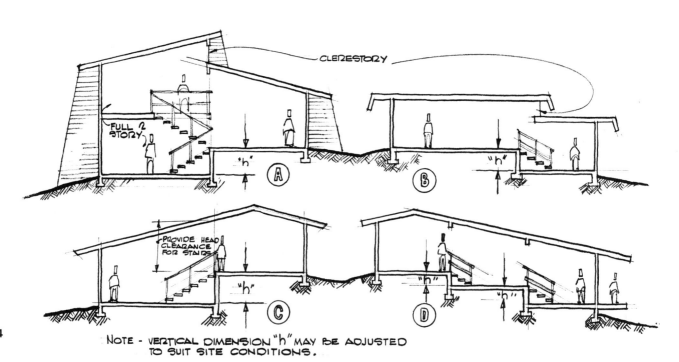

NOTE - VERTICAL DIMENSION "h" MAY BE ADJUSTED TO SUIT SITE CONDITIONS.

FIGURE 5-11   Possible split-level arrangements in section

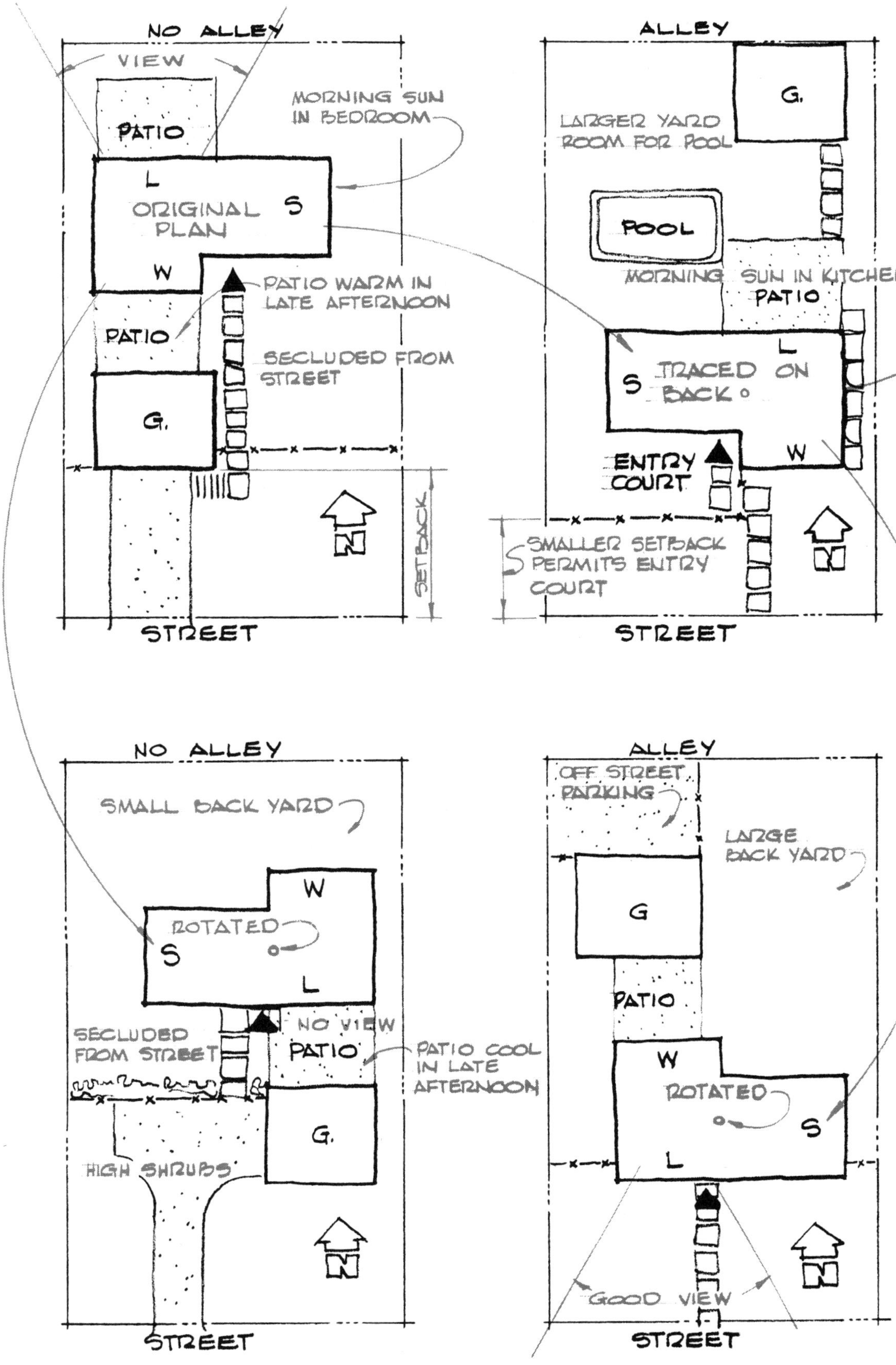
NO ALLEY
VIEW
PATIO
MORNING SUN IN BEDROOM
L
ORIGINAL PLAN
S
W
PATIO WARM IN LATE AFTERNOON
PATIO
SECLUDED FROM STREET
G.
SETBACK
STREET
ALLEY
G.
LARGER YARD ROOM FOR POOL
POOL
MORNING SUN IN KITCHEN
PATIO
L
S
TRACED ON BACK
W
ENTRY COURT
SMALLER SETBACK PERMITS ENTRY COURT
STREET
NO ALLEY
SMALL BACK YARD
W
ROTATED
S
L
SECLUDED FROM STREET
NO VIEW
PATIO
PATIO COOL IN LATE AFTERNOON
G.
HIGH SHRUBS
STREET
ALLEY
OFF STREET PARKING
LARGE BACK YARD
G
PATIO
W
ROTATED
S
L
GOOD VIEW
STREET

FIGURE 5-12 Manipulating of floor plans to solve problems of client or site

BUILDING SHAPE

Because building costs are high, it is desirable in most cases to design a structurally simple building and to use floor space efficiently. Therefore, the outline of the building should not have too many breaks and corners, required hall spaces should be kept to a minimum, and room shapes should be simple. Unnecessary jogs in a wall cost money but do not always contribute to the function of a building. In a residence, the hardest part of floor planning for a student is the bedroom wing. The problem of providing access to several rooms and storage places from minimal hall space is difficult. This job is compounded by the need to maintain simple room shape and desired room size.

For these reasons, several standardized wings containing one, two, three, and more bedrooms are included here (Fig. 5-13). All have rectangular rooms, minimum hall space, adequate closet space, and easy access to all facilities. There are, of course, many other ways to solve these problems, but if they do not develop immediately, it will save much time to use one of the provided layouts. The living-working areas are usually much simpler for the student to work out.

SPLIT-LEVEL PLANNING

There are many reasons why a split-level or multistory design may be more desirable or practical than a single story:

1. *Economy.* It is often cheaper to build a two-story building than one of comparable area on one level.
2. *Limitations of lot size.* A lot may be too small to include the required building area within the setbacks.
3. *Land profile.* A split-level plan usually works better on a slope.
4. *Type of architecture.* Some types demand a multistory building.
5. *Esthetics.* The varying floor and plate heights of a split-level plan sometimes permit more interesting uses of space than are possible in a one-story house.

Some of the possible schemes for split-level and multistory construction are shown. The split-level sections shown are offset a half story. It is possible to have as many levels as desired, any vertical distance apart (Fig. 5-11).

LIGHT-COMMERCIAL PLANNING

The procedure for planning a commercial building is the same as that for a residence. The principal difference lies in the names of the use areas. Instead of "living," "working," and "sleeping," they might be "merchandising," "comfort," "working," "storage," and "outdoor," as described in Chap. 4 (Fig. 5-7). The same considerations regarding efficiency and simplicity apply and, because of business factors, are usually even more important. Traffic patterns are more important in the normal commercial building than in a residence. Individual areas, such as warehousing and merchandising, must be very accurately laid out in planning, owing to the critical space requirements of displays, aisles, large items of merchandise, and so on. Basically, however, the procedures in the design of either type of building are the same.

ELEVATIONS AND SECTIONS

At this point some rough sketches of the elevations should be drawn (Figs. 5-14 and 5-15). To do this, it is necessary to decide on the type of structural system to be used.

The first section drawings, though they will be subject to many changes during the planning process, should be carefully done. The draftsman must think in three dimensions at all times. For instance, the first one-line structural section, done to scale, will indicate the locations of walls, roof, ceiling, roof bracing and beams, bearing walls, and interior footings or floor reinforcement to support these walls. The rafter, floor, and ceiling joist sizes; the type and size of sheathing; and the size of interior footings can now be determined from this first section. If a trussed roof is used, no interior bearing walls are required. If a job-built roof is used, a bearing wall and roof bracing may be used to reduce the size and expense of structural members; for instance, a roof brace to the middle of a roof span will permit a reduction in the size of the rafters. If a bearing wall occurs over a concrete floor, an interior

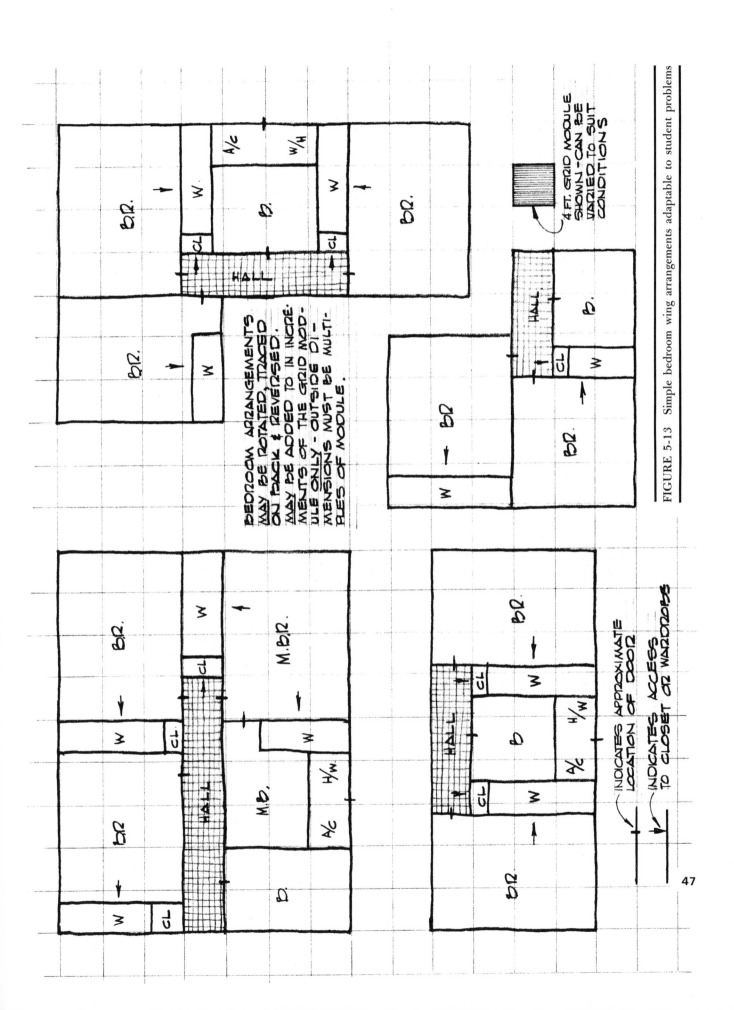

BEDROOM ARRANGEMENTS MAY BE ROTATED, TRACED ON BACK & REVERSED. MAY BE ADDED TO IN INCREMENTS OF THE GRID MODULE ONLY - OUTSIDE DIMENSIONS MUST BE MULTIPLES OF MODULE.

4 FT. GRID MODULE SHOWN - CAN BE VARIED TO SUIT CONDITIONS

— INDICATES APPROXIMATE LOCATION OF DOOR

— INDICATES ACCESS TO CLOSET OR WARDROBE

FIGURE 5-13 Simple bedroom wing arrangements adaptable to student problems

47

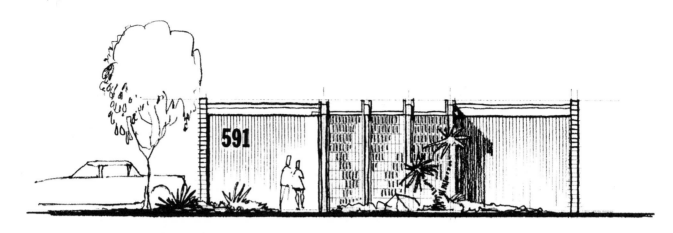

FIGURE 5-14   Preliminary elevation sketch of a laboratory-clinic

SOUTH ELEVATION

FIGURE 5-15   Preliminary elevation sketch of a residence

footing must be placed under it; if over a wood floor, the joists under it must be doubled or solid blocking installed. Read ahead in Chaps. 22 and 23 to clarify this (Fig. 22-5).

First, establish the type of floor system. Most people have strong ideas about wood versus concrete floors in a residence. The type of floor construction will affect the overall height of the building above the ground level. Generally, a concrete floor will be 6 to 8 in. above grade, while a wood floor will be 16 to 20 in. above grade. Use these approximate figures in working out your preliminary sketches. Concrete floors, because of economy and durability, are generally used in commercial and industrial structures.

Many types of structural systems are used; some of the more common types are described as follows:

1. *Walls.* Plate height is usually 8 ft 0 in. for a residence, 8 to 12 ft for a commercial building.
   a. Frame construction: Vertical members of wood or metal covered with any desired material.
   b. Masonry construction: Brick, stone, or concrete-block units laid in courses to form a wall.
   c. Other types should be investigated, such as modular post and beam construction, either wood or steel, using conventional finished or newly developed prefinished panels.
2. *Roof construction.*
   a. Double-pitched roofs, either gable or hip, are most common in residential construction. The pitch depends on local conditions and the type of roofing material desired. Clerestory windows may be easily built into a pitched roof.
   b. Single-pitched roofs are quite common in residential and commercial construction and are easily designed to use clerestories. Skylights and eggcrate patterns are often used with this type of roof.
   c. Flat roofs include pitches under 4:12 and may be single- or double-pitched.
   d. A-frame roofs are quite spectacular and are widely used in cabins, churches, and certain commercial buildings.
   e. Special types of roofs, such as hyperbolic paraboloids and other shell structures, should be left to the experts.
3. *Exterior finishes for frame construction.*
   a. Stucco.
   b. Wood sheathing.
   c. Plywood, metal, plastics, or other sheet materials.
   d. Masonry veneers.
   e. Ceramic tile.
   f. Wainscoting, using combinations of the above.
4. *Windows and doors.* Many types are available, and they may be used at the discretion of the designer.

Some simple structural shapes are shown in Fig. 5-16. The cross section is used with the floor plan to establish the size and shape of the elevations (Figs. 5-17 and 5-18). When size and shape are established, it is possible to experiment with window and door arrangements, materials, and so on. At this stage of development exact information is not required as long as one has settled on the general appearance of the

structure. Further information will be found in Chaps. 16 and 23.

DESIGN

Many different combinations of these structures and materials can be used, and the only rule possible is this: Combine them in a way that will suit the client and the conditions of the site. Avoid "period" architecture until you know more about the periods. You may discover that many types of period architecture worked well when they were developed but may not be adaptable to present ways of living and construction methods in many areas.

Because of space limitations and the purposes of the book, it is not practical to take up the subjects of proportion, texture, color, fenestration, and other factors of design. The best advice is to keep the design simple and functional and to be careful of applied decoration. Simplicity with function is often good design.

USE OF PRELIMINARIES

The object of completing a set of preliminary studies is to provide the information required for a complete set of working drawings. At this stage the required drawings are a structural section, at least two elevations, the plot plan, and the floor plan, plus ideas for fireplaces or other masonry work, windows, doors, interior and exterior finishes, major cabinet work, and all features peculiar to the type of building being developed (Figs. 5-19 and 5-20). In most cases these drawings do not have to be completely detailed, but they should clearly indicate the designer's intentions.

All notes regarding materials, windows, doors, fixtures, appliances, and special equipment should be recorded. Enough information must be included to draw or call out the object properly on the working drawings. Finished drawings are based on these preliminaries. When in doubt about how to proceed on a certain drawing, look it up in its proper chapter.

When the preliminary studies are complete, look them over carefully. Check them with such questions in mind as: Does the building fit the site? Is storage space adequate? Is there enough room provided for

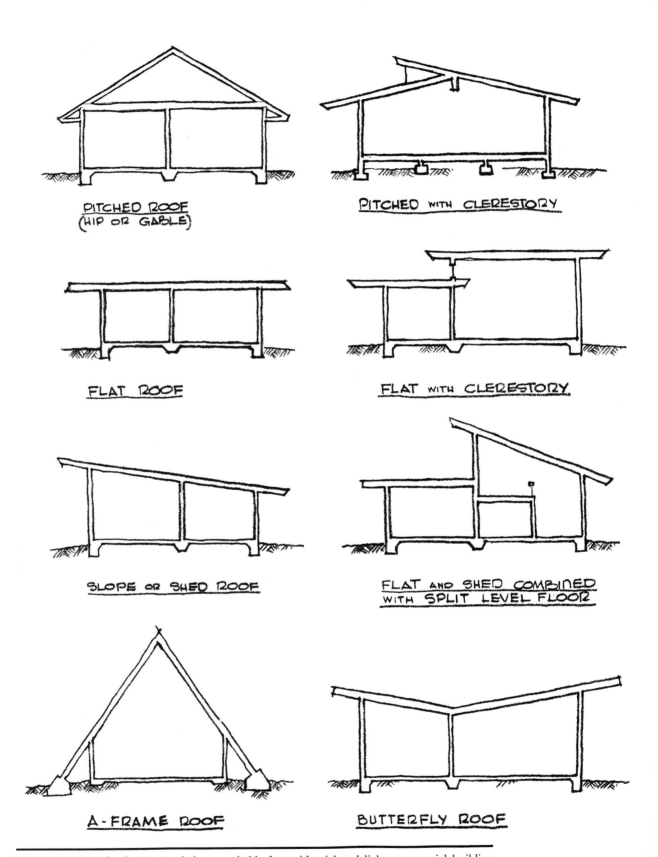

PITCHED ROOF
(HIP OR GABLE)

PITCHED WITH CLERESTORY

FLAT ROOF

FLAT WITH CLERESTORY

SLOPE OR SHED ROOF

FLAT AND SHED COMBINED
WITH SPLIT LEVEL FLOOR

A-FRAME ROOF

BUTTERFLY ROOF

50   FIGURE 5-16 Simple structural shapes suitable for residential and light-commercial building

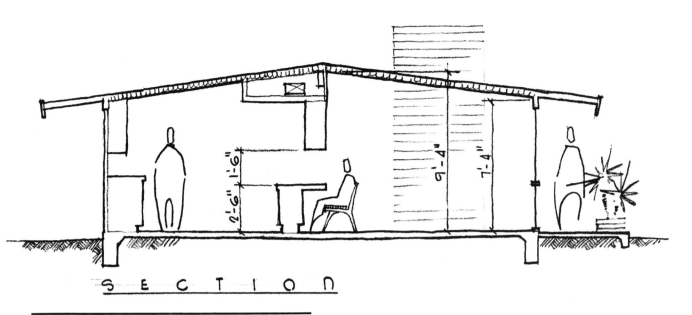

FIGURE 5-17   Sketch of cross section for a residence

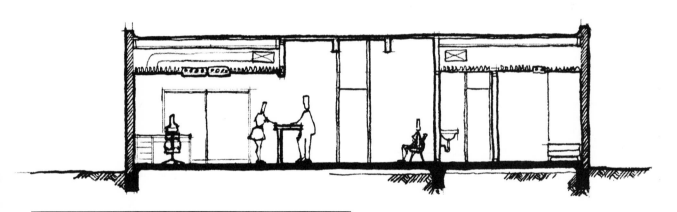

FIGURE 5-18   Sketch of cross section for a laboratory-clinic

equipment to be used in the building? Is the orientation correct? When student and instructor agree that the sketches are complete, work can begin on the working drawings.

The final data sheet shown in the Appendix is a useful device for organizing information for a residence (see A-2). The sheet should be clipped to the other sketches and drawings which represent the final form of the project. Keep this packet in a safe place, because all finished working drawings will be based on the information it contains. In addition, good organization at this point will save much drafting time later.

THE NEXT STEP

Now that the preliminary drawings have been completed, the student must decide on the next step: either to start the working drawings or to prepare a presentation drawing. Regardless of one's level of experience, it is possible to proceed with the working drawings at once, since this book discusses developing the preliminaries into the various working drawings in logical order and one at a time. From the standpoint of a student draftsman, the question of whether to attempt a presentation drawing depends on his experi-

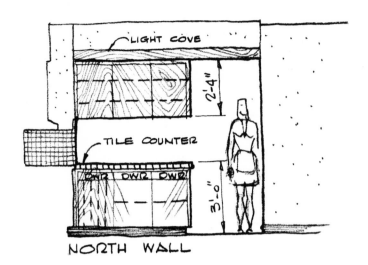

LIGHT COVE

2'-4"

TILE COUNTER

DWR DWR DWR

3'-0"

NORTH WALL

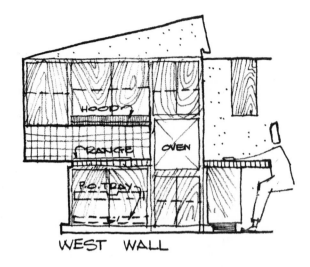

HOOD

RANGE   OVEN

P.O. TRAY

WEST WALL

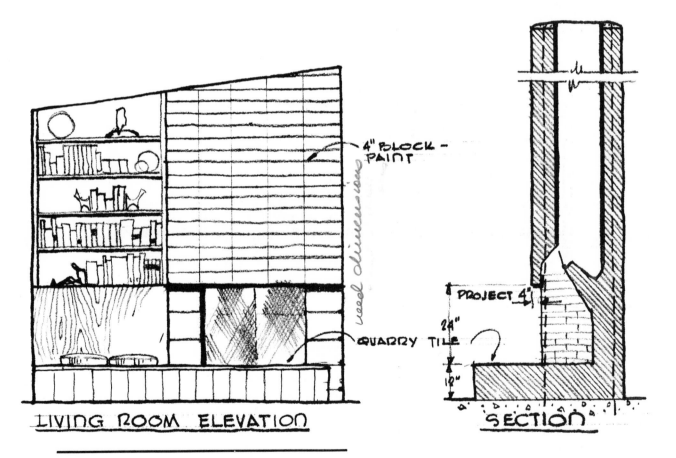

4" BLOCK - PAINT

real dimensions

QUARRY TILE

LIVING ROOM ELEVATION

PROJECT 4"

24"

10"

SECTION

FIGURE 5-19   Sketches of interior details of a residence

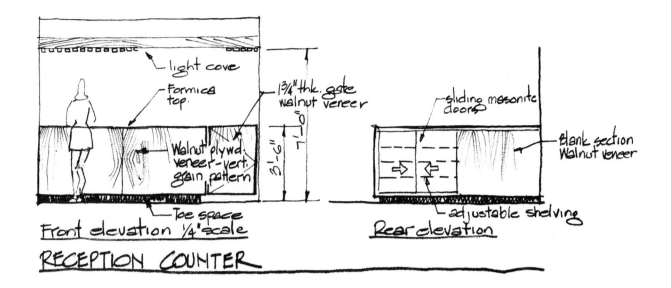

Front elevation ¼" scale

RECEPTION COUNTER

Rear elevation

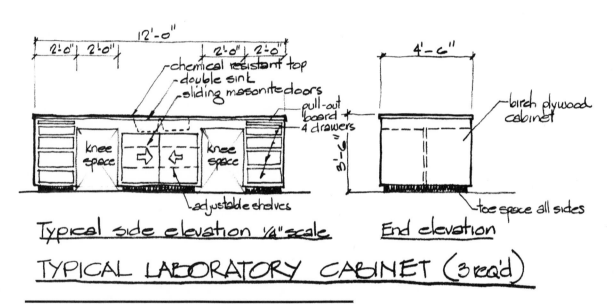

Typical side elevation ¼" scale

TYPICAL LABORATORY CABINET (3 req'd)

End elevation

FIGURE 5-20   Sketches of interior details of a laboratory-clinic

ence and understanding. It would usually be unwise to attempt such a drawing at this point in a first project. The principal reason is that the execution of a presentation drawing demands an understanding of each of the different types of working drawings to be used. Naturally, a beginning student would not have a sufficient background of knowledge for this until the completion of at least one full set of working drawings. It is useful, however, from the standpoint of learning, to do the presentation drawing after the

working drawings are finished. Granted that this puts the cart before the horse, doing the drawing is still a good experience in drafting.

STUDY SUGGESTIONS

1. Break the floor plan of a house or commercial building down into its "use areas" outlined by balloons. Change the overall shape of the plan, or

use a differently shaped site, and try to keep the areas in the same relationships. Can this always be done easily?

2. Study the kitchen arrangements shown in a women's magazine. Try to use some of the details on your own project.

3. Discuss the problems of room arrangement, window and door location, and traffic patterns with several housewives. Remember that these factors are considered extremely important by women, whose job it is to decorate and maintain a home.

STUDENT PROBLEM

1. Using the checklist and sketches developed in the Student Problem in Chap. 3, start developing a one-line floor plan to accurate scale ($\frac{1}{8}$ in. or $\frac{1}{4}$ in. = 1 ft).

2. Along with step 1 above, develop a kitchen as suggested in the client checklist. Be very careful of sizes of equipment, width of aisles, access, and the housewife's most-used traffic pattern. Relate the size and shape of the kitchen to the floor plan. "Architectural Graphic Standards" and "Time-Saver Standards" contain many useful data for kitchen design.

3. Draw a typical vertical section through the building. Check Chap. 8, "Orientation," for the size of overhang. Note all structural parts and surface materials (scale: $\frac{1}{2}$ in. or $\frac{3}{8}$ in. = 1 ft).

4. Using the checklist, the scale floor plan, and the section, develop a front and a side elevation (same scale as floor plan).

5. Sketch your ideas for special interior elevations such as the fireplace or indoor planters.

6. Put all the final preliminaries and notes in a folder. Don't lose it! This folder is the most important part of the entire project. It will take time to develop, but if it is properly done, it will save much more time later.

CHAPTER 6
MATERIALS AND
DATA SOURCES

MATERIALS

There is a vast number of materials available for use in building, and more are being developed every day. The architect and builder must choose wisely from these materials if the finished building is to satisfy all the conditions and people involved. Each material must satisfy many demands based on such diverse factors as cost, availability, strength, durability, appearance, weight, compatibility with other materials, and so on. Most similarly used materials can satisfy a large number of requirements, but each will be superior or inferior to others in some small way. It is the job of the designer to make wise choices in this area, based on the uses of the building and his client's wishes.

Certain materials are so far superior in performance to others that there are no substitutes for them. For instance, concrete and masonry are used in foundations and other below-grade applications. No other materials will perform as well for the same cost. Many other "best" materials are available in certain areas. Sometimes their only advantage over other materials is ease of availability or low cost. Such factors tend to reduce the number of choices which must be made by the student.

CLASSIFICATION

Because of the great number of available materials, most of which can be used in many ways, the job of classification and description becomes extremely difficult. It is possible to classify materials by their physical characteristics, such as tensile strength or compressive strength; by their principal use, such as foundation or sheathing; or by their origin, such as metal or wood. In fact, a good description of each of the most-used building products would fill a large book. Therefore the method used here must necessarily be simplified, and only the most widely used materials can be described.

For convenience, construction materials will be grouped into four categories, some of which overlap. They are structural, sheathing, insulation, and surface treatment or waterproofing. Since all materials do not possess some useful degree of every quality, only a few useful criteria will be applied to each material. Cost is always implied in judging the worth of any building material.

STRUCTURAL USES

Foundation materials must possess great compressive strength, stability, and resistance to soil chemicals and organisms. Concrete and masonry rate high in all of these qualities. Steel is used in special situations such as for pilings, but is not competitive in price for building simple footings and walls.

Materials used for load-bearing walls must have high compressive strength and stiffness and must be capable of taking sheathing fasteners such as nails. Wood and metal studs and masonry have all these qualities; wood and masonry are most often used in residential construction because they are usually cheaper. RIGID STIFF

Beams, joists, and rafters should have high tensile strength, stiffness, and relatively low weight and should be capable of taking sheathing fasteners. Wood, steel, and aluminum are excellent materials for such use. Wood and steel are most often used, but aluminum is used when its low weight offsets its higher unit cost.

SHEATHING

When used as structural sheathing, a material needs qualities of tensile strength, lightness, and stiffness. Wood boards, plywood, and plastic or metal sheets

satisfy these needs. Wood boards and plywood are most used on small jobs because of availability and lower cost.

Nonstructural veneers used for exterior walls carry no loads; therefore the main criteria for such veneers are appearance, durability, and low maintenance. Brick, tile, cement plaster, native stone, and wood are common veneer materials.

Unpainted interior wall and ceiling surfaces are chosen on the basis of their color, texture, and ease of maintenance. Plaster, acoustic plaster, acoustic tiles, prefinished plywood, and plastic-faced laminates are often used in this way.

WATERPROOFING AND SURFACE TREATMENTS

Waterproofing and surface treatments, including paints and stains, must be impermeable, stable, long lasting, and capable of resisting mechanical stress. Asphaltic and plastic materials are applied to walls below grade and must be of the best quality, as they stay in place for the life of the building. Asphaltic materials are most widely used because of their dependability and low cost. Built-up roofs are usually waterproofed with tar over sheathing. Tiles or shingles of wood, metal, or asphaltic materials are also used for waterproofing roofs. Roof materials are generally chosen because of their appearance or fitness for a certain type of architecture.

Flashings, or sheet materials applied at breaks or changes of material in a surface, such as at window frame edges, prevent the flow of air or water through the joint. These materials must be impervious, must resist tearing or cracking, and if visible, they must be inconspicuous. Copper, coated steel, and asphalt-impregnated felt are the most often used flashings.

INSULATION

Most insulating materials are both thermal and acoustic insulators. They are available in loose form or as paper-backed batts, sheets, or tiles of several degrees of compaction. Some insulating boards have a small amount of structural value. The lighter the material, the greater its insulating value. The qualities desired in concealed insulating materials are resistance to the passage of heat or sound, resistance to rot, and ease of application. Fiber glass, rock wool, expanded plastic, and fireproof cellulose are widely used as wall and ceiling insulation. Visible insulation must have similar qualities in addition to a pleasing appearance. It is usually applied in sheets or tiles.

EQUIPMENT AND APPLIANCES

There are thousands of manufactured articles designed for building, ranging from cement, tiles, bricks, steel joists, lighting fixtures, stoves, ovens, and water heaters to entire structural systems. Only a few of these products are easily available in any one part of the country. For this reason, catalogs are printed for architects and other interested people. The largest catalog file, "Sweet's Architectural Catalog File," includes 39 sections in 12 or more large volumes. The number of sections and the total size of the set increases steadily from year to year as new products are added. This catalog is compiled and distributed by McGraw-Hill, Inc., and the loose-leaf information sheets are paid for by the advertisers who use the service. The file is distributed free to most architects and builders in the United States. The filing system for the catalog is very simple, and it is possible to investigate any material or product through its pages. Some of the material is very detailed and specific, and from it the draftsman can determine practically every fact concerning, for example, an air conditioner. He can find the model number, capacity for heating and cooling, physical dimensions, materials of construction, appearance, and type and number of the matching thermostat.

Every draftsman must be able to use such a useful device as Sweet's File. Every school drafting room should have one, even if it is a few years out of date. Old sets use the same filing system, and the important thing is to learn to use the system easily and rapidly.

TECHNICAL INFORMATION

Many sources of technical information are available to the architect and draftsman. Much of the information is compiled in easy-to-use tabular form; much

more is in the form of reference books and textbooks on structural, air-conditioning, electrical, and other fields of engineering. In the library a student can probe as deeply as he wishes into any subject.

The tables and forms in the back of this book require very little engineering knowledge, yet structures designed with their aid will be sound. This is because all of these tables are designed with an adequate safety factor. They are suitable for student use; however, large buildings and complex structures require the services of a professional engineer. One should be cautious in using tabular engineering data under unusual conditions. In all cases, the total structural system of a project should be evaluated by an engineer before construction starts; in fact, in some states an engineer or architect must vouch for the structural soundness of any project before it can be built.

Most of the tabular information is compiled by manufacturers of products whose use demands such tables. Lumber associations produce joist and rafter tables, span tables for plywood sheathing, and load-limit tables for built-up beams. Producers of heating and cooling equipment supply forms and charts for the sizing of air-conditioning components. Manufacturers of modular kitchen cabinets furnish detailed drawings and tables which key the model numbers of units to their physical dimensions.

It is important for the serious drafting student to investigate every available source of information relating to all aspects of his project. The longer the student works on architectural drafting, the more he will realize that drafting includes much more than linework and lettering.

RECORDING INFORMATION

It is important to record and carefully file for later use all information concerning materials, appliances, and structural parts. Any information which is incomplete or has been lost will have to be looked up again. Such notes may be made directly on the preliminary drawings or on a separate sheet of paper. The source of all notes should be recorded with the notes. For instance, the file number of an oven listed in Sweet's should be written down. If further information is needed later it can easily be located.

For a building material, record the name, size,

shape, and method of fastening it in place. For an appliance, note the manufacturer, catalog number, name of the appliance, and its height, length, and depth. For a large piece of equipment such as an air conditioner or hot-water heater, include the output in heat units, capacity, or other important data; for example, "G.E. #B186C unit air conditioner, 100,000 Btu/hr heating, 3 ton cooling," or "Rheem #506L water heater, 50 gal cap."

Structural information should include material, quality or grade, name of member, nominal size, and spacing; for example, "Douglas fir, construction grade, ceiling joist, 2 × 6, 16″ o.c." Make sketches if the written data might later be misinterpreted.

A nationally recognized body, the Construction Specifications Institute, has prepared a numerically organized format in an attempt to standardize material classification. All work is organized into 16 basic divisions with all building materials classified therein. The numerical system applied to the material literature simplifies the filing and retrieval of information (see Chap. 28).

STUDY SUGGESTIONS

1. Look through the index in Sweet's File or other material files and note the number and types of categories.
2. Visit a large building-supply house and note the sizes and construction of commonly used building items.

STUDENT PROBLEM

The rough plot plan, floor plan, section, foundation plan, and elevations, as well as manufacturers' catalogs and structural tables, should be available at this point.

Investigate the qualities, sizes, shapes, and methods of using all of the structural and finish materials to be used in the project. Record all the pertinent information about each appliance and material; it will all be needed in the working drawings. Place it all in the folder described in the Student Problem, Chap. 5.

CHAPTER 7
BUILDING RESTRICTIONS AND STANDARDS

DEFINITION

Building restrictions are general limitations on building or property improvements which are imposed by various agencies, such as local building departments, local planning boards, and health departments, or by federal and individual tract or development control. These restrictions cover such aspects of building as allowable material stresses, room sizes and relationships, fire protection, plumbing, electrical and air-conditioning design, setbacks, and easements.

PURPOSE

The purpose of building restrictions and standards is to protect the structure and the interests of all people and institutions involved in the project. For instance, if the rafters are improperly designed for the locality, the roof might collapse under the weight of snow.

BUILDING CODES

Building codes are concerned with the health and safety of the occupants of the building. Several model building codes are used in the United States. The Uniform Building Code (U.B.C.), from which the following excerpts are taken, is used in the western states. Codes are generally divided into four basic sections: occupancy requirements, construction types, engineering regulations, and detailed regulations; they vary from one part of the country to another.

The section on occupancy requirements deals with

such planning factors as type of use, allowable building area, location on property, exiting provisions, and lighting, ventilation, and sanitation facilities. A typical directive states that "all living rooms, kitchens, and other rooms used for living, dining, or sleeping purposes shall be provided with windows with an area not less than twelve square feet nor one-eighth of the floor area of such rooms."

The section on construction types defines and identifies basic types of construction. These construction types are classified in accordance with their fire-resistive qualities. The classifications are Type I, reinforced concrete; Type II, combinations of steel and concrete; Type III, combinations of masonry, wood, and steel; Type IV, all steel; and Type V, all wood or combustible materials. A typical directive under Type V construction in the Uniform Building Code is as follows: "Type V buildings three stories in height shall have all exterior walls of the first story covered with solid sheathing, as specified in this section. Such sheathing, when of wood, shall be applied diagonally."

The section on engineering regulations deals with the quality and design of construction materials. It is divided into parts concerning design loadings and material characteristics for masonry, wood, concrete, and steel. A universally observed restriction taken from the section on wood materials specifies the minimum size of wood studs: "Except as otherwise provided, exterior stud walls and bearing partitions for buildings of two stories or less shall consist of not less than 2 in. by 4 in. studs; for buildings of three stories, the studding shall be not less than 3 in. by 4 in. or 2 in. by 6 in. to the bottom of the second floor joists, and 2 in. by 4 in. for the two upper stories."

The section on detailed regulations includes excavations, foundation systems, floor and roof construction, stairs and exiting, building appendages, fire-resistive standards, wall cladding, heat-producing appliances, fire-extinguishing systems, and so on. A typical directive states that "the rise of every step in a stairway shall not exceed $7\frac{1}{2}$ in. and the run shall be not less than 10 in."

ZONING ORDINANCES

Zoning ordinances are set up by local authorities and are usually similar in details to ordinances of other areas with similar problems. They establish regulations controlling land use, population density, and location, use, and height of structures and their related facilities. Zoning ordinances always include land-use maps of the area concerned (Fig. 7-1). Land-use zones are based on population density and use, such as single family dwelling, multifamily dwelling, commercial, and manufacturing. Local planning commissions are responsible for setting up and enforcing the zoning ordinances. A typical single family dwelling setback requirement states that "every lot shall have a front yard with a minimum depth of 25 ft or 25% of the depth of the lot, whichever is less."

LENDING AGENCIES

The agency which lends the money for any building naturally exerts a large amount of control over all aspects of the project. The Federal Housing Administration, the largest insurer of building financing in the United States, has set up its own regulations and standards ("Minimum property standards for one and two living units"). These are sometimes more stringent than local ordinances. Banks, savings and loan companies, and insurance companies usually adopt similar standards for their mortgage holders.

DEED RESTRICTIONS

Some restrictions are found in the legal description of the land on which the building is constructed. A few such restrictions are rights of way, special setbacks, utility easements, minimum building areas, and architectural controls. The size and shape of the actual building site is usually found on the tract or development map (Fig. 7-2). Such maps are made by the developer of the land; they also show the streets, curbs, and gutters. They are filed with the appropriate city, county, and state offices with whose ordinances they must comply. This information is always available from the assessor or planning commission, as well as from realty companies and tract offices.

Because most zoning restrictions are rigidly enforced, and since responsibility for conforming lies with the designer, the designer must investigate all the restrictions applicable to his project.

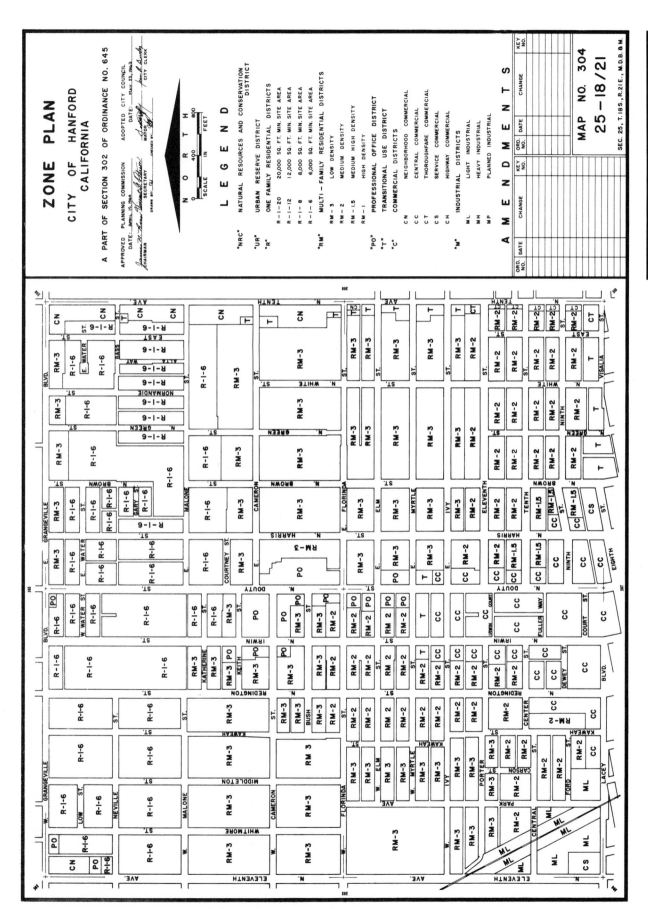

FIGURE 7-1 Extract from typical zoning map

61

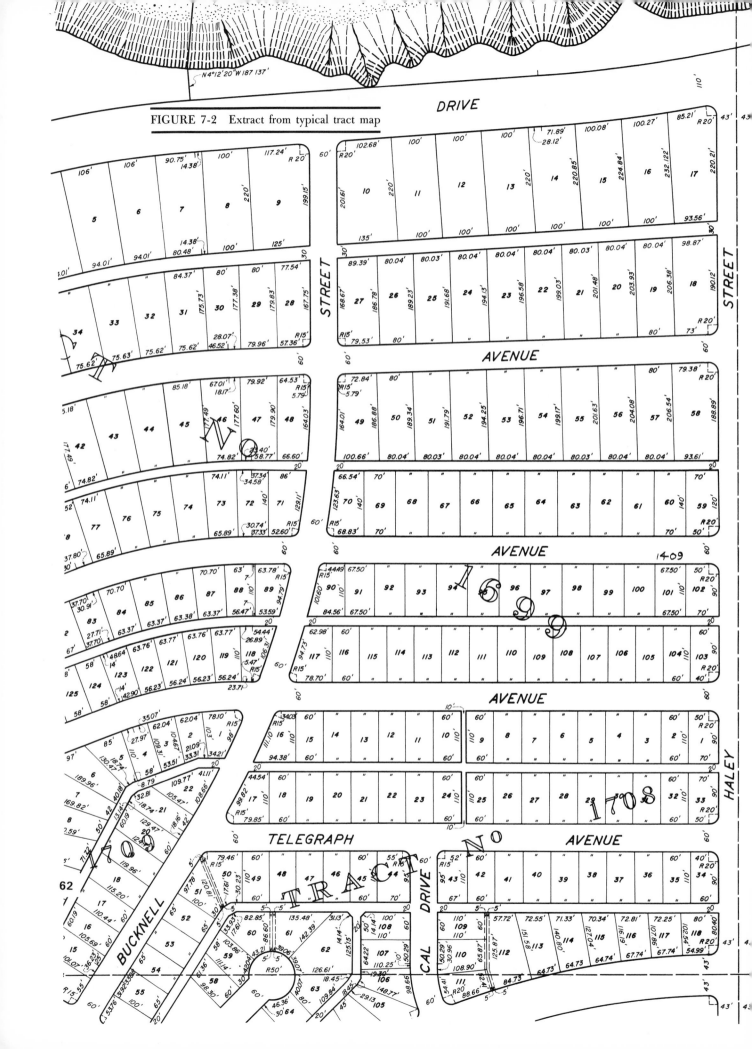

FIGURE 7-2 Extract from typical tract map

STUDY SUGGESTIONS

1. Visit the local building department and determine which codes and ordinances apply to your project.
2. Select a certain local building and determine:
   a. Fire zone in which it is located
   b. Its occupancy type
   c. Its construction type

STUDENT PROBLEM

Much reading is required to establish a working knowledge of the national and local restrictions applicable to any building project. If the required documents are not available in the classroom, either the student must use the extracts in this book, or the instructor should supply the most important items of information.

Investigate the restrictions which affect your building and make the notes and sketches which will govern the working drawings.

CHAPTER 8
ORIENTATION

DEFINITION AND PURPOSE

Though a floor plan may now work well from the standpoint of interior circulation, it must still be related to its surroundings. It is a mistake to assume that a good floor plan will work well on any site. The process of placing a building on the site to take most advantage of the surroundings is called *orientation*. Orientation should always be considered as the floor plan is developed to avoid major changes at a late stage of planning. Orientation will have an effect on every drawing in the set. In fact, as mentioned before, the first sketches drawn should show the relationship of the basic living areas, garage, and outdoor living areas to the site (see Fig. 5-1).

Important aspects of the structure which are most affected by the sun and weather are size and location of windows, extent of the roof overhang, type of roof, size and type of the heating and cooling plant, insulation, location of outdoor living areas, and landscaping.

REQUIRED INFORMATION

Before orienting the building, it is necessary to have an accurate drawing of the site showing the north arrow; streets; alleyways; property lines; easements; locations of utilities; locations of existing buildings; and location, type, and size of all trees that might be saved. If the site is hilly, contour lines are needed. It is also necessary to know how far back from the property lines the building must be set. These requirements are determined by local zoning ordinances and deed restrictions. Look them up. Visit the site if possible.

THE SUN

One of the most important factors affecting the orientation of a structure is its relation to the sun. In considering the effect of the sun on the building it is necessary to know both the vertical and horizontal angles of the sun at any time of the year. Charts and tables showing these angles may be found in many references.

The horizontal and vertical angles of the sun vary with the date, time of day, and latitude, or distance from the equator, of the place in question. A few obvious remarks should be made here. The vertical angle of the sun with the ground is steeper in summer than in winter. In the northern hemisphere it is steeper in southern than in northern latitudes at any given time. The horizontal angle of the sun between sunrise and sunset is larger in the summer than in winter. The principal reason that summer is warmer than winter is due to the steeper vertical angle of the sun, plus the longer daylight hours.

When orienting a building to the sun, one should have a plan view of the site and building, tentative cross sections of the structure drawn to scale, and the sun tables (Fig. 8-1 and A-3). Using these data, one may establish three important functional aspects of the structure:

1. The extent of the roof overhang above the largest window areas
2. The location and size of these windows
3. The location of treillage (sun screens) or landscaping to control the sun in relation to the house and outdoor living areas

It is possible to determine the shadow line of the roof or canopy overhang at any time of the day and year. This is best done by graphic means, using orthographic projection in conjunction with the sun tables. It is assumed that any student using this book can do such a construction (Fig. 8-2).

LOCAL REQUIREMENTS

Unfortunately, no ironclad rules may be made concerning the amount of sun required for a given building. This naturally depends on the latitude of the building, the direction it faces, its surroundings, the size and location of window areas, general weather conditions, the function of the windows, and the desires of the client. It is wrong to assume that most existing buildings in an area are correctly oriented. Do not copy the orientation of the building next door; decide what is needed and plan windows, overhangs, and so on correctly. Some effective methods of controlling the sun are shown in Fig. 8-3.

Some general rules follow:

1. Buildings in far northern latitudes will tolerate more of the sun's heat than those in the south. This refers mainly to windows facing south and west. Except in northern latitudes, little sun comes in from the north other than in the early morning and late evening hours during the summer. Since the sun in the morning is seldom objectionable in most areas, windows to the east are sometimes desirable. The western sun is harsh and glaring in the summer in all latitudes, therefore large west windows are seldom desirable even in northern climates. This is, however, a matter of taste. Factors which tend to cancel this disadvantage are a beautiful view to the west, sheltering trees which will shield the windows from glare, or an extensive west overhang or sun screen. West windows are seldom desirable in hot, southern climates. (The word *window*, as used here, refers to large window areas.)
2. In any part of the country, the direction which the large window areas of the building face is the most important factor in sun control. Generally speaking, a southern exposure is better than any other for a building on a plot without trees. By designing the south roof overhang properly, it is possible to keep the sun out in the summer and let it come in at any desired date in the fall and spring. This condition tends to keep the building cool during hot weather and warm during the winter, which makes possible a substantial saving in heating and cooling costs. The amount of heat energy obtained in the winter naturally depends mainly on the area of south-facing windows exposed to the sun.

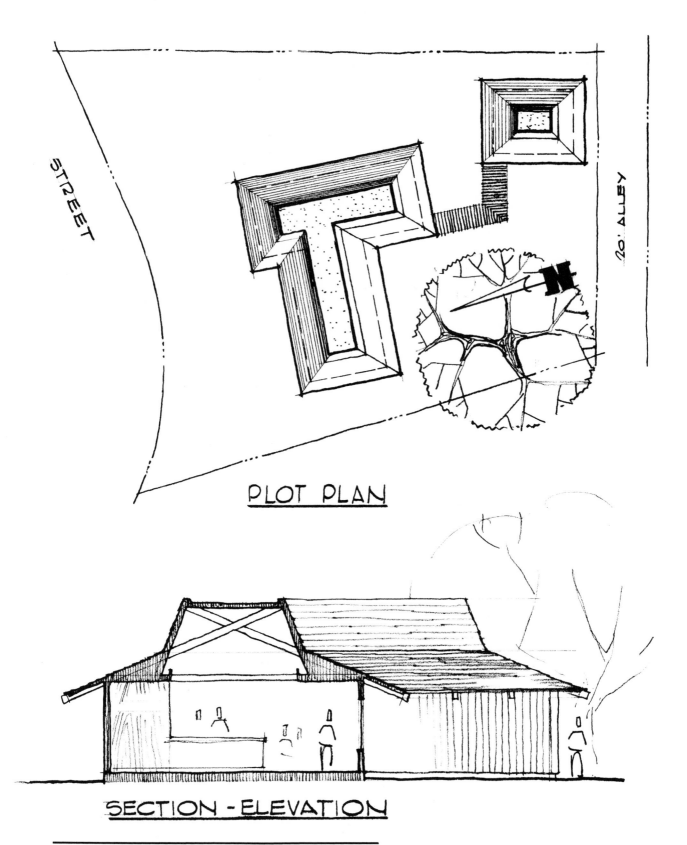

PLOT PLAN

SECTION - ELEVATION

66   FIGURE 8-1 Drawings required to make a study of orientation

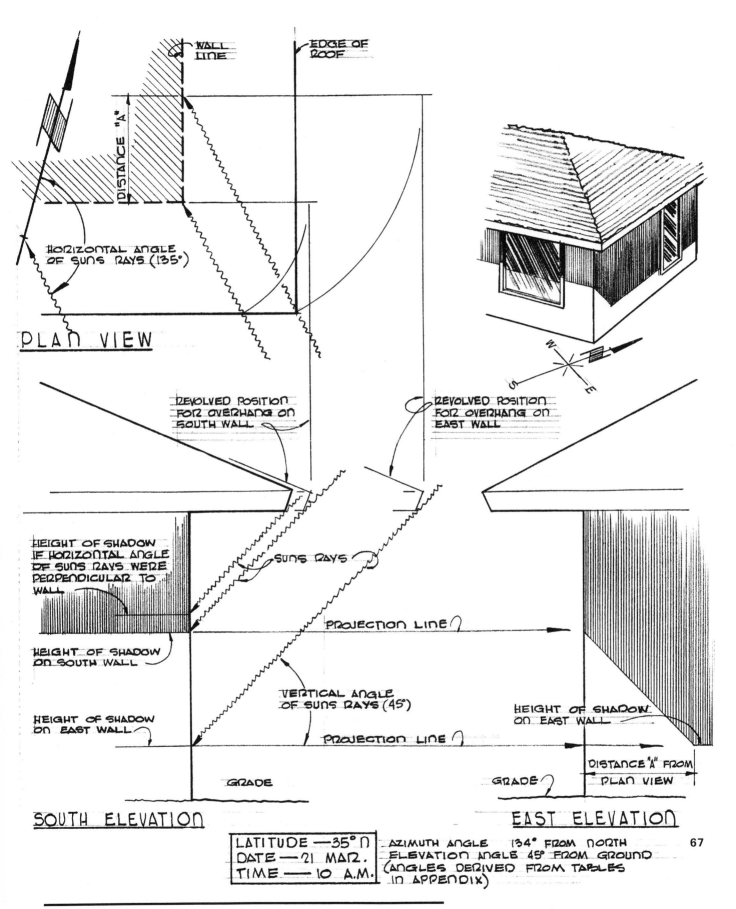

PLAN VIEW

WALL LINE

EDGE OF ROOF

DISTANCE "A"

HORIZONTAL ANGLE OF SUNS RAYS (135°)

REVOLVED POSITION FOR OVERHANG ON SOUTH WALL

REVOLVED POSITION FOR OVERHANG ON EAST WALL

HEIGHT OF SHADOW IF HORIZONTAL ANGLE OF SUNS RAYS WERE PERPENDICULAR TO WALL

SUNS RAYS

HEIGHT OF SHADOW ON SOUTH WALL

PROJECTION LINE

HEIGHT OF SHADOW ON EAST WALL

VERTICAL ANGLE OF SUNS RAYS (45°)

HEIGHT OF SHADOW ON EAST WALL

PROJECTION LINE

GRADE

GRADE

DISTANCE "A" FROM PLAN VIEW

SOUTH ELEVATION

EAST ELEVATION

LATITUDE —35° N
DATE —21 MAR.
TIME —10 A.M.

AZIMUTH ANGLE 134° FROM NORTH
ELEVATION ANGLE 45° FROM GROUND
(ANGLES DERIVED FROM TABLES IN APPENDIX)

67

FIGURE 8-2 Construction used to determine shadow lines at any given time

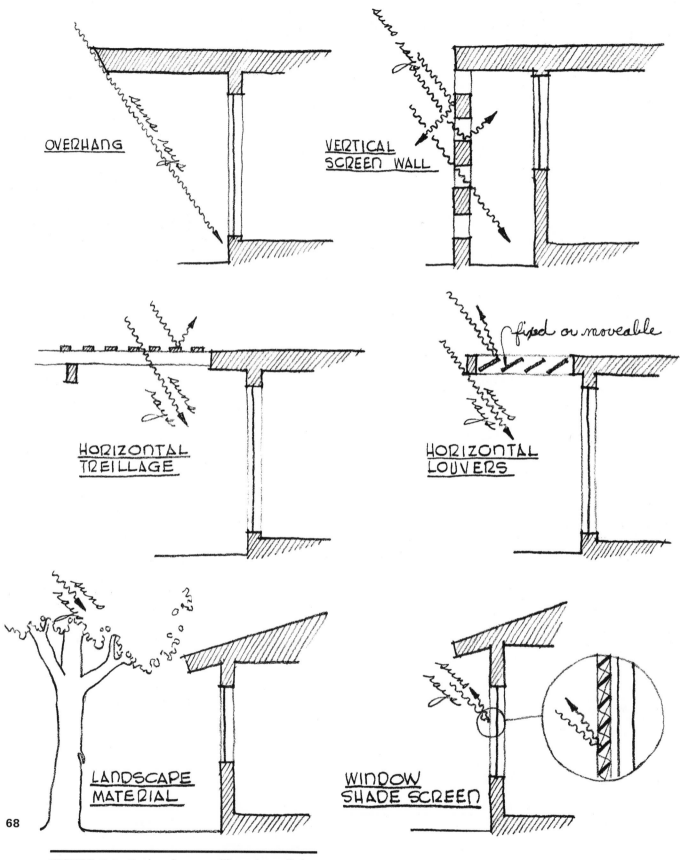

OVERHANG

VERTICAL SCREEN WALL

HORIZONTAL TREILLAGE

HORIZONTAL LOUVERS

fixed or moveable

LANDSCAPE MATERIAL

WINDOW SHADE SCREEN

FIGURE 8-3 Devices for controlling solar radiation

3. The near surroundings of the building have a great effect on its orientation. A wooded lot offers more choice of orientation than a bare lot. Large trees usually have a greater effect than any other nearby feature in modifying the above rules. For instance, a house can be comfortably faced due west if there is sufficient tree shelter. On the other hand, large areas of paving or water to the south will reflect much heat energy from below, so be sure to consider these conditions.

4. The larger the window area, the more it must be considered in the control of heat. Heat gain from the sun is important; so is heat loss from the building to the outside. Be careful of large windows to the north in northern climates or areas where strong north winds are prevalent. Such windows should be well draped or provided with double glazing.

5. Though sun angles vary according to latitude, weather conditions of cities in the same latitude can differ greatly. For instance, San Francisco, California; Pueblo, Colorado; and St. Louis, Missouri, are all very close to lat 38°N, but have widely varying weather conditions. San Francisco is on the coast, its weather moderated by the Pacific Ocean. The yearly temperature range is small, humidity high, rainfall average, and snowfall negligible. Pueblo is on a high plateau; this condition emphasizes the differences between seasons. The yearly temperature range is great, humidity is generally low, rainfall is scant, and snow falls in the winter. St. Louis lies in the Mississippi River Basin at a low altitude. Here the yearly temperature range is great, the humidity is high, there is much rain, and it snows in the winter. It can be seen that houses designed for these three cities would differ greatly, though they are at the same latitude. Always remember to provide for local weather conditions.

6. The client's wishes are an important factor in deciding the orientation of the building. One person may want a great deal of sun from all angles; another may want only the early morning sun; another may want the morning or afternoon sun in a particular room. One may like many windows, and another may consider privacy more important than sun and view. Remember that the building is being designed for an individual client's use.

SIMPLIFIED PROCEDURE FOR ESTABLISHING EAVE LINE

The mechanical problem of establishing the length of the overhang above a large south-facing window is very simple. Note: This method works only when the wall in question faces almost due south (Fig. 8-4). Any other exposure will require supplementary constructions.

1. The client and designer should first determine the date on which the sun will be permitted to enter the large windows. This decision is based on all the variables previously listed.

2. Find the vertical angle of the sun on the desired date in the sun table (see A-3), and draw a line at this angle from the bottom of the window.

3. The point at which this line strikes the rafter line will determine the extent of the roof overhang. Establish the fascia board or the edge of the roof structure at this point. In the hot months, the sun will be at a steeper angle and will not reach the window. In the cooler months, the sun will be at a shallower angle and will enter the window.

OTHER EXTERNAL CONDITIONS

Other conditions that affect orientation and that are not so dependent on the sun include the following:

1. The outside temperature range through the year will affect many details of a building. In a cold climate a square building would lose less warmth than a rambling building of the same floor area, and would thus be more economical to heat. Also, smaller windows would be desirable for the same reason. The alternative to small windows would be double glazing or storm windows. Of course more insulation and better weather stripping are required to keep the structure comfortable. In any climate, good insulation is needed for effective air conditioning.

2. Where prevailing winds blow across an area, houses should be faced so that outside living areas are protected. The side facing the wind should have few large window areas; this prevents excessive heat loss. In extreme cases, houses have been built with

69

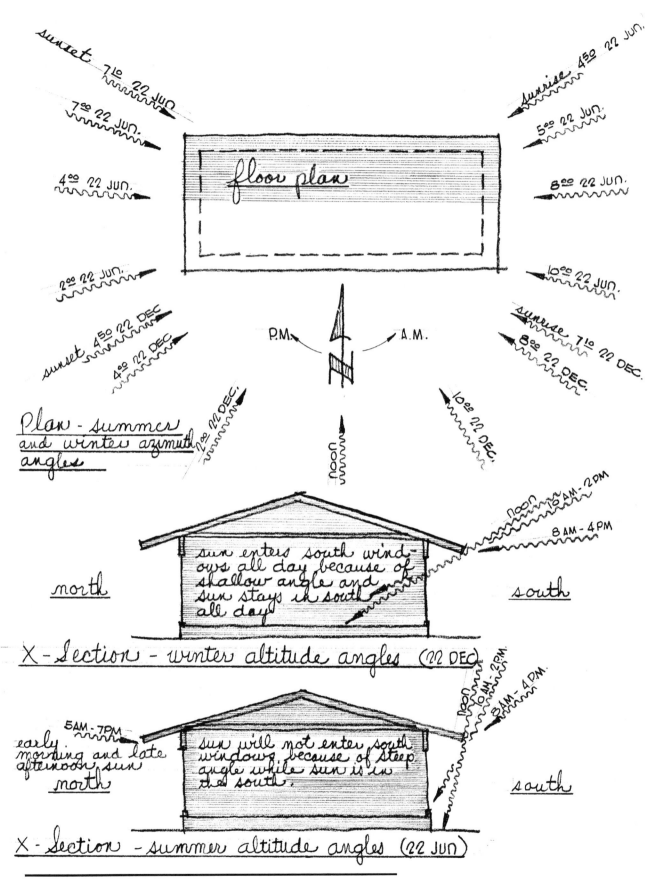

sunset 7¹⁰ 22 JUN.
7⁰⁰ 22 JUN.
4⁰⁰ 22 JUN.
2⁰⁰ 22 JUN.
sunset 4⁵⁰ 22 DEC
4⁰⁰ 22 DEC.

floor plan

sunrise 4⁵⁰ 22 JUN.
5⁰⁰ 22 JUN.
8⁰⁰ 22 JUN.
10⁰⁰ 22 JUN.
sunrise 7¹⁰ 22 DEC.
8⁰⁰ 22 DEC.

P.M.   A.M.
N
noon

2⁰⁰ 22 DEC.
10⁰⁰ 22 DEC.

Plan - summer
and winter azimuth
angles

noon   10 AM - 2 PM
8 AM - 4 PM

north

sun enters south wind-
ows all day because of
shallow angle and
sun stays in south
all day

south

X - Section - winter altitude angles (22 DEC)

noon 10 AM - 2 PM
8 AM - 4 PM

5 AM - 7 PM

early
morning and late
afternoon sun
north

sun will not enter south
windows because of steep
angle while sun is in
the south

south

70 X - Section - summer altitude angles (22 JUN)

FIGURE 8-4 Sun angles throughout the year on a south-facing building

the lower half of the windward wall below grade.

3. In an area of heavy rainfall, provide extensive covered areas between buildings and adequate cover over entrances. Gutters and downspouts are needed also. In desert areas, however, gutters are usually eliminated in residential structures.

4. The roof of the building must be designed to support or shed snow if heavy snows are expected.

5. If the site has a desirable view, sometimes a compromise may be made between efficiency and esthetics. For instance, in a hot climate where the site offers a view to the west, either some arrangement should be made to protect the view windows or the view should be ignored. On the other hand, if the view is to the south, there is no problem.

6. One feature of a house that yields great dividends and is closely related to orientation is insulation in roof and walls. Any heating or cooling system needs insulation for efficient operation. Weather stripping of doors and windows is usually done when a building is insulated.

7. Further compromises with thermal efficiency, lot size, traffic, and personal preference must be made so that service areas, access between areas, and automobile parking can be provided. The clothesline, garbage can, and garage should be close to the kitchen or rear entrance of a residence for obvious reasons. When parking areas are needed, they should be convenient to the main entrances of the building, the garage (or loading dock), or both. Be sure to consider these areas when orienting the building.

STUDY SUGGESTIONS

1. Evaluate, on the basis of orientation, some existing building with which you are familiar. Try to improve on it.

2. Study a magazine article or text on orientation, and decide which factors are of most importance in your locality.

STUDENT PROBLEM

1. Determine the date on which it is desirable to have the sun enter the south windows in your area. Using the sun table (A-3), determine the extent of overhang which will permit the sun to enter south windows on this date. Apply this information to the structural section.

2. As an experiment, try this same overhang with other types and pitches of roof to determine the advantages or disadvantages of each.

CHAPTER 9
LANDSCAPING

VALUES OF LANDSCAPING

Any building, no matter how well or poorly designed, may be improved by landscaping. The soft lines of trees and shrubs set off the sharp lines of the building, and the presence of growing things moderates the weather around the structure. To prove this, compare the appearance and livability of a brand-new house on a bare plot with its well-established neighbors. Certain commercial buildings demand landscaping, and any building in a hot climate is greatly improved by trees and vegetation.

Many books are written on landscaping, and there are several schools of thought regarding the arrangement of plantings. Good books on the subject are available at any library. If you are especially interested, check one out.

RELATIONSHIPS BETWEEN LANDSCAPING AND ORIENTATION

This chapter is closely related to the chapter on orientation, and the two should be considered together. Only the functional side of landscaping can be presented here. Its important uses are protecting from sun and wind, screening objectionable views and framing desirable ones, using trees and shrubs as fences, and setting off the lines of the building (see Figs. 5-1, 8-1, and 9-1).

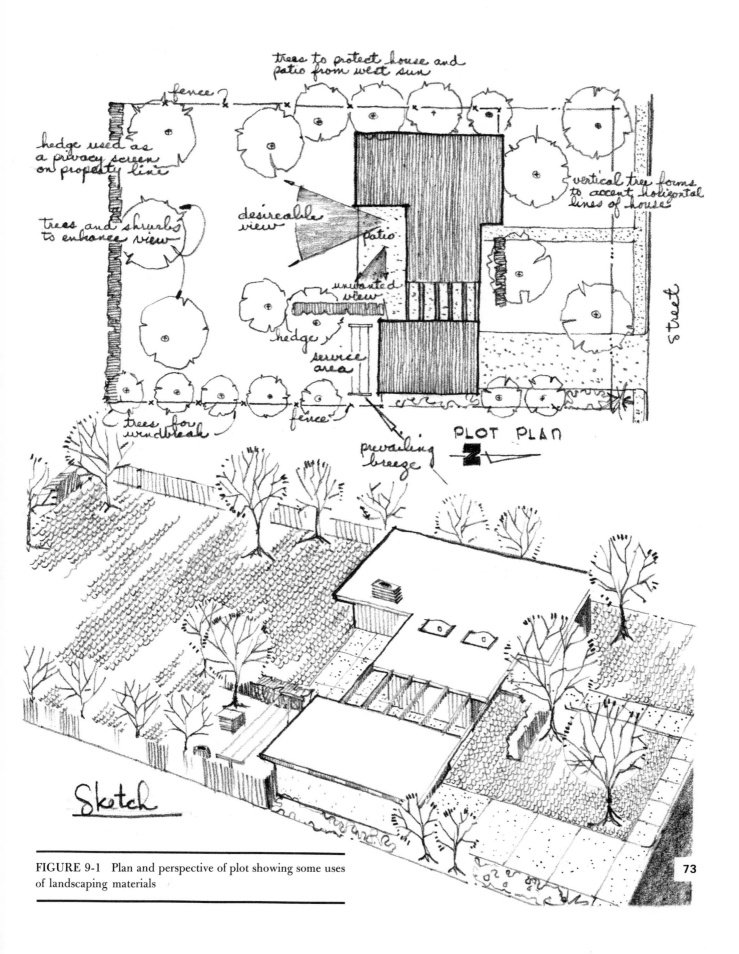

trees to protect house and
patio from west sun

fence?

hedge used as
a privacy screen
on property line

vertical tree forms
to accent horizontal
lines of house

desireable
view

trees and shrubs
to enhance view

patio

street

unwanted
view

hedge

service
area

PLOT PLAN

trees for
windbreak

fence

prevailing
breeze

Sketch

FIGURE 9-1   Plan and perspective of plot showing some uses
of landscaping materials

73

1. *Trees and shrubs as sun and wind protection* (mainly covered in "Orientation"). A knowledge of the path of the sun and direction of prevailing winds is of first importance in planning the location of plantings. To merely shut out the sun or wind, plant a dense hedge or row of trees in the proper spot. To provide a comfortable shaded area near the house, plant a large tree. For summer shade and winter sun, plant a tree that loses its leaves in winter. For constant shade, plant evergreens. A few trees to the west of a house in a hot climate will decrease the summer heat load considerably. This will save the owner a substantial amount of money that might otherwise have been spent on cooling.

2. *Trees and shrubs in relation to the view.* The view from any window may be either improved or concealed by proper plantings. To conceal it, plant a screen in front of it. To set it off, plant trees and shrubs to frame it. Usually a large, open, growing tree will greatly improve the effect of the view seen through it.

3. *Trees and shrubs as fences.* Many types of plants may be used in a hedge to make an excellent fence. Any thorny hedge will keep people and large animals out of a property as effectively as barbed wire. Most close-growing hedges are almost as good. One advantage of a growing fence is that it never needs painting, though it will need pruning. Usually it will look better than most cheap fence materials.

4. *Trees and shrubs to set off the building.* When planted in front of the building, trees and shrubs provide soft lines to offset and soften the lines of the structure. They also give a feeling of space and scale to the architectural features of the building.

TREATMENT OF THE GROUND

In addition to large plantings, ground covers, grass, and paving areas are extremely important to the design of a good landscape plan.

1. *Ground covers.* Ivy, strawberry, and other low-growing plants provide ground protection, color, and texture in areas away from traffic.

2. *Grasses and other lawn materials.* These will serve the same purposes as ground covers, and in addition will withstand foot traffic.

3. *Brick and natural stone.* Suitable for walks, patios, and walls, they provide a rich color and texture, and will take a great deal of traffic.

4. *Concrete.* It can be used in the same ways as stone and is extremely durable, but it lacks the richness of natural materials.

5. *Plant-mix surfacing, or black top.* A useful material for large areas of paving because of its economy.

DESIGN

When planning the landscape, keep it simple and functional. Avoid "pretty" patterns and complicated arrangements of plantings. Remember that a beautiful geometric design, as seen on a plan, does not guarantee a beautifully landscaped plot. From the usual points of view, the observer is aware of space and volume as well as area in a landscaped plot.

In mild or hot weather, outdoor spaces can be used to advantage for dining, entertaining, or simple enjoyment. Well-designed outdoor spaces can add greatly to the useful living area of any project.

Since landscape architecture is a profession in itself, this chapter has treated it only briefly. Interested students will profit from reading Garrett Eckbo's "Landscape and the Art of Its Design" (McGraw-Hill Book Company), or any other good text.

STUDY SUGGESTIONS

1. Read a book on landscaping, and try to work the ideas you like into your own project.
2. Identify some of your local trees, and decide which ones will work best for specific conditions.

STUDENT PROBLEM

1. From a functional point of view, plan the major landscaping over the site, or plot plan. Consider shade, sun, privacy, and view. The structural section must be considered as well as the plan at this point. Use care in placing areas of ground covers and paving materials. Consider durability, beauty, suitability to the local area, and maintenance.
2. Place fences and overhead coverings, or treillage, if they are needed.

CHAPTER 10
REGIONAL DIFFERENCES
IN DESIGN
AND CONSTRUCTION

LOCAL CONDITIONS

Many different types of construction are found throughout the country. The differences are brought about principally by climate, availability of materials, and regional architectural trends and tastes. Because these factors overlap in many ways and their effects are further complicated by local and personal factors, the student should investigate conditions and preferences in his own area.

Many weather factors have already been treated in Chap. 8. Other construction and design features affected by weather will be pointed out here. Hot and cold weather affect overall design, particularly regarding outdoor living, insulation, structure, and heating

and cooling requirements. The frost line in winter affects the depth of footings, perimeter insulation at foundation walls, and insulation of plumbing lines. Basements are used in cold climates principally because the foundation walls must be excavated to basement depth anyway. Older houses in these areas used gravity heating, and gravity heating works best with a basement. The extra storage of basements plus personal preferences also favor their use. Basements are seldom used in the hot desert areas of California and Arizona. Cold weather also limits the use of large window areas. Rain and snow conditions affect the building greatly. Foundation drains, gutters, downspouts, and well-protected outdoor areas may all be needed in an area of severe winters. In arid sections,

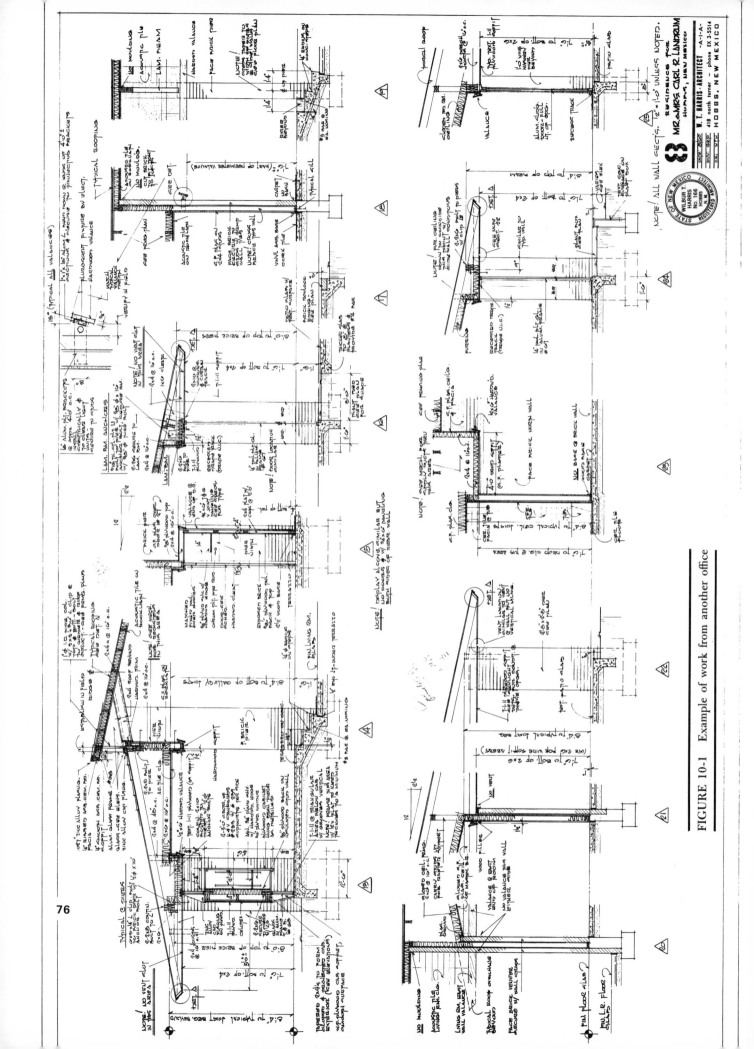

FIGURE 10-1 Example of work from another office

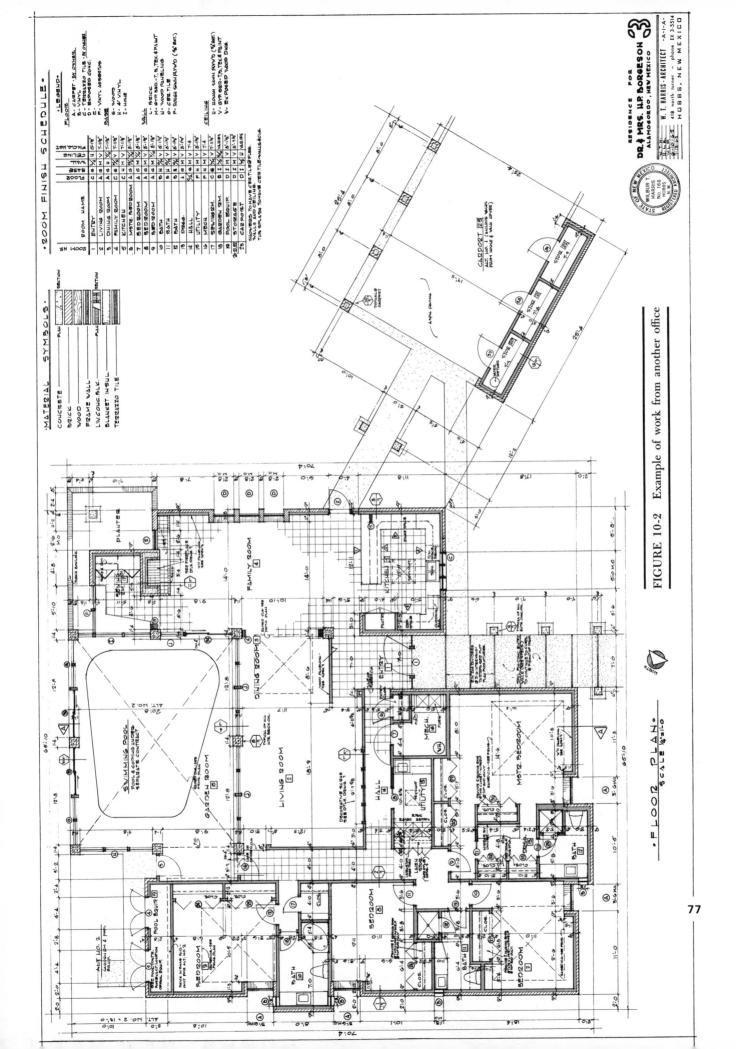

FIGURE 10-2 Example of work from another office

77

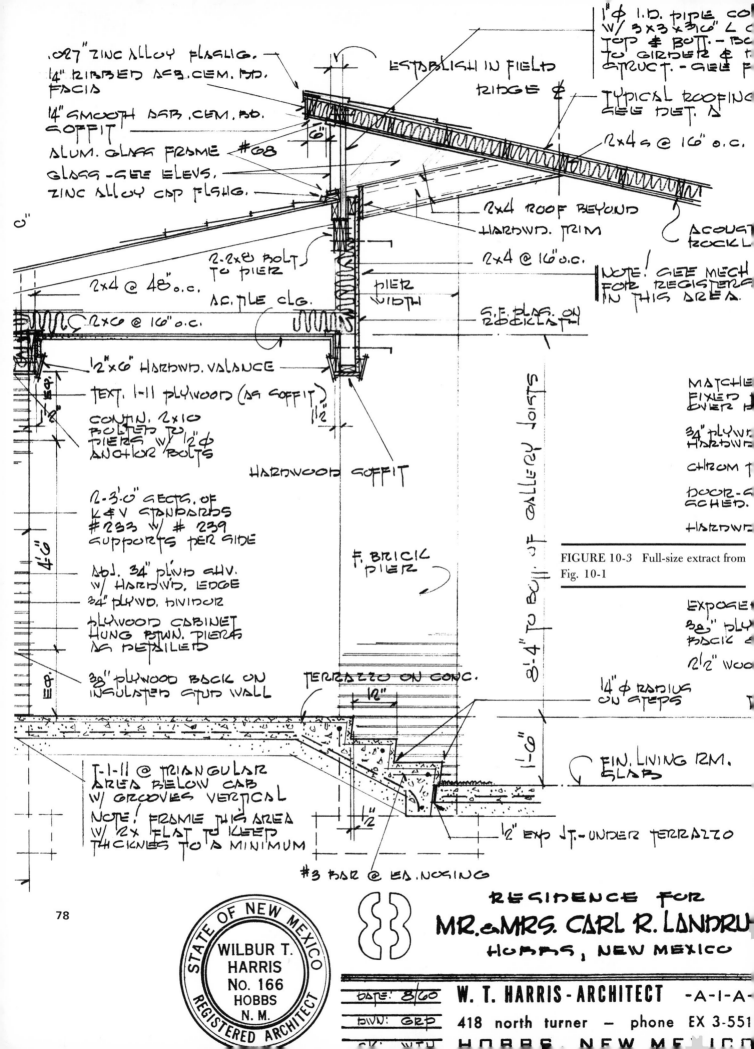

.027" ZINC ALLOY FLASHG.

1/4" RIBBED ASB. CEM. BD. FACIA

1/4" SMOOTH ASB. CEM. BD. SOFFIT

ALUM. GLASS FRAME #68

GLASS - SEE ELEVS.

ZINC ALLOY CAP FLSHG.

ESTABLISH IN FIELD

RIDGE ¢

1" ⌀ I.D. PIPE CO
W/ 3×3×3/16" L O
TOP ¢ BOTT. - BO
TO GIRDER ¢ S
STRUCT. - SEE F

TYPICAL ROOFING
SEE DET. A

2×4s @ 16" O.C.

2×4 ROOF BEYOND

HARDWD. TRIM

ACOUST
ROCKL

NOTE! SEE MECH
FOR REGISTERS
IN THIS AREA.

2-2×8 BOLT
TO PIER

AC. TILE CLG.

2×4 @ 48" O.C.

2×6 @ 16" O.C.

PIER
WIDTH

S.E. PLAS. ON
ROCKLATH

1/2"×6" HARDWD. VALANCE

TEXT. 1-11 PLYWOOD (AS SOFFIT)

CONTIN. 2×10 BOLTED TO PIERS W/ 1/2"⌀ ANCHOR BOLTS

2-3'.0" SECTS. OF K&V STANDARDS #233 W/ #239 SUPPORTS PER SIDE

ADJ. 3/4" PLYW. SHV. W/ HARDWD. EDGE

3/4" PLYWD. DIVIDER

PLYWOOD CABINET HUNG BTWN. PIERS AS DETAILED

3/8" PLYWOOD BACK ON INSULATED STUD WALL

HARDWOOD SOFFIT

F. BRICK PIER

TERRAZZO ON CONC.

12"

T-1-11 @ TRIANGULAR AREA BELOW CAB W/ GROOVES VERTICAL

NOTE! FRAME THIS AREA W/ 2× FLAT TO KEEP THICKNESS TO A MINIMUM

1/2"

#3 BAR @ EA. NOSING

1/2" EXP. JT. - UNDER TERRAZZO

8'.4" TO BOTT. OF GALLERY JOISTS

MATCHE
FIXED
OVER

3/4" PLYWO
HARDW

CHROM

DOOR-S
SCHED.

HARDW

FIGURE 10-3 Full-size extract from
Fig. 10-1

EXPOSE
3/8" PLY
BACK

2 1/2" WO

1/4" ⌀ RADIUS
ON STEPS

1'.0"

FIN. LIVING RM.
SLAB

78

RESIDENCE FOR
MR. & MRS. CARL R. LANDRU
HOBBS, NEW MEXICO

DATE: 8/60

DWN: GRP

W. T. HARRIS - ARCHITECT - A-I-A-

418 north turner — phone EX 3-551

HOBBS NEW MEXICO

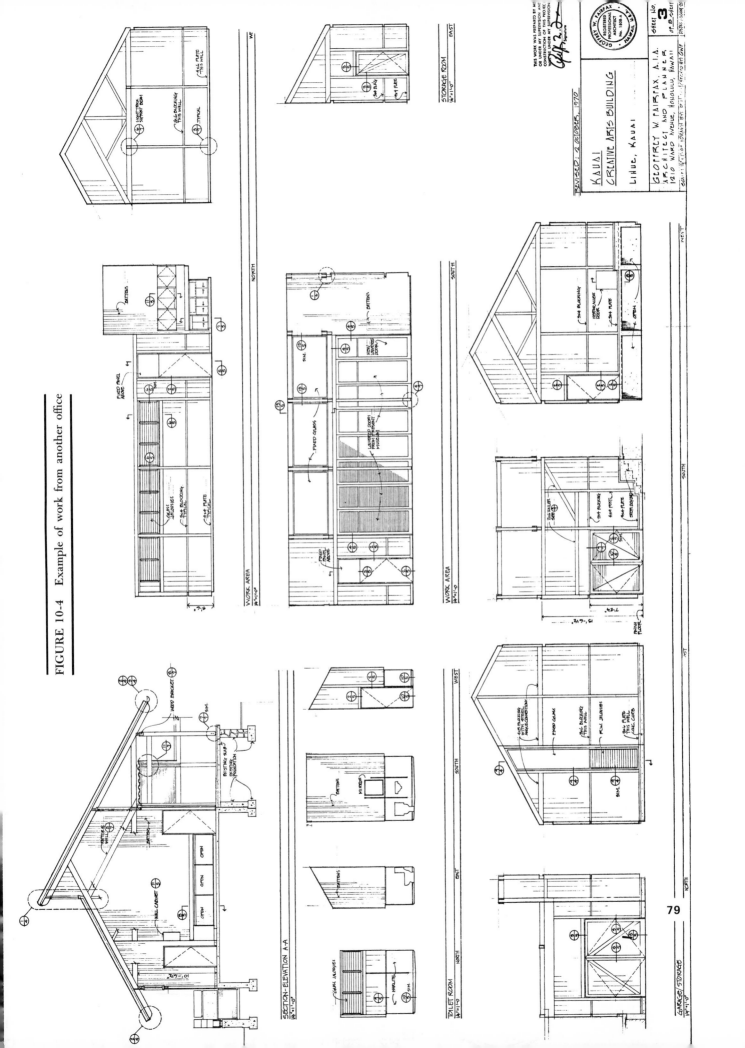

FIGURE 10-4 Example of work from another office

79

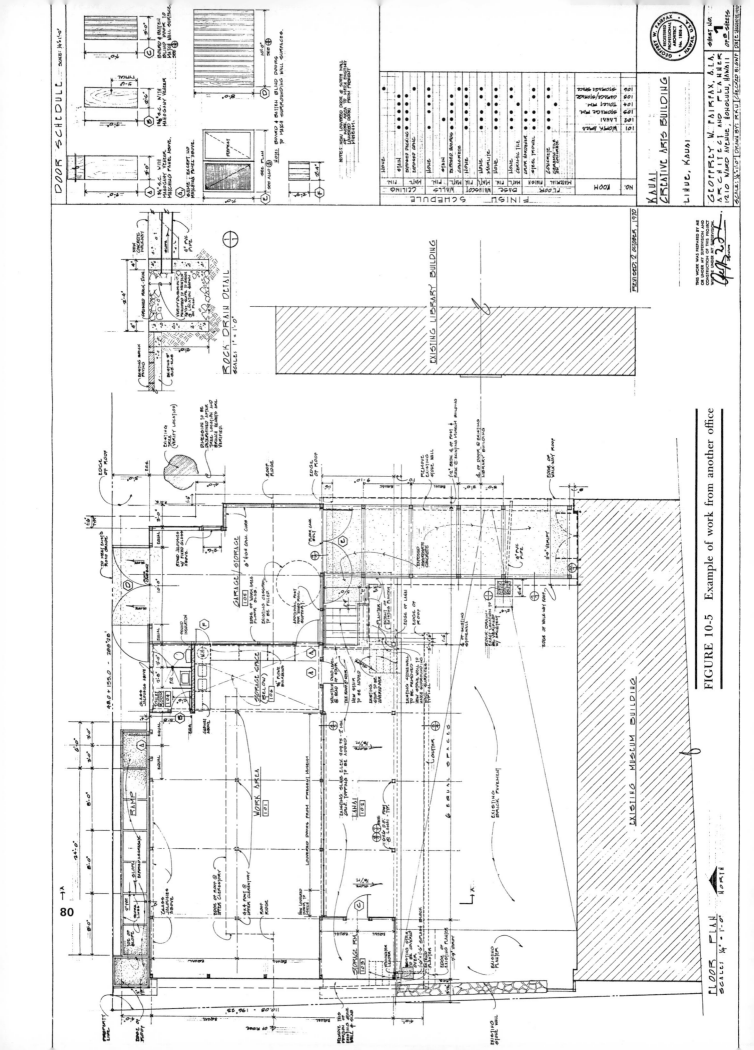

FIGURE 10-5 Example of work from another office

FIGURE 10-6   Full-size extract from Fig. 10-4

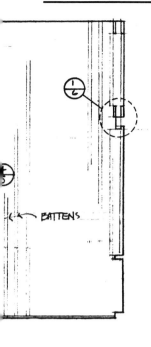

← BATTENS

SOUTH

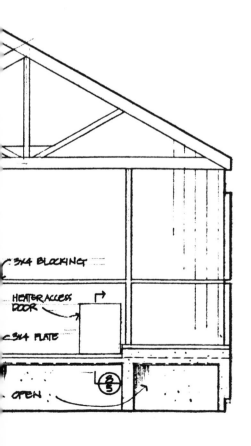

← 3x4 BLOCKING

HEATER ACCESS
DOOR

← 3x4 PLATE

③
⑤

← OPEN

WEST

STORAGE ROOM
1/4" = 1'-0"   EAST

③
⑤

③
⑤
3x4 BLKG
↓

← 4x4 PLATE

THIS WORK WAS PREPARED BY ME
OR UNDER MY SUPERVISION AND
CONSTRUCTION OF THIS PROJECT
WILL BE UNDER MY SUPERVISION.

Signature

REVISED: 2 OCTOBER, 1970

KAUAI
CREATIVE ARTS BUILDING

LIHUE, KAUAI

GEOFFREY W. FAIRFAX
REGISTERED
PROFESSIONAL
ARCHITECT
No. 1808-A
HAWAII   81

GEOFFREY W. FAIRFAX, A.I.A.
ARCHITECT AND PLANNER
1210 WARD AVENUE, HONOLULU, HAWAII

SHEET NO.
3
OF 8 SHEETS

SCALE: 1/4" = 1'-0"   DRAWN BY: P.H.   CHECKED BY: GWF   DATE: AUGUST 25

drains, gutters, and downspouts are usually omitted.

Wind, particularly hurricanes and cyclones, must be considered in the design of the structure. A basement or shelter is usually included in the plan as a safety factor, and the entire structure must be strengthened to withstand the extreme forces expected. Wall and roof bracing, foundation and roof ties, and so on normally exceed the requirements for other geographical areas.

Earthquakes, while not related to weather, are a regional factor which has to be considered. Foundation ties, wall bracing, and roof bracing must be made stronger to resist seismic forces.

Even though all other design considerations are the same, the easy availability and economy of certain local materials, and the dearth of others, have a large effect on the structure. For instance, redwood is most used in California and other West Coast areas because it is grown only there. Structural brick walls are seldom used in areas far from a brickyard. These are only a few of the obvious examples.

LOCAL DESIGN RESTRICTIONS

Architectural and constructional details of many buildings are limited by local pressures and tastes. People in certain areas feel compelled to build of brick, wood, or another particular material because most buildings in the area are so built. Some clients are forced by local custom to build in Cape Cod, Spanish Provincial, Ranch, or some other style; the feeling in other localities seems to encourage experiment and originality in construction. Many regional design and construction features, however, can be effectively adapted to other areas; tradition and lack of imagination tend to limit their use.

Such factors are impossible to ignore but are not usually noticed by the average person until he has reason to move from one part of the country to another. A draftsman, however, should always be aware of these factors in order to understand the differences between his drawings and those produced in other regions.

The illustrations shown here are examples of good solutions to conditions in widely separated parts of the country (Figs. 10-1 to 10-6).

REVIEW QUESTIONS

1. Look at the drawings and photos in a national magazine of buildings in other parts of the country. Are they different in appearance and construction from comparable buildings in your own area? Why?
2. Why are many residences in northern Maine square in shape? Why are many residences in Arizona rambling?
3. Do you think there are many commercial buildings of Spanish Colonial design in Boston, Massachusetts? Why?
4. Would you expect to find a newly constructed one-story wood-frame commercial building in the financial district in New York City? Why?
5. Why are coal-fired basement furnaces seldom found in San Diego, California?

STUDY SUGGESTIONS

1. Make a study of residential building practices and types in three widely distant parts of the country. This information can be found in any national architectural magazine.
2. In view of what you have learned from the above suggestion, try to adapt some of these practices to your own locality.

CHAPTER 11
PRESENTATION DRAWINGS

DEFINITION AND PURPOSE

Upon the completion of a set of preliminary drawings which seem to satisfy the client, the usual practice is to prepare a presentation drawing for the client's approval (Figs. 11-1 and 11-2). The purpose of the presentation drawing is to bring together the solution thus far to the client's problem, to convey to the draftsmen the designer's intent, or to sell the project to a financial institution. If it is approved, work can then start on the working drawings; if not, changes may easily be made before any further time and expense are involved. Presentation drawings are not working drawings, and the building contractor seldom sees them. If the student plans to do such a drawing

before the working drawings, this chapter should be studied; if not, he should proceed to the next chapter.

COMPOSITION OF PRESENTATION DRAWINGS

The types of drawings which may appear on the presentation drawing, named in the order of their importance, are floor plan, elevations, plot plan, sections, interior elevations, and exterior or interior perspectives. A very simple drawing might include only a floor plan and an elevation or two; an elaborate one might use all of the drawings mentioned. A good format for a student drawing would include a floor

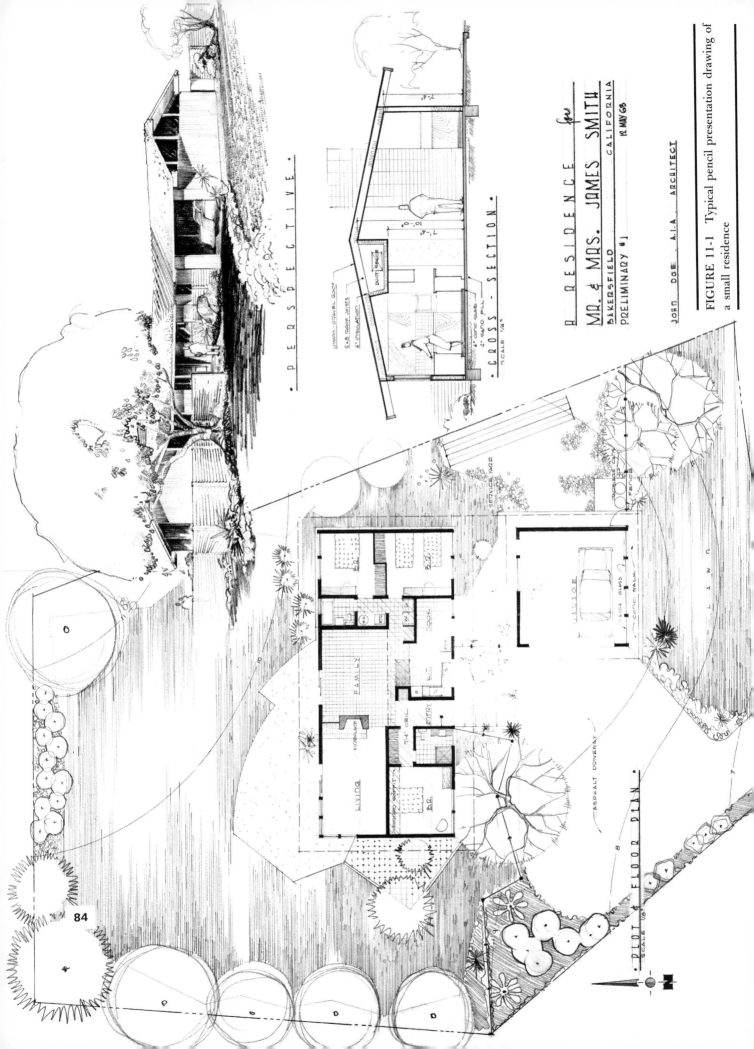

84

· PERSPECTIVE ·

· CROSS - SECTION ·
· SCALE 1/4" ·

A RESIDENCE for
MR. & MRS. JAMES SMITH
BAKERSFIELD   CALIFORNIA
PRELIMINARY #1   12 MAY 68

JOHN   DOE   A.I.A   ARCHITECT

FIGURE 11-1   Typical pencil presentation drawing of
a small residence

· PLOT & FLOOR PLAN ·
· SCALE 1/8" ·

· P E R S P E C T I V E ·

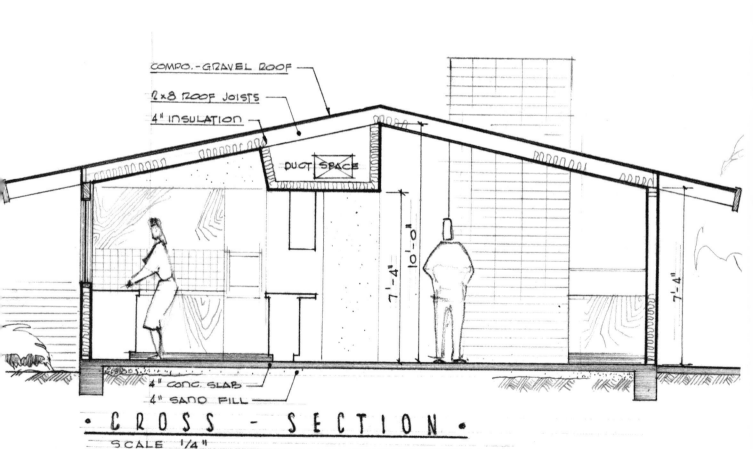

COMPO.-GRAVEL ROOF

2 x 8 ROOF JOISTS

4" INSULATION

DUCT SPACE

10'-0"

7'-4"

7'-4"

4" CONC. SLAB

4" SAND FILL

· C R O S S - S E C T I O N ·

SCALE 1/4"

FIGURE 11-2 Full-size extract from Fig. 11-1

85

A R E S I D E N C E *for*

M R. & M R S. J A M E S S M I T H

plan, two elevations, and a structural section. Usually the drawings are not completely dimensioned, because it is reasonable to expect that changes will be made before working drawings are started. At this stage, the effect of the total project should be emphasized rather than completeness of detail. One purpose of a presentation drawing is to "sell" the client.

Characteristics of the types of drawings used for presentation are described here:

1. Floor plans show only overall dimensions and room sizes, the walls are sometimes filled in very dark for visibility, and all the rooms are identified. Prevailing breeze and north arrows should be included as well as front and rear entrance indications. Electric outlets are omitted. Furniture and equipment, patios, parking areas, and landscaping close to the building should be shown. The roof overhang is generally drawn as a dashed line. Scale is indicated, usually $\frac{1}{8}$ or $\frac{1}{4}$ in. to the foot.

2. While one or more exterior elevations may be shown, the front elevation is always drawn. To indicate scale, conventionalized human figures are placed close to the building. Shrubs and trees, sometimes "transparent," are indicated. For realism shadows are drawn in, particularly the shadow of the roof overhang. It is good practice, but not necessary, to draw elevations to the same scale as the floor plan for ease in relating the two drawings.

3. The plot-landscaping plan should be quite complete, eliminating only dimensions and utilities, except the septic tank where required. Usually great care is taken in drawing in the landscaping, paving and streets, and fences or screens. Sometimes the plot and floor plan are combined, drawn at a scale larger than the usual plot plan. The usual scale varies between $\frac{1}{50}$ and $\frac{1}{16}$ in. to the foot.

4. When a cross section through the building is shown, important dimensions such as plate height, beam and rafter sizes, and roof pitch should be given. The scale may be $\frac{1}{4}$ to $\frac{3}{4}$ in. to the foot. Indicate all surface materials used.

5. When interior elevations are used, they commonly show only important wall areas. The scale is $\frac{1}{8}$ to $\frac{1}{4}$ in. to the foot.

6. Exterior or interior perspectives are usually drawn of the entrance or other important features of the building and sometimes of the entire project. The perspective is usually approximate rather than projected, and a viewpoint is chosen which will enhance the architectural features of the building.

MEDIA

Presentation drawings may be done in pencil, felt pen, crayon, colored pencil, charcoal, ink, pastels, water colors, or oil colors, depending on the purpose of the drawing and the budget involved. The style of drawing is much more casual than that used on working drawings. Pencil is most often used, generally on tracing paper so that the drawing may be duplicated. However, if the job is a large one it may be done in color, particularly pastels, water colors, or tempera.

WHITE ON BLACK

A dramatic effect can be achieved in a drawing by the use of a white line on a dark background. Several means are available for producing such drawings: white ink on a dark surface; scratchboard, in which the dark surface is removed to expose the white underlayer; and photography. The simplest method consists of photographing an existing drawing and then printing it reversed. The principal advantage of this method is that no new technique need be learned (Fig. 11-3).

Many different materials are used: tracing paper, drawing paper, illustration board, or textured papers. Common sizes used are 20 by 30 in. and 30 by 40 in., although any available paper size is suitable. A special type of presentation drawing is the brochure type, assembled in book form on standard-size sheets, usually $8\frac{1}{2}$ by 11 in. Each sheet has one drawing, and the sheets are bound in an attractive folder.

FORMAT

Certain printed information is required on the presentation drawing for identification, such as the title preceded by the word *proposed*, for example, "Proposed Residence for J. Jones." The client's address and/or the location of the building should be shown, as well as the name and address of the architectural firm or student involved.

· P E R S P E C T I V E ·

COMPO.-GRAVEL ROOF
2×8 ROOF JOISTS
4" INSULATION

DUCT SPACE

10'-0"
7'-4"
7'-4"

4" CONC. SLAB
4" SAND FILL

· C R O S S - S E C T I O N ·
SCALE 1/4"

FIGURE 11-3 White on black rendering (photo negative of Fig. 11-2)

A RESIDENCE for
MR. & MRS. JAMES SMITH
BAKERSFIELD CALIFORNIA

The composition of the material on a presentation drawing is more a matter of artistic taste than formula or rule. The student should examine the work of a professional and try to achieve a similar effect in technique and organization (Fig. 11-2). A pleasing, artistic style of drawing is more important to the success of a presentation drawing than it is to a working drawing. Good style requires artistic ability and constant practice.

SHORTCUTS

Because most presentation drawings are done quickly, it is an advantage to use any device which will save time or produce a good effect. Some of these simple, effective devices are:

1. *Templates.* They are available for practically any feature desired—landscape, furniture, machinery, and so forth.
2. *Transfer letters.* These letters are purchased in sheets of any size or lettering case. They are placed on the drawing as desired and rubbed off with a hard instrument. Their adhesive backing holds them firmly to the paper.
3. *Rubber stamps.* Any large city has firms which specialize in making rubber stamps from their customers' drawings. These stamps save a great deal of time in rendering often-used objects such as trees and shrubs on landscape plans.

REVIEW QUESTIONS

1. In your own words define a presentation drawing.
2. Do any of the building trades use presentation drawings in their work?

3. What is the principal advantage of doing presentation drawings on tracing paper?
4. What types of drawings, for example, floor plan, may appear on a presentation drawing?
5. A presentation drawing shows exactly how the proposed building will look. True or False? Explain.

STUDY SUGGESTIONS

1. Cut some presentation drawings out of magazines or newspapers and study them. Pick a style you like, and apply it to a practice drawing of your own.
2. Practice sketching shrubbery, trees, conventionalized human figures, and automobiles whenever you have free time.

STUDENT PROBLEM

This problem is optional at this point; it may also be done after completion of the working drawings.

1. Assemble the preliminary drawings and plan a pleasing format on a piece of paper of the size that will be used for the working drawings. Include a combination floor–landscape plan, a full structural section, a rendered elevation, and a title. Use any desired scales; trace existing drawings where possible.
2. For extra credit, draw a perspective of the house viewed from the front. Render it on tracing paper showing trees, shrubs, an automobile, and two human figures at different distances.

CHAPTER 12
RELATIONSHIPS
AMONG DRAWINGS

AGREEMENT AMONG DRAWINGS

No working drawing can be drawn in isolation from the others. Neither can changes in one be made without considering the effect of those changes on the others (Figs. 12-1 and 12-2). The major drawings of a set, such as plot plan, foundation plan, structural sections, floor plan, elevations, and interior elevations, must agree in all respects. Other drawings, such as electrical, plumbing, ventilating, and air-conditioning plans, are closely related to one another and especially to the floor plan. Some drawings, such as particular miscellaneous details, are related closely to only one or two of the others. For instance, cabinet details must agree with the interior elevations and the floor plan.

These are only a few of the possible combinations. Some obvious reasons for being careful are: Many drawings are traced in part from the floor plan; agreement in projection must exist among all drawings; clearance must be maintained among footings, beams, pipes, ducts, and so on; and plumbing, electrical, and duct connections must be provided for appliances.

PRELIMINARY PLANNING

Certain construction features must be checked closely; for example, stairs usually require a minimum of 6 ft 6 in. of headroom from the tread. This problem must be worked out orthographically in the prelimi-

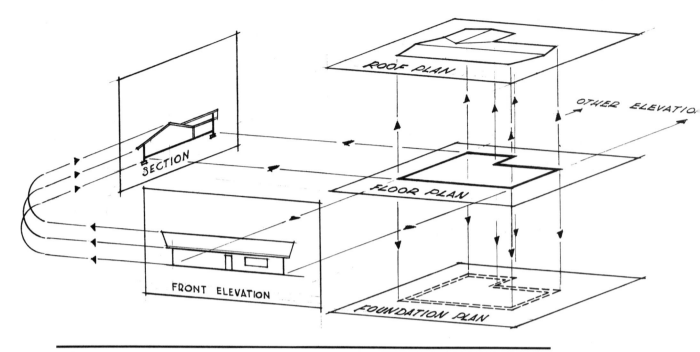

FIGURE 12-1 Relationships in projection among some of the more important drawings in a set

nary drawings, because the working drawings cannot easily be changed later. An error in the size of the stairwell could be an expensive mistake to correct. Another common problem is providing adequate clearance for pipes and ducts in restricted attic spaces. Though the drawings sometimes indicate plenty of clearance, the sheet-metal man and the plumber often find that their jobs conflict because of a draftsman's oversight. Other problems arise because of the space requirements of under-the-floor and under-the-slab ducts and footings, roof bracing, ducts, plumbing vents, and wall thickness. Problems which are more difficult to anticipate involve the intersections of oblique roof and ceiling planes with sloping pipes or ducts. These are difficult to detail exactly.

CHANGES IN DRAWINGS

The following is an example of the amount of work caused by a change. If the location of the heating-refrigerating plant were changed after completion of the working drawings, changes would have to be made in the floor plan, foundation plan, plumbing plan, electrical plan, heating and air-conditioning plan, and

possibly the roof and floor framing plans, elevations, and plot plan. In case of conflict among drawings, large-scale details take precedence over other drawings because of the obvious increase in accuracy achieved by drawing at larger scale.

In many situations it is necessary to start drawing a detail from some existing or otherwise fixed point. This point could be the height of a canopy, from which window heights would be derived, or the corner studs in a frame wall, which would locate the edge of a window jamb. Sometimes the size of a door or window frame will determine the spacing of the module lines of an entire building. The size of any modular building material, such as cinder block, will restrict the size and location dimensions of the building to multiples of this module.

DRAFTING-ROOM PROBLEMS

Agreement among drawings becomes more complicated in a large drafting room in which several draftsmen may be working on different drawings of a set at the same time. Although the main responsibility for solving this problem lies with the architect or head

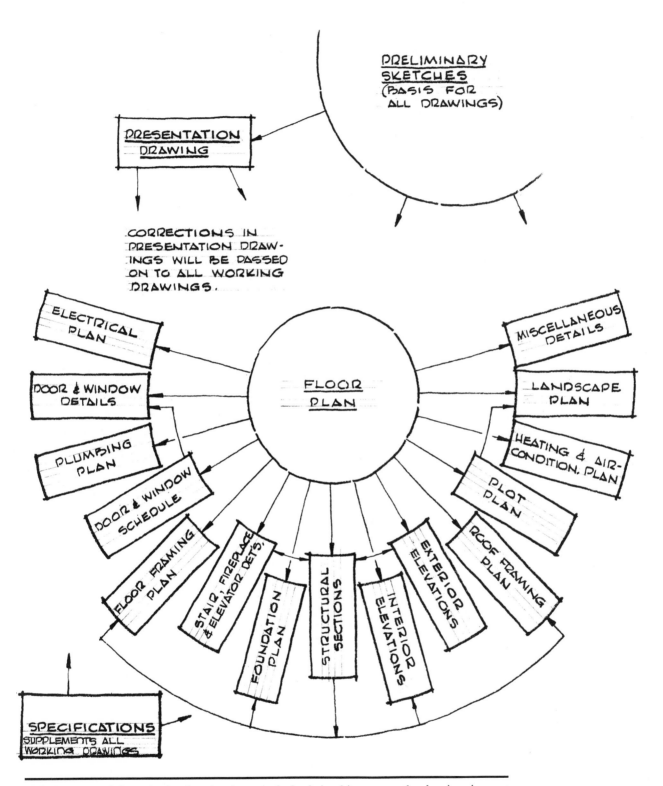

PRELIMINARY
SKETCHES
(BASIS FOR
ALL DRAWINGS)

PRESENTATION
DRAWING

CORRECTIONS IN
PRESENTATION DRAW-
INGS WILL BE PASSED
ON TO ALL WORKING
DRAWINGS.

ELECTRICAL
PLAN

DOOR & WINDOW
DETAILS

PLUMBING
PLAN

DOOR & WINDOW
SCHEDULE

FLOOR FRAMING
PLAN

STAIR, FIREPLACE
& ELEVATOR DETS.

FOUNDATION
PLAN

STRUCTURAL
SECTIONS

INTERIOR
ELEVATIONS

EXTERIOR
ELEVATIONS

ROOF FRAMING
PLAN

PLOT
PLAN

HEATING & AIR-
CONDITION. PLAN

LANDSCAPE
PLAN

MISCELLANEOUS
DETAILS

FLOOR
PLAN

SPECIFICATIONS
SUPPLEMENTS ALL
WORKING DRAWINGS

FIGURE 12-2   Schematic drawing showing principal relationships among the drawings in a set

draftsman, each draftsman, in the interest of his employer's reputation and his own job, should be aware of the relationship of the drawing on which he is working to all the other drawings.

Most of the drawings of the set are developed together in normal office practice to avoid conflict and unnecessary changes, since a minor change in one drawing could affect several others to a great degree. The most important drawings in the set from the standpoint of their influence on all of the others are the floor plan, structural sections, schedules, plot plan, exterior elevations, and stair and fireplace sections. In unusual structures some large piece of equipment, such as a hoist or a large machine, may also have a great effect on the total structure.

See Fig. 12-2, which shows the relationships among drawings. It can be seen that the basic drawings must be accurately worked out at the start, even though they may be completed in some other order.

REVIEW QUESTIONS

1. Name three working drawings affected by an inside staircase.

2. Point out some possible points of conflict between the heating and air-conditioning plan and the second-floor plan.

3. Name a fixture or appliance used in a residence which if moved would affect at least three working drawings.

4. How many working drawings in a set are supplemented by the specifications?

5. How many working drawings in a set are affected by a fireplace?

6. In view of your answers to the above questions, can you see the reason for using care in drawing the preliminaries?

7. Does the draftsman have any responsibility for the agreement of his own drawing with others?

STUDY SUGGESTIONS

1. Look over a set of working drawings, and locate points of agreement among several drawings.

2. Make any change you wish in one existing working drawing, and then pencil in all the changes called for on the other drawings. Try several different types of change.

CHAPTER 13
WORKING DRAWINGS

DEFINITION AND PURPOSE

From this point on, all drawings described are called *working drawings*. The term working drawing is used in all fields of drafting, and the general definition, as stated in French and Vierck's "Fundamentals of Engineering Drawing," 2d ed. (McGraw-Hill Book Company, 1966) is: "A working drawing is any drawing used to give information for the manufacture or construction of a machine or the erection of a structure. Complete knowledge for the production of a machine or structure is given by a *set* of working drawings conveying all the facts fully and explicitly so that further instructions are not required." (See Figs. 13-1 and 13-2.) To satisfy this definition, architectural working drawings must include:

1. *Orthographic projection:* The true shape of all features described.
2. *Proper dimensioning:* The true size of all features described.
3. *Call-outs:* Complete notes regarding items not fully described by size and shape.
4. *Construction details, sections:* Enlarged drawings of construction features not completely shown in small-scale drawings or of features which are hidden.
5. *Electrical plan, plumbing plan, heating and ventilating plan, and so on:* Classification of different kinds of information for clarity and completeness of description.
6. *Specifications:* Bid documents, general information, and specific instructions.

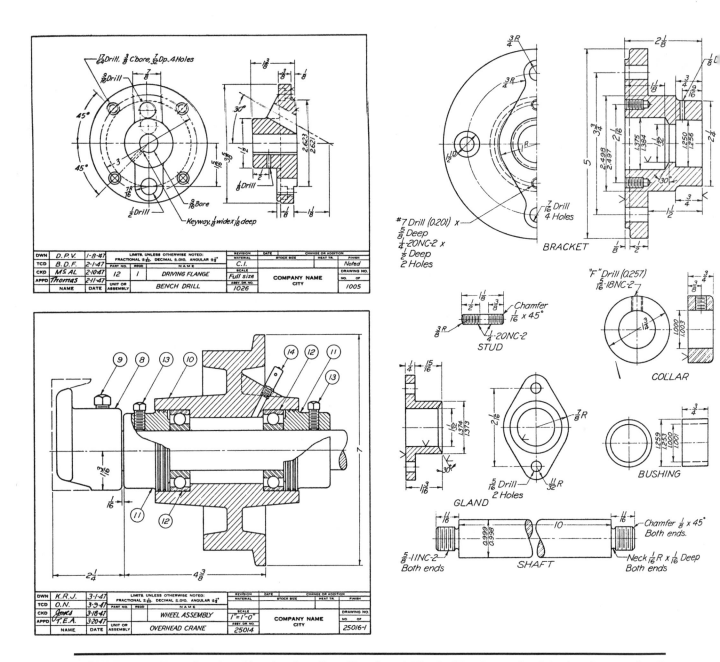

FIGURE 13-1 Examples of working drawings (from French and Vierck, "Fundamentals of Engineering Drawings")

In other words, a perfect set of working drawings would contain all the information needed by a builder to complete a building exactly as specified by the architect. In practice, however, continual inspection of the structure is made by the architect, by city or county building inspectors, and sometimes by the client to ensure compliance with the drawings. Specifications are included in any complete set of working drawings; they will be covered in Chap. 28.

MATERIALS AND EQUIPMENT

On the assumption that students in the class have had at least a year of mechanical drawing before using this book, terms such as *orthographic projection* and descriptions of objects such as *45° triangle* will be omitted from the following discussion on working drawings. Explanation will be made only when terms peculiar to architectural drawing are encountered.

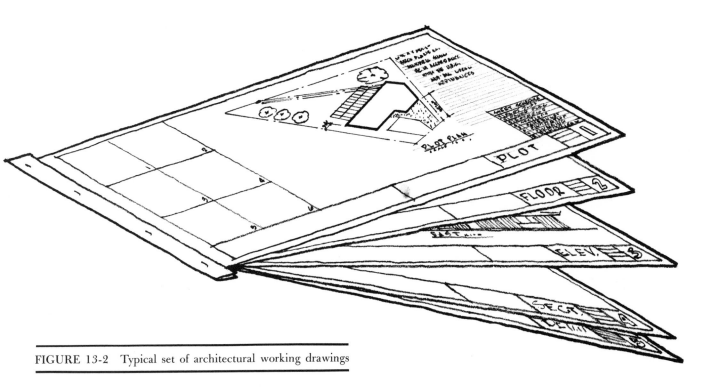

FIGURE 13-2 Typical set of architectural working drawings

Tools and equipment used by architectural draftsmen:

1. *Pencils:* Wood or automatic. Weight of lead varies according to individual preference; H to 4H are commonly used.
2. *Pencil pointer:* Sandpaper or mechanical type.
3. *Triangles:* Average sizes, 45° by 10 in., 30–60° by 10 in.
4. *T square or drafting machine:* Both used. This is a matter of personal preference.
5. *Scale:* Architect's and engineer's.
6. *French curves, circle, ellipse, plumbing and electrical templates:* To cut drafting time and improve the appearance of the drawing.
7. *Erasers, erasing shields, erasing machines, dry cleaner, and brush:* For use in correcting mistakes and keeping drawings clean.
8. *Drawing boards, drafting tables:* Common sizes of boards, 20 by 26 in., 24 by 30 in., 30 by 40 in. A table can be made by putting legs on a flush door. Size and type are determined by storage space available or the sheet size desired. For school use, where storage is a problem, 20 by 26 in. is the usual size, and an 18- by 24-in. sheet size is convenient. These are, however, much smaller than the 24- by 30-in. sheet size often used in professional practice.

Types of paper used:

1. *Opaque or transparent paper:* Used for rough studies until the final outlines of the drawing are determined. The finished drawing may be traced from this copy.
2. *Tracing paper or plastic film:* Used for finished drawings. Use of good-quality paper is important. No matter what the price, paper is much cheaper than the drafting time expended on it.

LINEWORK

Standards of linework:

Use ASA recommendations; emphasize black linework, consistency in drawing each type of line, and cleanliness, or absence of stains and smudges. The style of drawing is a matter of taste and ability; the student should copy some professional example. Never sacrifice legibility for "style." For speed and accuracy, use electrical, plumbing, and other templates wherever possible.

BASES FOR LINEWORK STANDARDS

The choice of linework of varying thickness and darkness is based on the relative importance of the feature,

95

ease of reading the print, and artistic effect. Cutting-plane and profile lines are drawn heavier than the most important object lines. Cutting-plane lines are thick in all fields of drafting, while profile lines emphasize principal features of the drawing. It is recommended that the most important object outlines be drawn in a heavier black line than objects of lesser importance.

Dashed lines either represent hidden objects or are used in a conventionalized way to represent objects above the cutting plane on a floor plan; these dashed lines are thinner still than the others and black.

Dimension, extension, and center lines, which do not represent objects, are drawn black and as thin as possible. Trees and shrubs, whose size and shape are estimated, may be drawn with dimension lines.

Call-outs, or leaders, are drawn like dimension lines but at an angle or curved so that they will not be mistaken for other lines of the drawing.

Texture and hachure lines do not show outlines of or changes in a surface; therefore they are drawn thin and grey to avoid confusion.

Construction, projection, and lettering guide lines are not intended to be reproduced; therefore they are drawn very thin and light grey in color. Check the illustrations in this book for the exact appearance of the "alphabet" of lines.

VARIATIONS

Linework standards differ somewhat from one geographic area to another. Variations from the standards stated here are permissible as long as the drawings print and read well. For example, this book recommends that a dimension line be used for landscape materials. Some draftsmen and architects use a fairly thick, grainy line for trees and shrubs, more for artistic than for practical reasons. Both methods communicate well, and the two are equally acceptable. However, the student should not try to mix styles, as he does not yet have the experience and judgment necessary for these decisions. He should follow a consistent scheme until he becomes proficient in its use.

VISIBILITY

Decisions concerning the visibility of lines are usually difficult for beginning draftsmen. These decisions can be made easily if a few simple principles are followed:

1. Outlines of a measurable object such as concrete or walls follow the rules of orthographic drawing. If they are behind or under some other object, they are shown as hidden lines.

2. Landscape materials are considered to be transparent; therefore they do not follow the rules of visibility. In other words, the outline of a tree should be drawn over everything below it, and it can overlap any other plant material without the use of hidden lines. A shrub underneath a solid overhang should not be drawn at all, but should be called out by note. If it is necessary to show plants close to the building, the overhang should be shown in dashed lines or omitted.

3. Textures are not needed on a drawing but are usually used for artistic reasons and for visual separation of areas. Therefore they are never shown as hidden lines, and they should be omitted when they occur under or behind any solid object.

4. There is no problem of visibility with extension, center, call-out, and cutting-plane lines. They do not change their character under any conditions.

5. Strictly speaking, the only lines which should be shown on a structural section are the ones which are actually cut by the cutting plane. For clearness in reading the drawing, however, other lines behind the cutting plane are shown, for instance, the rafter, joist, and roof bracing. When such lines cross one another, the most important one is shown as an object line and the other is shown as a hidden line.

REPRODUCTION

Practically all working drawings must be reproduced; sometimes when a large project is involved, as many as 50 sets of drawings may be made. The originals, or tracings, are kept on file and changes may later be made on them, while the reproductions, or "blue-prints" as the layman calls them, are given to the contractors or workmen for actual construction purposes. There are several methods of making reproductions. However, the most-used methods have basic similarities, and all have the same end in view—to make a true copy of an original drawing. The two processes involved are exposure and development. All processes produce either dark lines on a light background or vice versa. Exposure is made in the most common processes by placing a sensitized paper behind the tracing and exposing them both to a strong light. Development is a result of either exposing this sensitized sheet to a gas, usually ammonia, or wetting it with a chemical solution. The portion of the sheet which was covered by a pencil mark will develop and show as dark on light, or light on dark, depending on the process.

A discussion of each type of reproduction process and its advantages and disadvantages is not of great importance, inasmuch as every city of fair size has a blueprint service which offers a choice of at least two common processes. Of great importance, though, is a knowledge of one step in the procedure, namely, exposure. The machine cannot tell the difference between an important line and a stain, spot, or smudge; it reproduces them all. Also, a faint or indistinct pencil line will reproduce as a faint or indistinct line on the reproduction. This is the main reason for using black, consistent linework and keeping the drawing clean.

CLEANLINESS

People's hands are covered with a film of oil or moisture which can be absorbed by the paper and trap dirt and dust. Keep your hands off the drawing surface by resting them on a small piece of scrap paper. Erase the first sign of dirt immediately. On tracings, erase both sides of the paper when mistakes are made; graphite from the original will stick to the back of the tracing and will sometimes show on the prints. Any drawing that is not entirely legible or that lacks any small detail is not a good working drawing. Remember, the building is built from the reproductions, not the originals.

FORMAT OF SHEET

A suitable format—the size, style, and arrangement of material on the drawing—should be chosen which will be complete, economical of space, and pleasing to the eye (see A-4). It should be used consistently on all drawings in the set so that the person reading the drawings will be able to find desired information quickly. The format may be copied from an existing drawing, or the student may decide to develop his own; if so, the following factors must be considered:

1. Margins: $\frac{1}{2}$ in. on the top, bottom, and right side, and 1 in. on the left side. Margins are provided not only for appearance, but also to prevent the loss of information near the edges in case the tracing does not register perfectly with the sensitized sheet. The larger margin at the left is necessary so that the set of drawings may be bound together at the left.

2. A record or title strip should contain essential information not shown on the actual working drawing. It should be placed so that it will be prominent as the reader turns each sheet while going through the set; therefore, it should be placed at the bottom or the bottom right of every sheet. The title strip should have as a minimum the following information:

   a. The office which produced the drawing, firm name, address, architect's (or student's) name and initials, and initials of the person who checked the drawing (head draftsman or instructor).

   b. The client for whom the drawings were produced, job number and title of each drawing, and address of the job.

   c. The title of the drawing itself, revisions, the date completed, and the sheet number, for example, sheet 4 of 7 (usually placed at the lower right corner for easy reference). The total number of drawings in the set should always be shown (seven in this case) so that the person reading the plans can be sure he has not lost any of the last sheets. The title, for example, Plot Plan, is usually placed in the record strip and also within the margins under the drawing, since there may be more than one type of drawing to a sheet. Each drawing on the sheet should be clearly labeled.

   d. The scale should always appear within the margins under the title of each drawing or detail.

ARRANGEMENT OF DRAWINGS

The following information on procedures and order of linework refers to all drawings in the set, not to any one drawing in particular. Before starting the working drawings, it is good practice to decide in advance which information should be placed on each sheet, then to make an outline of the full set. In an

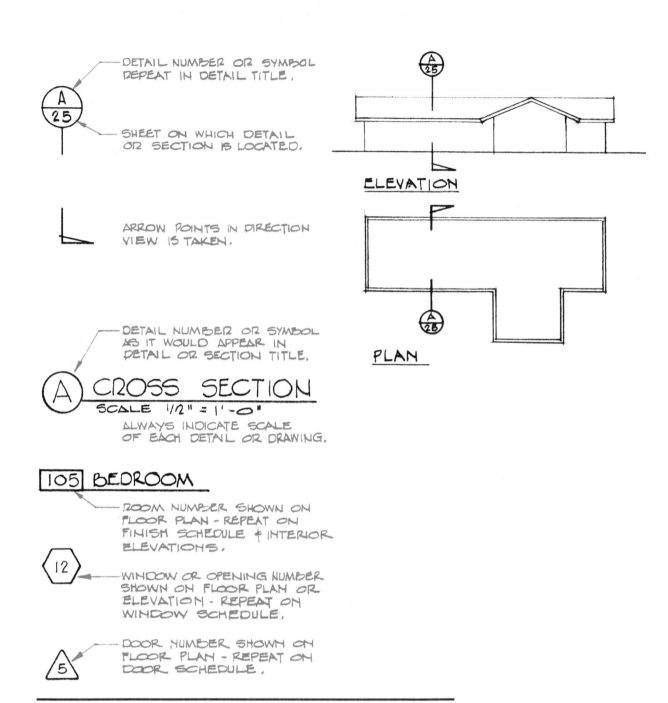

DETAIL NUMBER OR SYMBOL
REPEAT IN DETAIL TITLE.

A
25

SHEET ON WHICH DETAIL
OR SECTION IS LOCATED.

ARROW POINTS IN DIRECTION
VIEW IS TAKEN.

DETAIL NUMBER OR SYMBOL
AS IT WOULD APPEAR IN
DETAIL OR SECTION TITLE.

A CROSS SECTION
SCALE 1/2" = 1'-0"
ALWAYS INDICATE SCALE
OF EACH DETAIL OR DRAWING.

105 BEDROOM

ROOM NUMBER SHOWN ON
FLOOR PLAN - REPEAT ON
FINISH SCHEDULE & INTERIOR
ELEVATIONS.

12

WINDOW OR OPENING NUMBER
SHOWN ON FLOOR PLAN OR
ELEVATION - REPEAT ON
WINDOW SCHEDULE.

5

DOOR NUMBER SHOWN ON
FLOOR PLAN - REPEAT ON
DOOR SCHEDULE.

A
25

ELEVATION

A
25

PLAN

FIGURE 13-3   Typical reference symbols used on architectural working drawings

office this is the responsibility of the architect or lead draftsman. It is necessary so that the work load can be divided among several draftsmen working on the same project at the same time. To divide the work it is necessary to know only the total number of views or drawings per sheet, their overall size (with allowance for dimensioning where necessary), and the working space available. The sheets should be arranged generally in the order of their use on the job. A typical arrangement of a simple set of drawings with their sheet numbers might be (Fig. 13-2):

1. Sheet 1, Plot Plan, Sheet Schedule
2. Sheet 2, Foundation Plan
3. Sheet 3, Floor Plan
4. Sheet 4, Elevations
5. Sheet 5, Interior Details

The drawings are arranged in this way because they are used in this order from the start of actual construction. On a large project it is necessary to classify drawings to a greater degree than this. On a small job it is assumed that foundation details are on the same sheet as the foundation plan; the window, door, room finish, and electrical schedules are on the floor plan; the structural sections are on the elevations; and cabinet details are on the interior details. When special sheets are needed for structural, electrical, plumbing, or similar information, they may be inserted where desired.

REFERENCES BETWEEN DRAWINGS

Every set of working drawings uses keying symbols that make it possible to locate information and refer from one sheet to another. Specific symbols vary from office to office, and some systems are more complex than others. The system described here is simple but effective, and can be learned in a few minutes. The symbols may be any shape—circle, square, diamond, hexagon, and so on—as long as they are used consistently.

Large sections and sectional details are keyed on the plan or elevation by two numbers, one above the other—inside a circle in our example (Fig. 13-3). The top number refers to the number of the detail, the bottom number to the sheet on which it appears. Detail 3/5 is not the same as detail 3/6. When used with a large cutting plane, such as a principal structural section, the circle is attached to one or both ends of the cutting-plane line on the plan. On the sectional drawing it is placed below the drawing, sometimes with a verbal description (Fig. 13-3).

When used on a plan or elevation to show a small sectional detail such as a window jamb, footing, or handrail, the circle is attached to a small line which crosses, at a right angle, the place at which the section is taken (Fig. 13-3). A circle of the same size, containing the detail number only, is used as a title for the detail. Sometimes a verbal description is added, for example, "Typical end wall footing." The scale should always be shown with the section.

Another symbol, used on large projects, is the room number. It is usually placed inside a square before the room name on the plan, and under the interior elevations of the walls of the room (Fig. 13-3).

Window and door symbols are described in Chap. 15.

PROCEDURE

Before starting any sheet, a study should be made of the various symbols and conventional practices to be used on that particular drawing. This will shorten drafting time considerably and eliminate much erasing. Check the dimensions of the drawing for overall size. Next, space the views on the working area for appearance, room for dimensioning, and titles. Generally a large drawing on a sheet will be more pleasing to the eye if it is spaced equally at the sides with slightly more space at the bottom than the top. This will frame the drawing effectively and leave room for the title and scale below. Using construction lines, indicate the major outlines of the drawing and the location of the title. At this point check with the instructor; he may be able to point out some small error or suggest an improvement.

The order of linework suggested here should be followed generally; however, minor changes may be made to suit individual preference (Fig. 13-4). The principal object of this method is to avoid unnecessary corrections and erasures of hard, black lines which are difficult to get rid of completely.

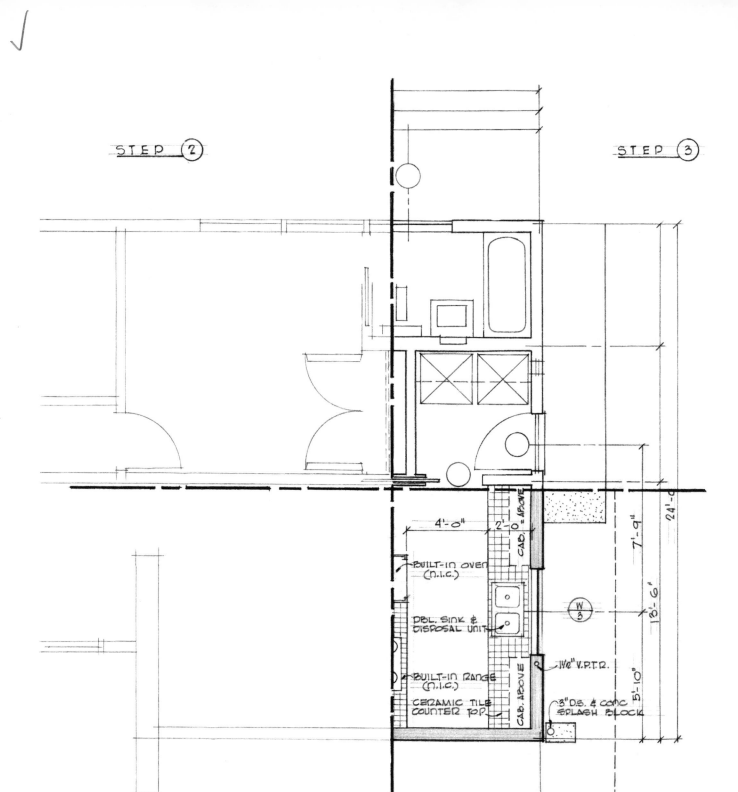

FIGURE 13-4 Steps in the development of a floor plan (all other working drawings should proceed in the same order of work)

Using construction lines:

1. Place all major outlines of drawing on the sheet.
2. Locate center lines and edge lines of important features, walls, doors, and openings.
3. Draw in smaller details—trim, mullions, small footings, and so on.
4. Check with instructor.

Using finished lines:

1. Draw in main outlines, partitions, openings, and so on (object lines).
2. Draw in minor details (object lines).
3. Dimension (dimension lines).
4. Letter in notes and dimensions, particularly where they occur within the outlines of the drawing.
5. Draw in textures and shading.
6. Profile the drawing if desired. Profiling consists of drawing a heavy line around the outline of the view.
7. Complete lettering on drawing and record strip.
8. Check with instructor.

This procedure will apply to any working drawing, and reference will be made to this chapter in the chapters which follow.

REVERSED TRACING

Many drawings are superimposed on the outline of the floor plan—plumbing, electrical plans, and so forth. On a large project, the outline of the floor plan is printed several times on a special transparent paper. These copies can be drawn on like tracing paper and all information can be printed at once. The plumbing, electrical, heating, or other information can be placed as desired. The principal reason for using this method is the economy of reproducing a drawing rather than redrawing it.

When only a small number of drawings are to be made, the following method works well (Fig. 13-5).

1. Turn the tracing of the floor plan over.
2. Trace the walls, windows, doors, and locations of large appliances on a new piece of tracing paper. Ignore all lettering.

3. Put the original tracing away, and place the second copy, penciled side down, on the board.
4. Draw in the desired information.

The reason for this procedure is that any correction or erasure of, for instance, the electric circuits will not disturb the lines of the walls and other lines, which are on the other side.

DRAFTING STYLES

Drafting styles vary greatly, depending on the locality, the office, and the individual draftsman. Any style is good if the drawings are legible, accurate, and complete. Most offices try to standardize the appearance of their drawings; therefore, the draftsman should keep an open mind regarding his style, and he should be prepared to learn another when he takes a job in an office.

The factors which produce a pleasing, readable style of drafting are simple to state but demand constant practice to develop. An artistic style is not an end in itself. Drawings are read by many people of varying degrees of experience and intelligence; therefore, readability is the most important requirement. Some of the devices which create a style are:

1. *The artistic ability of the draftsman.* Probably the most important factor, it guides him in his use of the various devices.
2. *Varying weights of line.* Used consistently for each symbol, they make a drawing pleasing and easy to read. Lines slightly thinner or heavier than those in the alphabet of lines may be used for particular symbols, such as thin object lines for structure beyond the section, extra-heavy object lines for outlines and profiling.
3. *Arrangement of drawings on the sheet.* Space should be efficiently used, yet plenty of room must be left for titles, notes, and call-outs.
4. *Distinctive titling for drawings.* The judicious use of stenciled letters, underlining, and visible guide lines will enhance the appearance of almost any drawing.
5. *Delineation of gratings, wood, brick, and stone textures on all drawings.* This device is most useful on elevations, but is also often used on plans.

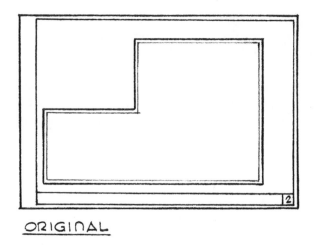

ORIGINAL

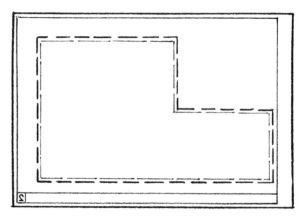

STEP 1 - INVERT ORIGINAL

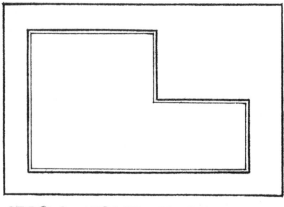

STEP 2 - TRACE ON NEW SHEET

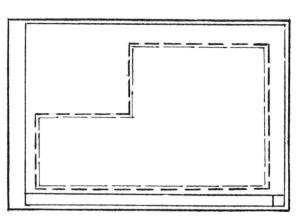

STEP 3 - INVERT NEW SHEET

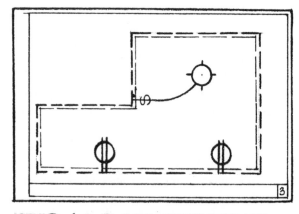

STEP 4 - PLACE DESIRED IN-
FORMATION.

NOTE : THIS DRAWING NOT TO
ANY SCALE. LINES ON TOP
SURFACE OF PAPER ARE SHOWN
SOLID. LINES ON BACK ARE
SHOWN DASHED.

FIGURE 13-5 Method of tracing a plan on the back of the sheet for use with electrical and other plans

Textures must not be allowed to interfere with the readability of notes and dimensions. Practically speaking, textures are not required, since the outline of each material plus proper notes will tell the builder all he has to know.

6. *Lettering shape, size, and arrangement.* On many drawings extensive notes must be placed in restricted areas; they should be placed as close as possible to the object they describe. For these reasons the draftsman should be able to produce small, compressed, and legible notes when they are needed.

7. *Pencil technique.* Crossed corners, increased pencil pressure at the ends of lines, graceful call-outs, attractive arrows, and so on all have to do with the way a person holds and handles a pencil. These techniques are the product of constant practice by the draftsman.

Until the student acquires the skill and taste required to develop his own style, he should copy the work of a professional architect (Figs. 13-6 to 13-8). An experienced draftsman with a practiced eye and a feeling for linework can produce excellent linework with a wide range of pencil grades, sometimes even with apparently inefficient methods. The student, however, should maintain a consistent pencil grade and should use the pencil in the best position: at a slight angle in the direction of the line and perpendicular to the paper when viewed along the line. There are two reasons for the effectiveness of this position. First, the line will be drawn at a slight distance from the guide, which makes it easier to evaluate and to correct if it is too light or too thin. Second, there is no chance that the pencil might slip under the guide and create an inaccurate or doubled line. The position sometimes seems awkward at first, but if it is learned correctly it will be a great aid in the development of a good technique.

TIME-SAVING METHODS

Because architectural drafting time is expensive and architectural practice is a competitive business, any saving in labor costs is desirable. Of course, the result must be as good and complete as that which other methods produce. Some firms use the following methods with great success:

1. *Freehand architectural working drawings done over blue-lined grid paper.* This practice eliminates the use of instruments, whose use consumes time. When done by a competent draftsman, the end result compares favorably with instrumental drawing (Fig. 13-9).

2. *The inclusion of small detail drawings, done on small sheets, with the specifications (Fig. 13-10).* As many projects in a given geographical area use many identical construction details, much drafting time can be saved by keeping such details on single sheets in a filing cabinet. When needed, they can be printed in any required number. Also, the reuse of this material by the office secretary is an additional economy. Foundation, window, door, and miscellaneous details are most often used in this way.

THE DRAFTSMAN IN ARCHITECTURAL PRACTICE

Office practices vary widely among architectural firms. Office size, type of practice, locality, and the personalities of the people involved are responsible for these variations. For these reasons it is difficult to describe the situation a young draftsman would find on his first job. However, he can be sure that because of his lack of experience, only a limited range of jobs will be delegated to him in any office. Our approach will be to describe the responsibilities of each of the people in a small architectural practice limited to residential and small commercial projects. This will help the student to see his part in the overall picture; it will also indicate to him the studies on which he must concentrate if he is to advance in his field.

THE "TYPICAL" OFFICE

The office we describe here will consist of two architects in partnership; one trainee, a graduate of an architectural school; one lead draftsman; one experienced draftsman; one beginning draftsman; and one receptionist-secretary. Since the receptionist-secretary does few jobs usually done by draftsmen except to produce, deliver, and mail prints, her job will not be described.

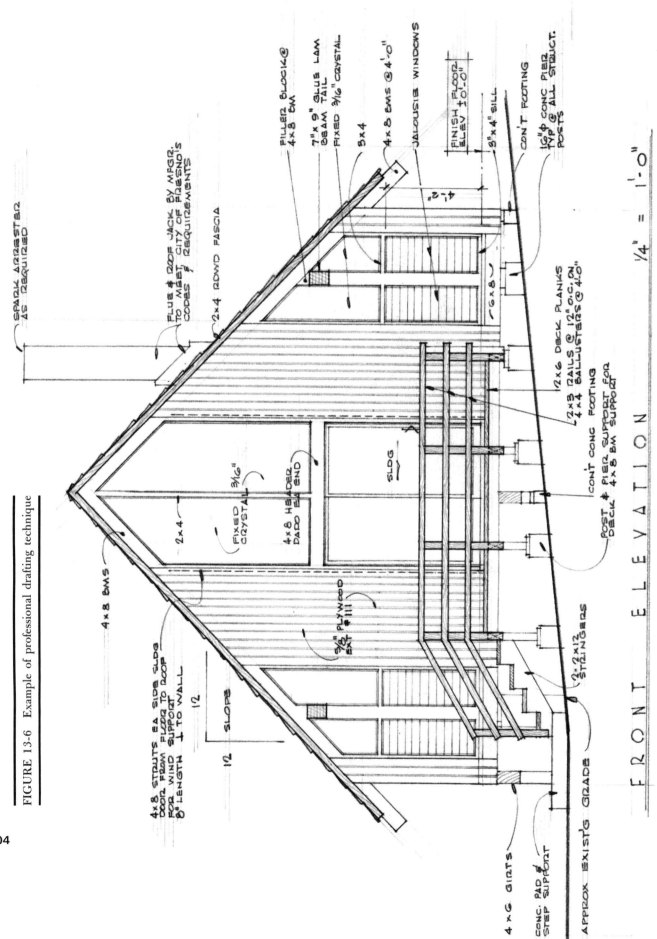

FIGURE 13-6 Example of professional drafting technique

104

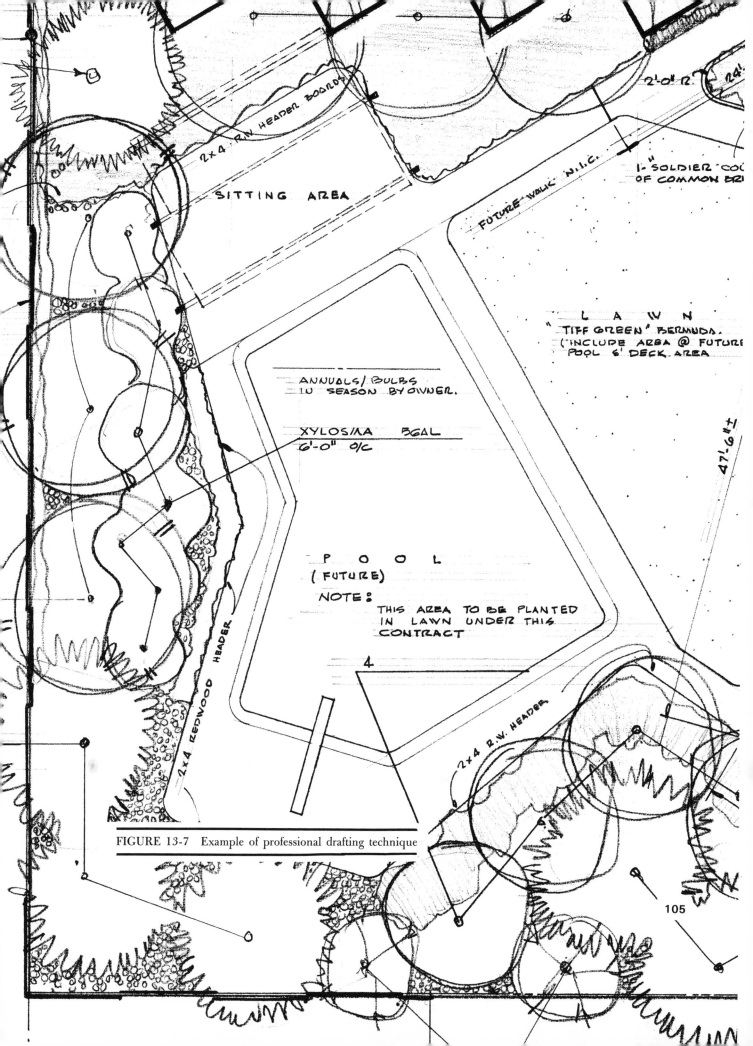

FIGURE 13-7 Example of professional drafting technique

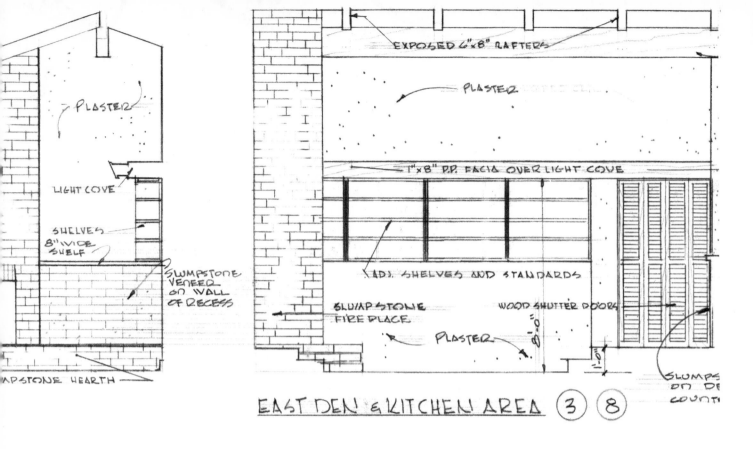

PLASTER

LIGHT COVE

SHELVES
8" WIDE SHELF

SLUMPSTONE VENEER ON WALL OF RECESS

...PSTONE HEARTH

EXPOSED 6"×8" RAFTERS

PLASTER

1"×8" R.R. FACIA OVER LIGHT COVE

ADJ. SHELVES AND STANDARDS

SLUMPSTONE FIRE PLACE

PLASTER

WOOD SHUTTER DOORS

8'-0"

1'-0"

SLUMPS... ON DE... COUNT...

EAST DEN & KITCHEN AREA ③ ⑧

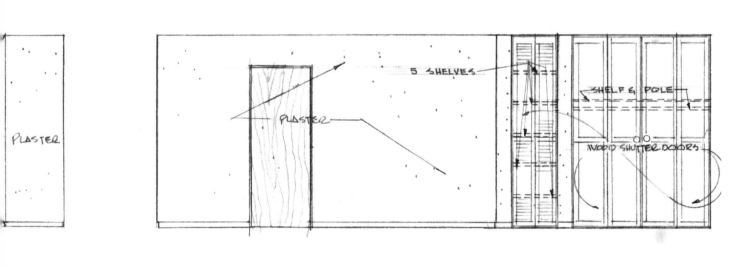

PLASTER

PLASTER

5 SHELVES

SHELF & POLE

WOOD SHUTTER DOORS

...M ④

SOUTH MASTER BEDROOM ④ (REVERSED)

FIGURE 13-8   Example of professional drafting technique

106

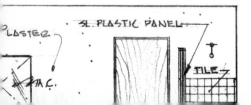

...PLASTER

SL. PLASTIC PANEL

TILE

PLASTER

SLID. PLASTIC PANEL

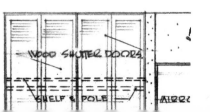

WOOD SHUTTER DOORS

SHELF & POLE

MIRR...

EDUCATION

An architectural student graduating from school today has completed at least five years of college, concentrating on art, design, mathematics, science, and specific engineering courses.

It is recommended, but not mandatory, that a draftsman have two years of college in drafting and related technical subjects. After getting his job, the draftsman should take night-school or extension courses to improve his competence, and hence his pay.

RESPONSIBILITIES

The principals in the firm are independent businessmen as well as artist-engineers, and consequently must perform many more functions than their employees. Their strictly architectural functions include meetings with clients; overall design of their projects; coordination of effort with engineers, contractors, and local officials; building inspection; cost estimating; selection and approval of sites and materials; specification writing; delegation of responsibility in the office; training of their employees; and so on. Their business responsibilities include billing and payroll, correspondence, purchasing of supplies and equipment, filing, and so on. Most of this work is executed by the secretary, who also does the typing. It is the architects' duty to see that all these jobs are done properly and on time.

The recent graduate works for other architects to gain the practical experience needed to complete his education. He works under the direction of the senior architects and usually takes on more responsibility as he gains experience. Depending on their interests and particular abilities, some recent graduates concentrate on design and others on specification writing; most work at the drafting board, inspect buildings in progress, and help train new draftsmen.

THE DRAFTSMAN

The principal job of the draftsman is the production of working drawings from preliminaries or sketches done by the architect. Draftsmen with particular ar-

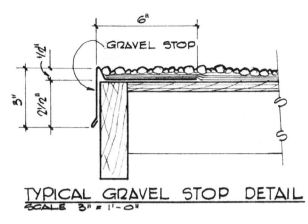

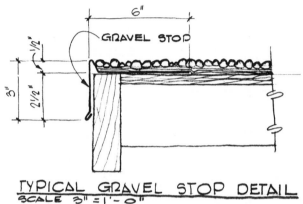

FIGURE 13-9   Comparison of instrumental and freehand detail

tistic ability make perspective and presentation drawings of projects. Much drafting time is spent in lettering, tracing, producing new drawings, and making small alterations on existing drawings. Building codes, zoning ordinances, engineering references, and product files must be constantly consulted to ensure correctness and completeness of the drawings. Many offices have their own print-making equipment, which is generally operated by anyone who has free time; others have their printing done by duplicating firms. Other jobs of the draftsman include delivering prints, purchasing supplies, and perhaps even sweeping the office.

The lead draftsman does all of these things and in addition directs the work of the junior draftsmen. He must assign and check all the drawings in progress to make certain that each is correct and correlates with other drawings. In most cases he transmits the architects' instructions to the draftsmen.

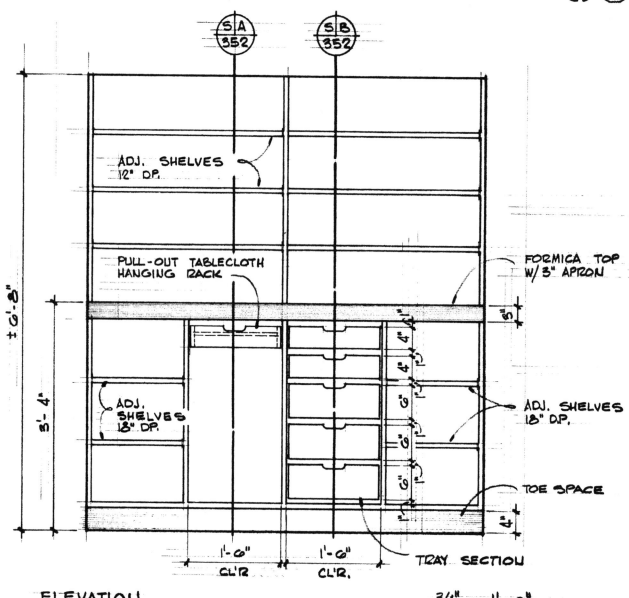

S A / 352

S B / 352

ADJ. SHELVES 12" DP.

PULL-OUT TABLECLOTH HANGING RACK

FORMICA TOP W/ 3" APRON

ADJ. SHELVES 18" DP.

ADJ. SHELVES 18" DP.

TOE SPACE

TRAY SECTION

± 6'-8"

3'-4"

4"

1'-6" CL'R.

1'-6" CL'R.

ELEVATION   3/4" = 1'-0"

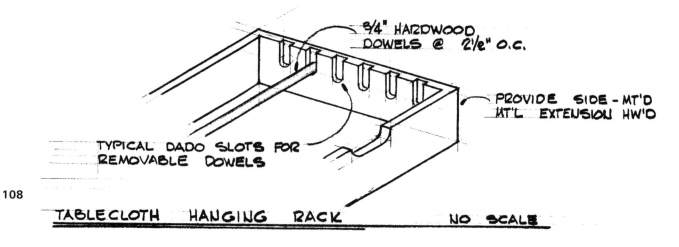

3/4" HARDWOOD DOWELS @ 2½" O.C.

PROVIDE SIDE-MT'D MT'L EXTENSION HW'D

TYPICAL DADO SLOTS FOR REMOVABLE DOWELS

TABLECLOTH HANGING RACK   NO SCALE

108

DINING ROOM - CHINA CLOSET

REVIEW QUESTIONS

1. Name five architectural working drawings.
2. What are two reasons why a draftsman should use templates?
3. Is the use of cheap tracing paper a wise economy?
4. Describe in your own words what good linework looks like.
5. What is the most important step in the process of making either a dark or a white line reproduction?
6. Why are margins needed on drawings?
7. What order of linework will you use on your working drawings?
8. Why is the outline of the floor plan drawn on the back of the tracing paper for the electrical plan?

STUDY SUGGESTIONS

1. If you can, borrow a set of working drawings and look them over. Did they print clearly? Is the format suitable for your use? Is the style pleasing to you? Is the lettering architectural and legible? Is the reference system easy to use? Remember, your drawings will be judged in the same way.
2. Draw some details on a sheet of paper, using several weights of line. Place a piece of tracing paper on top and trace each of the details. Note the weight of line required to read the drawing easily through the tracing paper. It is very important to make drawings traceable, because much time can

be wasted by constantly lifting the top sheet to check.
3. Draw or trace a few details on a sheet of tracing paper; try to copy the styles of several drawings you like. You will find that pleasing techniques require study and analysis to determine exactly what it is that creates the effect. You will notice that consistent linework is the common element in all successful styles.
4. Practice several types of lettering at all sizes from $\frac{1}{16}$ to $\frac{1}{4}$ in. in height. Try extended and compressed lettering, long notes in small spaces; experiment with underlines and visible guide lines. When you find a type of lettering that satisfies you, practice it until it becomes a habit.

STUDENT PROBLEM

1. Trace part of an existing drawing on a small piece of tracing paper. Experiment with varying thickness and blackness of line; try several weights and styles of lettering. Print this sheet and then compare the original and reproduced lines. Use this information as a basis for the linework of your working drawings.
2. Decide on the number of drawings which will comprise the set. Lay out each sheet, determine the scale of each drawing, and provide a sheet index on the first sheet (Plot Plan). It is a good idea to sketch "dummy" sheets to small scale for ease in visualizing the finished set. Decide on a sheet format to be used for all drawings of the set.

CHAPTER 14
FLOOR PLAN

DEFINITION AND PURPOSE

The most important drawing of a set is the floor plan, since all other drawings are derived from it in some way (Figs. 14-1 and 14-2). For instance, the outline of the foundation plan is traced from the floor plan, the elevations are projected or measured from it, and the sizes of roof and ceiling members are based on the spans between walls. All the building trades find at least part of their information on it. The main purpose of the floor plan, which is a horizontal section through the building usually taken just below the tops of the windows and doors, is to show the location of the walls, partitions, and all openings. A very simple floor plan would show only this, but most show much more detail.

DRAFTING THE FLOOR PLAN

The floor plan is copied from the final preliminary drawings, but before starting, the student should check with Chap. 12. The procedure for drawing the floor plan is as follows:

1. A one-line floor plan is drawn in light lines. Lines for outside walls indicate the outside face of studs or the outside face of masonry. Lines for interior partitions indicate the center lines of walls. It is best to place the drawing with the main entrance facing the bottom of the sheet.
2. The thickness of the walls showing doors, windows, and so on is shown by standard symbols. The symbols for the various wall constructions

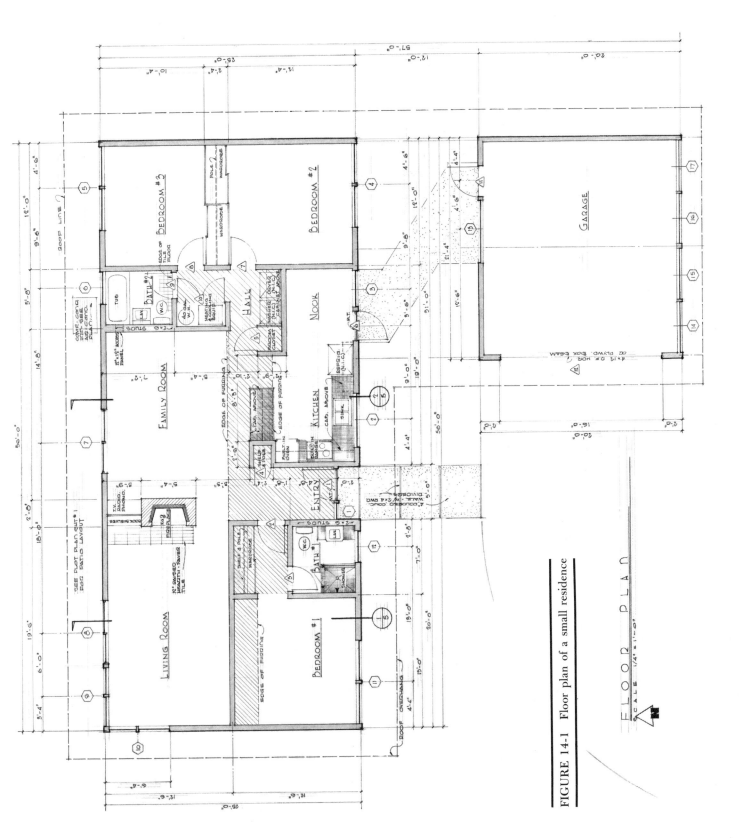

FIGURE 14-1 Floor plan of a small residence

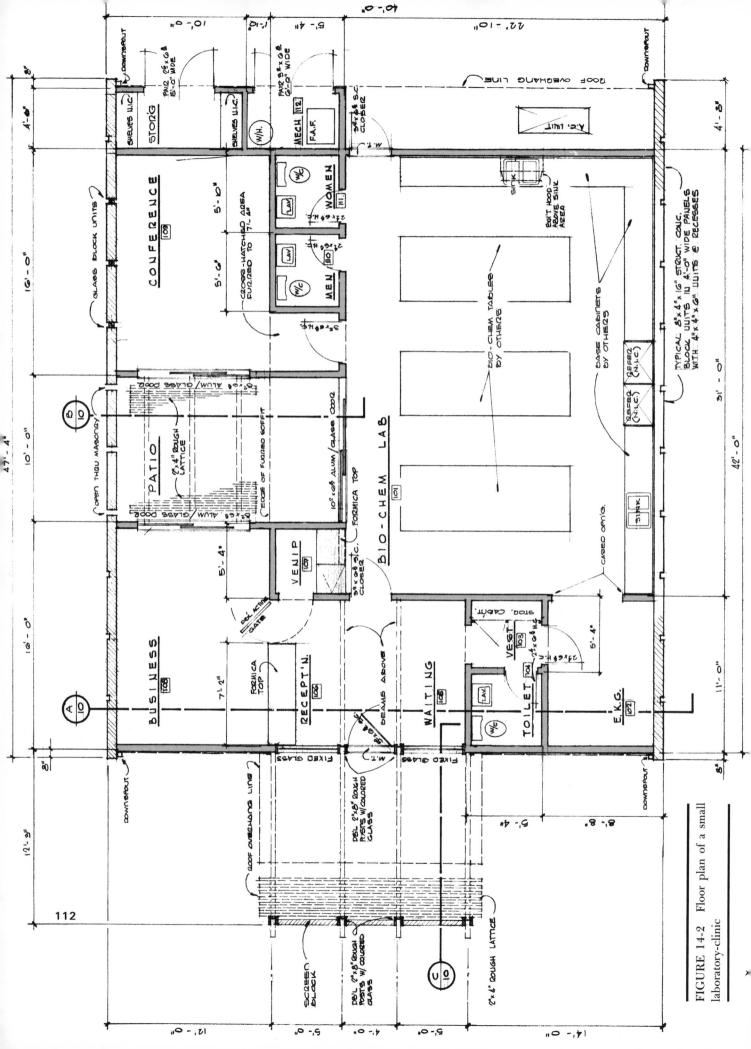

FIGURE 14-2 Floor plan of a small
laboratory-clinic

are listed in the Appendix (see A-5). Note: All pochéing is applied to the back of the tracing.

3. Landings, steps, walks, and handrails are shown in outline and noted. Any change in floor elevation must be indicated by a line plus a call-out or note.

4. Fireplaces, masonry planters, or dividers are shown crosshatched. Hearths are shown in outline and described by note.

5. The locations and sizes of heating and air-conditioning equipment and water heaters are shown in solid lines. Type, capacity, and catalog number are noted near the equipment or may be written into the specifications.

6. Large plumbing fixtures are drawn to scale, while hose bibbs and other small items are drawn as symbols. Where needed, plumbing access panels are called out by note.

7. Any cabinet work or built-in equipment, such as a stove or oven, is shown in solid lines; upper cabinets are normally indicated as dashed lines (here conventional practice violates the rules of projection).

8. Furred, or lowered, ceiling areas are shown by dashed lines and called out by note.

9. The individual rafters in an open-beam ceiling should be shown by conventional center lines and their size and spacing called out. Supporting beams are shown as dashed lines and called out.

10. The extent of floor materials, such as carpet, tile, slate, or materials of varying thickness, must be shown by a solid line and noted.

11. Sound insulation is indicated by a serpentine line between the wall lines and noted. Thermal insulation is not generally drawn on the floor plan but is described in a general note.

12. Attic access doors, or scuttles, are indicated by dashed lines and called out by note. They are generally located in hall ceilings, storerooms, or other inconspicuous places.

13. Where space is reserved for equipment which is not included in the bid, the equipment is drawn in outline and noted NIC (not in contract).

14. The dimension lines are drawn in.

15. All lettering, notes, reference symbols, title, and scale are placed. The full-scale extracts from the floor plan show the use of most of these symbols (Fig. 14-3).

SIMPLE FLOOR PLANS

In a complete set of plans for a large project such information as plumbing, electrical, heating, and air conditioning is placed on separate sheets, that is, on a plumbing plan, electrical plan, and heating and air-conditioning plan. On small jobs, this information may be placed on the floor plan. Separate sections in this book are devoted to these special drawings, but when the information is to be placed on the floor plan, the following instructions should be employed (see Fig. 14-4):

1. *Electrical.* Electric outlets, switches, and switch legs are shown by the symbols listed in the Appendix. Any outlet, whether on the floor, ceiling, or wall, is merely located where desired. The only wiring generally indicated is the switch leg from the outlet, or outlets to the switch, or switches controlling them. If special light fixtures are desired, the manufacturer's name and catalog number are placed beside the outlet. The location of the service-entrance switchgear should be shown, generally at the rear of the building, and the size of the main fuses and number of branch circuits noted. The symbols used are described in the electrical schedule on the same sheet. For speed and consistency in drafting, use a template for all symbols. For more complete information see Chap 27.

2. *Heating and air conditioning.* Heating and air-conditioning units are shown in actual size by outline, and the manufacturer, catalog number, type of unit, and capacity are noted. Heating and cooling registers, return-air grilles, radiators, fans, and so on are located by note and described by size and type. For additional information see Chap. 26.

3. *Plumbing.* Plumbing fixtures are shown true size in outline. Care must be taken to provide adequate space around each fixture as required by local building codes and ordinances. Plumbing lines are not usually shown on the floor plan. Use a plumbing template for all fixtures. For additional information see Chap. 25.

4. *Schedules.* Although the use of window, door, and room-finish schedules is preferred on most drawings, when there are only a few windows and doors this information may be placed beside each opening on the floor plan. Type, brand, and material of

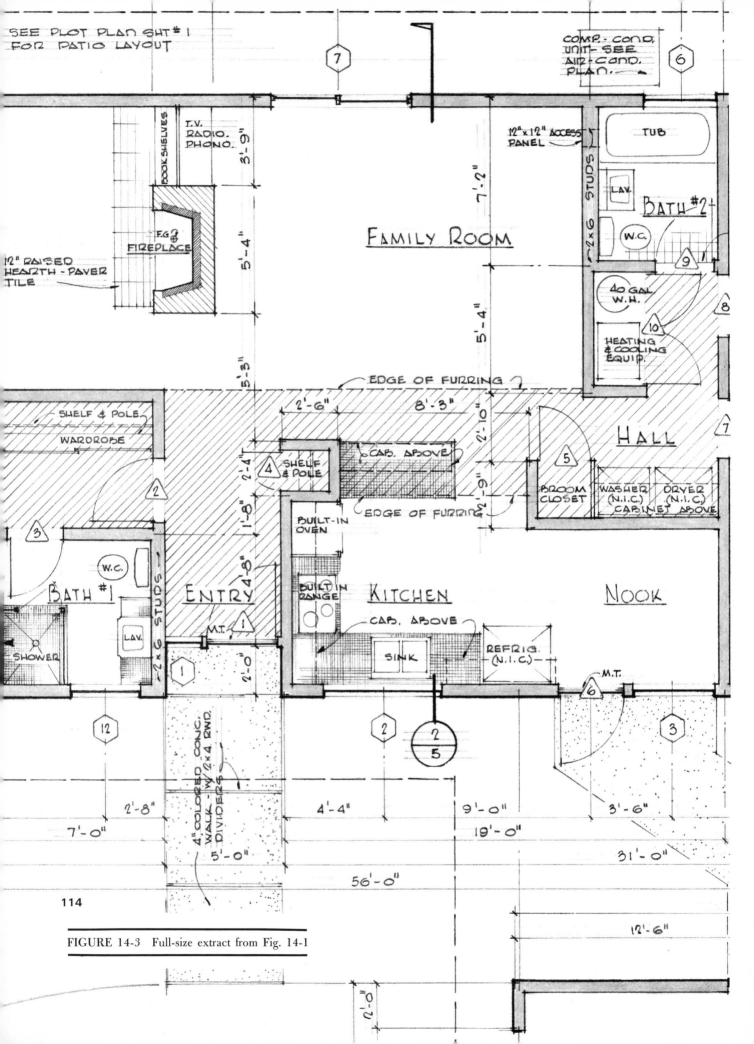

FIGURE 14-3   Full-size extract from Fig. 14-1

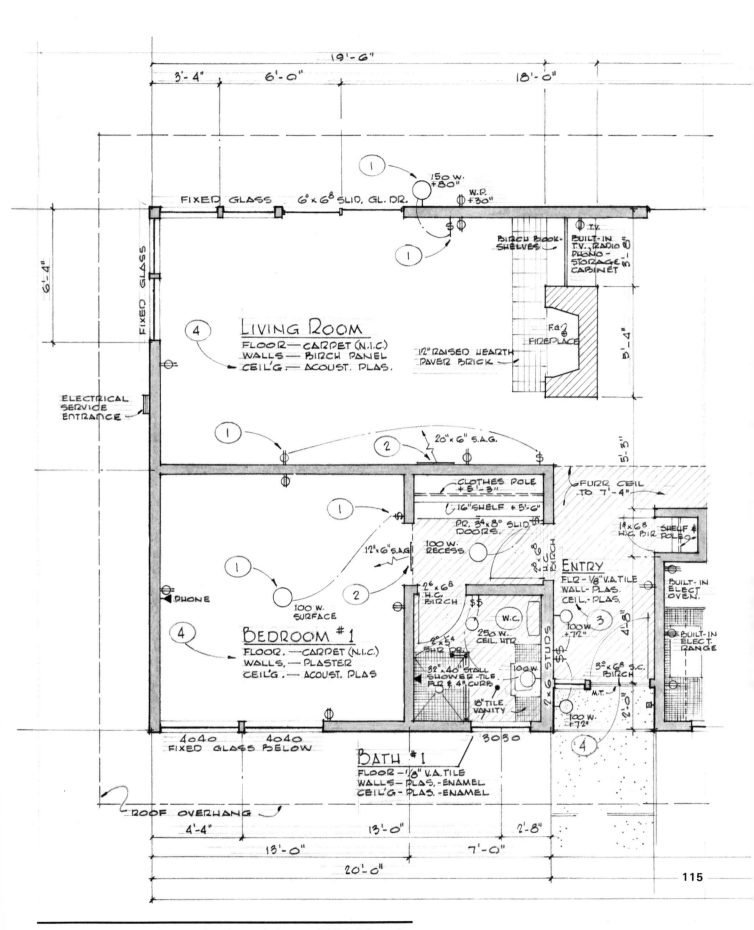

FIGURE 14-4   Floor plan showing door, window, and finish information

115

windows should be written in the form of a general note beside the plan. The size of the door is noted at each door symbol, and the material and type of finish are also in the form of a general note. The description of wall, floor, and ceiling finish is lettered near the room name. A complete treatment of the use of the various schedules is given in Chap. 15.

DIMENSIONING

Dimensioning is extremely important and should be consistent. If the drawing is small compared with sheet size, the spacing between dimension lines may be large; if the area is limited, the spacing must be smaller. The clear space between the wall line and the nearest dimension line should be at least $3/4$ in. so that notes may be entered close to the building. Space between dimension lines may be $1/4$ to 1 in., depending on space, to avoid crowding the figures. For a neat appearance, use the same spacing on all sides of the building.

In architectural practice, dimension lines are continuous, with figures above the line (Fig. 14-1). This practice increases speed in drafting. All lettering should read from the bottom or right-hand edge of the sheet; figures are placed above the line. One may use conventional arrows, small circles, or slant lines (hash marks) through the intersection of the dimension line with the center line or extension line. Hash marks are recommended because of speed in drafting. Circles and arrows have special meanings in modular dimensioning. Distances are always expressed in feet and inches. Whenever distances are in even feet, zero inches have to be shown. For distance less than a foot, place zero feet before the number of inches. Each continuous row of dimensions must add up to the overall dimension. It is possible to have gaps in the row of dimensions as long as all important points are located.

Although there are variations in practice, dimensions can be arranged in the following order from the wall line:

1. Distances between door and window center lines and the outside of the end walls or offsets (see illustrations for examples of dimensioning)

2. Distances between center lines of interior walls and outsides of end walls

3. Distances between wall breaks and outside of end walls

4. Overall dimensions, outside wall to outside wall

All outside walls and wall breaks are shown by extension lines to the faces of studs, not to the surface finish. All centers of openings or walls are shown by center lines. Short interior partitions may be dimensioned in the floor plan, while cabinet work, drainboards, and similar features are dimensioned on the detail sheets.

With modular constructions such as concrete block, the dimensions indicate the outside surface of the walls and the edges of openings. The distances are multiples of the sizes of the blocks used.

One important symbol, the north-pointing arrow, should be placed with the title and scale at the bottom of the drawing on all floor plans. Place an entrance symbol at the main entrance.

MULTISTORY PLANS

Thus far it has been assumed that the building is of one-story construction. In the case of a two-story building or a building with a basement, several factors must be considered (Figs. 14-5 and 14-6). The first-floor plan should be drawn first. The basement and second story can then be traced from the first-floor plan. The exterior walls of the basement and second story may be in a line with the first-floor walls or set back from them, or the second floor may be cantilevered out from the first-story walls. If the walls of an upper floor are set back, structural support must be provided underneath and shown by dashed lines on the floor below. If the top floor is cantilevered, a dashed line is used to show the location of the wall below. Interior walls do not necessarily have to line up unless they are used as bearing walls or unless they contain vents or piping from the wall below. Stairways must be carefully lined up and provision made for head room. Remember to provide space for vertical heating ducts from the basement to the second floor. Basements may be equal to the size of the first floor or smaller. They may be completely below ground or may have one or more walls exposed, as

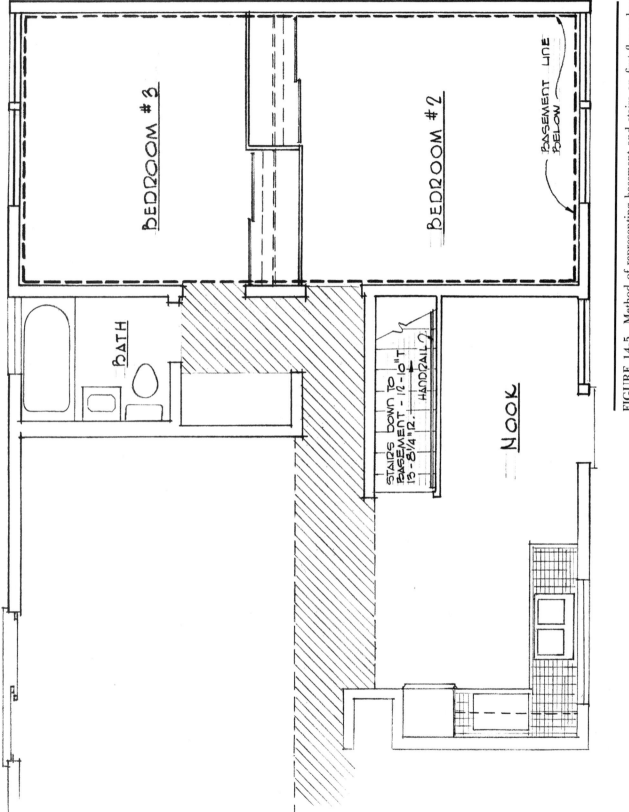

FIGURE 14-5 Method of representing basement and stairs on first-floor plan

BEDROOM #3

BEDROOM #2

BASEMENT LINE
BELOW

BATH

STAIRS DOWN TO
BASEMENT - 12-10"T
13 - 8¼"12.

HANDRAIL

NOOK

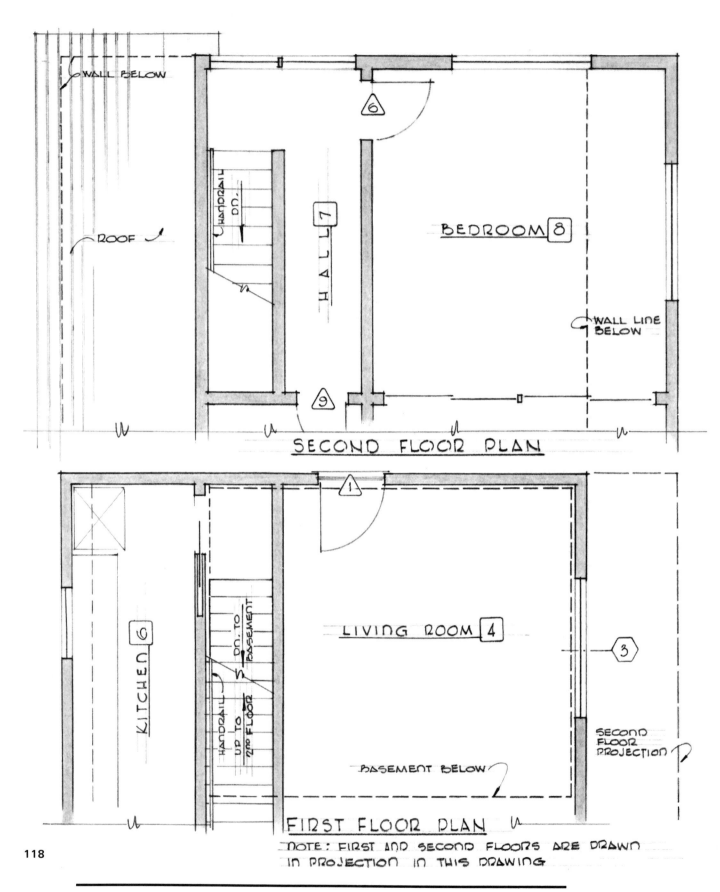

FIGURE 14-6 Methods of representing stairs, basement, setback, and contilevered second story

on a sloping site. In any case, floor plans of the basement and second floor are required. The same procedures are used for drawing the second-floor and basement as for the first-floor plan. Further information regarding basement types and plans will be found in Chap. 22.

REVIEW QUESTIONS

1. Which one drawing is used by the most building tradesmen? Explain.
2. At $\frac{1}{4}$ in. = 1 ft 0 in. scale, draw a 10-ft section of the following types of wall in plan.
   a. Stud wall
   b. Post and beam, 32 in. between posts
   c. Brick veneer over stud wall
   d. Concrete block wall, 8 in. thick
3. What are three types of specialized information which may either appear on the floor plan or be placed on separate drawings?
4. What information concerning a door or a window, aside from its plan-view symbol, must be shown on the floor plan?
5. Draw a typical row of dimensions showing the proper use of center lines, extension lines, arrows, and figures. Label the function of each line of dimensions with a call-out and note, for example, "overall dimensions."

STUDY SUGGESTIONS

1. Look over a completed floor plan drawn by an architect or draftsman; try to identify the various symbols for walls, fixtures, and so on.
2. Visit a residence which is under construction, and ask the foreman if you might compare his drawings with the actual construction.
3. Study the symbols and notes used on a floor plan before starting the drawing.
4. Make a freehand floor plan of your own kitchen and one other adjacent room. Use all of the proper symbols and notes.
5. Practice lettering!

STUDENT PROBLEM

If the instructor approves your preliminary floor plan, use it. If it is not approved, you may use the one-line floor plan provided (Fig. 3-4), which satisfies the demands of the client checklist (Prob. 2, Chap. 3). A basic plot plan is also provided (Fig. 3-4) which agrees with the floor plan. It will still be necessary for you to do the rest of the planning and to provide the information concerning appliances, doors, etc.

Place the preliminary $\frac{1}{4}$-in. scale floor plan on the board and trace the finished floor plan from it. Follow the procedures described in this chapter.

CHAPTER 15
DOOR, WINDOW, AND ROOM-FINISH SCHEDULES

DEFINITION AND PURPOSE

The door, window, and room-finish schedules furnish much information which is often difficult to place elsewhere on the working drawings (Fig. 15-1). The principal advantage of using schedules is that the information concerning the doors, windows, and finish is organized logically and can be found in one place. Though schedules are usually used, some floor plans contain such a small amount of other detail that this information can be placed on the drawing as notes (see Fig. 14-4). It is the draftsman's responsibility to decide which method will work best for each set of drawings. There are two types of door and window schedules, pictorial and tabular.

TYPES

Pictorial door and window schedules are simply scale drawings, at $\frac{1}{4}$ or $\frac{1}{2}$ in. = 1 ft 0 in., of each of the types of doors and windows used (Fig. 15-2). Each unit is designed specially for the job or the needed information is copied directly from manufacturers' catalogs. Each illustration is further described by a note giving the manufacturer's name and catalog number, type, material, and finish of the unit.

Tabular door and window schedules use verbal descriptions in place of pictures, and the information is broken down into several categories for easy reference (Fig. 15-3). Though there are many variations in practice, the schedules described here are typical.

ROOM FINISH SCHEDULE

REMARKS

- (n) NATURAL FINISH
- (E) 3 COAT ENAMEL
- (W) 3 COAT FLAT WALL PAINT
- (S) STAIN FINISH
- (P) PRE-FINISHED
- (XS) EXTERIOR STAIN
- (XE) EXTERIOR TRIM PAINT.

NOTES

1. PAINT CONC. BLOCK FIREPLACE WITH TWO COATS-VINYL WALL PAINT.

FLOOR / BASE

NO.	NAME	FLOOR: EXPOSED CONCRETE	FLOOR: CARPET (N.I.C.)	FLOOR: VINYL ASBESTOS TILE	BASE: HARDWOOD	BASE: PINE	BASE: 4" VINYL TOPSET
1	ENTRY		O		E		
2	LIVING ROOM		O		n		
3	FAMILY ROOM		O		E		
4	KITCHEN			O			O
5	NOOK			O			O
6	HALL		O		E		
7	BEDROOM #2		O		E		
8	BEDROOM #3		O		E		
9	BATH #2			O			O
10	BATH #1			O			O
11	BEDROOM #1		O		E		
12	GARAGE	O				E	
	EXTERIOR						

WALLS – SOUTH / WEST

NO.	NAME	S: 1/2" GYPSUM BD.	S: HARDWOOD PANELING	S: TEXTURE ONE-ELEVEN PLYWD	S: MARLITE PANEL	S: D.F. PLYWD. WARDROBE	S: UNFINISHED	W: 1/2" GYPSUM BD.	W: TEXTURE ONE-ELEVEN PLYWD.	W: MARLITE PANEL	W: D.F. PLYWOOD WARDROBE	W: UNFINISHED
1	ENTRY								S			
2	LIVING ROOM		P					W				
3	FAMILY ROOM	W										
4	KITCHEN	E						E				
5	NOOK	E										
6	HALL	W						W				
7	BEDROOM #2	W						W				
8	BEDROOM #3					E		W				
9	BATH #2				P					P		
10	BATH #1				P					P		
11	BEDROOM #1								S			
12	GARAGE						O					O
	EXTERIOR			XS					XS			

WALLS – NORTH / EAST

NO.	NAME	N: 1/2" GYPSUM BD.	N: HARDWOOD PANELING	N: TEXTURE ONE-ELEVEN PLYWD.	N: MARLITE PANEL	N: D.F. PLYWD. WARDROBE	N: UNFINISHED	E: 1/2" GYPSUM BD.	E: TEXTURE ONE-ELEVEN PLYWD.	E: MARLITE PANEL	E: UNFINISHED
1	ENTRY							W			
2	LIVING ROOM		P								
3	FAMILY ROOM		P					W			
4	KITCHEN										
5	NOOK	E						E			
6	HALL	W						W			
7	BEDROOM #2					E			S		
8	BEDROOM #3	W							S		
9	BATH #2				P					P	
10	BATH #1				P					P	
11	BEDROOM #1										
12	GARAGE						O				O
	EXTERIOR			XS					XS		

CEILING / WAINSCOT / CABINETS & DOORS / TRIM

NO.	NAME	CEILING: 1/2" GYPSUM BD.	CEILING: 12"×12" ACOUSTICAL TILE	CEILING: UNFINISHED	CLG. HT.	WAINS. HT.	PINE CASEWORK	WHITE ASH CASEWORK	CERAMIC TILE COUNTER TOP	NOVOPLY DOORS	BIRCH DOORS	WHITE ASH DOORS	TRIM: PINE	TRIM: HARDWOOD	TRIM: REDWOOD
1	ENTRY	W			7'-4"						E		E		
2	LIVING ROOM		O		VARIES			n						n	
3	FAMILY ROOM		O		VARIES			n					E		
4	KITCHEN	E			VARIES			n	O						
5	NOOK	E			VARIES						E		E		
6	HALL	W			7'-4"		E				E		E		
7	BEDROOM #2	W			VARIES		E			E	E		E		
8	BEDROOM #3	W			VARIES		E			E	E		E		
9	BATH #2	E			VARIES						E		E		
10	BATH #1	E			VARIES		E		O		E		E		
11	BEDROOM #1				VARIES		E			E	E		E		
12	GARAGE			O	VARIES						E		E		
	EXTERIOR														XE

WINDOW SCHEDULE

SYM.	SIZE WDTH × HT.	TYPE	MANUFACTURE & CATALOG NO.	GLAZING	MATERIAL	REMARKS
1	1'-6" × 7'-4"	FIXED	JOB MADE	OBSCURE	REDWOOD	CUSTOM SIZE
2	5'-0" × 3'-0"	HORIZ. SLID.	E-Z SET ROLLING WINDOWS #5030	D.S. "B"	ALUM.	CUSTOM SIZE
3	3'-6" × 4'-0"		#3640			
4	4'-0" × 4'-0"		#4040			PAIR - WOOD MULLION BETWEEN
5	4'-0" × 4'-0"		#4040			
6	3'-0" × 3'-0"		#3030	OBSCURE		
7	6'-0" × 6'-8"	SLID. DOOR	ACME - 500 SERIES #6068-XO	1/4" PL.		
8	6'-0" × 6'-8"		#6068-OX	1/4" PL.		
9	5'-6" × 6'-8"	FIXED	JOB MADE	3/16" CRY.	REDWOOD	
10	6'-0" × VARIES			3/16" CRY		
11	4'-0" × 4'-0"	HORIZ. SLID.	E-Z SET ROLLING WINDOWS #4040	D.S. "B"	ALUM.	PAIR - WOOD MULLION BETWEEN
12	3'-0" × 3'-0"		#3030	OBSCURE		
13	6'-0" × 3'-0"		#6030	D.S. "B"		
14	5'-0" × VARIES	FIXED	JOB MADE	OBSCURE	REDWOOD	
15	5'-0" × VARIES					
16	5'-0" × VARIES					
17	5'-0" × VARIES					

DOOR SCHEDULE

SYM	SIZE WDTH × HT	THK.	TYPE	MANUFACTURE & CATALOG NO.	MATERIAL	FINISH	JAMB	REMARKS
1	3'-0" × 7'-4"	1 3/4"	FLUSH-SOLID	"SIMPSON"- 5 PLY SOLID CORE	BIRCH	ENAMEL	WOOD	PAINT GRADE - BIRCH VENEER.
2	2'-8" × 6'-8"	1 3/8"	FLUSH-HOLLOW	"SIMPSON"- 5 PLY HOLLOW CORE				
3	2'-6" × 6'-8"							
4	1'-8" × 6'-8"							
5	2'-4" × 6'-8"							
6	2'-10" × 6'-8"	1 3/4"	FLUSH-SOLID	"SIMPSON"- 5 PLY SOLID CORE				
7	2'-8" × 6'-8"	1 3/8"	FLUSH-HOLLOW	"SIMPSON"- 5 PLY HOLLOW CORE				
8	2'-8" × 6'-8"							
9	2'-6" × 6'-8"							
10	PR. 2'-4" × 6'-8"		FULL LOUVER					
11	3'-0" × 6'-8"	1 3/4"	FLUSH - SOLID					
12	16'-0" × 7'-0"		OVHD. GARAGE	"FILUMA" FIBERGLASS GARAGE	ALUM			FIBERGLASS FACE SKIN

FIGURE 15-1 Door, window, and room-finish schedules for a small residence

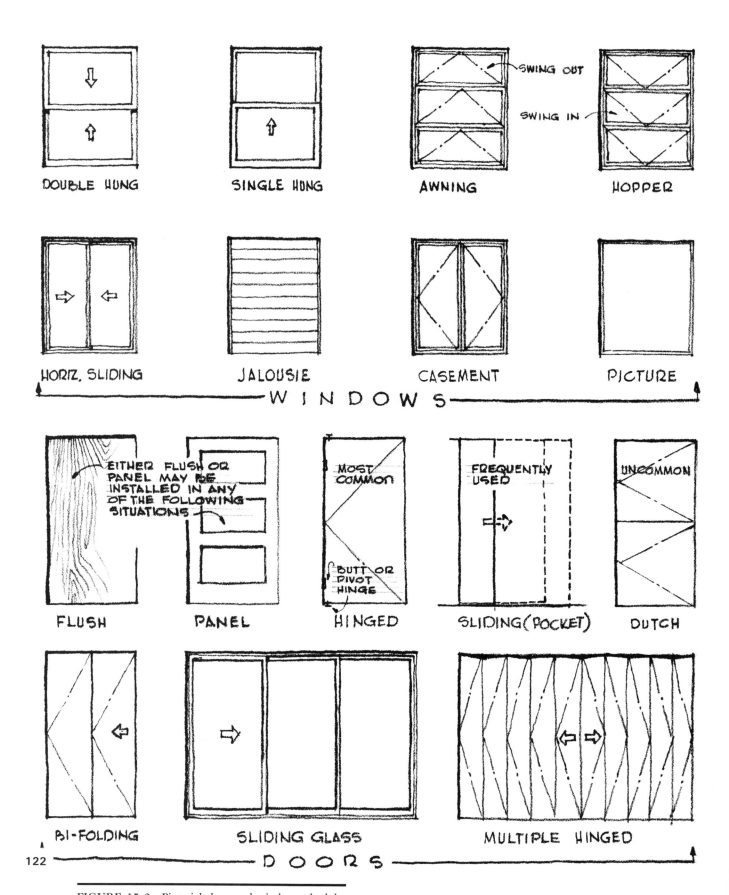

FIGURE 15-2 Pictorial door and window schedules

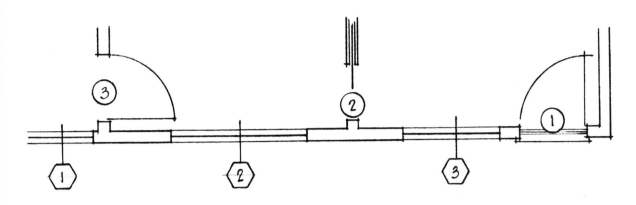

WINDOW SCHEDULE

SYM	SIZE	TYPE	MFGR. & CATALOG NO.	REMARKS	GLASS
1	6'-0"x3'-0"	HORIZ. SLID.	"TRIMVIEW"-TYPE T-2 #500-6030	SLIDING ALUMINUM, LACQUER FINISH VINYL WEATHERSTRIP, PLASTIC SCREENS	D.S. "A"
2	6'-0"x4'-0"	CASEMENT	"E-Z SET" DELUXE CASEMENT #3424 XW	DBL. VENT, ROTARY OPERATOR, LAQUER FINISH & PLASTIC SCREENS	7/32" OBSC.
3	4'-0"x6'-0"	FIXED		WOOD STOPS SET IN MASTIC. SEE DETAILS SHT. A-9	1/4" P.P.

DOOR SCHEDULE

SYM	SIZE	TYPE	MFGR. & CATALOG NO.	REMARKS	MATERIAL	THK	HOWE. TYPE
1	3'-0"x6'-8"	S.A. ENTRANCE TWO PANEL	"SIMPSON" SONATA	3 COATS EXT. TRIM PAINT	PINE	1¾"	A
2	2'-6"x6'-8"	SLIDING, H.C. FLUSH	"RODDIS" HOUSEMART HOLLOW	STAIN & LACQUER FINISH	ROTARY BIRCH	1⅜"	F
3	2'-8"x6'-8"	S.A., H.C. FLUSH	"RODDIS" HOUSEMART HOLLOW	STAIN & LACQUER FINISH	ROTARY BIRCH	1⅜"	C

FIGURE 15-3 Window and door schedules for a small residence, showing method of keying to floor plan

The ruled lines of tabular schedules may be drawn in india ink, which has the advantage that mistakes and deletions of lettering can be easily erased without disturbing the ruled lines. Another device is to place the lines on the back of the tracing and the lettering on the front; this also avoids problems of erasing.

WINDOW SCHEDULES

The headings used on a window schedule (Fig. 15-4) are listed here:

1. *Symbol:* The keying symbol or number
2. *Size:* The dimensions of the window

3. *Type:* Casement, double hung, horizontal sliding, fixed, and so on
4. *Manufacturer and catalog number:* Taken from the catalog
5. *Glazing:* Single or double strength, crystal, plate, obscure, and so on
6. *Material:* Wood, steel, aluminum
7. *Remarks:* Any further description

DOOR SCHEDULES

The headings used on a door schedule (Fig. 15-5) are listed here:

WINDOW SCHEDULE

SYM.	SIZE (WDTH × HT.)	TYPE	MANUFACTURE & CATALOG NO.	GLAZING	MATERIAL	REMARKS
1	1'-6" × 7'-4"	FIXED	JOB MADE	OBSCURE	REDWOOD	CUSTOM SIZE
2	5'-0" × 3'-0"	HORIZ. SLID.	E-Z SET ROLLING WINDOWS #5030	D.S. "B"	ALUM.	CUSTOM SIZE
3	3'-6" × 4'-0"	→	#3640	→	→	
4	4'-0" × 4'-0"	→	#4040	→	→	PAIR - WOOD MULLION BETWEEN →
5	4'-0" × 4'-0"	→	#4040	→	→	→
6	3'-0" × 3'-0"	→	#3030	OBSCURE	→	→
7	6'-0" × 6'-8"	SLID. DOOR	ACME - 500 SERIES #6068-XO	1/4" PL.	→	
8	6'-0" × 6'-8"	→	#6068-OX	1/4" PL.	→	
9	5'-6" × 6'-8"	FIXED	JOB MADE	3/16" CRY.	REDWOOD	
10	6'-0" × VARIES	→	→	5/16" CRY	→	
11	4'-0" × 4'-0"	HORIZ. SLID.	E-Z SET ROLLING WINDOWS #4040	D.S. "B"	ALUM.	PAIR - WOOD MULLION BETWEEN →
12	3'-0" × 3'-0"	→	#3030	OBSCURE	→	
13	6'-0" × 3'-0"	→	#6030	D.S. "B"	→	
14	5'-0" × VARIES	FIXED	JOB MADE	OBSCURE	REDWOOD	
15	5'-0" × VARIES	→	→	→	→	
16	5'-0" × VARIES					
17	5'-0" × VARIES	→	→	→	→	

FIGURE 15-4 Full-size extract from Fig. 15-1 (tabular window schedule for floor plan in Fig. 14-1)

DOOR SCHEDULE

SYM	SIZE WIDTH x HT	THK	TYPE	MANUFACTURE & CATALOG NO.	MATERIAL	FINISH	JAMB	REMARKS
1	3'-0" x 7'-4"	1¾"	FLUSH-SOLID	"SIMPSON"- 5 PLY SOLID CORE	BIRCH	ENAMEL	WOOD	PAINT GRADE - BIRCH VENE
2	2'-8" x 6'-8"	1⅜"	FLUSH-HOLLOW	"SIMPSON"- 5 PLY HOLLOW CORE	→	→	→	
3	2'-6" x 6'-8"	→	→	→	→	→	→	
4	1'-8" x 6'-8"	→	→	→	→	→	→	
5	2'-4" x 6'-8"	→	→	→	→	→	→	
6	2'-10" x 6'-8"	1¾"	FLUSH - SOLID	"SIMPSON"- 5 PLY SOLID CORE	→	→	→	
7	2'-8" x 6'-8"	1⅜"	FLUSH-HOLLOW	"SIMPSON"- 5 PLY HOLLOW CORE	→	→	→	
8	2'-8" x 6'-8"	→	→	→	→	→	→	
9	2'-6" x 6'-8"	→	FULL LOUVER	→	→	→	→	
10	PR. 2'-4" x 6'-8"	→	→	→	→	→	→	
11	3'-0" x 6'-8"	1¾"	FLUSH - SOLID	→	→	→	→	
12	16'-0" x 7'-0"		OVHD. GARAGE	"FILUMA" FIBERGLASS GARAGE	ALUM			FIBERGLASS FACE SKIN

FIGURE 15-5 Full-size extract from Fig. 15-1 (tabular door schedule for floor plan in Fig. 14-1)

125

1. *Symbol:* The keying symbol
2. *Size:* The dimensions of the door
3. *Thickness:* Front to back
4. *Type:* Panel, flush, dutch, sliding, overhead, rolling, folding, and so on
5. *Manufacturer and catalog number:* Taken from the catalog if required
6. *Material:* Wood, steel, aluminum, plastic
7. *Finish:* Varnish, paint, lacquer
8. *Jamb:* Wood, steel, and so on
9. *Remarks:* Any further description

ROOM-FINISH SCHEDULES

The room-finish schedule may be arranged similar to a door schedule, in which case descriptions of materials and finishes are lettered in opposite the room names. The type shown here lists all of the materials and finishes at the top of the sheet, and small circles are used to key them to the rooms (Fig. 15-6). This system saves space and lettering. Either method is suitable. The headings used on a room-finish schedule are listed here:

1. *Room:* The name of the room
2. *Floor:* Hardwood, concrete, carpet, tile, and so on
3. *Base:* Size and material
4. *Walls:* North, east, south, and west; gypsum board, plaster, tile, plywood
5. *Ceiling:* Plaster, open beam, suspended, acoustic tile, and so on
6. *Wainscot:* Tile, plywood, plastic, and so forth, plus height of wainscot
7. *Cabinets and doors:* Pine, birch, or ash casework; tile, micarta, or stainless-steel countertop
8. *Trim:* Door casing, window trim, ceiling molding, and so forth

The room-finish schedule is used together with the appropriate interior elevation to get a true picture of the inside walls of the building. Room-finish schedules are usually keyed to the floor plan by the room name, but some offices use a special keying symbol.

VARIATIONS IN FORM

The sizes of the columns used with any schedule depend on the amount of information to be placed within them as well as the space available. It is better to use a separate sheet for schedules than to try to crowd them into a small space. The schedules described here are broken down into seven to nine columns; other schedules are simpler but may still be adequate.

DRAFTING THE SCHEDULES

1. Collect all the notes pertaining to the schedules. Make a set of headings for each schedule and break down the information to fit them.
2. Determine the number of vertical entries needed for each schedule. Design the schedules to fit the available space. Provide a few blank spaces for any later entries.
3. Draft the schedules.

REVIEW QUESTIONS

1. Name two different types of door schedules.
2. Which of the above types of schedules takes the most drafting time?
3. How many types of doors and windows, based on the manner in which they operate, can you name? Use Sweet's File as a reference.
4. What advantages are inherent in each type of door and window as listed above?
5. How many applications can you think of in which acoustic tile would be superior to plaster for a ceiling? Vice versa?
6. Why is smooth-finished plaster used in kitchens and baths? Why is rougher-textured plaster used for other rooms?
7. Concrete, hardwood, linoleum, plastic tile, carpet, and terrazzo are all common flooring materials; discuss the reasons why each material should or should not be used in your project.

STUDY SUGGESTIONS

1. Look over a set of drawings for a large building, and note the extent of the schedules.
2. Check back and forth in these drawings between the interior elevations and the schedules to see how they are related.

Room-Finish Schedule

REMARKS (legend):

- N — NATURAL FINISH
- E — 3 COAT ENAMEL
- W — 3 COAT FLAT WALL PAINT
- S — STAIN FINISH
- P — PRE-FINISHED
- XS — EXTERIOR STAIN
- XE — EXTERIOR TRIM PAINT

FLOOR / BASE

NO.	NAME	EXPOSED CONCRETE	CARPET (N.I.C.)	VINYL ASBESTOS TILE	BASE: HARDWOOD	BASE: PINE	BASE: 4" VINYL TOPSET
1	ENTRY		●		E		
2	LIVING ROOM		●		N		
3	FAMILY ROOM		●		E		
4	KITCHEN			●			●
5	NOOK			●			●
6	HALL		●		E		
7	BEDROOM #2		●		E		
8	BEDROOM #3		●		E		
9	BATH #2			●			●
10	BATH #1			●			●
11	BED ROOM #1		●		E		
12	GARAGE	●				E	

WALLS — SOUTH

NO.	NAME	1/2" GYPSUM BD.	HARDWOOD PANELING	TEXTURE ONE-ELEVEN PLYWD	MARLITE PANEL	D.F. PLYWD. WARDROBE	UNFINISHED
1	ENTRY						
2	LIVING ROOM	W	P				
3	FAMILY ROOM						
4	KITCHEN						
5	NOOK	E					
6	HALL	E					
7	BEDROOM #2	W					
8	BEDROOM #3	W					
9	BATH #2				P		
10	BATH #1				P		
11	BED ROOM #1					E	
12	GARAGE						●

WALLS — WEST

NO.	NAME	1/2" GYPSUM BD.	TEXTURE ONE-ELEVEN PLYWD.	MARLITE PANEL	D.F. PLYWOOD WARDROBE	UNFINISHED
1	ENTRY		S			
2	LIVING ROOM	W				
5	NOOK	E				
7	BEDROOM #2	W				
8	BEDROOM #3	W				
9	BATH #2	W		P		
10	BATH #1			P		
12	GARAGE		S			●

WALLS — NORTH

NO.	NAME	1/2" GYPSUM BD.	HARDWOOD PANELING	TEXTURE ONE-ELEVEN PLYWD.	MARLITE PANEL	D.F. PLYWD. WARDROBE	UNFINISHED	1/2" GYPSUM BD.
2	LIVING ROOM		P					W
3	FAMILY ROOM		P					
4	KITCHEN							W
5	NOOK	E						
6	HALL	W						E
7	BEDROOM #2							W
8	BEDROOM #3	W						
9	BATH #2				P			
10	BATH #1				P			
11	BED ROOM #1					E		
12	GARAGE						●	

FIGURE 15-6 Full-size extract from Fig. 15-1 (tabular room-finish schedule for floor plan in Fig. 14-1)

3. Visit a building-supply firm and look at various types of doors, windows, and surface materials. Sketch them as they would be shown in plan, elevation, and section.

STUDENT PROBLEM

1. Assemble your preliminary notes and sketches. Determine the information required for the door, window, room-finish, and, if you wish, the electrical schedules. (Sometimes the door, window, and room-finish schedules are placed on the floor plan, and the electrical schedule on the electrical plan.) Decide on the type of schedule to use, and lay out a trial arrangement to be sure the information will fit the sheet.

2. Draft the schedules.

CHAPTER 16
EXTERIOR ELEVATIONS

DEFINITION AND PURPOSE

The purpose of the exterior elevations is to show the finished appearance of all outside aspects of the building (Figs. 16-1 and 16-2). Each elevation is an orthographic projection of one view of the building based on the floor plan and the structural sections. Other drawings, for instance the roof plan, are occasionally needed to find points not easily derived from these two. All surface materials are indicated, as well as the locations of important structural features—floor line, plate line, and window and door heights. Elevations are usually drawn at the same scale as the floor plan.

DRAWING BY DIRECT PROJECTION

When drawing the elevations, it is possible to use either direct projection or measurement. To fix the relationships of the three drawings firmly in mind, the beginner should try at least one job by direct projection. Basically, the procedure is the same as a "missing-view problem" in elementary drawing in which the floor plan is the top view, the structural section is the side view, and the elevation is the missing front view. This method is a rather cumbersome one to employ with a large building, but it works easily with a small one.

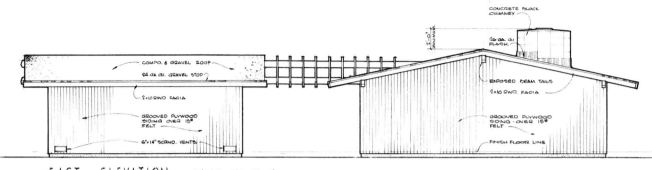

EAST ELEVATION   SCALE 1/4" = 1'-0"

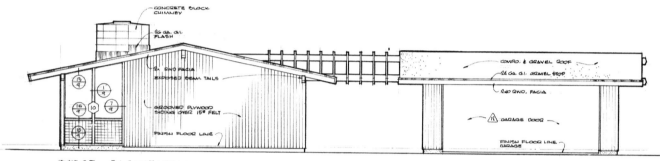

WEST ELEVATION   SCALE 1/4" = 1'-0"

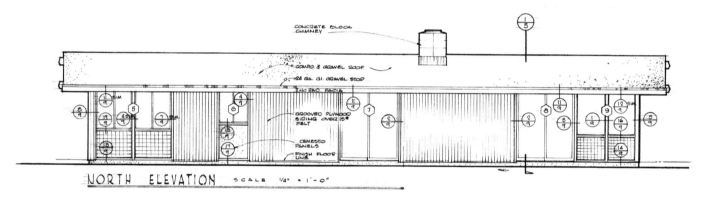

NORTH ELEVATION   SCALE 1/4" = 1'-0"

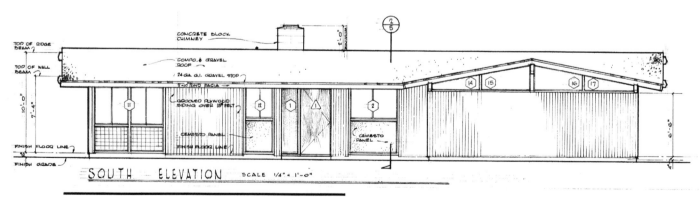

SOUTH ELEVATION   SCALE 1/4" = 1'-0"

130   FIGURE 16-1   Exterior elevations of a small residence

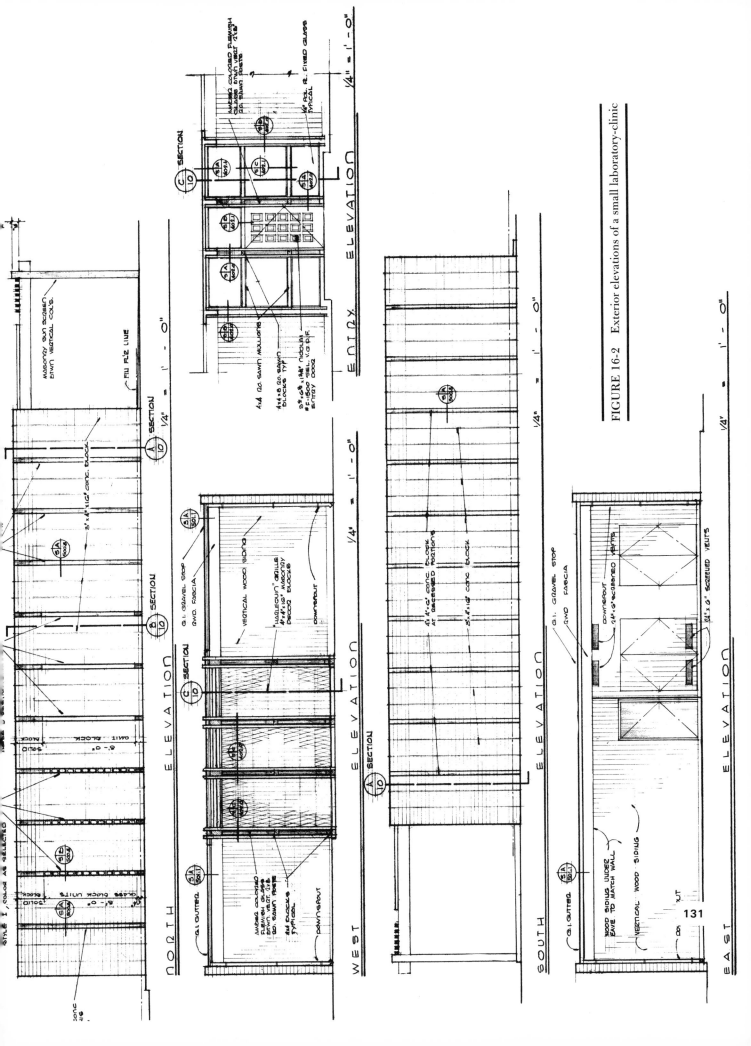

FIGURE 16-2 Exterior elevations of a small laboratory-clinic

131

REQUIRED DRAWINGS

Before starting, a copy of each of the different sections through the structure must be drawn at the same scale as the floor plan. These must be drawn on a separate sheet, not on the elevation drawings. It is important that the width of each section jibes with the width of the floor plan at the point where the section is taken and that all height measurements, roof pitch, and so on be taken accurately from the structural sections. It is a good idea to draw the roof plan over the floor plan (first draft, not finished drawing) for more accurate projection. First decide how many elevations will be required to give a complete description of the building; then space them by light outlines on the sheet or sheets required. Leave room for a title and scale under each elevation.

DRAFTING THE EXTERIOR ELEVATIONS

The steps in drawing the elevations by direct projection follow in logical order (Fig. 16-3).

1. Place the floor plan, with the outside wall facing down, directly above the space desired. This is important; if the outside wall is projected upward, a mirror image of that wall will result. To one side and in line with the desired space, place the required structural section or sections. All elevations will be exactly the same height overall.

2. Project a series of light lines from the floor plan to the working space. These lines represent length, or horizontal features of the building, such as ends of walls, eaves, windows, and doors. Project a series of light lines across from the sections to represent height, or vertical features of the building, such as grade line, floor line, window and door height, plate line, and ridge line.

3. Darken the lines slightly as needed, and erase those which might later be misleading. The result at this stage is a rough elevation lacking detail but giving a good idea of the ultimate appearance of that particular wall.

4. Repeat this procedure for all the required elevations. Rotate the floor plan for each view. Remove the floor plan and sections from the board.

5. Add all porches, railings, chimneys, trim and other small details in the order of their importance and line weight. Information needed to complete this part of the drawing is taken from many sources. The arrangement of window muntins is found in the manufacturer's catalog. The chimney is usually designed by the draftsman, and its height is determined by local building codes. Other sources include "Time-Saver Standards," "Architectural Graphic Standards," Sweet's File, construction details of the building, and the draftsman's judgment.

6. Place all notes, reference symbols, title, and scale (Fig. 16-4).

7. Draw in textures of all materials, and profile the drawing if desired.

SPECIAL CASES

The procedure in drawing a multistory or split-level structure is the same as that just described. The structural sections may be laid out one over the other on scratch paper if more than one section is needed (Fig. 16-5). Because the vertical distances from grade to all floor levels, window heights, plate lines, and eave and roof heights are the only important information taken from these sections, thicknesses of joists, beams, and so on do not have to be drawn. Heights of stepped foundations are set at a minimum of 6 in. above the grade at the uphill side (Fig. 16-5).

DRAWING BY MEASUREMENT

It is not mandatory that the elevations be directly projected from the floor plan and sections. The alternative is to measure from the drawings and transfer the required points to the sheet. A *tick strip*, or scrap of paper with "ticks" in line with walls, windows, and so on, may be used to transfer distances accurately. It is important, however, that the right end of the elevation appear on the right side of the sheet and that absolute agreement in projection exist among all drawings concerned. For these reasons, a knowledge of the method of direct projection is considered desirable. A few quick tests, easy to understand, can be made as the drawing progresses; they will detect

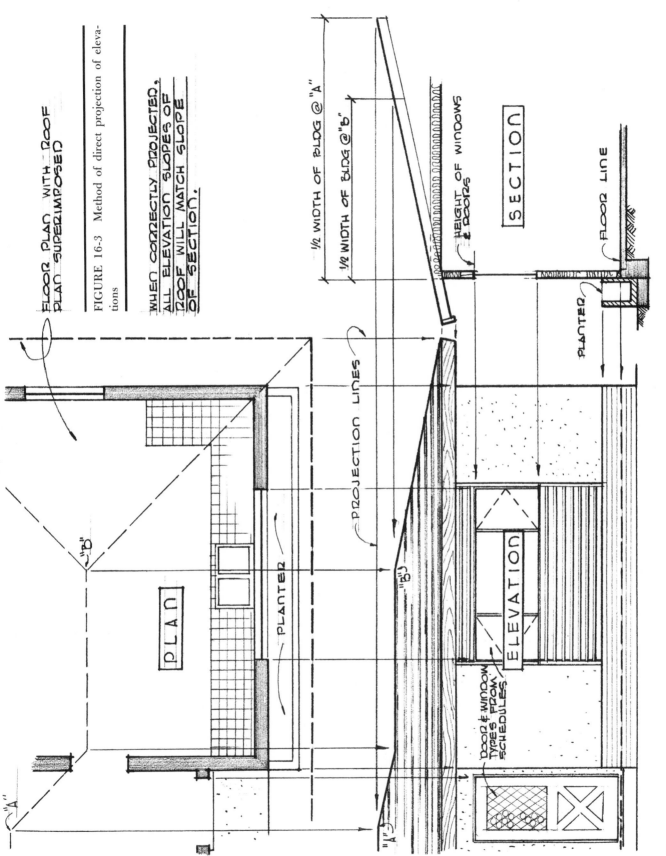

FLOOR PLAN WITH ROOF
PLAN SUPERIMPOSED

FIGURE 16-3   Method of direct projection of elevations

WHEN CORRECTLY PROJECTED,
ALL ELEVATION SLOPES OF
ROOF WILL MATCH SLOPE
OF SECTION.

½ WIDTH OF BLDG @ "A"

½ WIDTH OF BLDG @ "B"

HEIGHT OF WINDOWS
& DOORS

SECTION

FLOOR LINE

PLANTER

"B"

PLAN

PLANTER

PROJECTION LINES

"B"

"A"

ELEVATION

PLANTER

DOOR & WINDOW
TYPES FROM
SCHEDULES

"A"

133

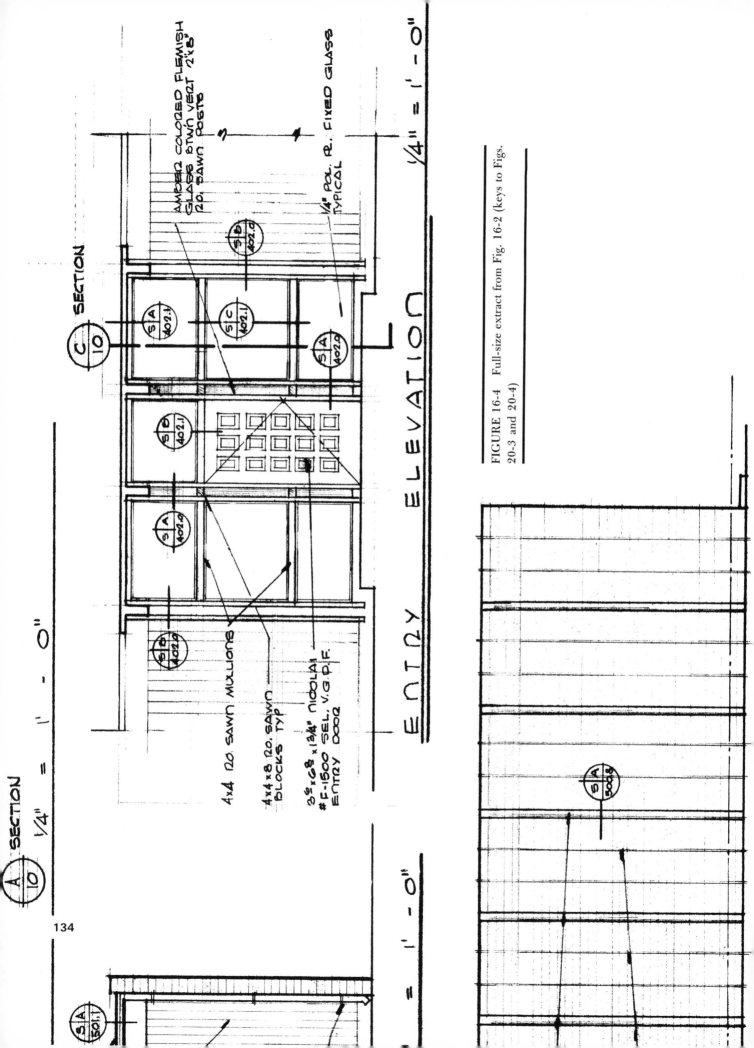

FIGURE 16-4   Full-size extract from Fig. 16-2 (keys to Figs. 20-3 and 20-4)

134

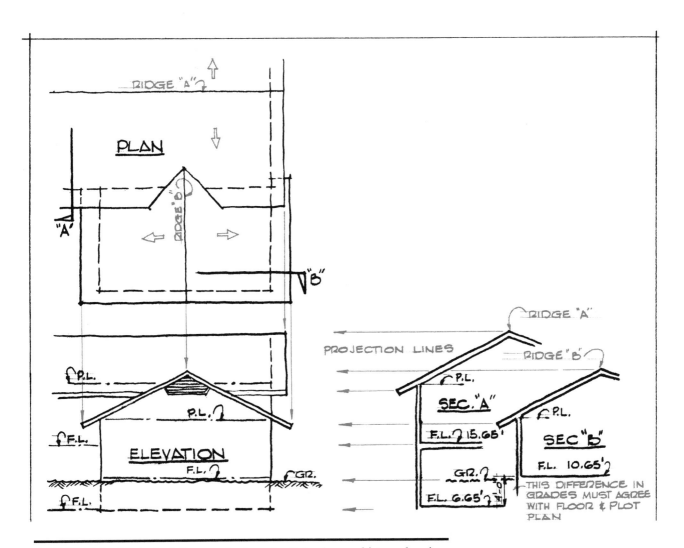

FIGURE 16-5   Method of direct projection of split-level or multistory elevations

serious error and avoid redrawing. For instance, if the north elevation happens to be high at the left side of the paper, the south elevation must be high at the right side. If the building has a pitched roof, like a hip roof, then the pitches of all roofs in all views will be identical with the roof pitch of the section. In addition, agreement in projection between selected points can be checked in all three drawings.

DEVELOPED AND ROTATED ELEVATIONS

If a building has a wing projecting from the main part at other than a right angle or if it has an odd plan form, say a circle, there are two ways of drawing the elevations. Direct projection, as shown above, is one way; development is the other. A developed elevation is produced by merely rotating the skewed section into the plane of projection and then projecting normally. A developed elevation of a circular building is produced by laying out the perimeter of the wall with windows, doors, and so on laid out in a straight line.

USE OF TEXTURE

Texture can be used on elevations in either of two ways, complete rendition of all textures or partial rendition (Fig. 16-6 and A-5). Taste or office practice

135

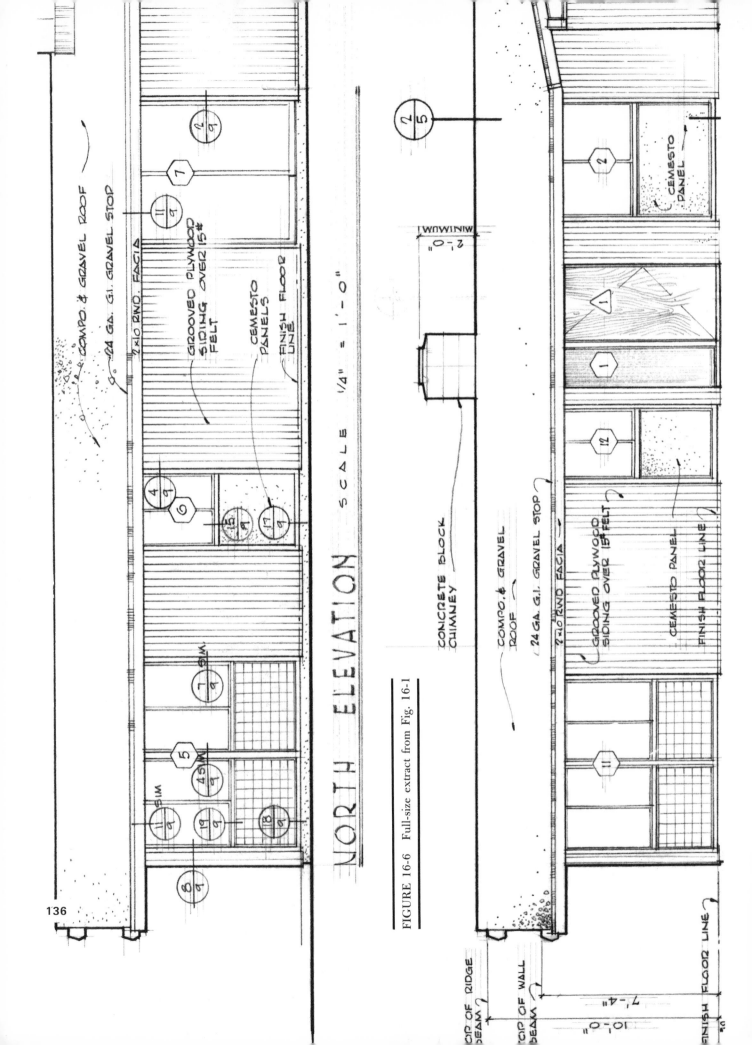

NORTH ELEVATION SCALE 1/4" = 1'-0"

FIGURE 16-6 Full-size extract from Fig. 16-1

136

usually determines which is to be used. The use of complete texturing takes more drafting time, but some architects prefer its appearance. Partial texturing is faster and, if done well, will appeal to many people. Textures for many materials are shown in the reference section, and their use is self-explanatory. In either case, the areas of each type of material should be called out by note.

REVIEW QUESTIONS

1. Try to draw an elevation based on the floor plan of a small building without reference to a structural section. Can you do it accurately? Why?
2. Sketch a developed elevation of an odd-shaped building, and compare it with the normal elevation. What are the advantages and disadvantages of each method?
3. Is it possible to draw a complete elevation from only a floor plan and a cross section? Explain.
4. What direct effect did the preliminary orientation sketches have on your elevation?
5. Is it possible to see a finished building as an accurate elevation? In other words, in orthographic projection?
6. Show how an elevation is related to several other working drawings.

STUDY SUGGESTIONS

1. Visit a building under construction, and compare the exterior of the building with the exterior elevations.
2. Try some sketches of your own project, using the floor plan and several cross sections of different shape, different sizes and proportions of doors and windows, and several combinations of exterior finishes. Some of these solutions may seem better to you than your first idea.

STUDENT PROBLEM

The floor plan and structural section are needed for constructing the elevations. Decide whether to draw a $\frac{1}{4}$-in. scale section to use for direct projection or to draw the elevations by measurement. Draw the required elevations.

CHAPTER 17
INTERIOR ELEVATIONS

DEFINITION AND PURPOSE

The interior elevations describe the interior walls of each room in the building. Each elevation is an orthographic projection based on the floor plan of the particular wall and the structural section at that point (Figs. 17-1, 17-2, and 17-3). Other drawings used to determine height are the fireplace section, cabinet sections, planter sections, and manufacturers' illustrations showing special equipment. All walls should be shown and identified in a complete set of drawings. Although not mandatory, this practice serves as a check for the draftsman in locating equipment; it also helps to assign responsibility when an error occurs in construction. However, on a minimum set of drawings, only the important walls are shown, such as the kitchen, fireplace, and special cabinet work. The scale of interior elevations is usually $\frac{1}{4}$ or $\frac{3}{8}$ in. = 1 ft. 0 in. but can be made larger to show more detail.

The procedure used in laying out accurate interior elevations is practically the same as that used for exterior elevations; the only difference is that the inside, rather than the outside, walls are projected (Fig. 17-4).

DRAFTING THE INTERIOR ELEVATIONS

Many features are common to the interior walls of any structure, and the following procedure is used for drawing all interior walls (Figs. 17-1 and 17-2):

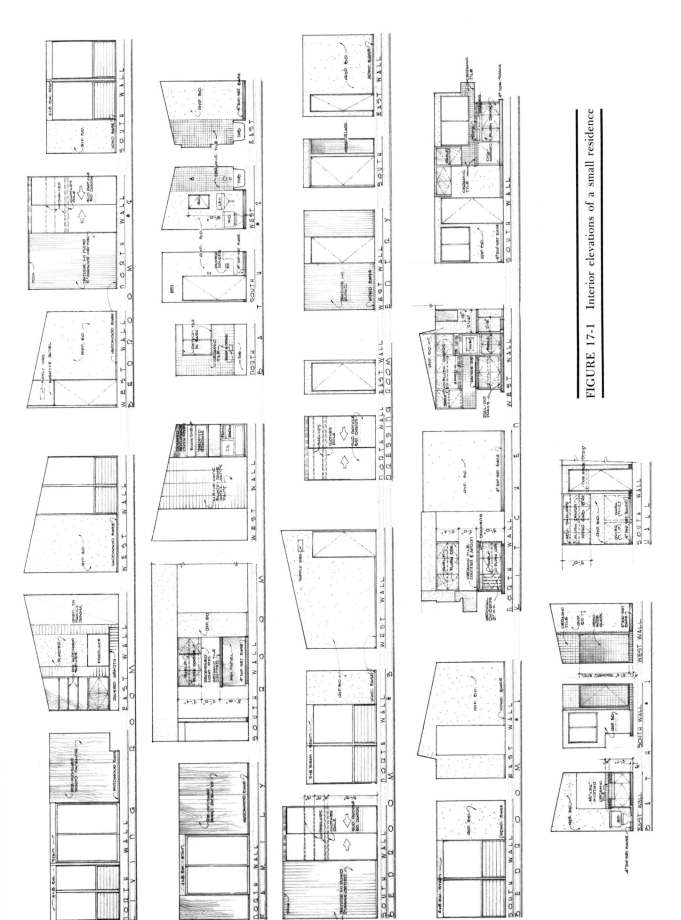

FIGURE 17-1 Interior elevations of a small residence

139

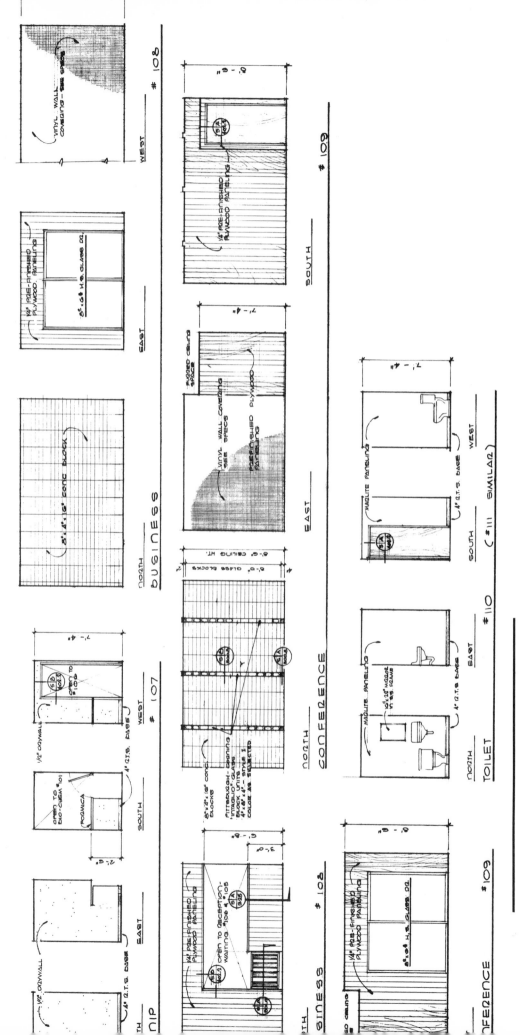

140

FIGURE 17-2 Interior elevations of a laboratory-clinic

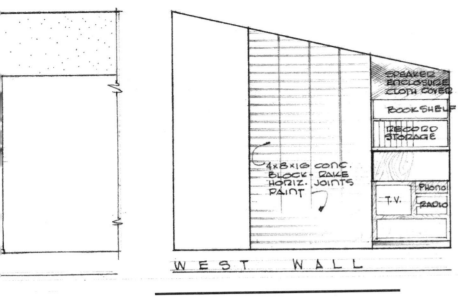

WEST WALL

NORTH
B A T

FIGURE 17-3   Full-size extract from Fig. 17-1

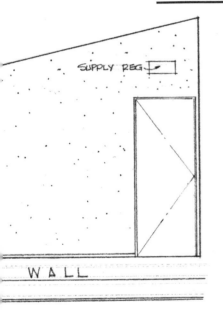

WALL

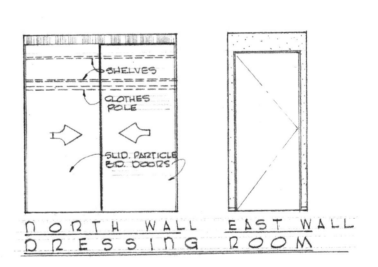

NORTH WALL   EAST WALL
DRESSING ROOM

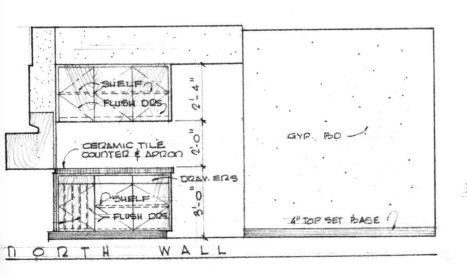

NORTH WALL

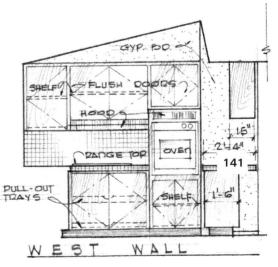

WEST WALL

141

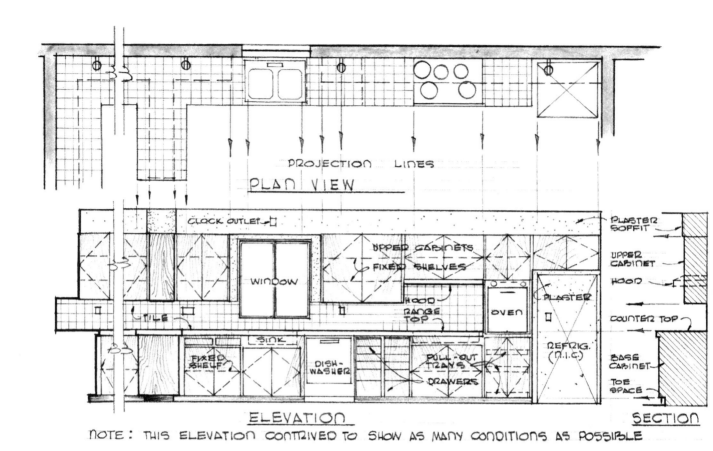

The figure contains the following hand-lettered labels:

PROJECTION LINES

PLAN VIEW

CLOCK OUTLET

PLASTER SOFFIT

UPPER CABINETS

FIXED SHELVES

UPPER CABINET

WINDOW

HOOD

HOOD

RANGE TOP

OVEN

PLASTER

COUNTER TOP

TILE

SINK

FIXED SHELF

DISH-WASHER

PULL-OUT TRAYS

DRAWERS

REFRIG. (N.I.C.)

BASE CABINET

TOE SPACE

ELEVATION

SECTION

NOTE: THIS ELEVATION CONTRIVED TO SHOW AS MANY CONDITIONS AS POSSIBLE

FIGURE 17-4 Method of direct projection of interior elevations

1. Project or measure the true width of the wall, and locate all windows, doors, stairs, and so on, from the floor plan. The space remaining is available for cabinet work, appliances, display cases, and the like.

2. Project or measure the height of all features of the wall from a section, or get the information from one of the schedules. In a room with a sloping ceiling show the ceiling area, beams, and so on, above the plate line.

3. Draw in the light outlines of all cabinets, shelves, wardrobes, and plumbing fixtures which are to be built in. Locate with light lines all stoves, refrigerators, and other appliances which must have space reserved for them and label NIC.

4. Wherever cabinets, soffits, and shelves return on a wall toward the observer, they should be drawn in heavy outline. Omit the lines of the wall and floor behind the cabinet, because these areas are not part of the wall being drawn. Also, this procedure makes the drawing easier to read.

5. Draw the outlines of varying wall materials, such as tile, stainless steel, and wood wainscoting.

6. Mark off the doors, drawers, shelves, toe spaces, and soffits of all cabinet work, display cases, and wardrobes.

7. Draw in all base molding, door and window trim, and so on, where needed.

8. Place all electric outlets, such as convenience outlets, wall switches, and wall fixtures, in the proper places.

9. Letter in all notes concerning surface materials and equipment.

10. Letter in all notes, titles, and scale.

11. Draw in the textures of all surface materials lightly.

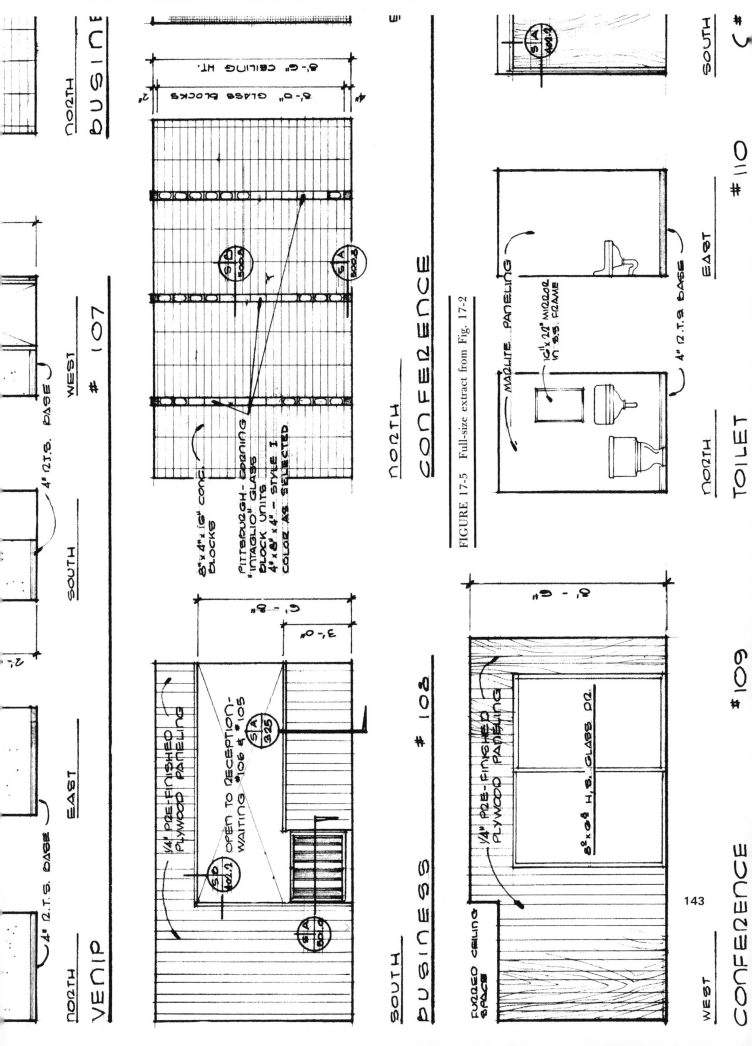

FIGURE 17-5 Full-size extract from Fig. 17-2

143

Refer to the appropriate chapters of the book for specific information on drawing cabinets, stairs, fireplaces, trim, tile, plumbing and electric fixtures, and so on.

KEYING SYMBOLS

Each drawing should be keyed to the others in the set (Figs. 17-2 and 17-5). Cabinet elevations must be keyed to the appropriate cabinet section. Door- and window-head jamb and sill conditions must be related to the correct sections. Store fronts and display cases should be keyed to their sections.

REVIEW QUESTIONS

1. What good reason is there for showing all the walls of all rooms of a building, even though some of them are practically blank?
2. Is it possible to draw an interior elevation from the floor plan of the wall without the cross section? Why?
3. In a frame and plaster structure, what is the main purpose of door trim?

STUDY SUGGESTIONS

1. Visit two buildings under construction, a typical frame residence and a high-quality commercial building. Compare construction features, such as windows, doors, hardware, and trim. Compare the drawings with the actual construction.
2. Inspect specific interior details, such as fireplaces, planters, room dividers, or cabinet work, in an architectural magazine. You may be able to use similar details on a future project.

STUDENT PROBLEM

The rough copy of the floor plan; the notes pertaining to all equipment which will appear in the interior elevations; and accurate sections of cabinets, fireplace, and so on, drawn at $\frac{1}{4}$ in. scale, will be needed for drawing the interior.

Every interior wall of the house should be shown in a complete set of drawings. However, for instructional purposes many walls which have very little detail may be omitted. The following walls would be acceptable in a set of student drawings: any walls of the kitchen which have cabinet work, two walls of the utility room, the fireplace and window wall of the living room, the linen closets, the wardrobe wall plus one other wall of a typical bedroom, two walls of the dining and/or family room, and any other wall which has cabinets, planters, or special case work. Of course, the decision on how much to include in the drawing is the responsibility of the instructor.

Draw the interior elevations.

CHAPTER 18
PLOT AND LANDSCAPING PLANS

DEFINITION AND PURPOSE

The plot plan is a plan view of the site, the building, and all outside work in connection with the job. The outside work includes all concrete and paving work, locations of utilities, and smaller structures, such as covered walks or arbors (Figs. 18-1, 18-2, 18-4, and 18-5). Landscaping can be shown on the plot plan but is usually on a separate drawing to avoid confusion (Fig. 18-3). Scale varies considerably depending on the size of the project and sheet size. Typical scale is $\frac{1}{16}$ in. = 1 ft 0 in.

PLOT PLAN

Before starting the plot plan, however, the student should be familiar with the use of contour lines and

polar coordinates and the problem of setbacks and easements. These subjects are not usually encountered in a first-year drafting course.

CONTOUR LINES

A contour line is a conventional means to show height on the flat surface of a drawing (Fig. 18-6). It is simply a line on a map which represents the intersection of an imaginary horizontal plane with the surface of the ground. The uniform vertical distance between contour lines is called the *contour interval*. The contour interval used on a small map may be as small as a fraction of a foot, or, on a large map, 100 ft. The usual contour interval used on small maps is 1 or 2 ft. Contours are labeled according to their height above mean sea level or any other convenient base

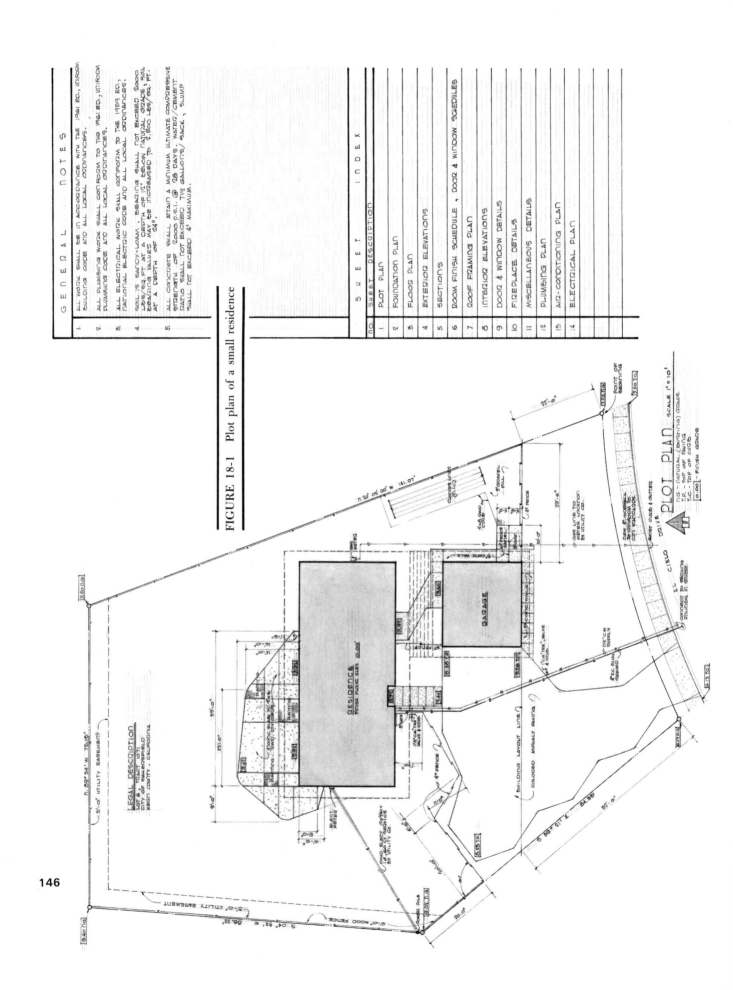

FIGURE 18-1 Plot plan of a small residence

146

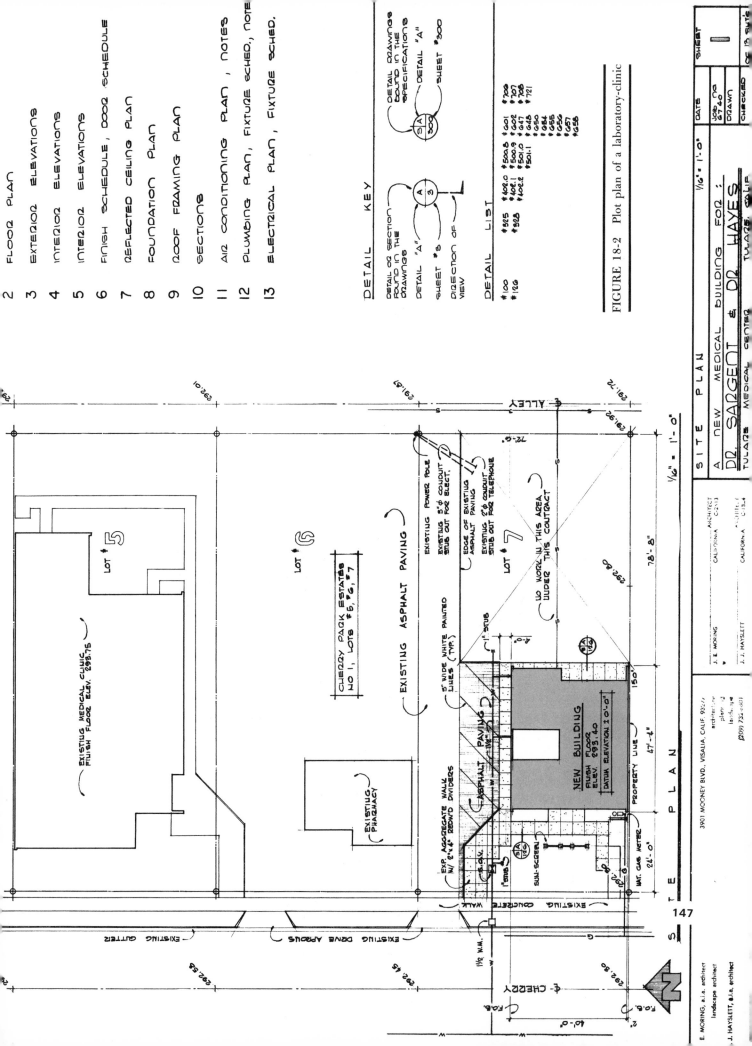

FIGURE 18-2 Plot plan of a laboratory-clinic

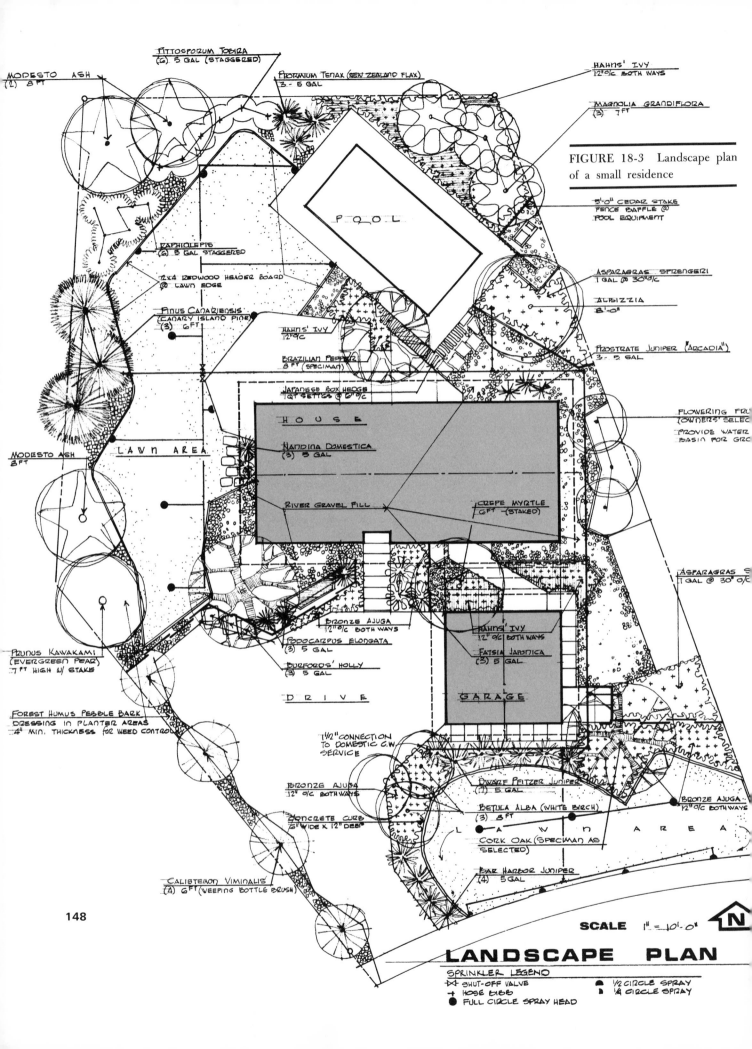

MODESTO ASH
(2) 8 FT

PITTOSPORUM TOBIRA
(6) 5 GAL (STAGGERED)

PHORMIUM TENAX (NEW ZEALAND FLAX)
3 - 5 GAL

HAHNS' IVY
12"O/C BOTH WAYS

MAGNOLIA GRANDIFLORA
(3) 7 FT

FIGURE 18-3 Landscape plan
of a small residence

5'-0" CEDAR STAKE
FENCE BAFFLE @
POOL EQUIPMENT

P O O L

RAPHIOLEPIS
(6) 5 GAL STAGGERED

2x4 REDWOOD HEADER BOARD
@ LAWN EDGE

PINUS CANARIENSIS
(CANARY ISLAND PINE)
(3) 6 FT

HAHNS' IVY
12"O/C

BRAZILIAN PEPPER
8 FT (SPECIMAN)

JAPANESE BOX HEDGE
QT SETIES @ 6" O/C

ASPARAGRAS SPRENGERI
1 GAL @ 30"O/C

ALBIZZIA
8'-0"

PROSTRATE JUNIPER ('ARCADIA')
3 - 5 GAL

FLOWERING FRU...
(OWNERS' SELEC...

PROVIDE WATER...
BASIN FOR GRO...

MODESTO ASH
8 FT

L A W N   A R E A

H O U S E

NANDINA DOMESTICA
(3) 5 GAL

RIVER GRAVEL FILL

CREPE MYRTLE
6 FT (STAKED)

ASPARAGRAS S...
1 GAL @ 30" O/C

PRUNUS KAWAKAMI
(EVERGREEN PEAR)
7 FT HIGH W/ STAKE

BRONZE AJUGA
12"O/C BOTH WAYS

PODOCARPUS ELONGATA
(3) 5 GAL

BURFORDS' HOLLY
(3) 5 GAL

HAHNS' IVY
12" O/C BOTH WAYS

FATSIA JAPONICA
(3) 5 GAL

FOREST HUMUS PEBBLE BARK
DRESSING IN PLANTER AREAS
4" MIN. THICKNESS FOR WEED CONTROL

D R I V E

G A R A G E

1 1/2" CONNECTION
TO DOMESTIC C.W.
SERVICE

BRONZE AJUGA
12" O/C BOTH WAYS

CONCRETE CURB
6" WIDE X 12" DEEP

DWARF PFITZER JUNIPER
(1) 5 GAL

BETULA ALBA (WHITE BIRCH)
(3) 8 FT

BRONZE AJUGA
12"O/C BOTH WAYS

L A W N   A R E A

CALISTEMON VIMINALIS
(4) 6 FT (WEEPING BOTTLE BRUSH)

CORK OAK (SPECIMAN AS
SELECTED)

BAR HARBOR JUNIPER
(4) 5 GAL

148

SCALE 1" = 10'-0" N

LANDSCAPE   PLAN

SPRINKLER LEGEND
SHUT-OFF VALVE
HOSE BIBB
FULL CIRCLE SPRAY HEAD
1/2 CIRCLE SPRAY
1/4 CIRCLE SPRAY

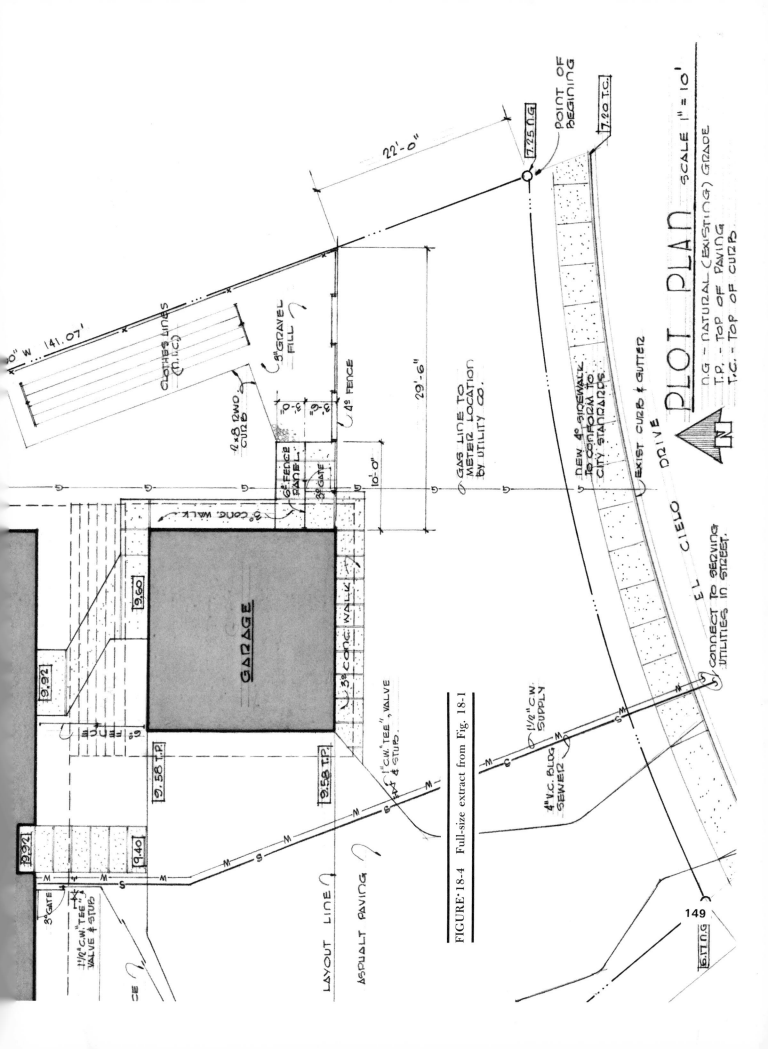

FIGURE·18-4 Full-size extract from Fig. 18-1

PLOT PLAN SCALE 1" = 10'

N.G - NATURAL (EXISTING) GRADE
T.P - TOP OF PAVING
T.C - TOP OF CURB

POINT OF BEGINNING

7.25 N.G

7.20 T.C.

22'-0"

CLOTHES LINES (T.I.C.)

W. 141.07'

3" GRAVEL FILL

4' FENCE

2×8 2ND. CURB

6' FENCE PANEL

3' GATE

3" CONC. WALK

29'-6"

10'-0"

3'-0"

4'-6"

GAS LINE TO METER LOCATION BY UTILITY CO.

GARAGE

9.60

CURB 6"

9.92

9.58 T.P.

9.58 T.P.

3" CONC. WALK

1" C.W. TEE, VALVE & STUB.

1½" C.W. SUPPLY

4" V.C. BLDG SEWER

NEW 4" SIDEWALK TO CONFORM TO CITY STANDARDS.

EXIST CURB & GUTTER

EL CIELO DRIVE

CONNECT TO SERVING UTILITIES IN STREET.

9.32

9.40

3" GATE

1½" C.W. TEE, VALVE & STUB.

LAYOUT LINE

ASPHALT PAVING

6.17 N.G

149

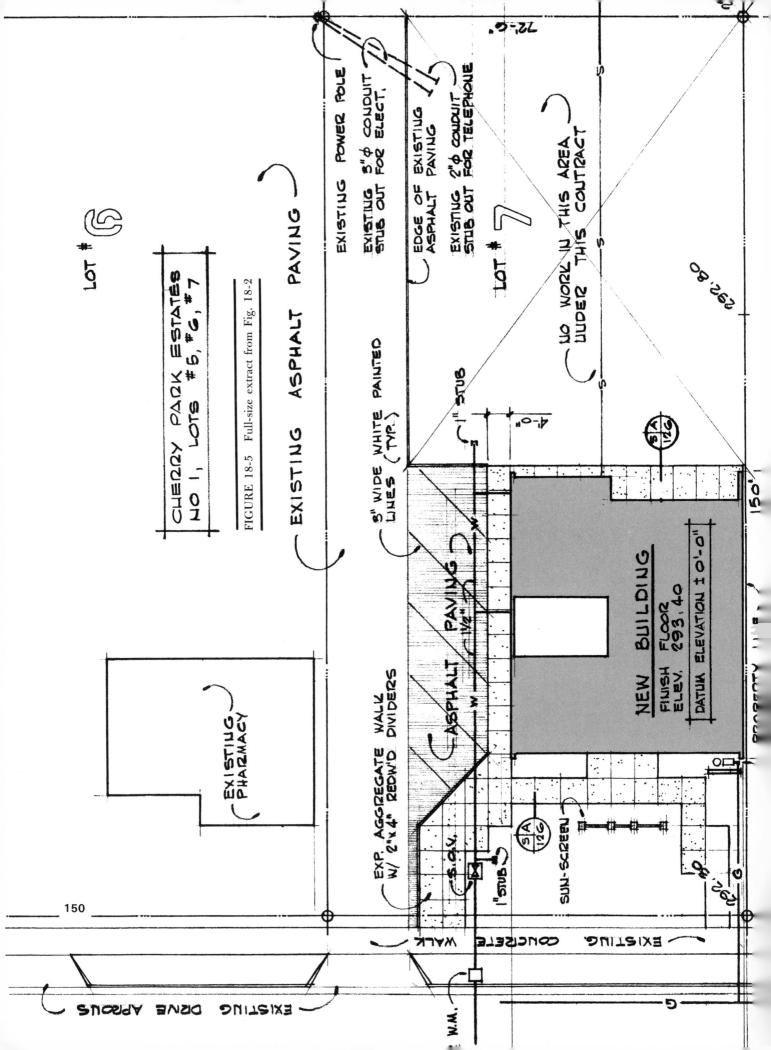

LOT # 6

CHERRY PARK ESTATES
NO 1, LOTS #5, #6, #7

FIGURE 18-5 Full-size extract from Fig. 18-2

EXISTING ASPHALT PAVING

EXISTING POWER POLE

EXISTING 5"∅ CONDUIT STUB OUT FOR ELECT.

EDGE OF EXISTING ASPHALT PAVING

EXISTING 2"∅ CONDUIT STUB OUT FOR TELEPHONE

LOT # 7

NO WORK IN THIS AREA UNDER THIS CONTRACT

EXISTING PHARMACY

EXP. AGGREGATE WALK W/ 2"x4" REDW'D DIVIDERS

5" WIDE WHITE PAINTED LINES (TYP.)

ASPHALT PAVING

S.O.V.

1" STUB

1" STUB

4'-0"

1 1/2"

SUN-SCREEN

NEW BUILDING

FINISH FLOOR ELEV. 293.40

DATUM ELEVATION ± 0'-0"

EXISTING CONCRETE WALK

EXISTING DRIVE APRONS

W.M.

72'-6"

150'

292.80

292.80

150

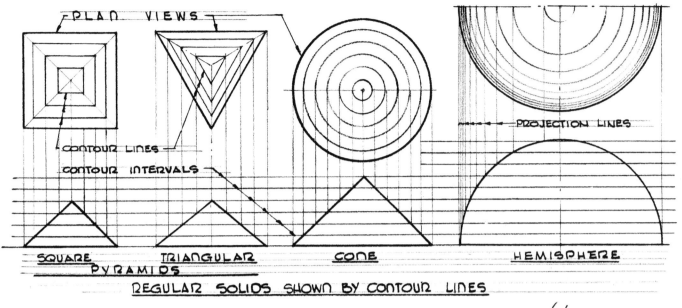

PLAN VIEWS

CONTOUR LINES

CONTOUR INTERVALS

PROJECTION LINES

SQUARE   TRIANGULAR   CONE   HEMISPHERE
PYRAMIDS

REGULAR SOLIDS SHOWN BY CONTOUR LINES

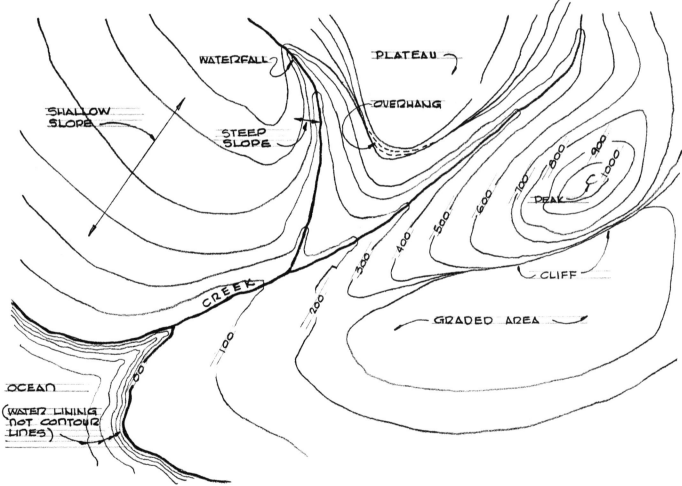

WATERFALL   PLATEAU

SHALLOW SLOPE   OVERHANG

STEEP SLOPE

CREEK

100 200 300 400 500 600 700 800 900 1000

PEAK

CLIFF

GRADED AREA

OCEAN
(WATER LINING
NOT CONTOUR
LINES)

NATURAL FEATURES OF THE EARTHS SURFACE SHOWN BY CONTOUR LINES

151

FIGURE 18-6   Contour lines used to demonstrate regular and irregular shapes

plane. A simple way of visualizing contours follows: If one were to draw lines at the varying water levels of a lake as the water level dropped, each line, when viewed from above, would represent a contour line, and all of them together would represent a contour map of the shore around the lake. With a little practice, a draftsman can easily visualize the shape of the land through the use of contour lines.

LOT LINES

Lots are usually laid out by surveyors by the use of polar coordinates; that is, each line around a lot is described by its length plus its angle in relation to true north or south, that is, *distance* and *bearing* (Fig. 18-7). The distance is laid off in feet and hundredths of a foot, rather than feet and inches. For example, 150 ft 9 in. would equal 150.75 ft. Angles, or bearings, are measured in relation to true north or true south. North and south are both read as 0°; east and

west are both read as 90°. To avoid ambiguity, the compass is divided into four quadrants of 90°—NW, NE, SE, and SW. Angles are labeled thus: N14°53′11″W; this reads "north fourteen degrees, fifty-three minutes, eleven seconds west." As there are sixty minutes to a degree and sixty seconds to a minute, the student may safely round this figure off to N15°W, because the ordinary protractor cannot be used to measure such small increments as minutes and seconds. For plot plans, $\frac{1}{2}$° accuracy is sufficient. When copying a lot from a map to a plot plan, start at the point of beginning (pob) which will permit each line to be laid out in order, head to tail, without using a reverse heading (Fig. 18-7). Lay off the bearing first, then the distance.

Other methods of expressing angular relationships are used, but all are based on a circle divided into 360°. The included angle between two lines or the included angle between a line and a base line may be indicated by an arc. The angle between a line and either north or south as 0° may be shown. A special

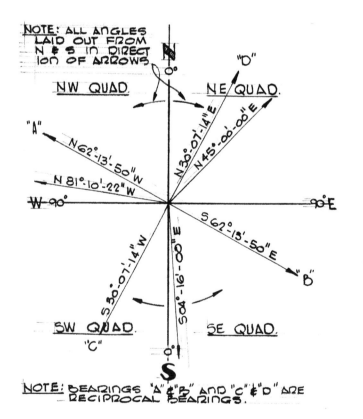

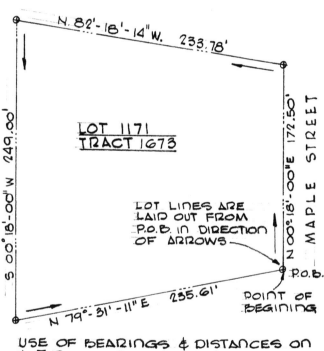

FIGURE 18-7 Use of polar coordinates to describe a plot of ground

case is the sun table used in this book. North is considered to be 0° and south 180°. No angle is larger than 180°. Angles to the east, or morning, read clockwise from north; angles to the west, or afternoon, read counterclockwise. It is easy to determine the method by which any angle is expressed by comparing the line with a north–south line or noting the arc used to dimension the angle.

EARTH SECTIONS

When designing a building to be located on a slope, it is necessary to construct one or more vertical sections through the lot. These sections will be used as a basis for many aspects of the completed building. Some of the more obvious of these aspects are the extent of excavation required, the size and placement of the foundation elements, and the appearance of the elevations.

The first requirement is an accurate contour map of the site at a contour interval of not more than one foot. It is easiest to draw the section by direct projection in the following manner: Draw a line on the contour map in the desired position; this is the section line. Next, draw on a piece of tracing paper a series of lines, at the same scale as the map, spaced equal to the contour interval. Label each of these lines in order with the elevations intersected by the section line. Place this tracing paper, with the lines parallel to the section line, on top of the map. Project the point of intersection of each contour line and the section line to the appropriate contour interval line. Connect the resulting series of points with straight lines; this profile will represent a very accurate section through the lot (Fig. 18-8).

SETBACKS AND EASEMENTS

Setbacks and easements limit the space on the lot within which buildings may be placed. Setbacks are listed in the building codes and zoning ordinances. They establish the distances from the front, rear, and sides of the lot beyond which the building may not be placed. They vary greatly, depending on the part of the country and type of building involved. The city and county building departments keep these restrictions on file for all areas under their jurisdiction

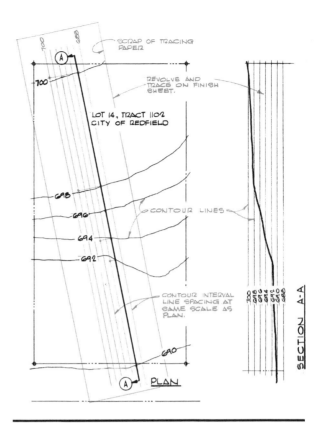

FIGURE 18-8 Method of taking an earth section from a contour map

(see A-38 and A-39). Easements are other areas within the lot over which construction may not be placed. Permission to use these areas at any time has been deeded to certain agencies for access to the facilities which they maintain. Easements are provided for power lines, sewer lines, and so on. The location and extent of easements are found on the subdivision maps (see Fig. 6-2).

DRAFTING THE PLOT PLAN

When drawing a plot plan, it is good practice to draw the project in the order of its construction, as follows (Figs. 18-1 and 18-2):

1. Lay out the lot and show contour if needed; flat lots do not have or need contour lines. Place the north arrow.
2. Indicate the streets and alleys.

3. Show locations of all utilities: electrical, gas, and water service; sewer lines; steam-heating lines; and so on.

4. Draw in any existing construction which will be left in place after construction starts.

5. In dashed lines draw any existing construction which will be removed before new construction. Indicate by a general note which construction is to be removed and by whom.

6. Lay off light lines representing the front, rear, and side setbacks allowed by ordinance. Construction is not permitted beyond these lines, except for walks, drives, and so on. Lay off any easements which cross the site; no construction should be placed in these areas.

7. Lay out the outlines of all buildings and roof overhangs.

8. Locate miscellaneous details, such as plumbing vents, advertising signs, fences, gates.

9. Draw in all concrete work, plant-mix surfacing, and areas of rock or gravel.

10. Dimension the building in relation to the lot lines. If the lot lines are at 90° angles to each other and the building is parallel to one of them, two dimensions are needed. If the building is not parallel to a lot line, locate one important corner of the building in relation to a corner of the lot with two dimensions. Show the distance from a lot line to another corner, on a wall common to the first corner. Dimension lines are always perpendicular or parallel to the lot lines.

11. Dimension concrete or paved areas by location and/or size, whichever is clearer.

12. Place all notes; all areas should be identified. The thickness of concrete and paving should be noted, and all utilities should be identified. Show elevations of the ground at the building and property corners. Show the elevation of each floor level of the structure.

LANDSCAPING PLAN

The landscaping plan is closely related to the plot plan. It shows the type and location of all trees, plants, lawn, ground cover, and so on, on the building site. Sometimes fences, lath houses, and benches are placed on the landscaping plan (Figs. 18-3 and 18-9).

DRAFTING THE LANDSCAPING PLAN

Following is a logical order of work:

1. Trace the plot plan omitting utilities and dimensioning.

2. Place all large trees and shrubs; draw them as mature plants, even though they may be small when planted. Mark the locations of the trunks as small circles.

3. Outline all planters and areas of lawn and ground cover.

4. Place small plants and hedges.

5. Identify all plants and planting areas by note. The common names for trees and shrubs are usually used by students.

6. Sprinkler systems are placed on the landscape plan (Fig. 18-3). Start from the water source and place the valves or automatic timing device. Run the water lines where needed, and identify all sprinkler heads. The information concerning pipes, valves, area covered by various sprinkler heads, and so on, may be found in the catalogs available from manufacturers.

COMBINED DRAWINGS

Many projects, usually residential ones, contain such a small amount of information that it would be pointless to use both a plot plan and a landscape plan. Therefore a combination plot, landscape, and roof plan (not roof framing plan) is drawn (Fig. 18-10). It shows the roof lines as object lines, the wall lines as hidden lines, and landscape materials the same weight as dimension lines, which can overlap anything else. Because of the relative importance of the house, concrete areas, and so on compared to indeterminate objects such as trees and shrubs, the drawing will be more readable this way.

The information usually omitted is the sprinkler system and the structural members of the roof. The drawing is titled "Plot Plan," and the scale should be fairly large to show enough detail: $\frac{1}{16}$ in. = 1 ft 0 in. to $\frac{1}{8}$ in. = 1 ft 0 in., depending on the space available.

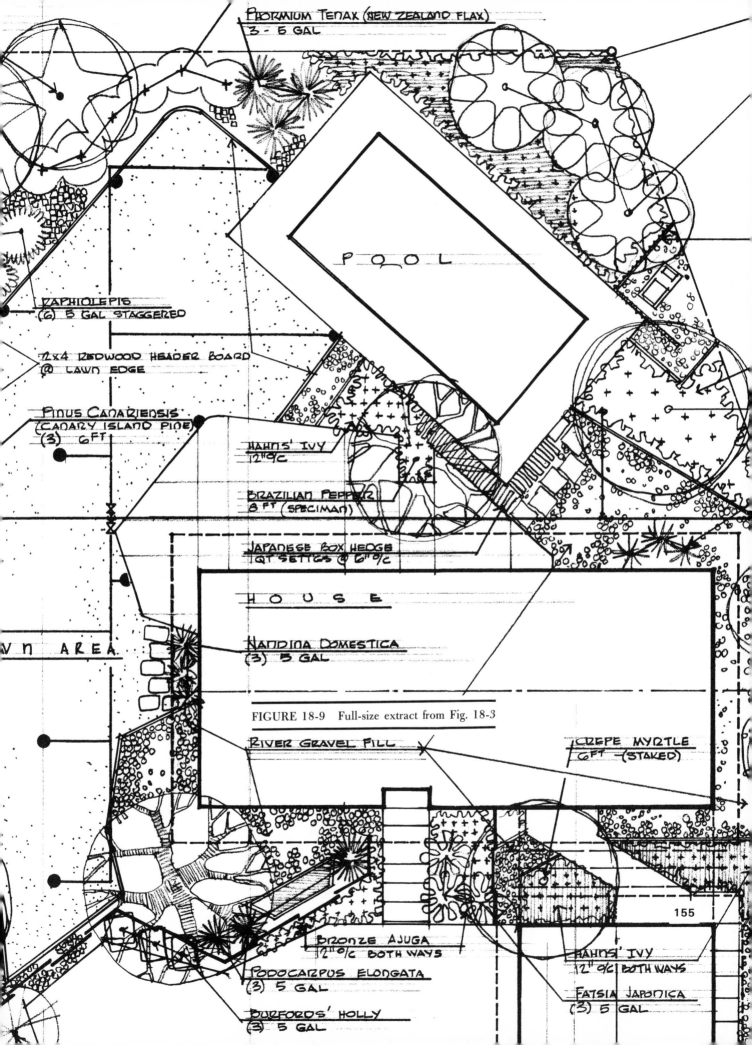

PHORMIUM TENAX (NEW ZEALAND FLAX)
3 - 5 GAL

RAPHIOLEPIS
(6) 5 GAL STAGGERED

2x4 REDWOOD HEADER BOARD
@ LAWN EDGE

PINUS CANARIENSIS
(CANARY ISLAND PINE)
(3) 6 FT

POOL

HAHNS' IVY
12" O/C

BRAZILIAN PEPPER
8 FT (SPECIMAN)

JAPANESE BOX HEDGE
(QT SETTES @ 6" O/C

HOUSE

NANDINA DOMESTICA
(3) 5 GAL

...VN AREA

FIGURE 18-9   Full-size extract from Fig. 18-3

RIVER GRAVEL FILL

CREPE MYRTLE
6 FT (STAKED)

155

BRONZE AJUGA
12" O/C BOTH WAYS

PODOCARPUS ELONGATA
(3) 5 GAL

BURFORDS' HOLLY
(3) 5 GAL

HAHNS' IVY
12" O/C BOTH WAYS

FATSIA JAPONICA
(3) 5 GAL

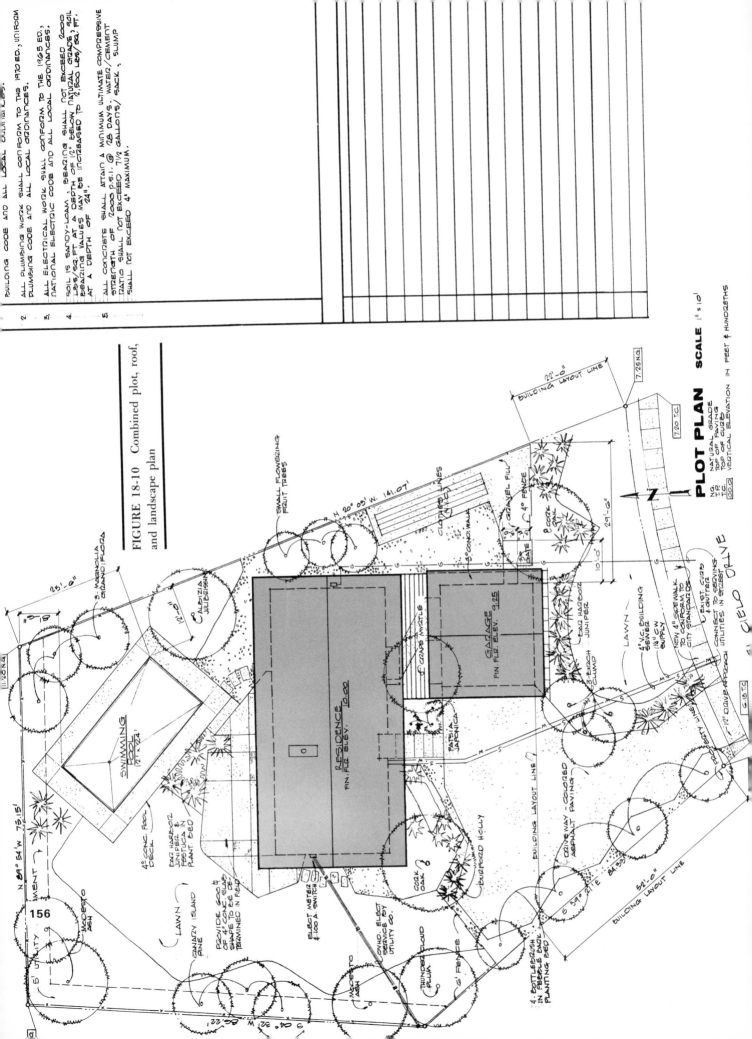

FIGURE 18-10 Combined plot, roof, and landscape plan

TREES AND SHRUBS

The methods of drawing trees, shrubs, and ground cover vary considerably, but the lines should usually be the weight of dimension lines (see A-40). In a plot plan that is part of a presentation drawing, trees and foliage are drawn in great detail, primarily to create an artistic effect. On a working drawing, circles drawn with a template or a compass are suitable for trees and shrubs. Some draftsmen devise their own symbols and lines for landscape features. In addition, landscape templates are available which increase speed in drafting. The type of rendition is a matter of taste or office practice.

A plant materials schedule, describing the name, size, and quantity of trees and shrubs, should be included on the drawing (Fig. 18-3).

REVIEW QUESTIONS

1. Round off the figure 37°21′37″ to ½°. Why is this done?
2. What is the angular difference between:
    a. N31°18′57″W and N18°01′32″W?
    b. N31°18′57″W and S18°01′32″E?
    c. N31°18′57″W and S31°18′57″E?
    Draw a rough sketch to avoid confusion.
3. Draw a contour map, at any convenient contour interval, of:
    a. A hemisphere resting on the flat side
    b. A cone resting on the flat side
    c. A square pyramid
    d. Any irregular object you desire
4. On your own landscape plan, why have you drawn the trees as you have? Appearance? Economy of time?
5. Using the diagram A-38, determine the following for an interior lot:

a. The minimum front yard setback for a residence.
b. The minimum side yard setback for a residence.
c. The minimum rear yard setback for a residence.
6. Using the diagram A-39, determine the following for a corner lot:
    a. The minimum front yard setback for a residence.
    b. The minimum distance from the garage or carport to the property line for a residence.
    c. The minimum side yard setback on the street side for a residence.
    d. The minimum side yard setback on the side opposite the street for a residence.
    e. The minimum rear yard setback for a residence.

STUDY SUGGESTIONS

1. Visit the assessor's office or a building-tract office, and check the map of a certain area against the land itself. Note the contour, locations of curbs and gutters, utilities, easements, and so on.
2. Check a finished building against the original plot and landscaping plans.

STUDENT PROBLEM

When starting the plot plan, remember to provide a space on the right side of the sheet for the sheet index. Copy the rough plot plan at a suitable scale to fit the assigned space.

1. Draft the plot plan.
2. Draft the landscape plan. (To start the landscape plan, trace only the required information from the plot plan; omit dimensions, roof overhang, and serving utilities.)

CHAPTER 19
STAIR
AND FIREPLACE
DETAILS

PLACE IN DRAWINGS

Fireplace and stair construction have no necessary relationship to each other; they are grouped together here only for convenience. Because these drawings have such a great effect on the total structure and affect other drawings in the set to such an extent, they are discussed separately. In a set of drawings, however, the stair and fireplace details are grouped with the miscellaneous details.

DEFINITION OF STAIR DETAILS

Stair details show the structure, stair size, posts, rails and balusters, materials, and method of attachment

to the structure. Sizes and clearances are dimensioned, and all materials are called out by note. The usual scale is full section $\frac{1}{2}$ in. = 1 ft 0 in., small sections, baluster, post, rail, newel, and so on; $1\frac{1}{2}$ in. = 1 ft or 0 in. to 3 in. = 1 ft 0 in. (Fig. 19-1).

PRELIMINARY DRAWINGS

Staircases must be carefully planned before working drawings are started. The procedure for laying out the longitudinal section follows (Fig. 19-2):

1. Establish the two floor levels.
2. Draw the thickness of the flooring and joists of the floor above to scale.

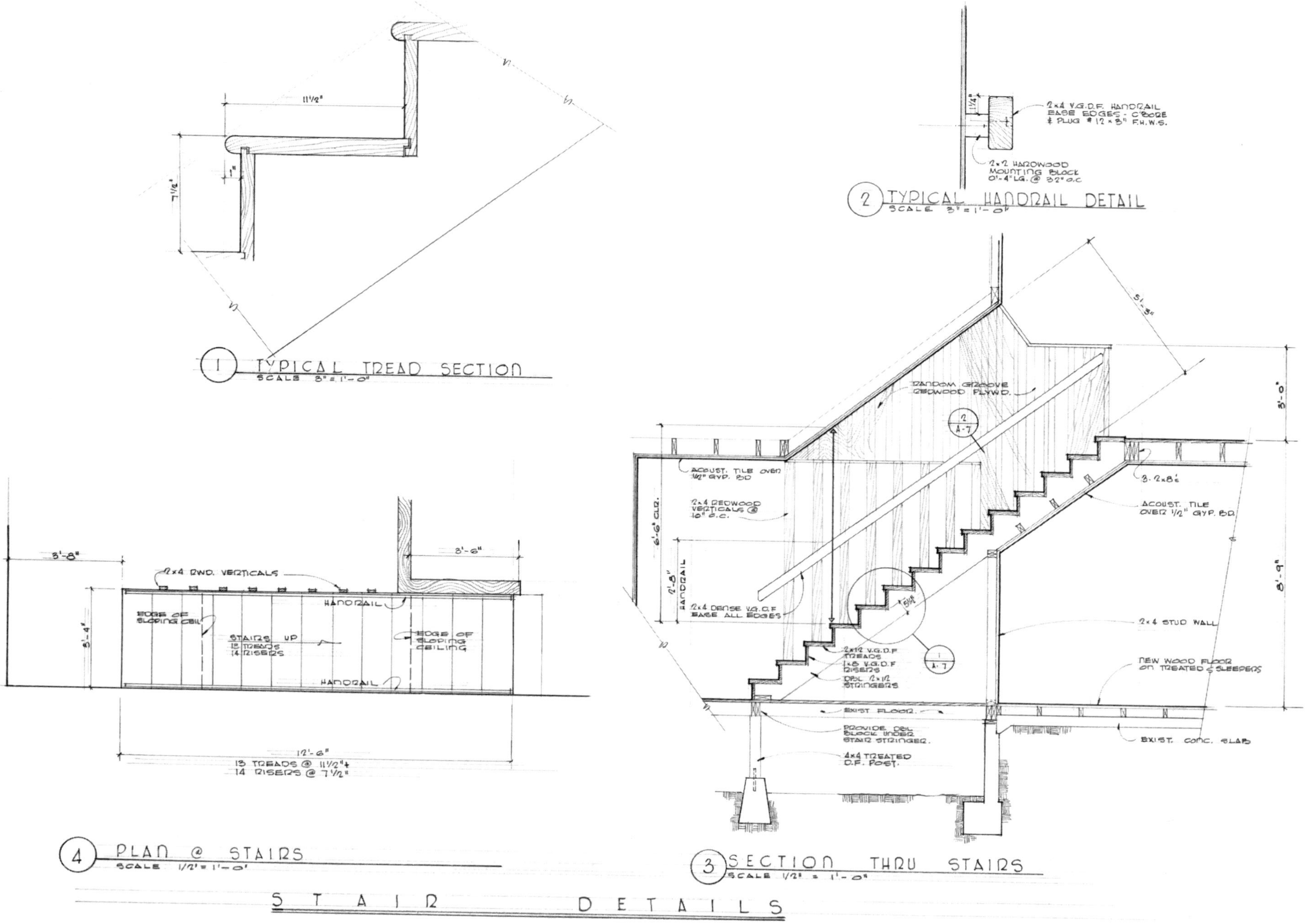

FIGURE 19-1 Stair details of a small residence (this drawing unrelated to the set of drawings developed in this book)

159

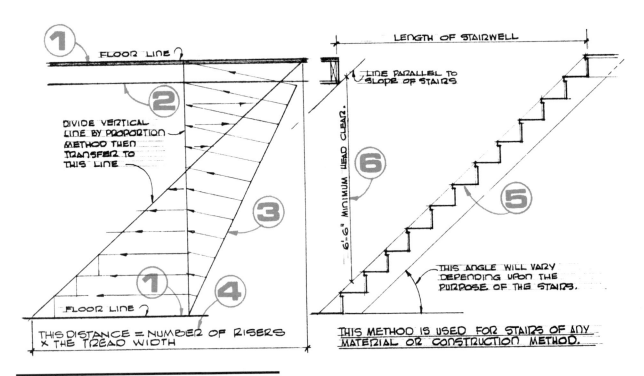

Labels in figure:

1 — FLOOR LINE

DIVIDE VERTICAL LINE BY PROPORTION METHOD THEN TRANSFER TO THIS LINE

2

3

1

4

FLOOR LINE

THIS DISTANCE = NUMBER OF RISERS X THE TREAD WIDTH

LENGTH OF STAIRWELL

LINE PARALLEL TO SLOPE OF STAIRS

6'-6" MINIMUM HEAD CLEAR.

6

5

THIS ANGLE WILL VARY DEPENDING UPON THE PURPOSE OF THE STAIRS.

THIS METHOD IS USED FOR STAIRS OF ANY MATERIAL OR CONSTRUCTION METHOD.

FIGURE 19-2   Procedure for laying out a staircase

3. Divide the vertical distance from finish floor to finish floor into equal increments of rise (approximately 7 in. is comfortable, 9 in. is maximum). Determine the run. (A simple formula is Run = 75 in./Rise. This formula works well for average stairs.)
4. Establish the angle of the staircase based on the dimensions of total rise and run.
5. Draw the outlines of the individual steps.
6. Place a construction line parallel to the staircase and 6 ft 6 in. vertically above the nose of the tread. This represents the minimum headroom. The open end of the stairwell will be at the point where this line passes through the bottom line of the top-floor construction. This method can also be used with a staircase which changes direction and with a circular staircase.

The working drawings will be based on the foregoing construction. Other drawings, such as the floor plan, floor framing plan, and interior and exterior elevations, are affected by the size, shape, and structure of the stairs.

DRAFTING OF THE STAIR DETAILS

The procedure in drawing the longitudinal stair section follows (Fig. 19-3):

1. Copy the construction just described.
2. Lay out the structural members of the staircase, for example, stringer, tread, riser. Construction methods vary in different parts of the country, so local methods should be followed.
3. Draw in treads, risers, and other members. (Construction lines show the *outline* of the stairs. Thickness of tread and riser must be subtracted to find the shape of the stringer.)
4. Place all notes, dimensions, title, and scale.

DETAIL SECTIONS

Detail sections are drawn in the same order from Step 2 above; they must agree in projection with the longitudinal section. Elevations of the stairs appear on either the interior or exterior elevations or both. Posts,

FIGURE 19-3 Full-size extract from Fig. 19-1

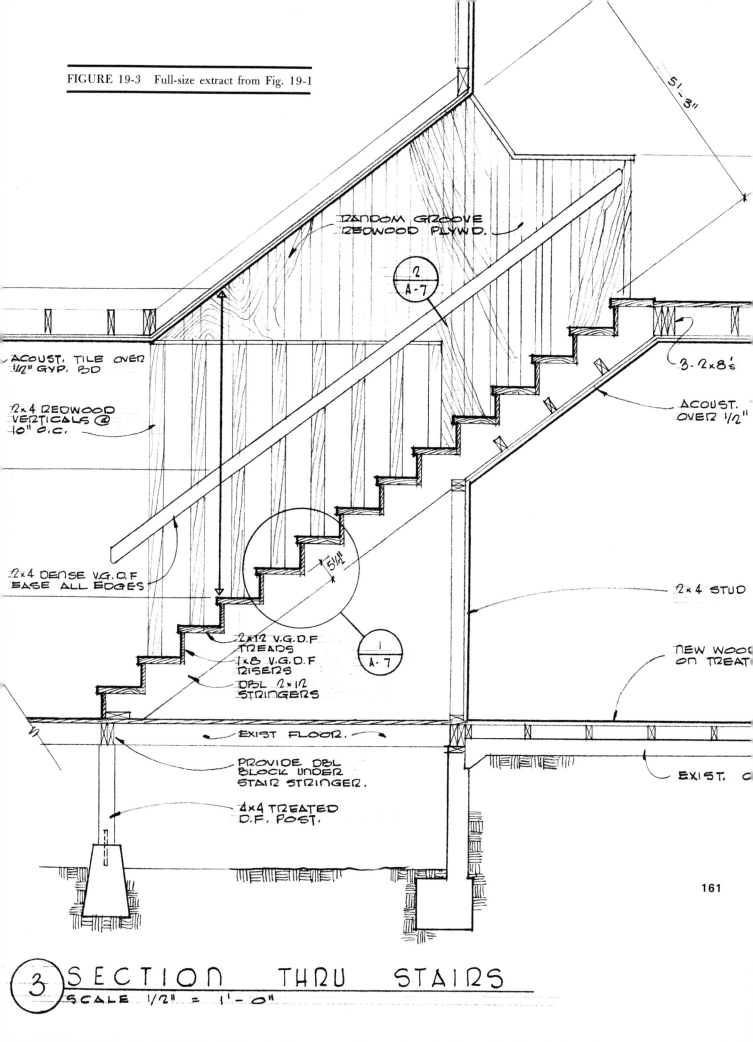

RANDOM GROOVE
REDWOOD PLYWD.

2 / A-7

ACOUST. TILE OVER
1/2" GYP. BD

2×4 REDWOOD
VERTICALS @
10" O.C.

3-2×8's

ACOUST.
OVER 1/2"

2×4 DENSE V.G.D.F
EASE ALL EDGES

5 1/2"

2×4 STUD

2×12 V.G.D.F
TREADS
1×8 V.G.D.F
RISERS
DBL 2×12
STRINGERS

1 / A-7

NEW WOOD
ON TREAT

EXIST FLOOR.

PROVIDE DBL
BLOCK UNDER
STAIR STRINGER.

EXIST. C

4×4 TREATED
D.F. POST.

161

3 SECTION THRU STAIRS
SCALE 1/2" = 1'-0"

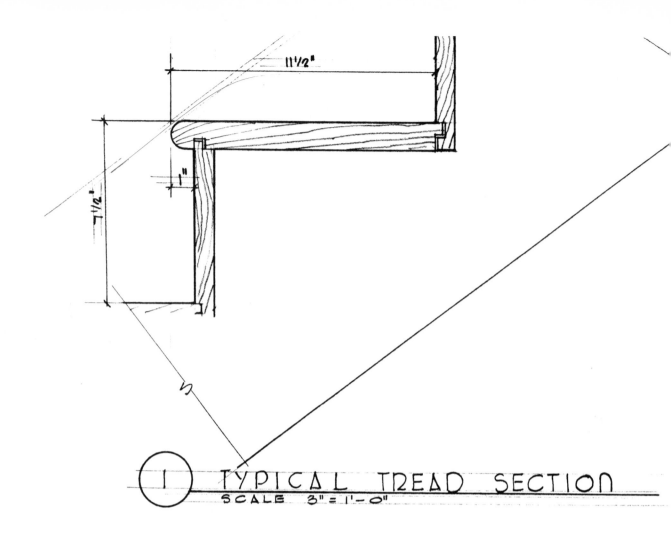

1 **TYPICAL TREAD SECTION**
SCALE 3"=1'-0"

11½"

1"

7½"

FIGURE 19-4 Full-size extract from Fig. 19-1

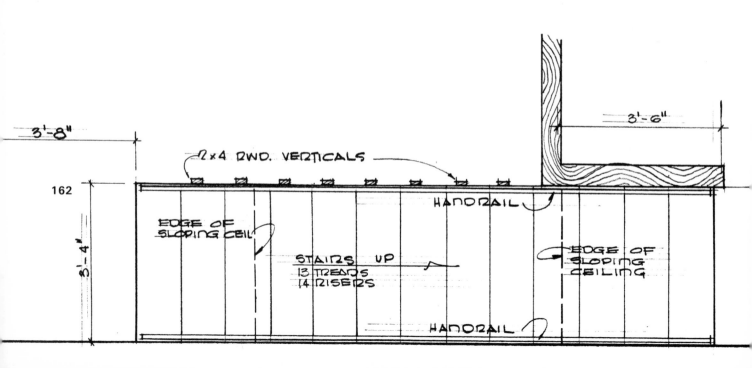

3'-8"

3'-6"

162

3'-4"

2×4 RWD. VERTICALS

HANDRAIL

EDGE OF
SLOPING CEIL

STAIRS UP
13 TREADS
14 RISERS

EDGE OF
SLOPING
CEILING

HANDRAIL

rails, balusters, and trim are shown in the elevations. Cross sections of these members are shown along with the other stair sections (Fig. 19-4).

The procedure in laying out a straight staircase (Fig. 19-2) applies also to a staircase with a platform half-way up or at a turn, to a staircase with winders (not advisable), and to a circular staircase (Fig. 19-5).

Elevators, dumbwaiters, and hoists also affect the structure to a great extent. Because of the wide variety of such devices and their relatively infrequent use in residential and light-commercial structures, they will not be discussed here. Information is available in "Architectural Graphic Standards" and various manufacturers' catalogs.

DEFINITION OF FIREPLACE DETAILS

Fireplace drawings show a section through the foundation, the fireplace, and the chimney to the cap, as well as detail sections (Fig. 19-6). A fireplace may be built of most masonry materials or common metals. It may be a ready-built unit or built on the job. Hardware is available for practically any shape of fireplace desired (Fig. 19-7). In addition, well-engineered metal fireplaces may be purchased from many sources and their installation is only a small problem. The drawing in Fig. 19-8 shows all construction—foundation, cleanout, hearth, firebox, smoke shelf, damper, flue, cap, and surrounding masonry. If the fireplace is a factory-built metal unit, installation drawings are available from the manufacturer. Dimensions are shown where needed; all materials are called out by note. Scale is usually $\frac{1}{2}$ in. = 1 ft 0 in.

FIREPLACE DESIGN

After the type of fireplace has been decided, its functional dimensions and parts must be established. All the outside dimensions of the finished fireplace are

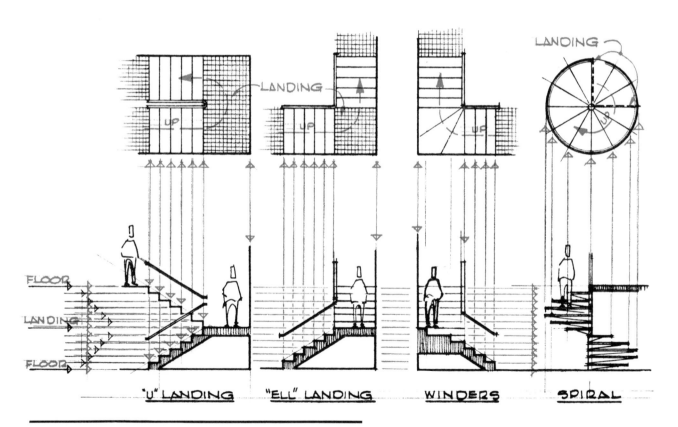

FIGURE 19-5 Orthographic views of various stair arrangements

163

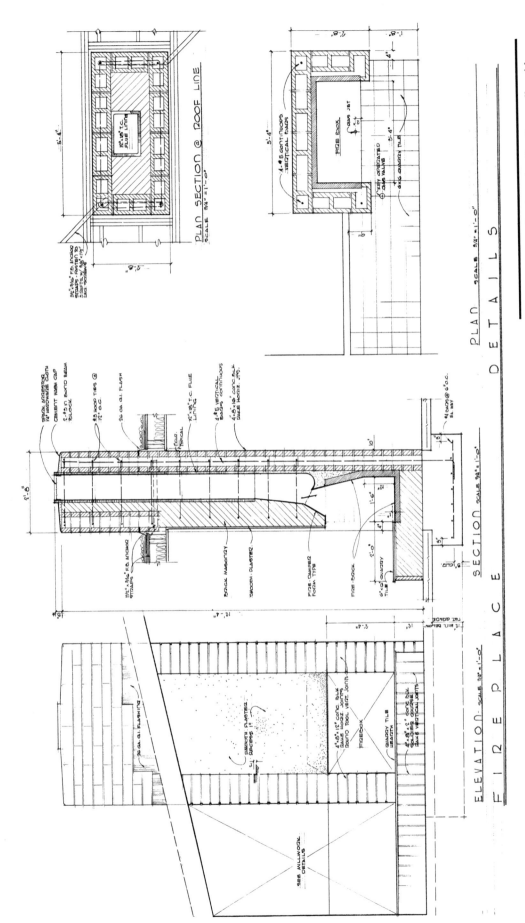

FIGURE 19-6 Fireplace details of a small residence

164

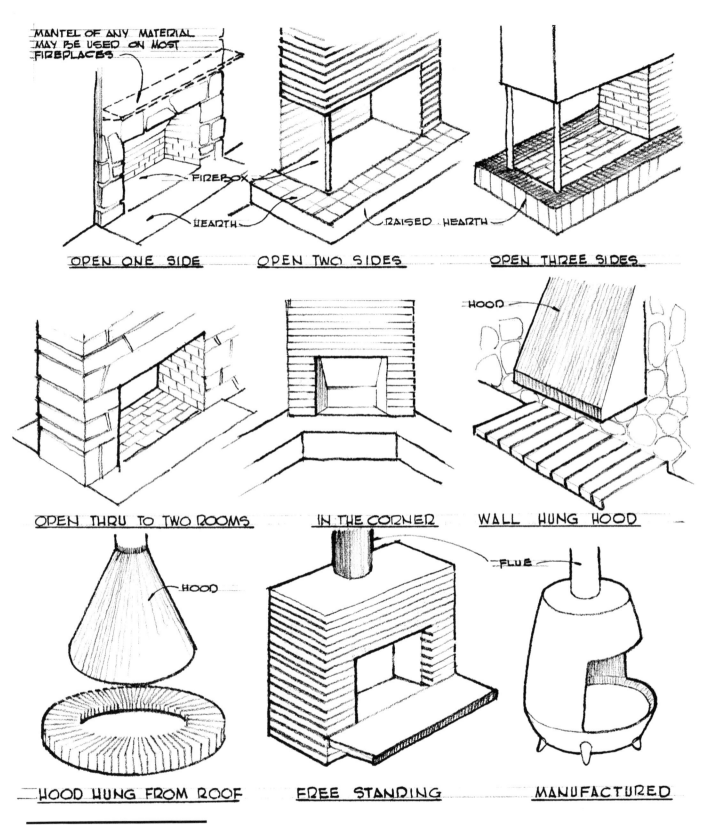

MANTEL OF ANY MATERIAL MAY BE USED ON MOST FIREPLACES

FIREBOX

HEARTH

RAISED HEARTH

HOOD

OPEN ONE SIDE   OPEN TWO SIDES   OPEN THREE SIDES

OPEN THRU TO TWO ROOMS   IN THE CORNER   WALL HUNG HOOD

HOOD

HOOD

FLUE

HOOD HUNG FROM ROOF   FREE STANDING   MANUFACTURED

FIGURE 19-7   Types of fireplaces

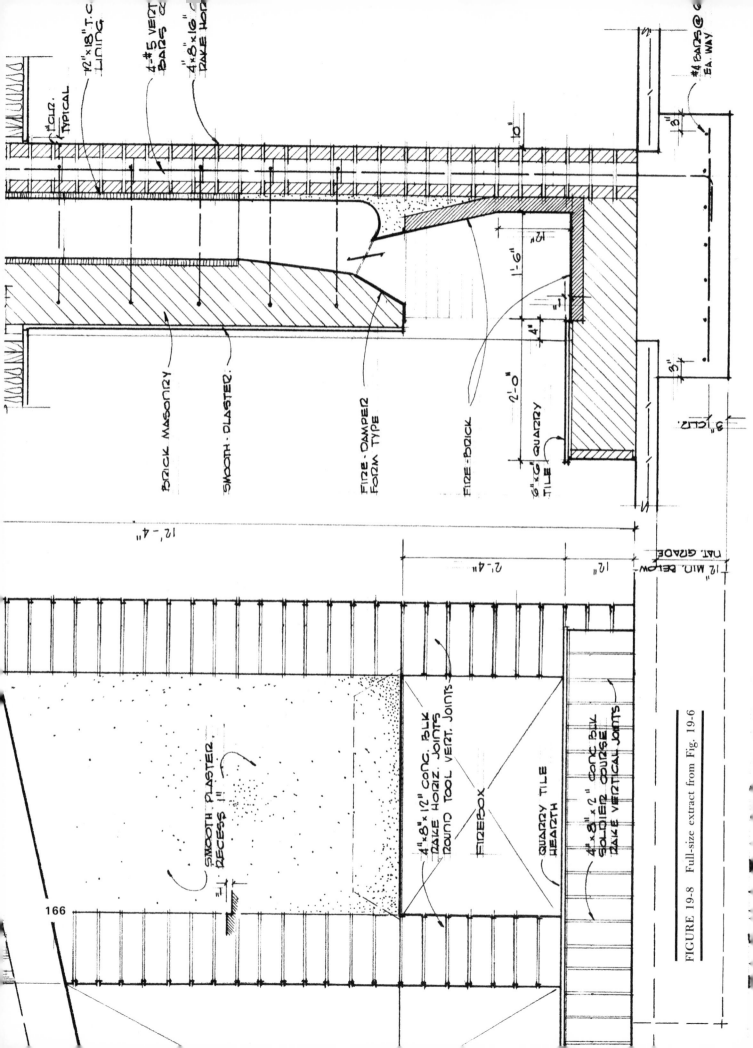

FIGURE 19-8 Full-size extract from Fig. 19-6

166

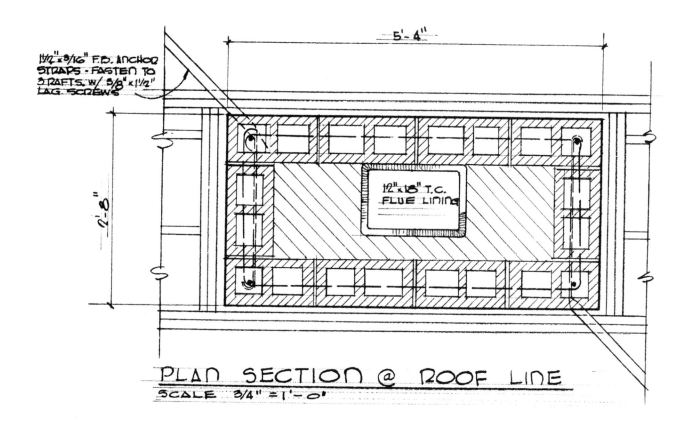

PLAN SECTION @ ROOF LINE
SCALE 3/4" = 1'-0"

1½" x 3/16" F.B. ANCHOR STRAPS · FASTEN TO RAFTS. W/ 3/8" x 1½" LAG SCREWS

5'-4"

2'-8"

12" x 18" T.C. FLUE LINING

FIGURE 19-9 Full-size extract from Fig. 19-6

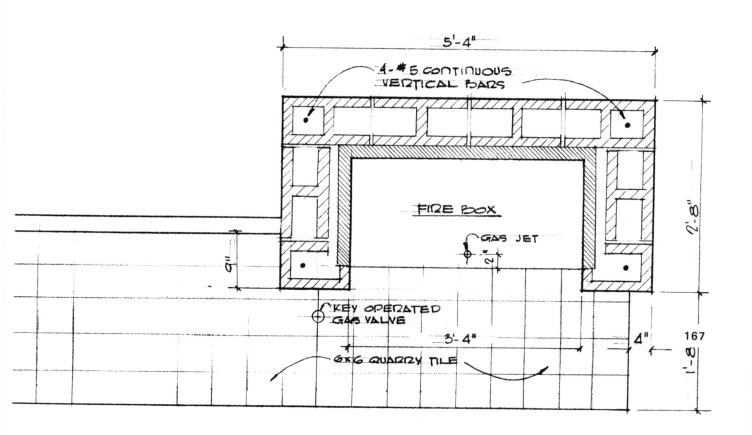

5'-4"

4-#5 CONTINUOUS VERTICAL BARS

FIRE BOX

GAS JET

9"

1'-8"

KEY OPERATED GAS VALVE

3'-4"

4"

6x6 QUARRY TILE

1'-8"

167

based on the following restrictive requirements: the height, width, and depth of the fireplace opening; the type and size of the damper; the size of the flue liner; the height of the chimney above the roof; and the thickness of noncombustible materials around the firebox and flue. The chimney and facade of the fireplace may be made larger, but not smaller, than these factors indicate. The technical information used in fireplace design is at the back of this book (see A-14).

DRAFTING OF THE FIREPLACE DETAILS

The procedure in drawing a vertical fireplace section follows:

1. Establish the groundline, or base, of the fireplace and the floor, roof, and ceiling structures as light lines.
2. Draw the inside of the firebox, smoke shelf, and flue.
3. Draw the outline of the masonry, or exterior finish, of the fireplace and the foundation.
4. Place smaller details such as damper, hearth, chimney cap, location of reinforcing steel, method of flashing, and chimney ties.
5. Dimension as needed.
6. Letter in all notes, title, and scale. Because of the height of a fireplace section, break lines are sometimes drawn across the flue to reduce its height.

HORIZONTAL SECTIONS

Horizontal sections are also taken to show the plan shape and the construction of the fireplace at flue, cleanout, and firebox (Fig. 19-9).

REVIEW QUESTIONS

1. Outline the procedure in designing a staircase.
2. What drawings are affected by the staircase?
3. What are the functional parts required in any fireplace?
4. What is the rule for establishing the height of a chimney above a roof? (Uniform Building Code.)

STUDY SUGGESTIONS

1. Check through an existing set of drawings to see the effects of the stairs and fireplace on each drawing.
2. Visit a building-supply house, and look at the fireplace and staircase hardware available, such as fireplace forms, dampers, hoods, complete fireplaces, metal treads, rails, and balusters.
3. Further tables and planning information are available from many sources, such as "Time-Saver Standards" and "Architectural Graphic Standards." Study these.

STUDENT PROBLEM

The stair and fireplace details may be drawn on the same sheet or placed in empty spaces on other sheets.

1. Work out the problem of designing the stairs.
2. Design the fireplace, using the tables in the back of the book.
3. Make working drawings of the stairs and fireplace, including the large-scale sections.

CHAPTER 20

DOOR
AND WINDOW
DETAILS

DEFINITION AND PURPOSE

Though much information regarding windows and doors is shown on the floor plan, elevations, and schedules, additional details are required to make installation and construction clear to the builder. These details usually include sections through each window and door as well as plan or elevation views where needed (Figs. 20-1 and 20-2). All parts used in construction are called out by note. Heights, clearances, openings, and sizes of special millwork are dimensioned. Parts furnished by certain manufacturers are described by note. Door and window details are drawn at large scale for ease of reading, $1\frac{1}{2}$ or 3 in. = 1 ft 0 in. Where large numbers of standard

windows or doors are used, a typical detail is drawn to show the method of their installation (Figs. 20-3 to 20-7).

It is a simple job to show the method of connecting windows or doors to the building, but the design of a custom-built opening demands much knowledge of construction and millwork. The procedure shown here is typical of the type of work expected of a beginning draftsman. The design of millwork will not be discussed.

The sections required, in the order of their importance, are head, jamb, and sill or threshold (required in all cases); and transom, post, muntin, and mullion (where required). For reasons of logic and clarity, the sections should be arranged in order vertically, head

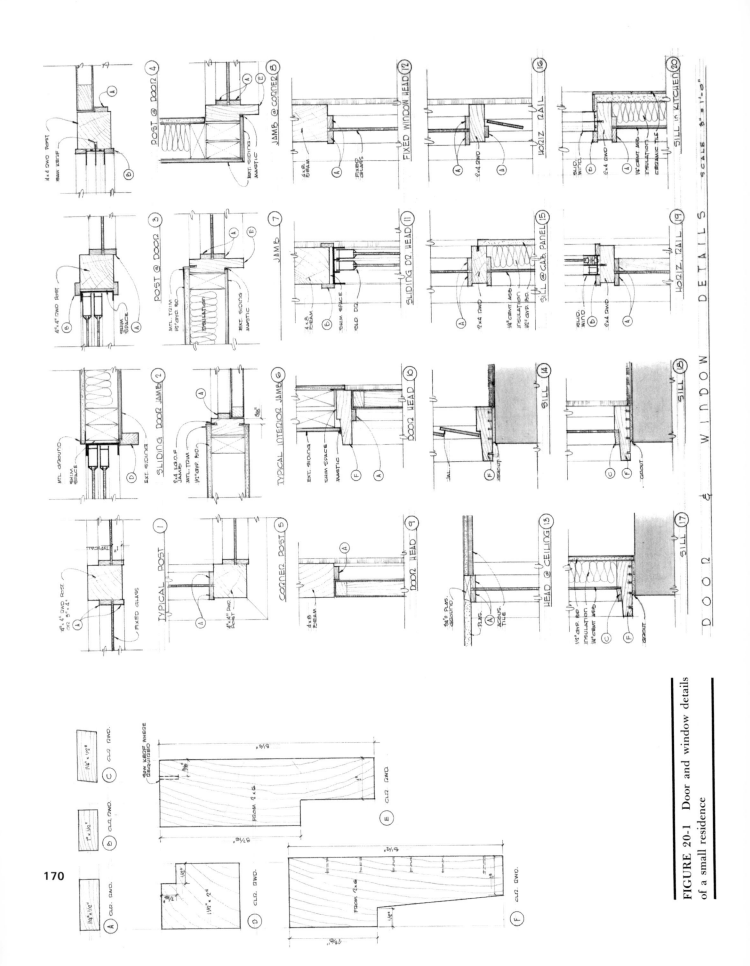

FIGURE 20-1 Door and window details of a small residence

170

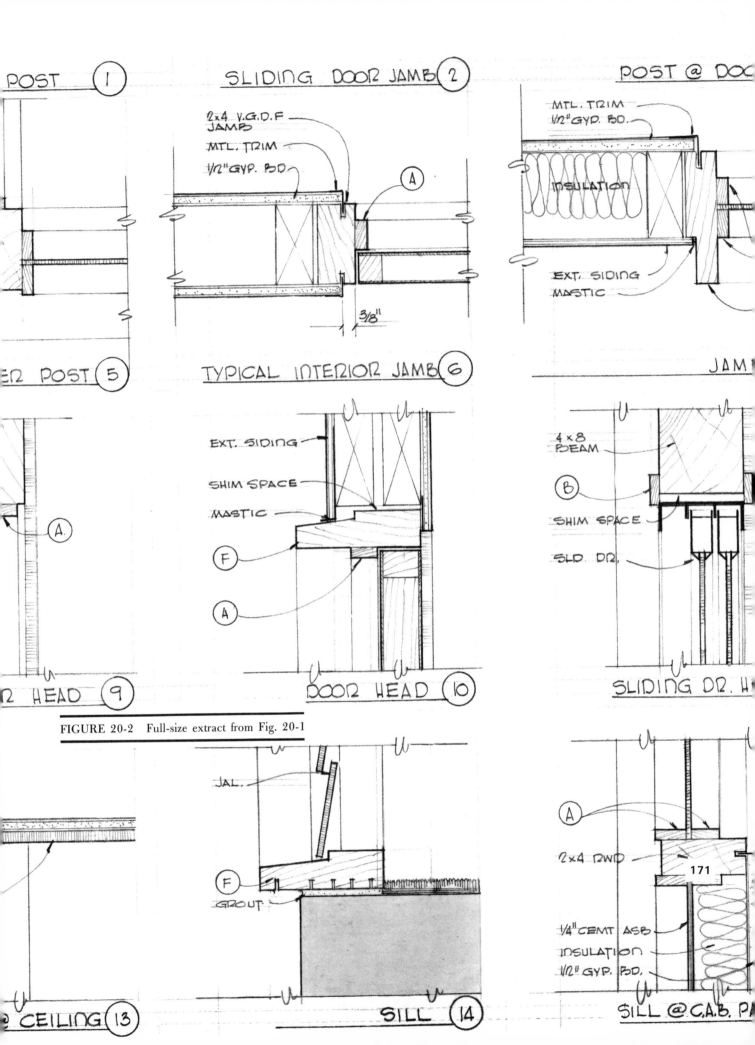

POST ①

SLIDING DOOR JAMB ②

2×4 V.G.D.F JAMB
MTL. TRIM
1/2" GYP. BD.

Ⓐ

3/8"

POST @ DOO

MTL. TRIM
1/2" GYP. BD.

INSULATION

EXT. SIDING
MASTIC

ER POST ⑤

TYPICAL INTERIOR JAMB ⑥

EXT. SIDING

SHIM SPACE

MASTIC

Ⓕ

Ⓐ

JAM

4×8 BEAM

Ⓑ

SHIM SPACE

SLD. DR.

Ⓐ.

HEAD ⑨

DOOR HEAD ⑩

SLIDING DR. H

FIGURE 20-2   Full-size extract from Fig. 20-1

JAL.

Ⓕ
GROUT

CEILING ⑬

SILL ⑭

Ⓐ

2×4 RWD

171

1/4" CEMT ASB
INSULATION
1/2" GYP. BD.

SILL @ C.A.B. P

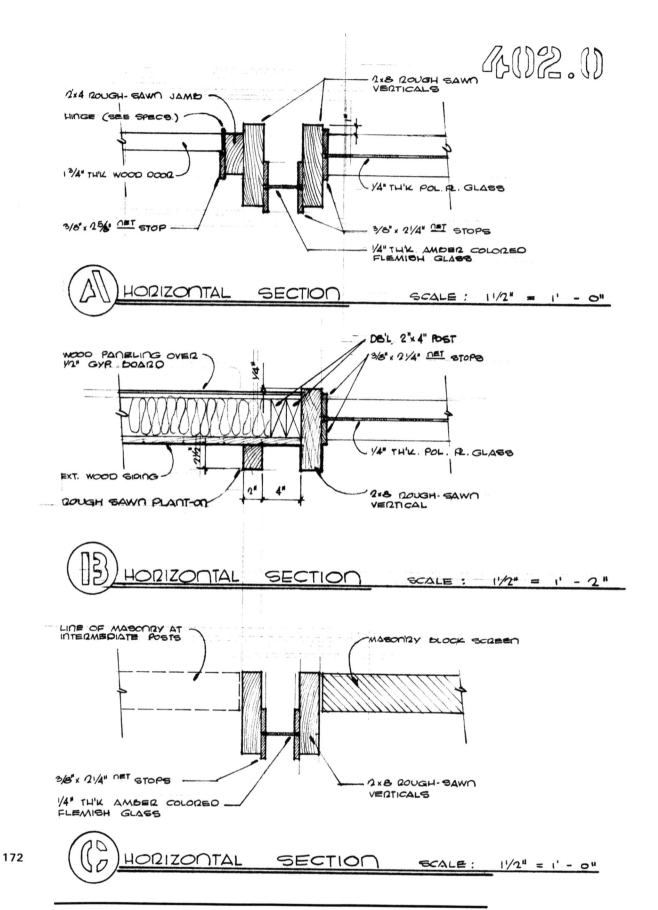

2x4 ROUGH-SAWN JAMB

HINGE (SEE SPECS.)

2x8 ROUGH-SAWN VERTICALS

1 3/4" TH'K WOOD DOOR

1/4" TH'K POL. PL. GLASS

3/8" x 2 5/8" NET STOP

3/8" x 2 1/4" NET STOPS

1/4" TH'K AMBER COLORED FLEMISH GLASS

Ⓐ HORIZONTAL SECTION   SCALE : 1 1/2" = 1'-0"

WOOD PANELING OVER 1/2" GYP. BOARD

DB'L 2"x 4" POST

3/8" x 2 1/4" NET STOPS

1/4" TH'K. POL. PL. GLASS

EXT. WOOD SIDING

ROUGH SAWN PLANT-ON

2x8 ROUGH-SAWN VERTICAL

Ⓑ HORIZONTAL SECTION   SCALE : 1 1/2" = 1'-2"

LINE OF MASONRY AT INTERMEDIATE POSTS

MASONRY BLOCK SCREEN

3/8" x 2 1/4" NET STOPS

1/4" TH'K AMBER COLORED FLEMISH GLASS

2x8 ROUGH-SAWN VERTICALS

Ⓒ HORIZONTAL SECTION   SCALE : 1 1/2" = 1'-0"

172

FIGURE 20-3   Window details keyed to elevations of a laboratory-clinic (Fig. 16-4)

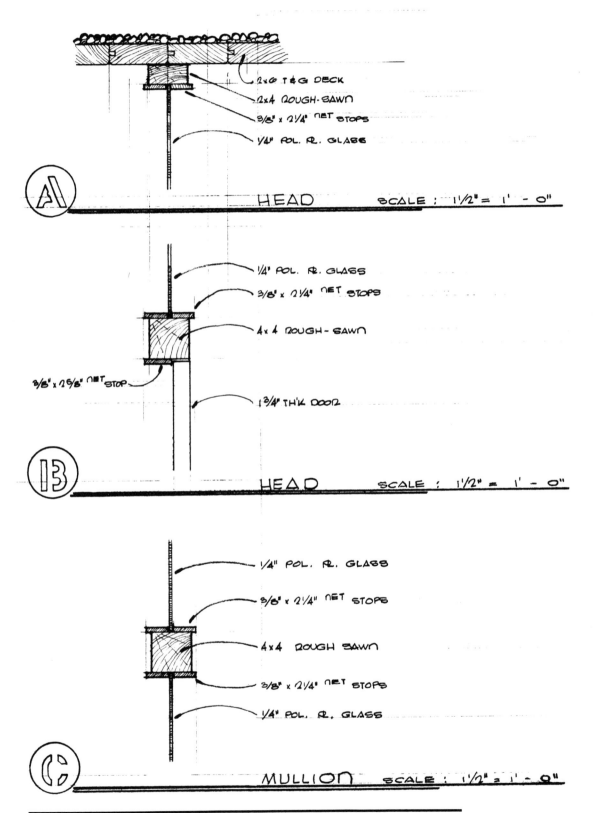

402.1

A) HEAD   SCALE : 1½" = 1' - 0"

2x6 T&G DECK
2x4 ROUGH-SAWN
3/8" x 2¼" NET STOPS
¼" POL. PL. GLASS

B) HEAD   SCALE : 1½" = 1' - 0"

¼" POL. PL. GLASS
3/8" x 2¼" NET STOPS
4x4 ROUGH-SAWN
3/8" x 2 5/8" NET STOP
1¾" TH'K DOOR

C) MULLION   SCALE : 1½" = 1' - 0"

¼" POL. PL. GLASS
3/8" x 2¼" NET STOPS
4x4 ROUGH SAWN
3/8" x 2¼" NET STOPS
¼" POL. PL. GLASS

173

FIGURE 20-4   Window details keyed to elevations of a laboratory-clinic (Fig. 16-4)

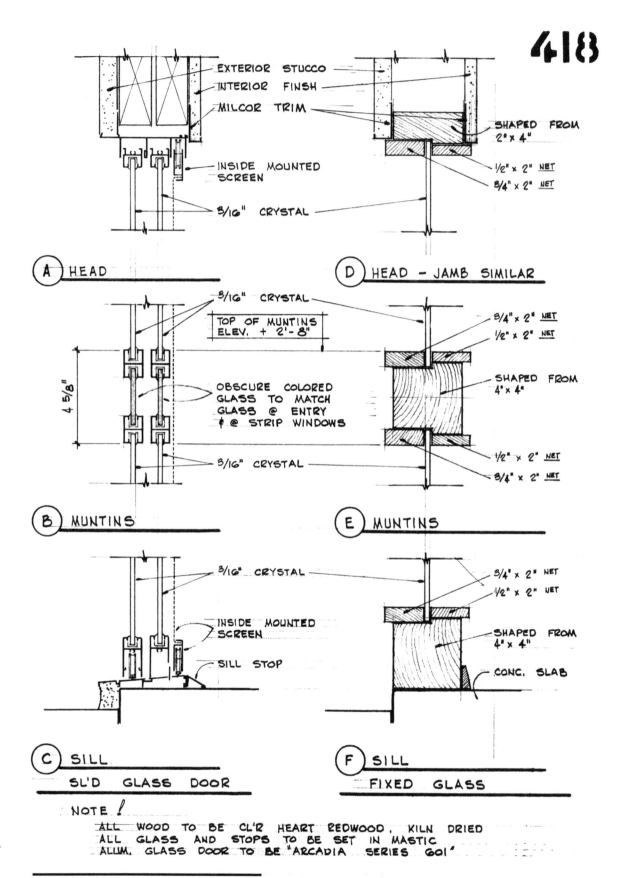

A HEAD — EXTERIOR STUCCO / INTERIOR FINISH / MILCOR TRIM / INSIDE MOUNTED SCREEN / 3/16" CRYSTAL

D HEAD - JAMB SIMILAR — SHAPED FROM 2" x 4" / 1/2" x 2" NET / 3/4" x 2" NET

B MUNTINS — 3/16" CRYSTAL / TOP OF MUNTINS ELEV. + 2'- 8" / 4 5/8" / OBSCURE COLORED GLASS TO MATCH GLASS @ ENTRY & @ STRIP WINDOWS / 3/16" CRYSTAL

E MUNTINS — 3/4" x 2" NET / 1/2" x 2" NET / SHAPED FROM 4" x 4" / 1/2" x 2" NET / 3/4" x 2" NET

C SILL — 3/16" CRYSTAL / INSIDE MOUNTED SCREEN / SILL STOP / SL'D GLASS DOOR

F SILL — 3/4" x 2" NET / 1/2" x 2" NET / SHAPED FROM 4" x 4" / CONC. SLAB / FIXED GLASS

NOTE!

ALL WOOD TO BE CL'R HEART REDWOOD, KILN DRIED
ALL GLASS AND STOPS TO BE SET IN MASTIC
ALUM. GLASS DOOR TO BE "ARCADIA SERIES 601"

174

FIGURE 20-5 Standard sliding door details

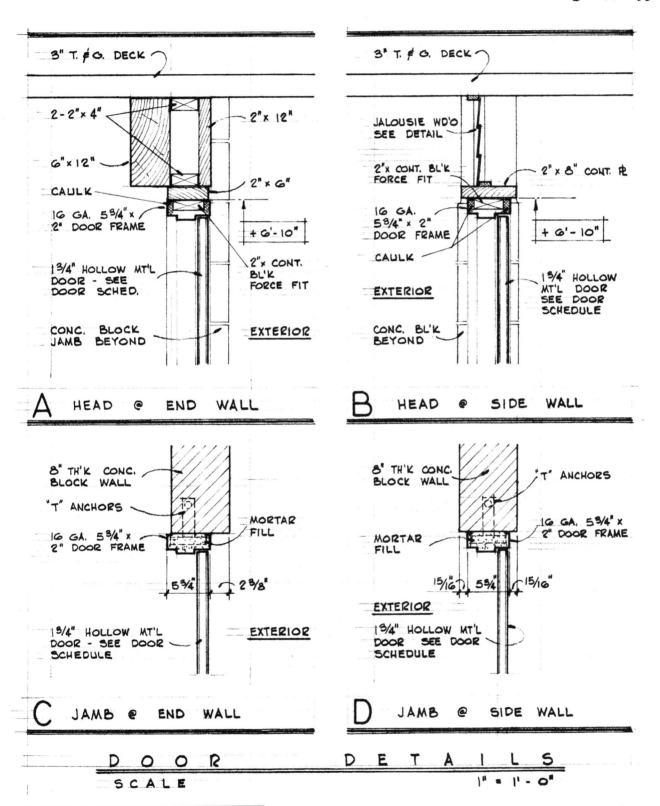

A HEAD @ END WALL

- 3" T. & G. DECK
- 2 - 2" x 4"
- 6" x 12"
- CAULK
- 16 GA. 5¾" x 2" DOOR FRAME
- 1¾" HOLLOW MT'L DOOR - SEE DOOR SCHED.
- CONC. BLOCK JAMB BEYOND
- 2" x 12"
- 2" x 6"
- + 6'-10"
- 2" x CONT. BL'K FORCE FIT
- EXTERIOR

B HEAD @ SIDE WALL

- 3" T. & G. DECK
- JALOUSIE WD'O SEE DETAIL
- 2" x CONT. BL'K FORCE FIT
- 16 GA. 5¾" x 2" DOOR FRAME
- CAULK
- EXTERIOR
- CONC. BL'K BEYOND
- 2" x 8" CONT. PL
- + 6'-10"
- 1¾" HOLLOW MT'L DOOR SEE DOOR SCHEDULE

C JAMB @ END WALL

- 8" TH'K CONC. BLOCK WALL
- "T" ANCHORS
- 16 GA. 5¾" x 2" DOOR FRAME
- MORTAR FILL
- 5¾"
- 2⅜"
- 1¾" HOLLOW MT'L DOOR - SEE DOOR SCHEDULE
- EXTERIOR

D JAMB @ SIDE WALL

- 8" TH'K CONC. BLOCK WALL
- "T" ANCHORS
- MORTAR FILL
- 16 GA. 5¾" x 2" DOOR FRAME
- 15/16"
- 5¾"
- 15/16"
- EXTERIOR
- 1¾" HOLLOW MT'L DOOR SEE DOOR SCHEDULE

DOOR DETAILS

SCALE 1" = 1'-0"

FIGURE 20-6 Standard exterior door details

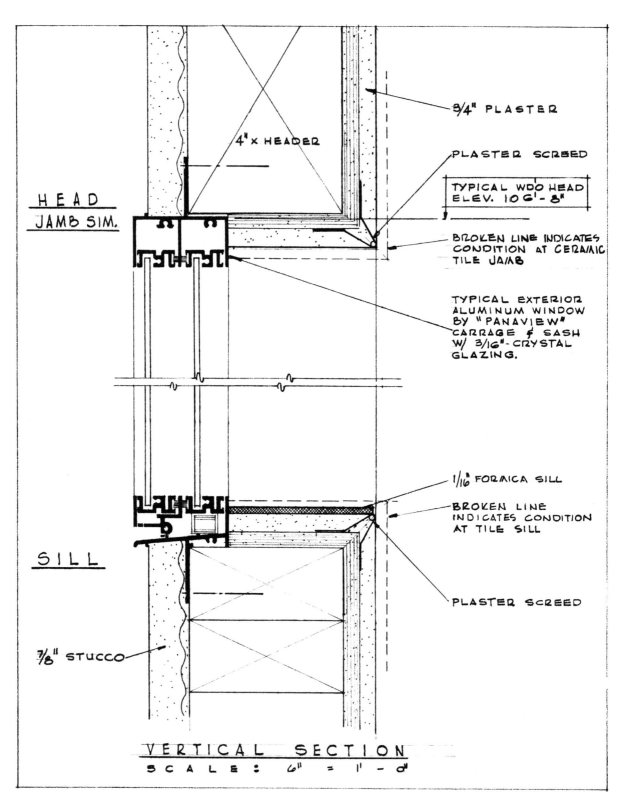

3/4" PLASTER

PLASTER SCREED

TYPICAL WDO HEAD
ELEV. 10 6'- 8"

BROKEN LINE INDICATES
CONDITION AT CERAMIC
TILE JAMB

TYPICAL EXTERIOR
ALUMINUM WINDOW
BY "PANAVIEW"
CARRAGE & SASH
W/ 3/16"- CRYSTAL
GLAZING.

1/16" FORMICA SILL

BROKEN LINE
INDICATES CONDITION
AT TILE SILL

PLASTER SCREED

<u>H E A D</u>
JAMB SIM.

4" x HEADER

<u>SILL</u>

7/8" STUCCO

<u>V E R T I C A L   S E C T I O N</u>
S C A L E : 6" = 1' - 0"

176

FIGURE 20-7   Standard sliding window details

or transom above, threshold or sill below, and from side to side, jamb to post to mullion to muntin to jamb.

DRAFTING THE WINDOW AND DOOR DETAILS

The same procedure is used in drawing a window or door detail (Fig. 20-1).

1. Draw a section through the wall showing the structure of the wall around the rough opening.
2. Copy the correct section from the manufacturer's literature in its proper relation to the opening.
3. Place weatherproofing and flashing as recommended.
4. Draw in exterior and interior finish materials.
5. Draw in blocking if required.
6. Draw in trim if required.
7. Letter in all notes, title, and scale.

Check as the work progresses to be certain that the construction of all sections is consistent all around the frame. Coordinate the sections with the exterior and interior elevations and the door and window schedules. Use the correct keying symbol to relate the sections to the elevations. Figures 20-5 to 20-7 show some commonly used door and window details.

REVIEW QUESTIONS

1. Define the following terms: stud, header, trimmer, stool, head, jamb, sill, threshold, mullion, post, muntin. Illustrate them in sketches.
2. In your locality, what are the advantages and disadvantages of casement, double-hung, awning, jalousie, or horizontal-sliding windows?
3. What advantages and disadvantages are inherent in the design of flush doors?

STUDY SUGGESTIONS

1. Visit a building-supply house, and inspect the various types of windows and doors.
2. Visit two buildings under construction, one of frame and the other of masonry construction. Compare the methods of framing windows and doors in both structures.

STUDENT PROBLEM

Copying window and door details from manufacturers' brochures is recommended. The design of custom door and window details would be difficult for a student; however, a fixed window detail would be within the student's ability. The extent of this drawing should be determined by the instructor. Draw the window and door details.

CHAPTER 21

MISCELLANEOUS DETAILS

DEFINITION AND PURPOSE

All small details difficult to classify elsewhere are placed on the "Miscellaneous" drawing. In case the draftsman feels that some detail might be misinterpreted by the builder, it should be clarified by additional drawings and notes. Notes and dimensioning should be complete. Sometimes isometric drawings are used to clarify details of construction. The scale of these drawings varies widely but is usually large, $1\frac{1}{2}$ in. = 1 ft 0 in. to full size.

The list of details shown below is by no means complete. It is intended merely to demonstrate the wide range of information found in the miscellaneous details. Procedures in drawing several of the most commonly used details are demonstrated. Much information can be derived from catalogs, brochures, and technical literature regarding particular items of equipment.

TYPES OF MISCELLANEOUS DETAILS

Some types of construction found in the miscellaneous details follow (Figs. 21-1 to 21-5):

1. All cabinet work
2. Range hoods
3. Planters

4. Screens and room dividers
5. Shower stalls
6. Ceramic tile, metal, and plastic surfacing
7. Attic louvers
8. Access panels
9. Suspended ceilings
10. Sun screens, patio covers
11. Signs and displays
12. Fences
13. Special equipment
    a. Overhead tracks
    b. Restaurant equipment
    c. Conveyors
    d. Letter slots
14. Flashings
15. Gutters, roof drains

CABINET WORK

The term *cabinet work* or *case work* covers all storage spaces not considered an integral part of the structure. Cabinet work may be job-built, shop-built, or manufactured, and it may be of wood or metal. There are three grades of wood cabinet work: standard, custom, and premium. Manufactured storage units may be purchased in a wide variety of sizes, materials, and finishes. Catalogs furnished by the manufacturers make planning for these units very simple.

Because of the wide variety of cabinet constructions and local building practices, this description must be in general terms. See "Time-Saver Standards" or "Architectural Graphic Standards."

DRAFTING THE CABINET DETAILS

The procedure in drawing the vertical sections for cabinet work, built-in furniture, wardrobes, and so on follows (Fig. 21-4):

1. Draw the floor, wall, and ceiling in light lines.
2. Check all heights and widths of cabinet work and sizes of component parts. Draw outlines as light lines.
3. Place shelves, drawers, breadboards, clothespoles, special hardware, and so on.
4. Draw in all finish materials.

5. Draw in drawer guides, forms or frames for finish materials, and so forth.
6. Dimension completely.
7. Place all lettering, notes, title, and scale.
8. Draw in textures where needed.

Partial horizontal sections are needed to show locations of structural parts, construction of face frame, and the like (Fig. 21-5). They are done in the same manner as and must be in projection with the vertical sections. Vertical and horizontal sections must be made at all points where the construction changes.

When using manufactured cabinet work, it is necessary only to fit the desired units into the available space and show all soffits, furring, and methods of attachment to the building. All units must be identified by note and dimensions. Special louvers, sunscreens, gutters, and downspout details may be taken directly from "Time-Saver Standards," "Architectural Graphic Standards," or various manufacturers' catalogs.

GUTTERS, LEADERS, AND DOWNSPOUTS

In most areas of the country, gutters must be provided around the roof to lead rainwater safely away from the building. Houses in some desert areas do not need gutters. In any building, however, it is wise to provide short gutters and diverters over the entrances to avoid discomfort during rain (Fig. 21-6).

Gutters are troughs, usually made of copper, aluminum, or galvanized iron, that are suspended under the eave line to catch the runoff. They should slope slightly toward the downspout to maintain the flow of water.

Leaders are sloping conductors used to carry the water from the gutter to the downspout.

Downspouts are the vertical conductors which carry the water to the point of disposal, usually a splash block or drywell.

Splash blocks are flat blocks of concrete placed below the downspout to break the force of the water and prevent erosion of the ground beneath the downspout.

Drywells are deep holes filled with permeable material such as rock or gravel. Their function is to carry the runoff down to the water table without erosion.

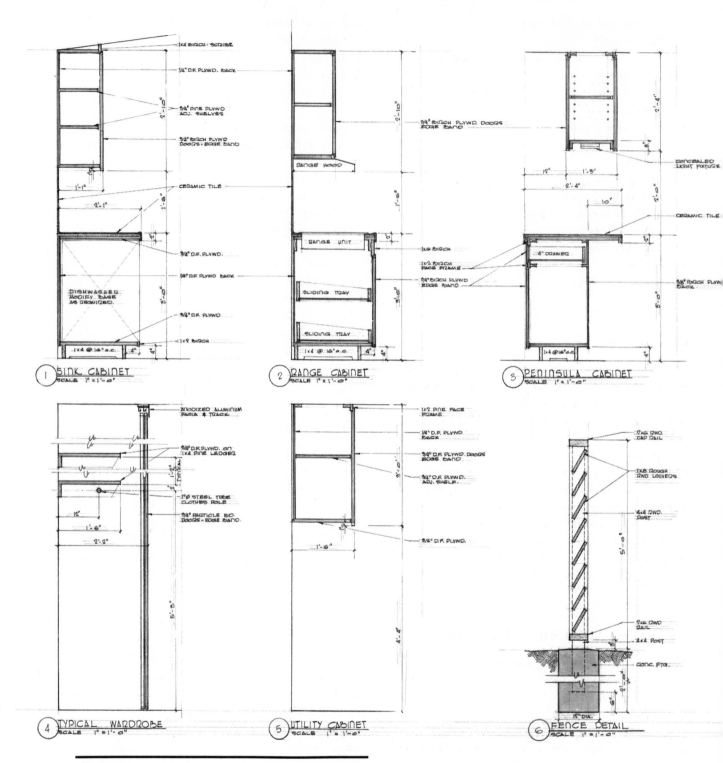

FIGURE 21-1 Miscellaneous details of a small residence

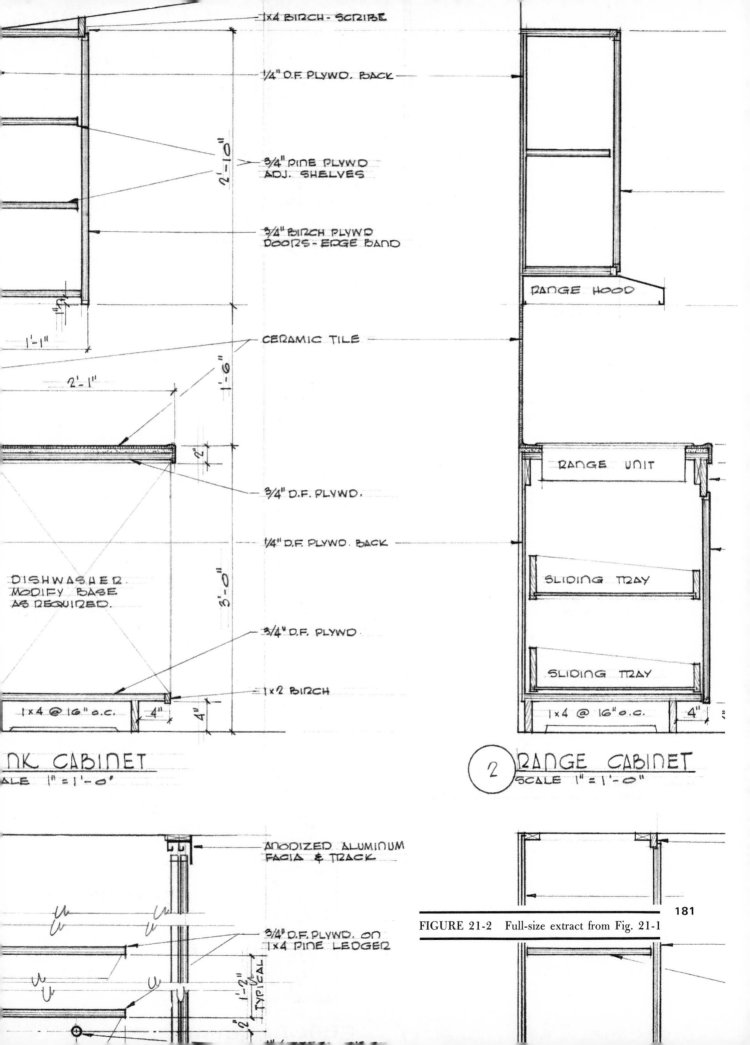

1x4 BIRCH - SCRIBE

1/4" D.F. PLYWD. BACK

3/4" PINE PLYWD
ADJ. SHELVES

2'-10"

3/4" BIRCH PLYWD
DOORS - EDGE BAND

CERAMIC TILE

RANGE HOOD

1'-1"

2'-1"

1'-6"

2"

3/4" D.F. PLYWD.

RANGE UNIT

1/4" D.F. PLYWD. BACK

DISHWASHER.
MODIFY BASE
AS REQUIRED.

3'-0"

SLIDING TRAY

3/4" D.F. PLYWD

SLIDING TRAY

1x2 BIRCH

1x4 @ 16" o.c.   4"   4"

1x4 @ 16" o.c.   4"

NK CABINET
ALE 1" = 1'-0"

② RANGE CABINET
SCALE 1" = 1'-0"

ANODIZED ALUMINUM
FACIA & TRACK

3/4" D.F. PLYWD. ON
1x4 PINE LEDGER

1'-2"
TYPICAL

2"

181

FIGURE 21-2   Full-size extract from Fig. 21-1

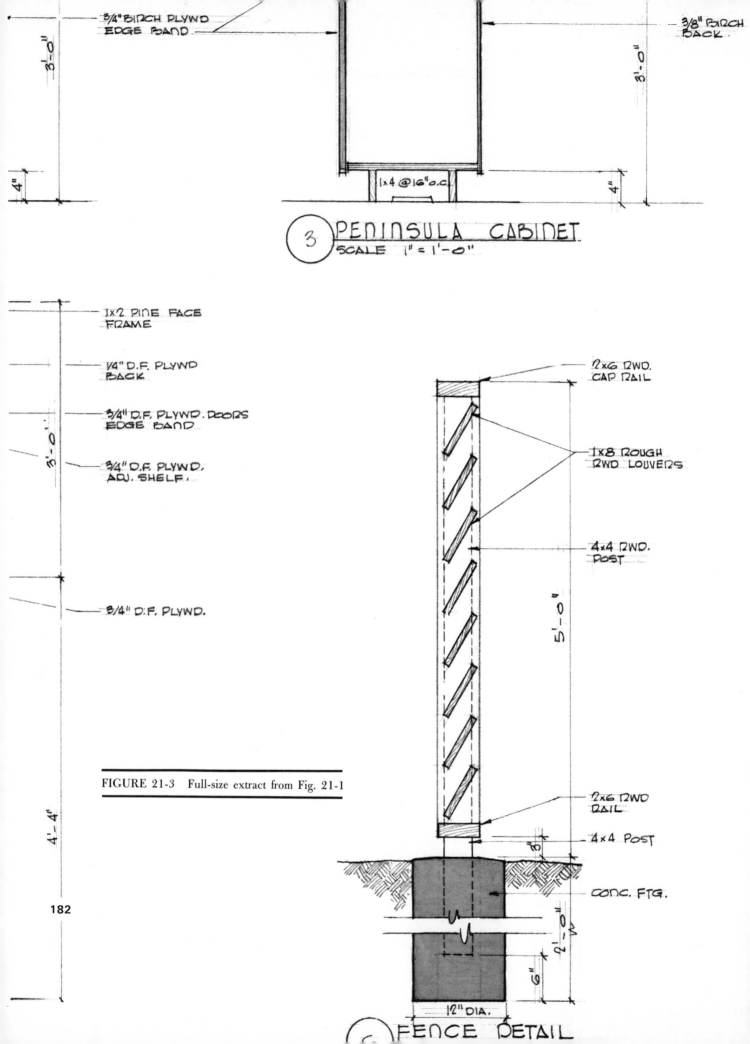

3/4"BIRCH PLYWD
EDGE BAND

3'-0"

4"

3/8" BIRCH
BACK

3'-0"

4"

1x4 @16"o.c.

③ PENINSULA CABINET
SCALE 1" = 1'-0"

1x2 PINE FACE
FRAME

1/4" D.F. PLYWD
BACK

3/4" D.F. PLYWD. DOORS
EDGE BAND

3/4" D.F. PLYWD.
ADJ. SHELF.

3'-0"

3/4" D.F. PLYWD.

FIGURE 21-3   Full-size extract from Fig. 21-1

182

4'-4"

2x6 RWD.
CAP RAIL

1x8 ROUGH
RWD LOUVERS

4x4 RWD.
POST

5'-0"

2x6 RWD
RAIL

4x4 POST

3"

CONC. FTG.

2'-0"

6"

12" DIA.

FENCE DETAIL

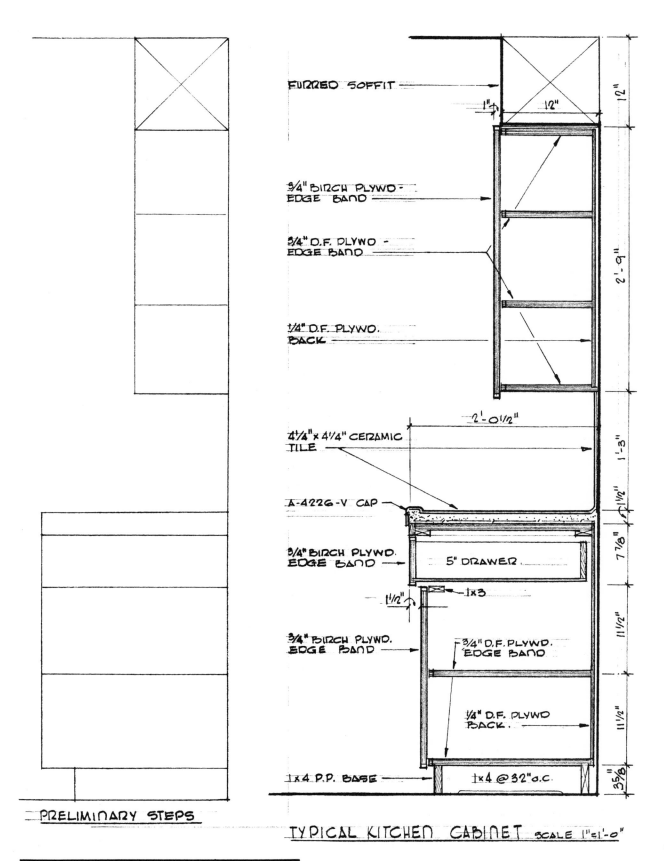

FURRED SOFFIT

3/4" BIRCH PLYWD - EDGE BAND

3/4" D.F. PLYWD - EDGE BAND

1/4" D.F. PLYWD. BACK

4 1/4" x 4 1/4" CERAMIC TILE

A-4226-V CAP

3/4" BIRCH PLYWD. EDGE BAND

3/4" BIRCH PLYWD. EDGE BAND

1x4 P.P. BASE

1"

12"

12"

2'-9"

2'-0 1/2"

1'-3"

1 1/2"

7 7/8"

5" DRAWER

1 1/2"

1x3

3/4" D.F. PLYWD. EDGE BAND

1/4" D.F. PLYWD BACK.

11 1/2"

11 1/2"

3 5/8"

1x4 @ 32" o.c.

PRELIMINARY STEPS

TYPICAL KITCHEN CABINET SCALE 1"=1'-0"

FIGURE 21-4   Procedure for drawing a cabinet detail

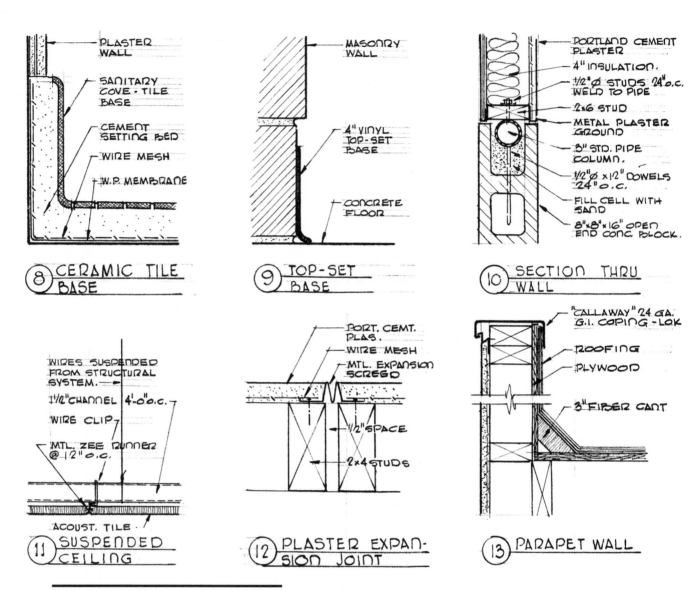

FIGURE 21-5 Typical miscellaneous details

Building code requirements for gutters and downspouts vary from place to place. The student should follow local practices.

FLASHINGS AND JACKS

Flashings are used to prevent the passage of liquids and gases through small openings which appear in a building. They are made of sheet materials, usually metal or waterproof paper, and are sometimes laid in, or coated, with a waterproof mastic. Flashings are used around openings in any surface, at changes in the direction of some surfaces, and at junctions between different surfaces. Following are some of the conditions encountered and the manner in which they are handled with flashings (Fig. 21-7).

1. Around windows and doors, reinforced waterproof paper or metal is fastened to the frame and placed behind the wall material.
2. Valley flashing is used on some roofs. Copper or coated steel sheet is laid in the valley and covered by the shingles except at the center. Membrane roofs require no flashing.
3. At a change of material in a wall (for example,

184

wainscot), sheet metal or paper is laid behind the top material and over the bottom material, or water table if used.

4. Between the fireplace and the roof, short overlapping sections of metal are laid in the horizontal mortar joint and bent downward and under the roof material for several inches.

5. In the case of pipes or conductors through a roof, a special flashing, called a jack, which fits the pipe snugly, is installed with its flange under the roof material. On shingle roofs, the flange is laid as a

shingle to prevent water from flowing through to the sheathing.

Other miscellaneous details are designed by either the architect or the draftsman. The procedure in drawing is the same as for other details. It is important to show enough sections, properly dimensioned, to make it possible for the builder to execute the drawings correctly. All sections must be related to the other drawings by the use of keying symbols (see Fig. 13-3).

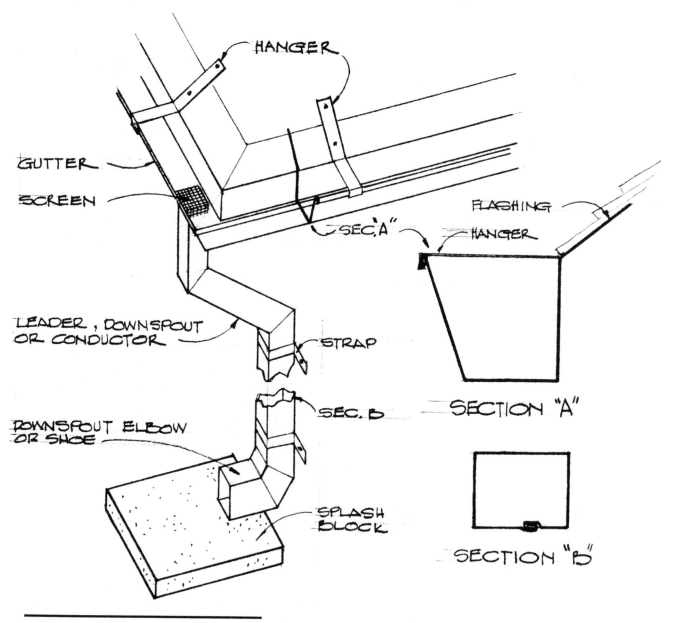

FIGURE 21-6   Gutter and downspout details

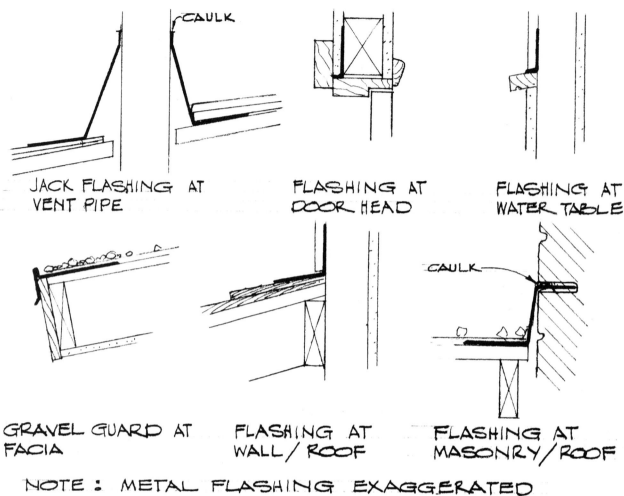

JACK FLASHING AT VENT PIPE

FLASHING AT DOOR HEAD

FLASHING AT WATER TABLE

GRAVEL GUARD AT FACIA

FLASHING AT WALL / ROOF

FLASHING AT MASONRY / ROOF

NOTE : METAL FLASHING EXAGGERATED

FIGURE 21-7   Flashings and jacks in section

REVIEW QUESTIONS

1. Why is it impossible to describe completely such details as base and window trim and baluster on a $\frac{1}{8}$ in. = 1 ft 0 in. floor plan or elevation?
2. Pick out any special detail from a catalog, and sketch a sectional detail of it as it would be installed in your building.
3. How many drawings in the set are affected by a shower stall?

STUDY SUGGESTIONS

1. Inspect a completed building and note the points requiring explanation in miscellaneous details.
2. Using several details as examples, decide how many building trades would need to use the drawings of these details.
3. Check a magazine such as *Progressive Architecture* for construction details which you might use in your own project.

STUDENT PROBLEM

We suggest that you restrict this drawing to the kitchen cabinet and fence details. Ideas can be found in catalogs, magazines, or professional working drawings. The instructor should designate the total number of details for this drawing. Draw the miscellaneous details.

CHAPTER 22

FOUNDATION PLAN

DEFINITION AND PURPOSE

The foundation plan shows the extent and location of all concrete footings, flatwork, and underpinning of the building (Figs. 22-1 to 22-7). Masonry fences, masonry walls above grade, and swimming pools are not included; they are usually shown on separate sheets. The primary purpose of the foundation is to distribute the weight of the building over the soil. The Appendix contains formulas and data for use in unusual situations. Most students, however, will follow local building codes in determining the sizes of footings, walls, and so on. Concrete is most often used in foundations, though stone and other masonry materials may be used.

TYPES OF FOUNDATIONS

Though there are many types of foundations and floor systems in use, only the two types most commonly used for residential and light-commercial structures will be discussed here, that is, wood floor and concrete floor construction. Wood floor construction uses outside foundation walls and interior supports of one type or another to carry the wood construction above grade. All forces from above are transmitted from these supports through the footings to the soil. In concrete floor construction, wall loads are carried through the footings to the soil; the floor loads are carried by the soil beneath the concrete slab.

Each system has certain advantages and disad-

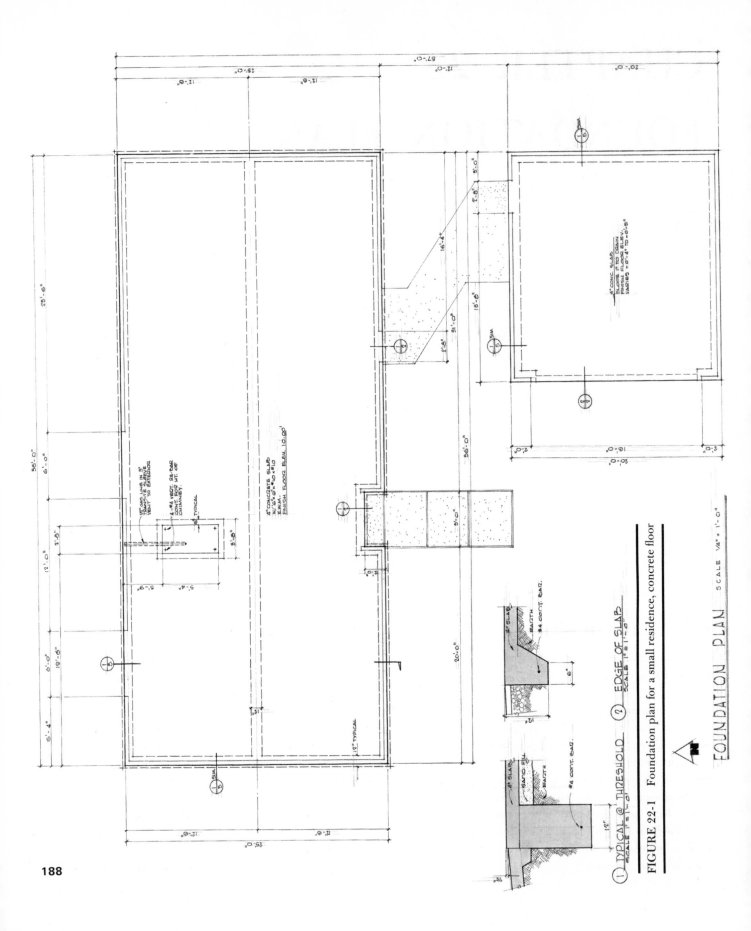

FIGURE 22-1   Foundation plan for a small residence, concrete floor

188

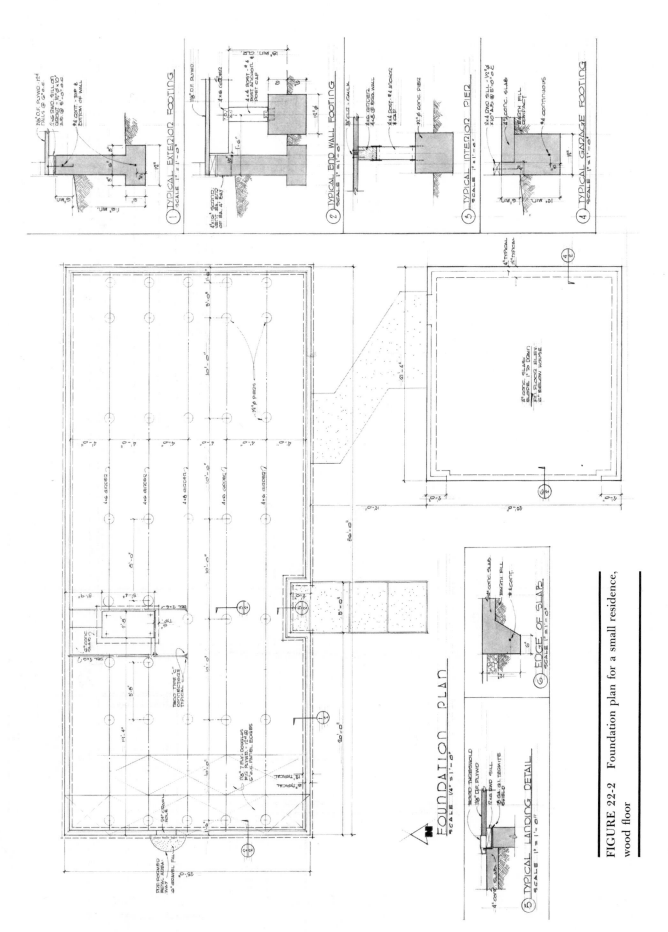

FIGURE 22-2 Foundation plan for a small residence, wood floor

189

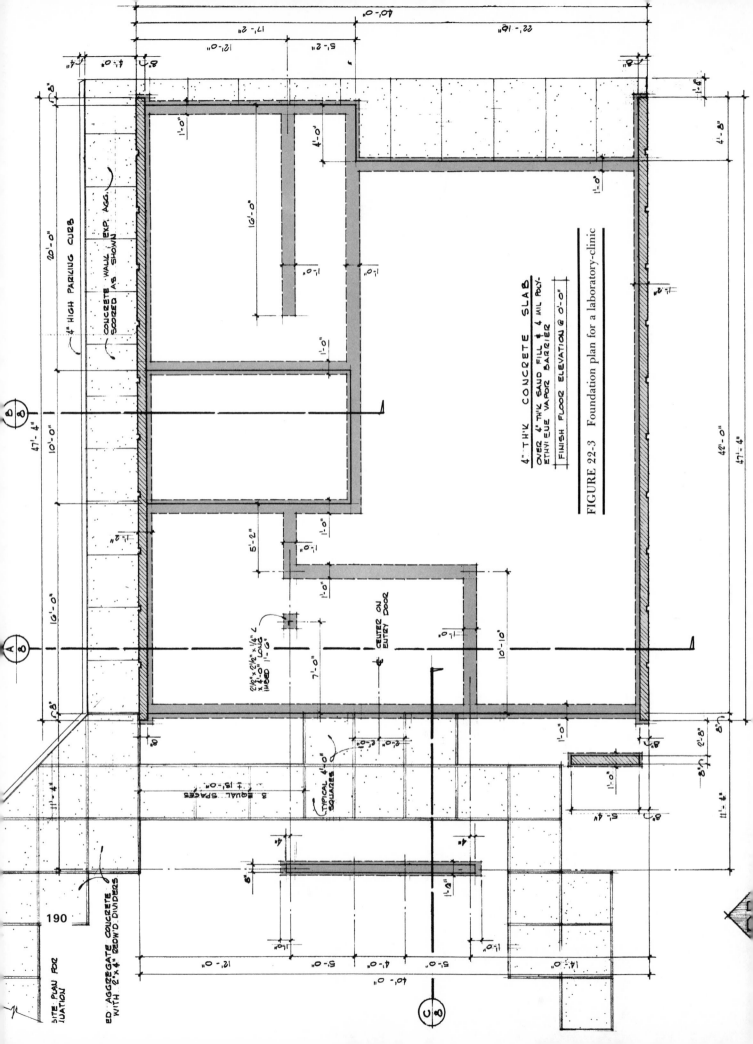

FIGURE 22-3   Foundation plan for a laboratory-clinic

190

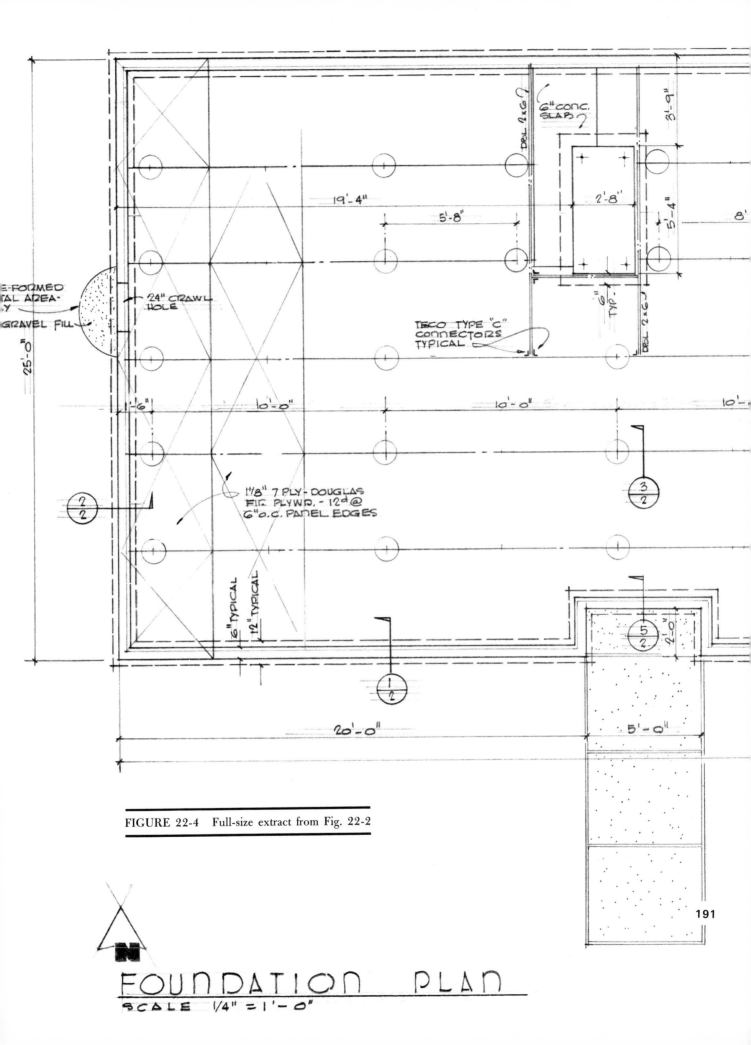

FIGURE 22-4   Full-size extract from Fig. 22-2

191

FOUNDATION PLAN
SCALE 1/4" = 1'-0"

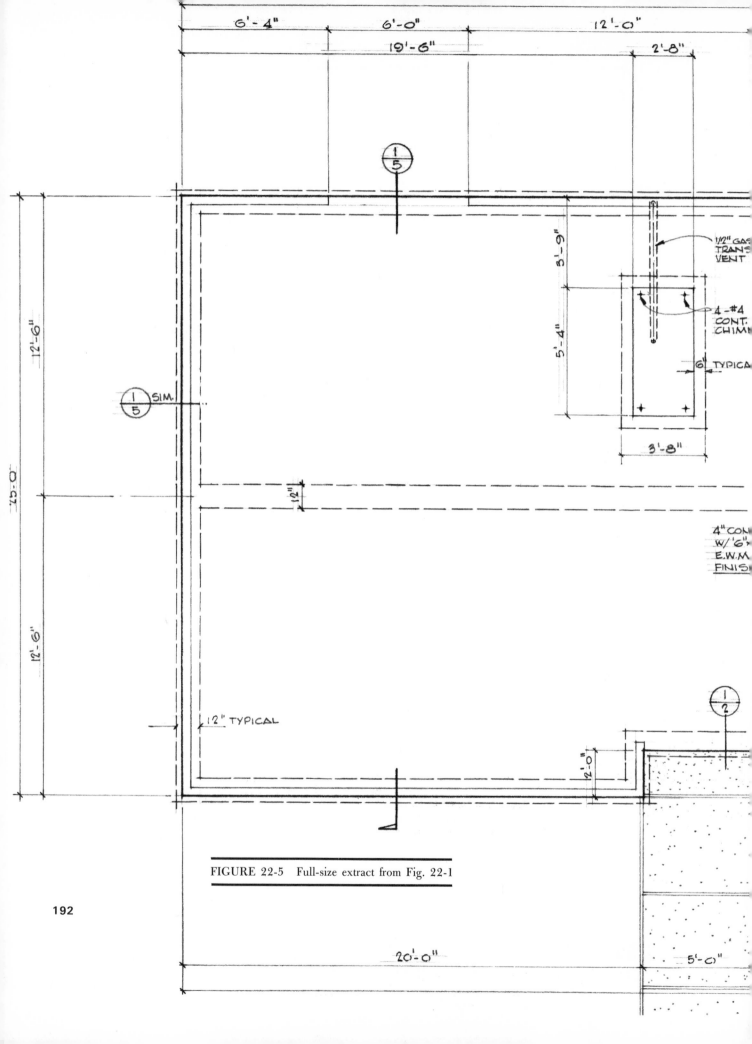

FIGURE 22-5   Full-size extract from Fig. 22-1

192

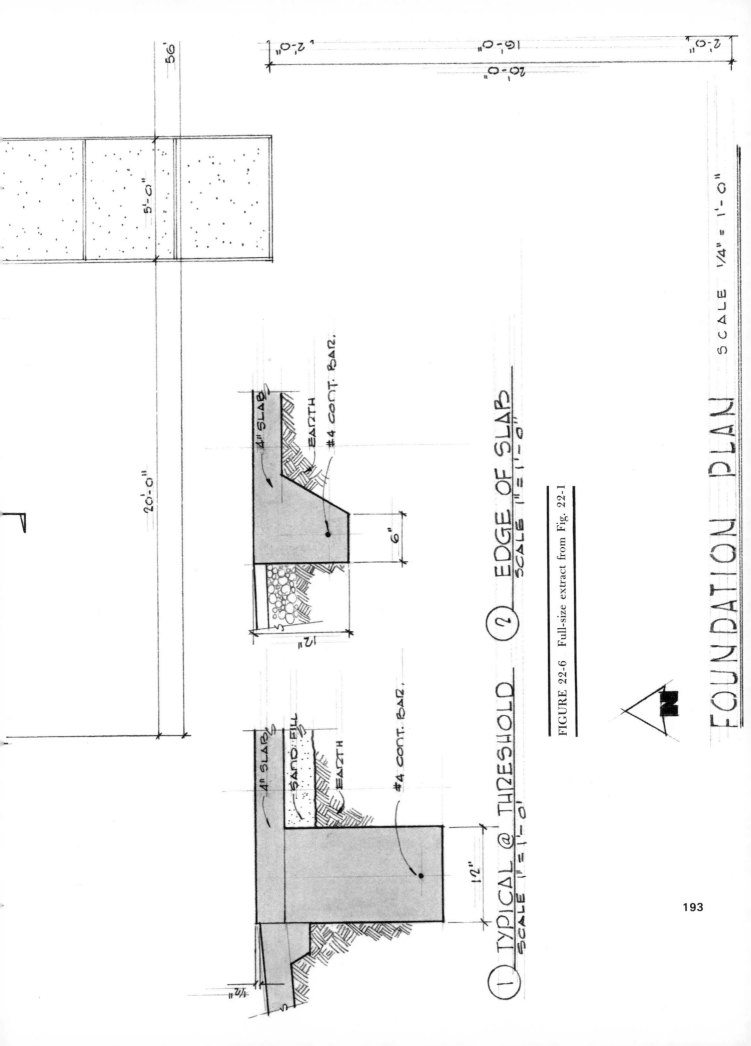

FIGURE 22-6 Full-size extract from Fig. 22-1

1 TYPICAL @ THRESHOLD
SCALE 1"=1'-0"

2 EDGE OF SLAB
SCALE 1"=1'-0"

FOUNDATION PLAN
SCALE 1/4" = 1'-0"

4" SLAB
SAND FILL
EARTH
#4 CONT. BAR.
12"

4" SLAB
EARTH
#4 CONT. BAR.
6"
12"

20'-0"

5'-0"

56'

2'-0"
6'-0"
2'-0"
20'-0"

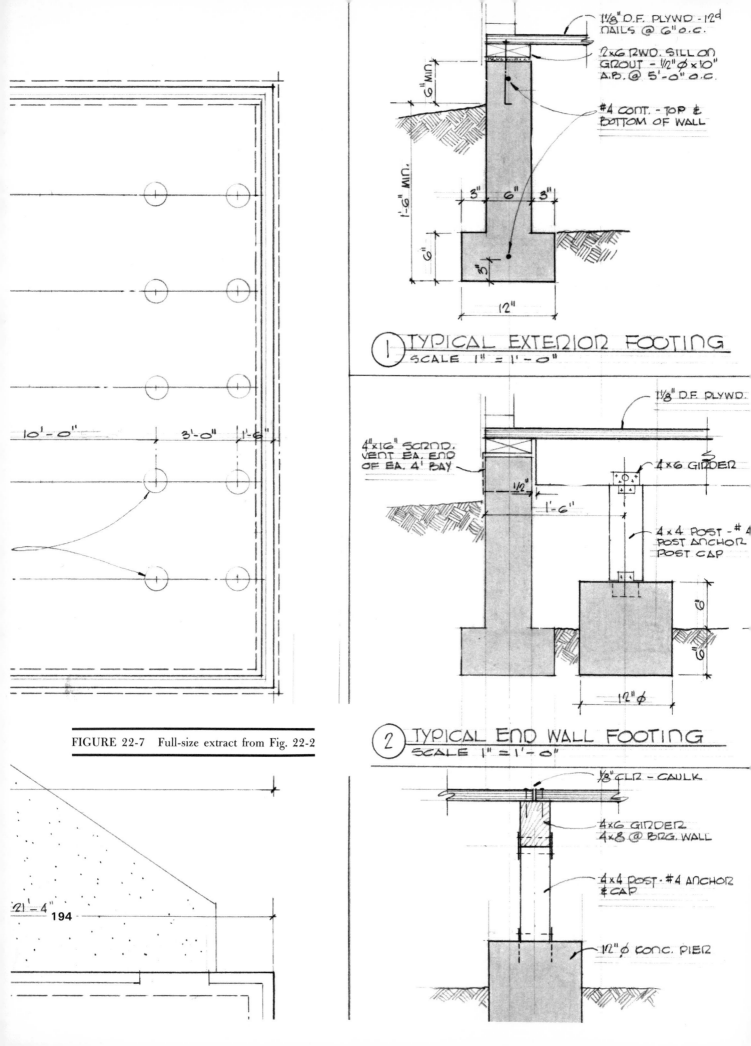

1⅛" D.F. PLYWD - 12ᵈ
NAILS @ 6" O.C.

2×6 RWD. SILL ON
GROUT - ½"∅ × 10"
A.B. @ 5'-0" O.C.

#4 CONT. - TOP &
BOTTOM OF WALL

6" MIN

1'-6" MIN.

6"

3"   6"   3"

5"

12"

① TYPICAL EXTERIOR FOOTING
SCALE 1" = 1'-0"

1⅛" D.F. PLYWD.

4"×16" SCRND.
VENT EA. END
OF EA. 4' BAY

½"

1'-6"

4×6 GIRDER

4×4 POST - #4
POST ANCHOR
POST CAP

6"

6"

12" ∅

② TYPICAL END WALL FOOTING
SCALE 1" = 1'-0"

⅛" CLR - CAULK

4×6 GIRDER
4×8 @ BRG. WALL

4×4 POST - #4 ANCHOR
& CAP

12" ∅ CONC. PIER

10'-0"   3'-0"   1'-6"

FIGURE 22-7   Full-size extract from Fig. 22-2

2'-4"   194

vantages. Wood floors have a texture and appearance that cannot be achieved with concrete. It is possible to work on the plumbing under a wood floor easily, and some people feel that a wood floor is more resilient than a concrete floor. Concrete floors are usually cheaper to build, warmer in winter, and cooler in summer than wood. They are quieter, because audible vibrations are not easily transmitted through concrete.

CHOICE OF A FLOOR SYSTEM

There are several methods of constructing both concrete and wood floor systems. The choice of methods depends on many factors; among them client preference, weather conditions, site conditions, availability of materials, and cost. Several methods of constructing both types of floor systems will be discussed and illustrated with actual scale working drawings. Choice of a system is the student's responsibility and should be based on local practice and the applicable building codes and ordinances.

CONCRETE FLOORS

Two systems are commonly used, the monolithic floor and footing and the separately cast floor and footing (Fig. 22-1). A monolithic floor and footing is poured in one piece, with forms only at the perimeter. In a separately cast floor and footing the foundation walls must be formed, poured, and stripped of forms before the floor can be poured. One advantage of this method is that the perimeter wall may be insulated with board insulation before the floor is poured.

A hardwood floor can be easily laid over a concrete slab floor by the following method. Coat the concrete floor with a thin layer of asphalt mastic and lay short sections of 1 by 4 boards, spaced 16 in. o.c., in the mastic. After the mastic sets, the hardwood can be nailed down in the usual manner (Fig. 22-6). Where a stone or tile surface is part of the floor, the required area of concrete can be depressed 2 in. or so and the stone or tile laid in a bed of grout to the specified height.

WOOD FLOOR SYSTEMS

All of the following floor systems are similar in the following ways. In each, a wood-sheathed surface is applied to a system of beams, joists, or girders; these are carried by posts and piers or by walls which rest on a concrete or masonry footing. A perimeter wall of masonry or concrete supports the outside edge. Any type of wood floor may be built over a basement.

Two-inch tongue and groove decking over beams supported by posts provides a stiff, bounce-free floor (Fig. 22-2). Plywood decking that is $1\frac{1}{8}$ in. D.F. can be substituted for the 2 in. tongue and groove, but the beam spacing must be closer (2 ft) to avoid a springy floor (Fig. 22-2). Spacing of the girders is determined from the tables in the back of the book. One-inch sheathing over joists set on dwarf walls is a very common system (Fig. 22-8).

All of these wood floor systems use the same perimeter wall, which is sized to support the building above. A basement wall is similar to any other perimeter wall except that it must be waterproofed, as it encloses a habitable space. A drain tile should be laid around the footing to lead groundwater away from the wall (Fig. 23-4).

A grade beam is a reinforced concrete beam partially supported by the earth. Its main support is derived from deep pilings cast with the beam at appropriate intervals. A floor system can be laid over it in the same way as over any other foundation component (Fig. 23-4).

ISOLATED PIER FOOTING

Small footings, or piers, inside or outside the main walls of the building are usually cast in place with a simple form (Fig. 23-4). Cardboard tubes are available in many diameters for casting piers and columns. It is possible to pour very long piers with relative ease; the finished job looks better than does conventionally formed concrete.

FOUNDATION WALLS ON A SLOPE

When a foundation wall runs downhill it must be stepped at the bottom. The steps must be at least

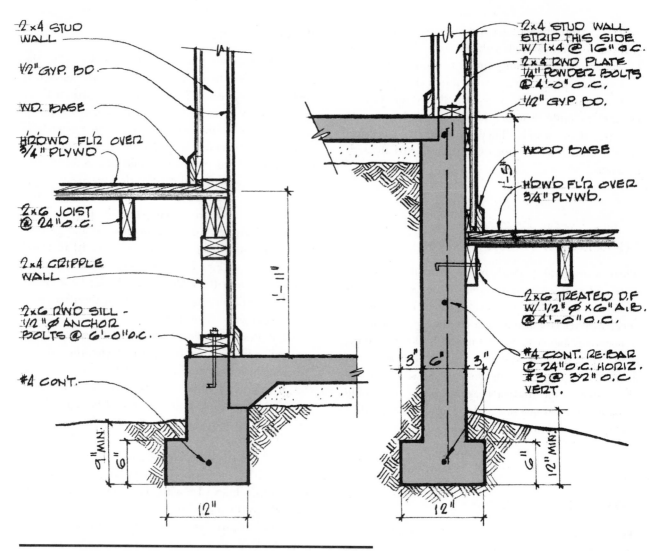

FIGURE 22-8   Conditions at transition from wood to concrete floors

4 ft in length and horizontal. This arrangement prevents the building from sliding downhill when the ground is saturated. The top of the foundation wall is set at a height 6 in. or more above finished grade at the uphill side (Fig. 22-9).

BEARING WALLS

All outside or perimeter walls are load-bearing, but not all interior walls are. Load-bearing interior walls must be located before the foundation plan can be started (Fig. 23-5). They can be identified by checking the structural section against the floor plan. Interior bearing walls are not needed under a trussed roof whose rafters have been sized to span from ridge to plate and have effective horizontal ties (usually ceiling joists). Interior bearing walls carry roof or upper-story loads directly or through bracing, and they need a footing. Masonry walls themselves are heavy enough to require a footing. Bearing walls or columns are required under the ends of beams which carry roof loads (beamed or cathedral ceilings).

In concrete floor construction a solid footing of concrete, about the size of the perimeter footing, must be placed under the interior bearing wall. In wood-joist floor construction, if the bearing wall parallels the joists, doubled joists are placed under the wall.

If the wall is at an angle to the joists, solid blocking must be nailed in under the wall.

REQUIRED INFORMATION

All foundation plans should include:

1. Plan views of:
   a. Foundation walls and footing of all buildings
   b. Interior footing or dwarf walls
   c. Piers and footing pads
   d. Walls below grade (basements)
   e. Locations of girders and beams supporting floors, walls, and so on
   f. Walks, driveways, and paved outdoor areas
   g. Other footings, curbs, gutters, and areaways
2. Cross-sectional details of all foundation work, usually drawn at $\frac{3}{4}$ in. = 1 ft 0 in. scale
3. Complete dimensioning and notes to go with the above drawings

PRELIMINARY STEPS

The foundation plan is based on the floor plan, as are all other plan views in the set. The best procedure is to trace the outline of the building from the floor plan in light lines. Show the center lines of any bearing walls, the locations of all outside entrances, and any isolated columns as light lines. Locate the inside of basement walls, planters, fireplaces, below-grade pits or above-grade slabs, and underground piping and ductwork in the same way. It is important to do this to avoid having concrete poured in the wrong places. These lines will determine the extent and location of foundation work.

Remove the floor plan from beneath the tracing to avoid possible damage, and then proceed with the foundation plan. It is assumed at this point that the student knows the sizes of all footings, walls, and flatwork; the locations and spacing of all girders and beams, and so on. This information is derived from local building codes and the design data in the Appendix. As a general rule, all foundation walls are drawn as visible lines and footings are drawn as hidden lines. The edges of flatwork and any breaks or changes in the elevation of the concrete are shown in visible lines. Any feature underneath the concrete is shown as a hidden line. In visualizing the plan view of any part of a structure, refer to the cross-sectional detail involved.

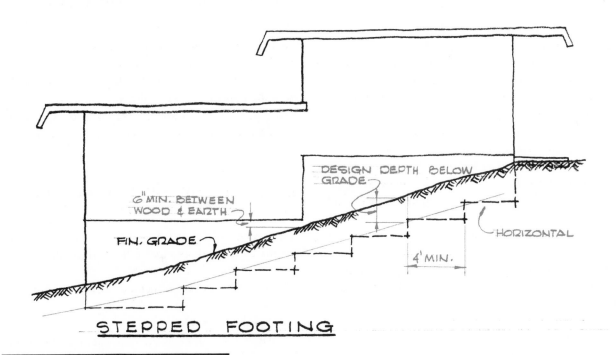

FIGURE 22-9 Stepped footings on a slope

SPLIT-LEVEL AND MULTISTORY BUILDINGS

When changes in level are encountered, it is necessary to have an accurate vertical section through the lot on which to base the location and sizing of foundation components (Figs. 22-8 and 22-9). The steps in foundation walls that run downhill are derived from the natural grade and the local building code; the extent of any excavation is also based on this vertical section.

Though there are many other types of construction, only the procedures for drawing the foundation plan of a wood-floored structure and a concrete-floored structure will be explained here. In each case it is assumed that the construction lines showing the outside walls, interior bearing walls, entrances, columns, inside of basement walls, masonry planters or fireplaces, below-grade pits or above-grade slabs, and underground piping are already placed.

DRAFTING THE FOUNDATION PLAN FOR A WOOD FLOOR

The procedure for drawing the foundation plan for a wood-floored structure follows (Fig. 22-2):

1. Size all concrete and wood structural parts (see A-6 to A-8).
2. Mark all breaks in the outside foundation walls (crawl holes, doors, windows), and locate porches.
3. Draw the outline of the foundation wall (usually 6 in. thick).
4. Draw the footings for the outside walls.
5. Draw the interior bearing walls or piers.
6. Draw the porches to the desired size in line with the entrances.
7. Draw in the locations of all columns, piers, and isolated footings.
8. Draw the basement walls and concrete steps if used.
9. Draw the fireplace and other masonry footings.
10. Draw any below-grade pits or above-grade slabs.
11. Draw in any under-floor ducts.
12. Show size and spacing of all floor joists with a double-pointed arrow.
13. Show the location of bearing walls as center lines. If parallel to joists, indicate doubled joists; if

perpendicular to joists, indicate solid blocking between joists.
14. Place all section-keying symbols.
15. Draw in dimension lines.
16. Draw all sections indicated by keying symbols. Show all typical constructions (wall, interior bearing wall, and so on) plus the places where different constructions come together (such as porch to foundation wall). Place the appropriate keying symbol under each section along with the scale.
17. Place all lettering, notes, title, and scale.

TRANSITIONS FROM WOOD TO CONCRETE FLOORS

Many split-level and multistory buildings use both wood and concrete construction, and it is important to show properly the construction at places where the two come together (Fig. 22-8). Where the finished floor levels must be the same height, the change between wood and concrete should occur at a partition to avoid problems of floor covering.

HABITABLE SPACES BELOW GRADE

When the floor of a habitable room of a building, including basements, garages, storage areas, and so forth, is below grade, it is necessary to waterproof the walls which extend below finish-grade. This may be done by applying sheet or liquid membranes, such as paint, asphalt, or bituminous materials to the side of the wall that comes in contact with the ground.

DRAFTING THE FOUNDATION PLAN FOR A CONCRETE FLOOR

The procedure for drawing the foundation plan for a concrete-floored structure follows (Fig. 22-1):

1. Size all concrete structural parts (see A-6 and A-7).
2. Locate all porches.
3. Draw the outline of the foundation wall showing wall breaks and centers of foundation bolts.
4. Draw the footings for the outside walls.

198

5. Draw the interior footings.
6. Draw porches in line with the desired openings.
7. Draw in the positions of all columns, piers, and isolated footings.
8. Draw the basement walls and concrete steps.
9. Draw the fireplace or other masonry footings.
10. Draw any below-grade pits.
11. Draw in under-floor ducts.
12. Place all section-keying symbols.
13. Draw in dimension lines.
14. Draw all sections indicated by keying symbols (see wood-floor construction).
15. Place all lettering, notes, title, and scale.

DIMENSIONING

Dimensioning of foundation plans is similar to the dimensioning of floor plans (Figs. 22-1 and 22-2). The outside line shows the overall size of the foundation. The second line shows all breaks, centers of interior footings or dwarf walls, centers of isolated footings, and so on. A third line is not needed. Locations and sizes of areas inside the building are dimensioned close to that area. The size of the foundation must jibe with the stud-to-stud size of the floor plan.

SECTIONAL DETAILS

The cross-sectional details shown here are sized to satisfy minimum requirements in a frost-free area assuming stable soil conditions (Figs. 22-5 and 22-6). The figures will have to be increased in areas of frost, earthquakes, hurricanes, or unstable soil. This information is available through local building departments. Some areas also demand insulation at the perimeter of slab floors. If the details shown conflict with local practice, follow the local practice.

KEYING SYMBOLS

The keying symbols used on foundation plans generally provide for two reference numbers (Figs. 22-1 and 22-2). The circle is about $\frac{1}{2}$ in. diameter, and the simplified cutting-plane line, or *flag*, touches the circle in line with the center; it is drawn long enough to go through the plan view of the detail. No matter what the position of the flag is, the circle is always divided horizontally into two equal parts. The top space has a number or letter representing the desired detail. The lower space refers to the sheet number on which the section view of the detail can be found. Other types of keying symbols may be used as long as they are easily understood. Form is considered unimportant if the meaning is clear.

REVIEW QUESTIONS

1. What is the main purpose of the foundation system?
2. What is the most common foundation material?
3. What are the two most commonly used types of floor construction?
4. What other drawing is the basis for drawing the foundation plan?
5. State the most important advantage of a wood floor.
6. How are interior bearing walls supported in a wood-floored house?
7. Which cross-sectional details are needed as a minimum on a typical foundation plan?
8. Draw and explain a foundation keying symbol.

STUDY SUGGESTIONS

1. Visit a residential building site, and compare the working drawings with the actual construction.
2. Visit your building department, and check typical foundation details.
3. Check out a book from the library on the subject of elementary structural design; read about the design of foundations.

STUDENT PROBLEM

The structural section and the floor plan must be consulted when drawing the foundation plan.

1. Locate all bearing walls, piers, and the like, and size them according to the information in the Appendix.
2. Decide on the type of footings and other foundation structures. Sketch them, using recommended sizes.
3. Locate any under-floor or through-floor parts and be certain that conflicts do not develop.
4. Draw the foundation plan and sections.

CHAPTER 23
STRUCTURAL SECTIONS

DEFINITION AND PURPOSE

Structural sections are views taken through the building at points which will best show the relationships of all structural and architectural parts of the building (Figs. 23-1 and 23-2). Sections can be taken through any object in any direction. Sections are commonly taken longitudinally or transversally through a structure, as with a structural section, or horizontally, as with a floor plan. Other small sections are taken in any direction which will best show the desired construction—stair, fireplace, window, door, and so on. All important dimensions are shown, such as plate height and roof pitch. Points of connection between various structural parts are shown, and all members

are noted concerning size and material (Fig. 23-3). Often, when the building is complex, several sections may be needed. Wherever there is a change in shape or construction methods, a new section must be drawn. Generally the structural sections are drawn on a separate sheet; however, on a small project they may be placed with another drawing. Structural sections are drawn at a fairly large scale to show detail—about $\frac{1}{2}$ to 1 in. = 1 ft 0 in.

Because construction practices and materials vary greatly from one part of the country to another, instruction in structural systems must be applicable to all areas. To this end, the phases of construction will be broken down into their logical parts—foundation, floor, wall, ceiling, and roof systems. With a few

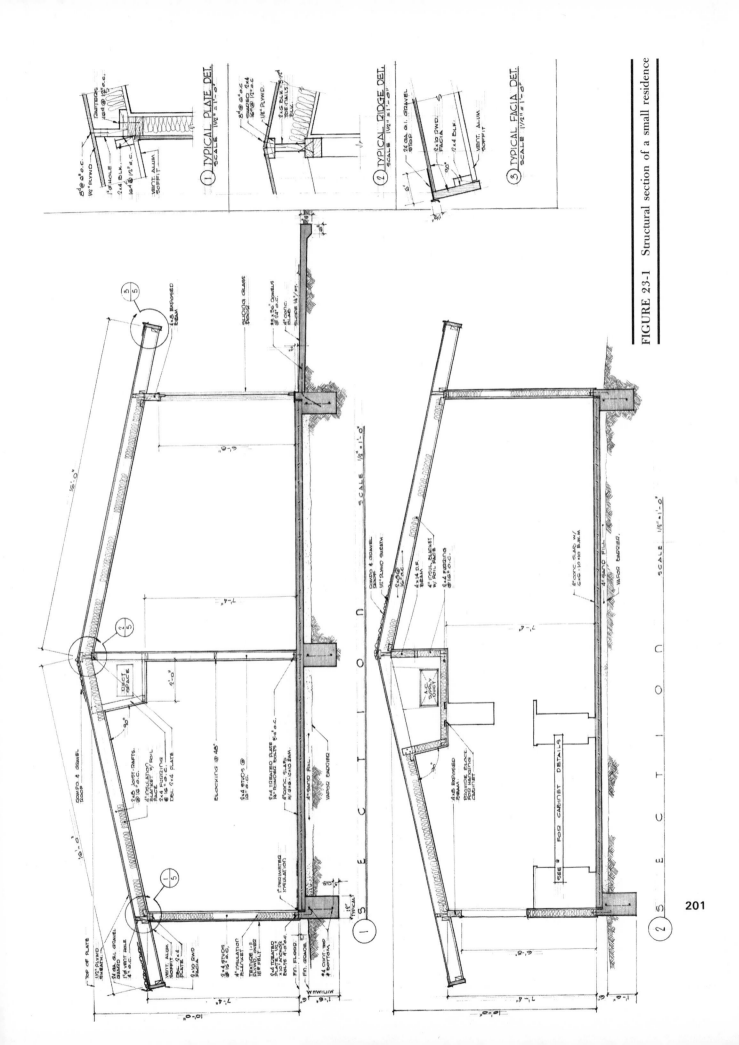

FIGURE 23-1 Structural section of a small residence

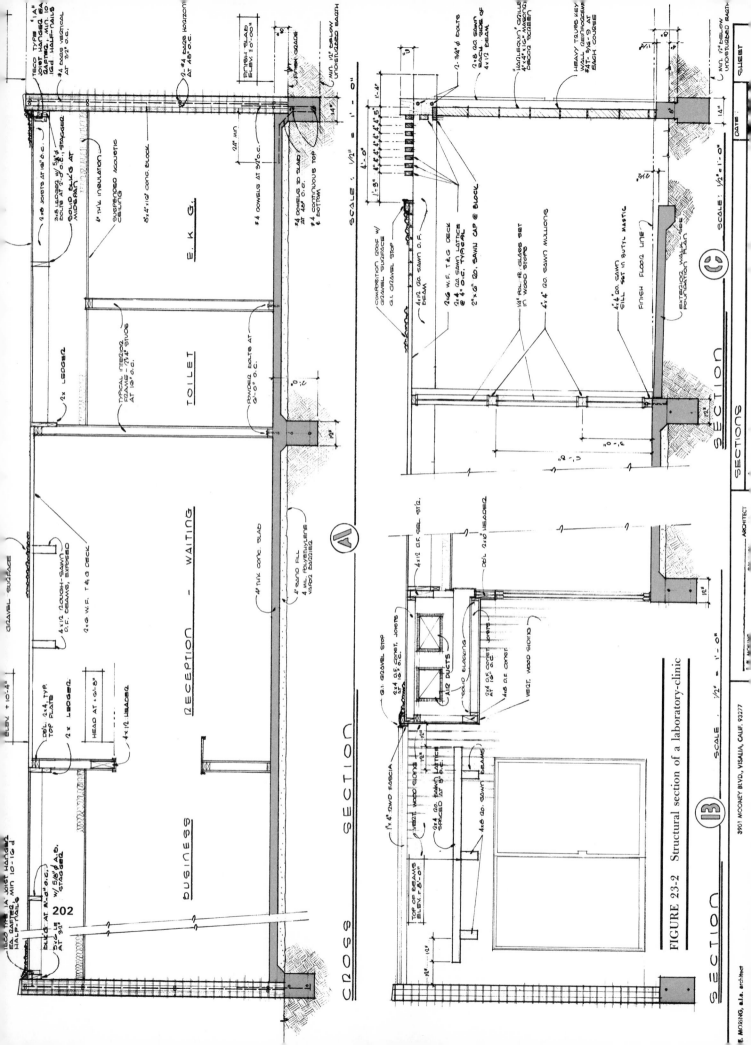

FIGURE 23-2 Structural section of a laboratory-clinic

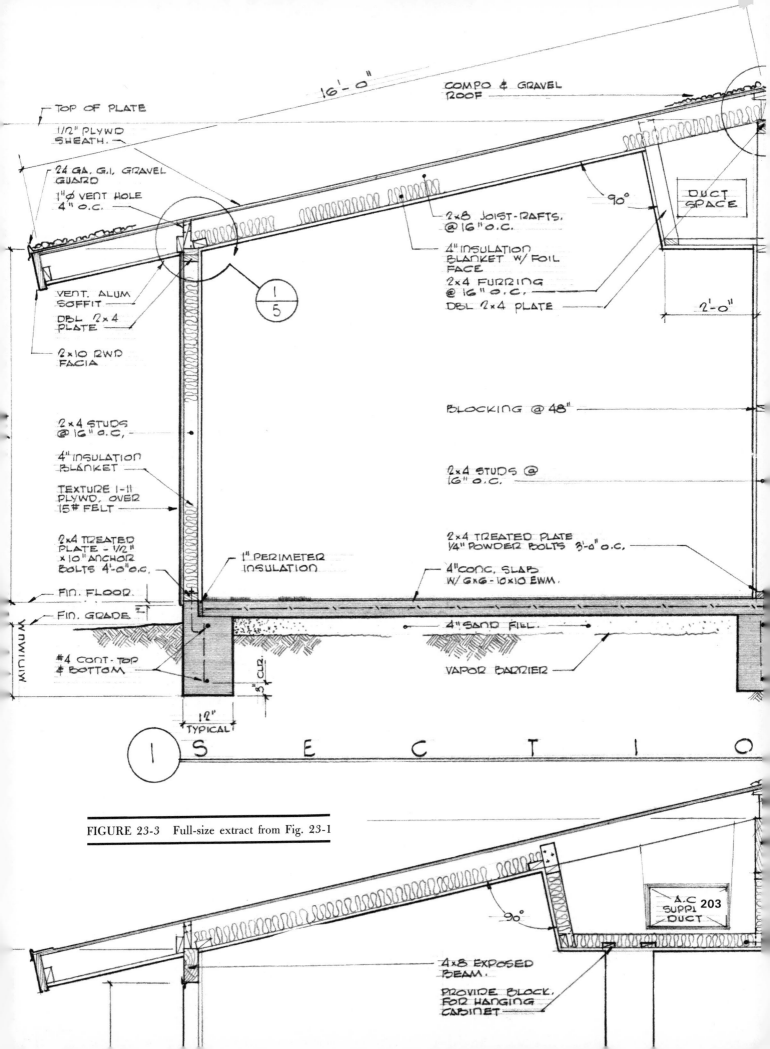

TOP OF PLATE

1/2" PLYWD SHEATH.

24 GA. G.I. GRAVEL GUARD

1"⌀ VENT HOLE 4" O.C.

16'-0"

COMPO & GRAVEL ROOF

2×8 JOIST-RAFTS. @ 16" O.C.

4" INSULATION BLANKET W/ FOIL FACE

2×4 FURRING @ 16" O.C.

DBL 2×4 PLATE

90°

DUCT SPACE

2'-0"

VENT. ALUM SOFFIT

DBL 2×4 PLATE

2×10 RWD FACIA

1/5

2×4 STUDS @ 16" O.C.

4" INSULATION BLANKET

TEXTURE 1-11 PLYWD. OVER 15# FELT

2×4 TREATED PLATE - 1/2" ×10" ANCHOR BOLTS 4'-0" O.C.

FIN. FLOOR.

FIN. GRADE.

MINIMUM

#4 CONT. TOP & BOTTOM

1" PERIMETER INSULATION

3" CLR.

12" TYPICAL

BLOCKING @ 48"

2×4 STUDS @ 16" O.C.

2×4 TREATED PLATE 1/4" POWDER BOLTS 3'-0" O.C.

4" CONC. SLAB W/ 6×6 - 10×10 EWM.

4" SAND FILL.

VAPOR BARRIER

1 S E C T I O

FIGURE 23-3   Full-size extract from Fig. 23-1

90°

A.C SUPPLY DUCT 203

4×8 EXPOSED BEAM.

PROVIDE BLOCK. FOR HANGING CABINET

exceptions, any type of foundation may be used with any type of floor, with any type of wall, and so on. Obviously though, masonry materials should not be placed above wood construction. It is best to use those types of constructions which are in common use locally.

DESIGN

All engineering decisions and computations which determine the nature of materials and the size and spacing of structural elements must be completed before any working drawing can be begun. In the structural design of a building it is necessary to work from the top down, because each member below must be designed to support the weight of the structure above. For drafting purposes though, it is better procedure to start below grade and work toward the top in the same order that the structure is erected. This is effective because all parts of the structure will have been sized by the time the working drawings start. For this reason, when any statement concerning the design of a part is made, remember that the necessary data are derived from the structure above.

STRUCTURES IN CONTACT WITH GROUND

Concrete and masonry are the only materials approved by building codes for foundations. Concrete, plain or reinforced, is the most commonly used material. The decision about what material to use depends on many factors: the type of construction above, availability of materials and labor, building codes, weather conditions, type of soil, cost, and so on.

FOOTINGS

The base of any structure is the footing, which distributes the weight of the building over the soil. The size of the footing varies with the type of soil and the weight of the building above. In areas of deep frost, the footing must be placed below the frost line. The decision whether to use reinforcing steel depends on the building code and design considerations. In

general, it is best to use reinforcing rods, at least, in the footing.

FOUNDATION WALL

The foundation wall transmits vertical forces from above to the footing. Walls may be extended up or down to form retaining walls or basement walls. They also isolate the wood construction from the effects of water, insects, and rot.

The thickness of foundation walls varies with the material in the wall, loads on the wall, and the footing below. The height of foundation walls varies from the usual minimum of 6 in. above grade to any desired height. Many building codes establish minimum wall heights and thicknesses. The use of reinforcing steel in walls increases strength and reduces mass. Size and spacing of steel in the foundation wall are determined by building code or local engineering practices (see A-6 and A-7). All of the foregoing applies equally well to solid concrete or masonry construction.

CONCRETE FLOORS

On- or below-grade concrete floors may be cast separately or integrally with the foundation footing or wall (Fig. 23-4). The usual thickness of a concrete floor is $3\frac{1}{2}$ in. (4 in. nominal), and it is often reinforced with welded wire fabric for strength and control of cracking.

WATERPROOFING

The footings, walls, and on-grade floors are all in contact with the earth and must be protected from groundwater. Below-grade walls, concrete floors, and footings are waterproofed on the earth side by the application of an impervious membrane. These films may be asphaltic or bituminous products (applied hot or cold, with or without a membrane) or plastic films or solutions. Concrete floors are sometimes further protected by a layer of gravel or crushed rock below the membrane. The large spaces between the rocks prevent the rise of water due to capillary action. In areas of poor soil drainage or excessive groundwater,

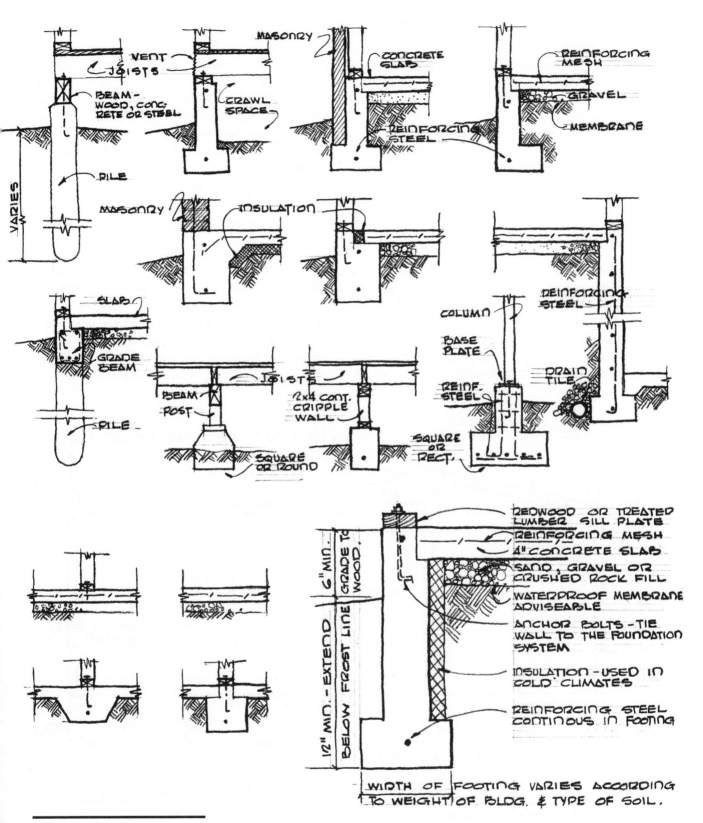

FIGURE 23-4 Types of footings

footing draintiles should be placed to conduct water away from the load-bearing surfaces.

Other types of footings include spread footings, piles, and caissons (Fig. 23-4). These are used to support concentrated loads of posts, columns, piers, and pilasters. Grade beams which carry wall loads bridge the spaces between footings; they are, however, partially supported by the soil. This completes the list of structural members which are in direct contact with the earth.

FLOOR SYSTEMS

Any floor system is designed to transmit live and dead loads from above, as well as its own weight, to the footings (Fig. 23-5). A dead load is the weight of the structure. A live load is any movable load. The most common types of floor systems include on- and above-grade concrete, wood-joist, steel-joist, and plank-and-beam. On-grade concrete floors have already

been described. Above-grade concrete floors in this discussion refer to floors not in contact with the earth. They must be designed to support their own weight plus live and dead loads from above. They must be supported by bearing walls, girders, or beams. These may be separate from or integral with the floor. Such floors always require reinforcing steel. The above-grade floor is an engineering problem beyond the scope of this book.

WOOD-JOIST FLOORS

Wood-joist floors are common in all parts of the country (Fig. 23-6). They are extremely simple to design and build. Tables are available which give the size and spacing of joists for any span and loading (see A-8). Any carpenter understands this type of construction. Joists are supported by bearing walls, girders, or beams of any common material. The size and spacing of the joists is related to the load, the

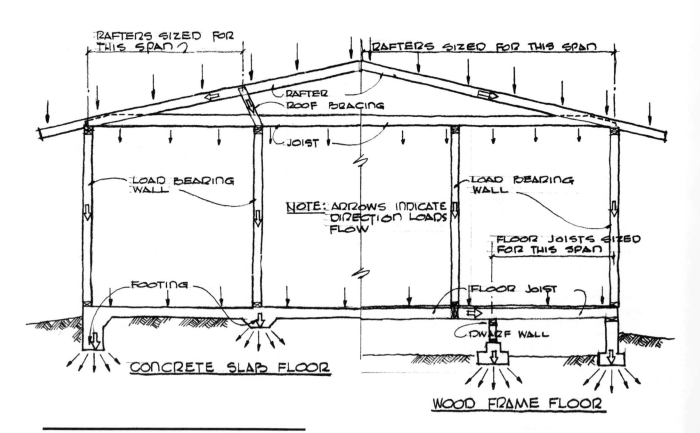

FIGURE 23-5 Forces acting on a simple structure

206

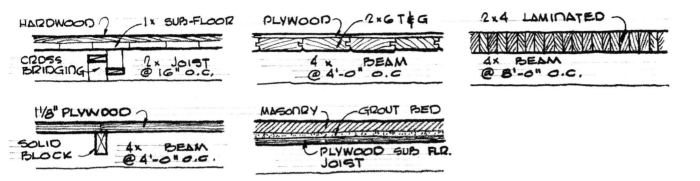

FIGURE 23-6   Typical floor constructions

span between supports, and the type of wood. The live and dead loads are specified in the local building code (usually 40 psf live load for a residence), and the span is equal to the distance betweeen supports. The type of wood depends on the locality.

Where spans between bearing walls are great, wood-joist floors are supported over basementless spaces on dwarf walls or piers and girders. They are supported over a basement or lower floor by girders or beams. Second-story floor joists serve as the ceiling joists over the first floor; they are found in a separate column of the joist table. Cross bridging is used between joists over long spans to stiffen the structure. Spans up to 8 ft do not require bridging. Solid blocking is placed between joists over dwarf walls or other supports and also under bearing walls at an angle to the joists. If the bearing wall is parallel to the joists, the joists are doubled under the wall. Basementless spaces must be ventilated; the requirements are set forth in local building codes. Subfloor materials used over wood joists are straight or diagonal wood sheathing, tongue-and-groove sheathing, and plywood. Finish floor materials used over the subfloor may be hardwood, plastic, ceramic tiles, or carpet.

STEEL-JOIST FLOORS

Steel joists perform the same functions as wood joists and, in addition, will span larger distances for their weight, are incombustible, and will not rot. They are used most often in commercial structures. AISC tables are available for the use of steel joists. Floor materials used over steel joists are the same as those used over wood joists; in addition, metal floor materials are available (Fig. 23-6). Some steel joists use bolted or welded clips to fasten other materials to them, while others are nailable with ordinary carpenters' tools and fastenings.

PLANK-AND-BEAM FLOORS

The plank-and-beam floor system differs from the joist system in that the supports (beams) are widely spaced, and heavy floor sheathing (planks) is used to span the larger spaces (see A-11). Tongue-and-groove sheathing permits the use of wider spacing of beams than does ordinary lumber. The beams are supported by the exterior wall, dwarf walls, posts, or piers.

In a system using wood, a rot- and insect-resistant wood sill or plate must be placed between the concrete or masonry and the wooden structure above. The sill is bolted to foundation bolts which are embedded in the concrete or masonry. In a structure with a concrete floor, the bottom plate of the wall is bolted to the concrete.

WALL STRUCTURES

In the usual frame construction the exterior, and sometimes the interior, walls are designed to support roof loads. Conventional 2- by 4-in. or 2- by 6-in. stud walls consist of a bottom plate, studs, and a double top plate. Intermediate bracing, or fire blocking, is placed horizontally near the middle of the studs. The double plates are overlapped at joints and all corners for continuity. This construction provides a strong ring around the top of the wall and also supports those rafters which fall between the studs. Spacing of studs is usually 16 in., but may be 12 or 24 in. Interior and exterior finish materials are nailed to the studs (Fig. 23-7).

POST-AND-BEAM WALLS

Post-and-beam walls are similar to stud walls with a few exceptions. The bottom plate is the same, but the vertical members are 4 by 4s at wider spacing, often 32 or 48 in. The top plate is a 4 in. beam—4 by 4, 4 by 6, or 4 by 8. The size of the beam depends on the size of the largest opening in the wall. These plates are joined with a simple lap joint at joints and corners. Advantages claimed for post-and-beam construction over stud construction are that the finished building has a neat modular appearance; there is less cutting and waste of finish materials; most lintels, trimmers, and so on are eliminated; and, when properly designed and built, construction goes faster. When

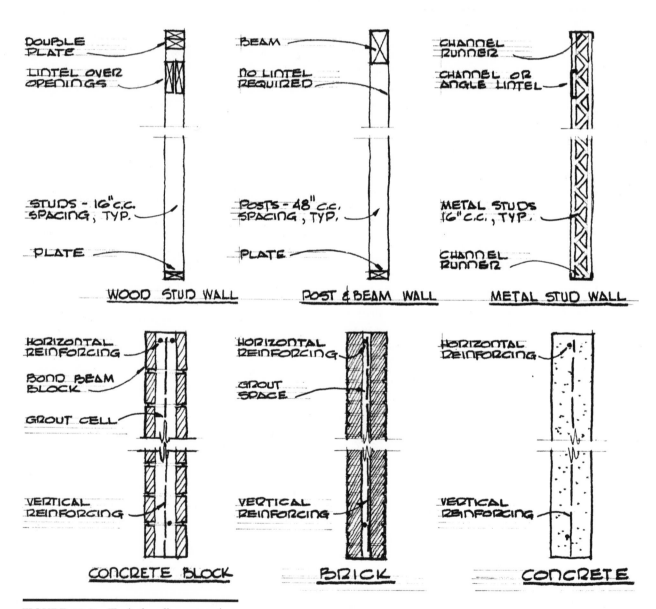

FIGURE 23-7 Typical wall constructions

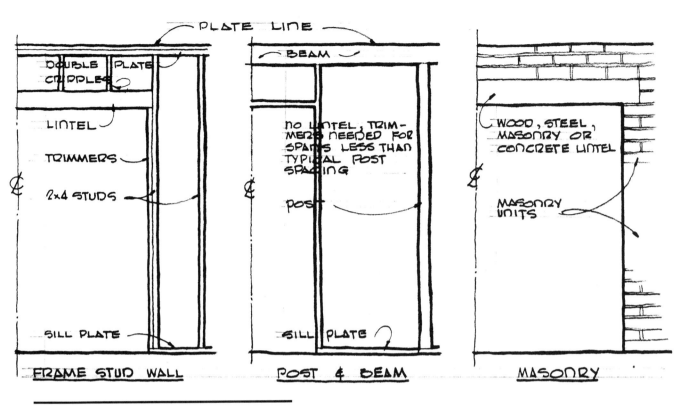

Labels in figure:

FRAME STUD WALL: PLATE LINE, DOUBLE PLATE, CRIPPLES, LINTEL, TRIMMERS, 2x4 STUDS, SILL PLATE

POST & BEAM: BEAM, no lintel, trimmers needed for spans less than typical post spacing, POST, SILL PLATE

MASONRY: WOOD, STEEL, MASONRY OR CONCRETE LINTEL, MASONRY UNITS

FIGURE 23-8   Typical supports in wall openings

openings such as doors, windows, arches, or fireplaces occur in a bearing wall, loads above the opening must be supported (Fig. 23-8). The problem of transferring the weight above the opening down to the floor is solved by the use of a stiff lintel which is supported by trimmers at each side. When the top plate in a post-and-beam wall is large enough, no header is required for an opening. Sizes of lintels vary with the size of the opening (Fig. 23-8 and A-12).

METAL-STUD WALLS

Metal studs are available which can be used with wood, masonry, or all-metal construction. They serve the same purposes as conventional studs and may be used at the same spacings. A U-shaped floor runner takes the place of the bottom plate; it is fastened to the floor with bolts, nails, or powder bolts. The studs are welded or wired to this channel. Blocking or cross bridging is used as fire blocking and stiffening. A U channel similar to the floor runner is used at the top.

Finish materials may be fastened by wire, bolts, screws, or welding; some types of studs will take nails.

NONBEARING WALLS

To this point, all the frame wall systems mentioned are suitable for use as bearing walls, exterior or interior. This same construction can be used for nonbearing walls. However, since nonbearing walls do not have to carry any vertical loads but their own weight, they may be lighter in construction than bearing walls, and lintels may be omitted over openings. It is permissible to use studs turned sideways in a nonbearing wall if space is critical. The resulting gain of 2 in. is sometimes important. In some parts of the country, nonbearing walls may consist of plywood, wood-fiber, or gypsum-board panels glued together without the use of studs. These walls are not usually recommended where noise between rooms is a problem, and since they are not standard wall thickness, their use is not advisable where doors must be framed in.

209

MASONRY WALLS

Masonry walls consist of modular, incombustible units laid up in courses, and they may be solid or grouted, with or without reinforcing (see A-13). There are hundreds of different masonry materials, and no attempt will be made to list all of them or to evaluate their merits. Several general statements can be made about the usual masonry construction, however, and it is the student's responsibility to decide on a suitable material which is used locally.

All masonry must be "keyed" or tied to the foundation wall or footing. This is done by the use of a depression, or "key," cast into the footing or slab. If the wall is to be reinforced with steel, reinforcing rods or dowels must be cast into the foundation at the proper spacing. Later, the spaces around the steel are grouted in. In earthquake areas, horizontal bond beams are required at the bottom, midpoint, and top of the wall (Fig. 23-7).

Most masonry walls require a mechanical tie completely around the wall at the plate line at least. This tie can consist of a complete ring of reinforcing rods grouted into the cavity or of a concrete bond beam on top of the masonry. Anchor bolts are set into a steel or wood plate to which a wood or steel roof may be fastened. When a concrete roof is used, reinforcing dowels extend from the bond beam into the roof slab.

Following are examples of the many types of masonry units:

1. *Concrete blocks.* Usual sizes are 16 by 8 by 8 in., 16 by 8 by 6 in., 16 by 8 by 4 in., and 12 by 8 by 8 in., but some manufacturers produce many other sizes. They are available in numerous shapes designed for particular purposes.
2. *Fired-clay bricks.* Usual sizes are 8 by $3\frac{3}{4}$ by $2\frac{3}{4}$ in., $2\frac{1}{16}$ by $5\frac{1}{2}$ by $11\frac{1}{2}$ in., and 2 by 4 by 12 in., though many others are made. Hundreds of colors, materials, and finishes are available.
3. *Terra-cotta tiles.* These are available in many sizes, shapes, materials, and finishes; it would be difficult to describe an average specimen. Some of these materials may not be used in many areas of the country for structural walls.
4. *Natural stone.* Stone-masonry materials are available in an infinite variety depending on locality;

they are usually not imported except in the case of expensive materials. Some stone is used only in walls as a structural material, while others are used as facings and veneers. For futher information refer to "Architectural Graphic Standards."

OPENINGS

Windows, doors, and other openings require lintels above to carry vertical loads. These lintels may be made of masonry, steel, or wood, depending on the local building code.

ROOF-CEILING STRUCTURE

The roof-ceiling structure above the walls serves several purposes. It provides shelter, supports the surface materials, and ties the walls together. In some cases it provides space for heating, ventilating, plumbing, and electric equipment and conductors (Fig. 23-9).

ATTIC SPACE

Two roofs which appear to be the same from the outside may be quite different in structure if one has an attic space and the other does not (Fig. 23-10). The one with the attic has a flat ceiling hung from joists which also act as ties across the building. When the ties are omitted, as is usual with a cathedral ceiling, a beam or beams must be provided to support the rafters between the walls (see A-9 and A-10). When an open-beam ceiling is desired, either exposed beams or rafter ties must be used. In either case the bottom of the roof decking usually shows as the ceiling finish. If desired, the bottoms of the rafters may be covered by plaster or some other finish material.

ROOF SHAPES

Hundreds of different combinations of roof shapes and materials can be developed, but the design of some of these systems requires an extensive engineering background. For this reason, the roof types discussed here will be limited to wood and metal with some

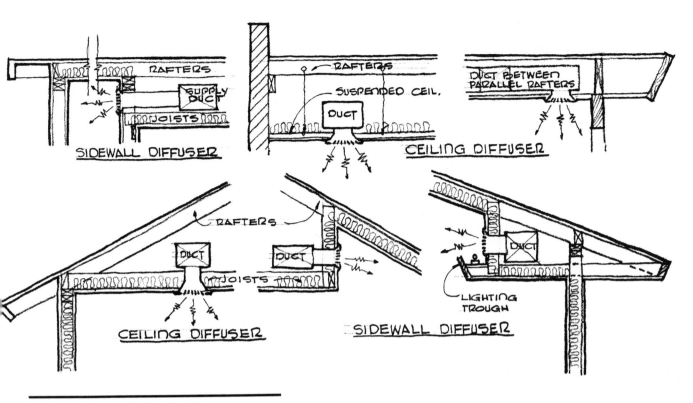

FIGURE 23-9 Typical roof-ceiling constructions

mention of concrete. Through the use of these materials many architectural effects can be achieved. The structural shapes possible include everything from a flat roof to an A frame, a butterfly section, or a warped surface (Fig. 23-10). Various types may be modified or combined to produce clerestory windows or skylights. The possibilities are limited only by the requirements of the structure and the designer's ingenuity.

The most commonly used roof systems can be divided into two general groups, flat and pitched. Any roof steeper than 4:12 pitch is called a pitched roof. Any roof shallower than 4:12 is called a flat roof. These two groups can be further classified into systems, such as a simple-span system and a trussed system.

SIMPLE-SPAN SYSTEM

In the simple-span system, the main structural member may be a rafter or a beam. Rafters and 1-in. sheathing are most often used for ordinary gable and hip roofs. Rafters and 2-in. tongue-and-groove decking are often used for open-beam ceilings. There are many other possible constructions. Wood or metal rafters and wood, metal, or concrete decking can be used. Such roofs are common on residences and some small commercial structures; 24 ft is usually the maximum span used for this type of construction. The sizes of all structural parts of the roof can be found in tables based on the spans involved and the materials used (see A-10 and A-11).

TRUSSED SYSTEM

Trussed systems permit large clear spans and speed up construction on large projects (Fig. 23-10). For this reason trusses are often used in large commercial buildings or large tracts of residences; they are seldom used in custom residences. Trusses are usually designed by engineers and fabricated and erected with special equipment. Many types of wood and metal

211

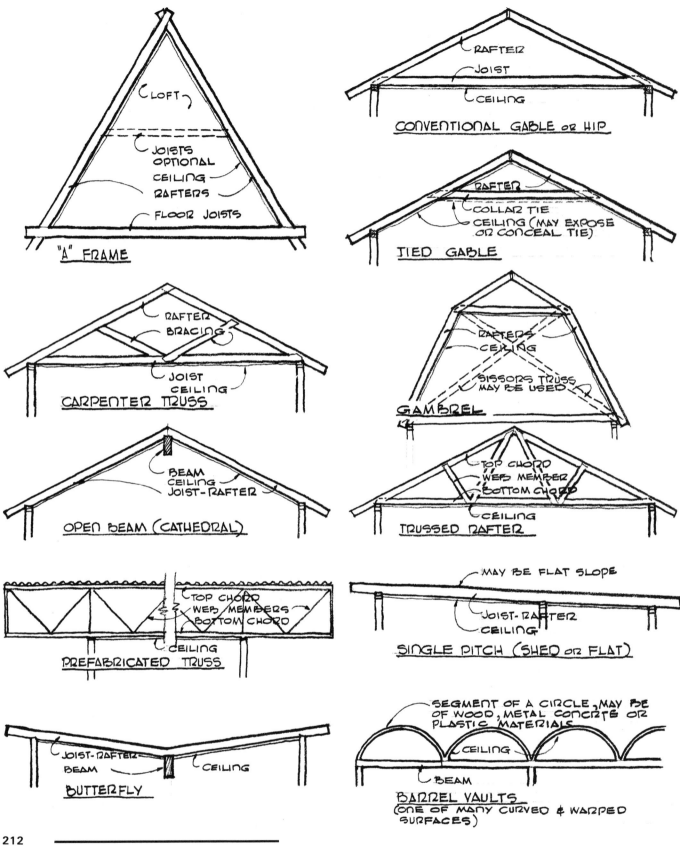

"A" FRAME

LOFT

JOISTS
OPTIONAL

CEILING

RAFTERS

FLOOR JOISTS

CONVENTIONAL GABLE or HIP

RAFTER

JOIST

CEILING

TIED GABLE

RAFTER

COLLAR TIE

CEILING (MAY EXPOSE
OR CONCEAL TIE)

CARPENTER TRUSS

RAFTER

BRACING

JOIST

CEILING

GAMBREL

RAFTERS

CEILING

SCISSORS TRUSS
MAY BE USED

OPEN BEAM (CATHEDRAL)

BEAM

CEILING

JOIST-RAFTER

TRUSSED RAFTER

TOP CHORD

WEB MEMBER

BOTTOM CHORD

CEILING

PREFABRICATED TRUSS

TOP CHORD

WEB MEMBERS

BOTTOM CHORD

CEILING

SINGLE PITCH (SHED or FLAT)

MAY BE FLAT SLOPE

JOIST-RAFTER

CEILING

BUTTERFLY

JOIST-RAFTER

BEAM

CEILING

BARREL VAULTS
(ONE OF MANY CURVED & WARPED
SURFACES)

SEGMENT OF A CIRCLE, MAY BE
OF WOOD, METAL CONCRETE OR
PLASTIC MATERIALS

CEILING

BEAM

212

FIGURE 23-10   Types of roof construction

trusses are available for various spans; they are listed in Sweet's File. The design of trusses is beyond the scope of this book.

OTHER SYSTEMS

Warped-surface systems are the least common types of roof in use. Concrete is a perfect material for most complex shapes such as conoids, domes, vaults, and hyperbolic paraboloids. Wood and metal can be used for simple warped surfaces, while plywood is especially suitable for barrel vaults and folded-plate roofs.

One type of structure which does not fit readily into the foregoing discussion is the A frame (Fig. 23-10). This system is adaptable to cabins and certain types of commercial buildings.

SURFACE MATERIALS FOR ROOFS

Many methods of weatherproofing the roof are available. Students should choose materials and methods used locally. A brief list of the most common roof materials follows (Fig. 23-11):

1. *Overlapping units:* Including wood shingles and shakes, asphalt shingles, slate, flat and mission tiles, asbestos shingles, and plywood sheets. These materials must be placed on a sloping surface to avoid leaking. Building codes and manufacturers' recommendations concerning the degree of slope must be followed.
2. *Membrane roofs:* Including built-up building paper and asphalt, fiber glass and plastic binder, and concrete. Many other types of fibers are used with many types of binders or waterproofing. These materials may be applied by painting, rolling, spraying, or hot mopping. Membrane roofs may be placed flat or at any desired angle. Some types, particularly bituminous roofs, may be covered with a layer of small rock. This provides mechanical protection and radiant insulation but will limit the pitch of the roof to less than $3:12$.
3. *Metal roofs:* Copper, terneplate, aluminum, lead, galvanized iron, and so on may be used in several ways. The most common joints are overlapping, standing-seam, flat-locked, and soldered. Other methods are also used.

ASSEMBLING A SECTION

Practically any combination of foundation, floor, wall, ceiling, and roof constructions can be sheathed or covered with most exterior and interior materials. Because decisions as to which combination to use are based on diverse factors, it would be difficult to detail the many possibilities here (see Chap. 6). For this reason a number of detailed sectional drawings are included here to demonstrate constructions which meet the demands of many areas of the United States (Figs. 23-12, 23-13, and 23-14).

From the viewpoint of the draftsman, the most useful information used in detailing sections is the various methods of fastening finish materials and veneers to the structure. With this information plus a knowledge of the desired structure, the draftsman can properly detail any condition he might encounter. Of course, the applicable local codes and restrictions must be followed in all details.

DRAINS AND GUTTERS

Gutters, drains, or scuppers must be placed at the eaves or low points of the roof and be connected to downspouts. Pipes, vents, chimneys, and the like which pass through a roof must be provided with waterproof flashings. Flashings must be placed at all valleys in any type but a membrane roof. Gutters, flashings, and so on are described in Chap. 21.

This discussion of roof systems omits most of the methods of construction and special terms; however, they are shown in the accompanying illustrations. Pictures are easier to understand than complex verbal descriptions. The student should avoid the use of any complex roof system in his drawings, because the design of such a roof demands a considerable engineering and practical background.

FASTENINGS

Many means of connecting the structural members of a building are available. For the purpose of this book, only methods applicable to wood will be discussed (Fig. 23-15).

1. Nails are widely used in small structures. They are cheap, available everywhere, and all workmen are

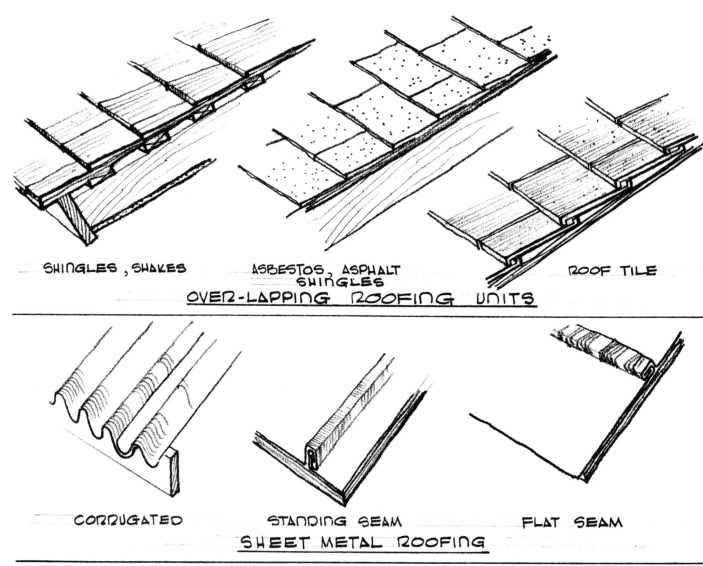

SHINGLES, SHAKES   ASBESTOS, ASPHALT SHINGLES   ROOF TILE

OVER-LAPPING ROOFING UNITS

CORRUGATED   STANDING SEAM   FLAT SEAM

SHEET METAL ROOFING

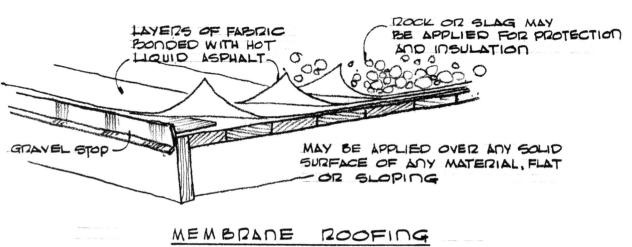

LAYERS OF FABRIC BONDED WITH HOT LIQUID ASPHALT

ROCK OR SLAG MAY BE APPLIED FOR PROTECTION AND INSULATION

GRAVEL STOP

MAY BE APPLIED OVER ANY SOLID SURFACE OF ANY MATERIAL, FLAT OR SLOPING

MEMBRANE ROOFING

214

FIGURE 23-11   Types of roof covering

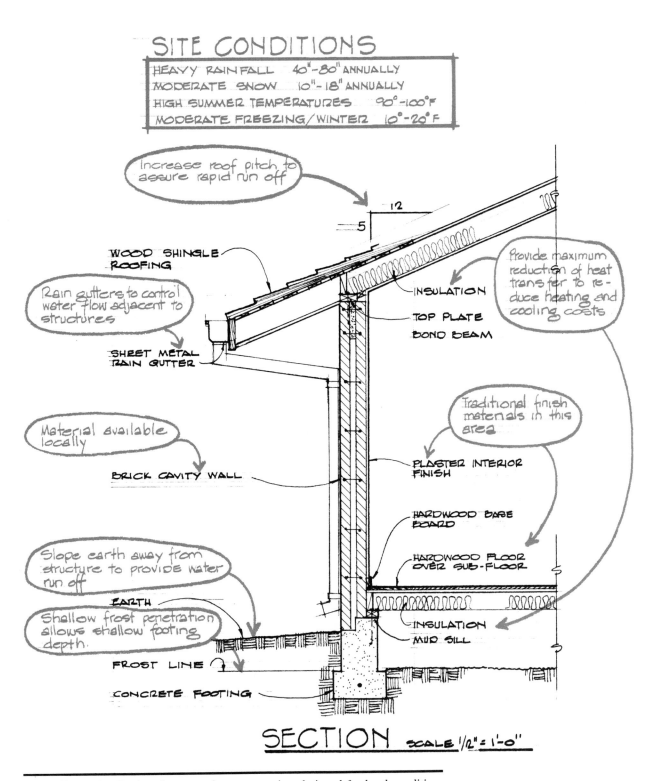

SITE CONDITIONS

HEAVY RAINFALL	40" - 80" ANNUALLY
MODERATE SNOW	10" - 18" ANNUALLY
HIGH SUMMER TEMPERATURES	90° - 100° F
MODERATE FREEZING / WINTER	10° - 20° F

Increase roof pitch to assure rapid run off

WOOD SHINGLE ROOFING

Rain gutters to control water flow adjacent to structures

SHEET METAL RAIN GUTTER

Material available locally

BRICK CAVITY WALL

Slope earth away from structure to provide water run off

EARTH

Shallow frost penetration allows shallow footing depth.

FROST LINE

CONCRETE FOOTING

12
5

INSULATION

TOP PLATE
BOND BEAM

Provide maximum reduction of heat transfer to reduce heating and cooling costs

Traditional finish materials in this area

PLASTER INTERIOR FINISH

HARDWOOD BASE BOARD

HARDWOOD FLOOR OVER SUB-FLOOR

INSULATION
MUD SILL

SECTION SCALE 1/2" = 1'-0"

FIGURE 23-12   Section demonstrating construction designed for local conditions

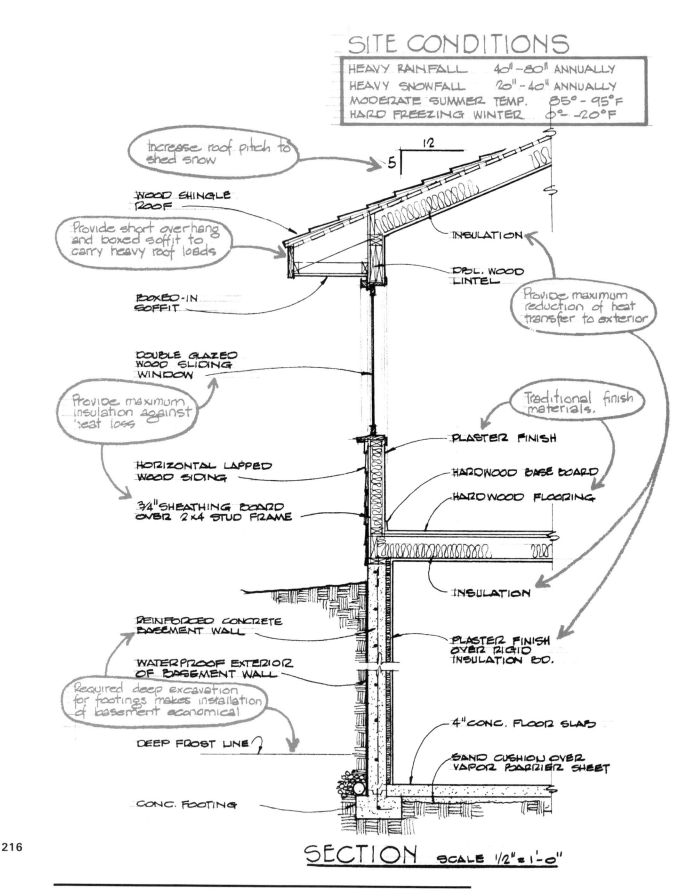

SITE CONDITIONS

HEAVY RAINFALL	40" – 80" ANNUALLY
HEAVY SNOWFALL	20" – 40" ANNUALLY
MODERATE SUMMER TEMP.	85° – 95° F
HARD FREEZING WINTER	0° – 20° F

Increase roof pitch to shed snow

5 | 12

WOOD SHINGLE ROOF

Provide short overhang and boxed soffit to carry heavy roof loads

INSULATION

DBL. WOOD LINTEL

BOXED-IN SOFFIT

Provide maximum reduction of heat transfer to exterior

DOUBLE GLAZED WOOD SLIDING WINDOW

Traditional finish materials.

Provide maximum insulation against heat loss

PLASTER FINISH

HARDWOOD BASE BOARD

HORIZONTAL LAPPED WOOD SIDING

HARDWOOD FLOORING

3/4" SHEATHING BOARD OVER 2x4 STUD FRAME

INSULATION

REINFORCED CONCRETE BASEMENT WALL

PLASTER FINISH OVER RIGID INSULATION BD.

WATERPROOF EXTERIOR OF BASEMENT WALL

Required deep excavation for footings makes installation of basement economical

4" CONC. FLOOR SLAB

DEEP FROST LINE

SAND CUSHION OVER VAPOR BARRIER SHEET

CONC. FOOTING

216

SECTION SCALE 1/2" = 1'-0"

FIGURE 23-13   Section demonstrating construction designed for local conditions

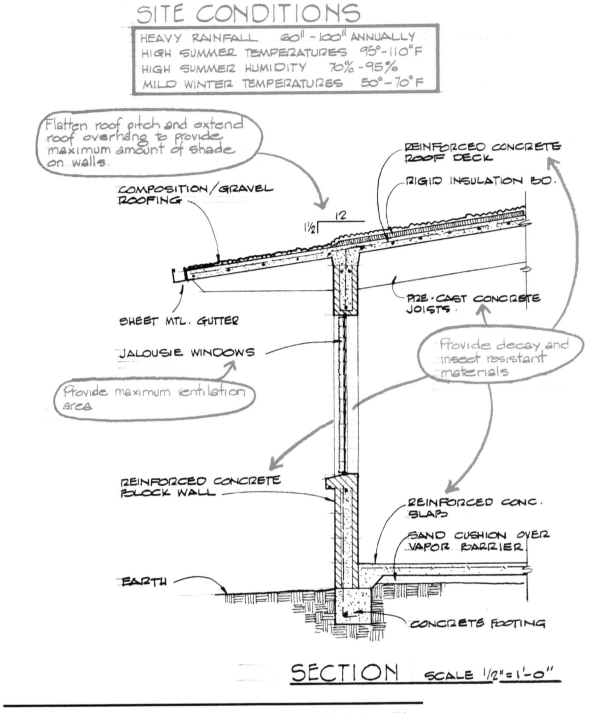

SITE CONDITIONS

HEAVY RAINFALL	60" - 100" ANNUALLY
HIGH SUMMER TEMPERATURES	95° - 110°F
HIGH SUMMER HUMIDITY	70% - 95%
MILD WINTER TEMPERATURES	50° - 70°F

Flatten roof pitch and extend roof overhang to provide maximum amount of shade on walls.

REINFORCED CONCRETE ROOF DECK

RIGID INSULATION BD.

COMPOSITION/GRAVEL ROOFING

1½ 12

PRE-CAST CONCRETE JOISTS

SHEET MTL. GUTTER

JALOUSIE WINDOWS

Provide decay and insect resistant materials

Provide maximum ventilation area

REINFORCED CONCRETE BLOCK WALL

REINFORCED CONC. SLAB

SAND CUSHION OVER VAPOR BARRIER

EARTH

CONCRETE FOOTING

SECTION SCALE ½"=1'-0"

FIGURE 23-14 Section demonstrating construction designed for local conditions

217

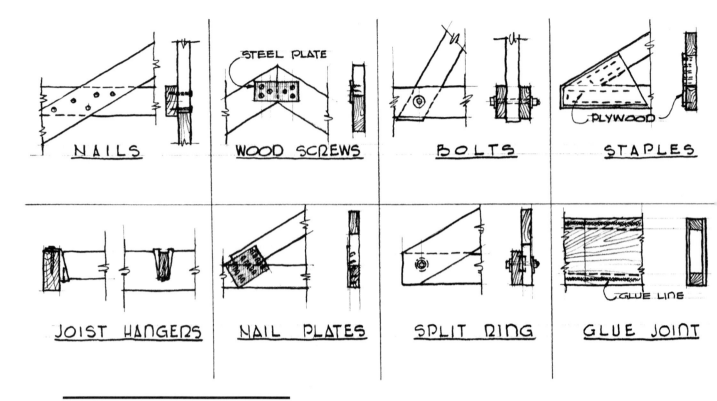

FIGURE 23-15   Typical connecting devices

familiar with their use. On the other hand, they sometimes split the wood, and the resulting joints are relatively weak.

2. Screws are less often used but are useful for attaching beam-seat connections, steel plates, and so on. They are slower to use and more expensive than nails.

3. Bolts are often used in large structures for assembling trusses, attaching beams and plates, and so forth. They make possible very secure joints. They are expensive for some uses and require the drilling of holes.

4. Staples are adaptable to such uses as building box beams and plywood-gusseted trusses. Because air-driven guns are used, staples are faster to drive than nails.

5. Joist hangers are used to eliminate the notching of beams and to reduce carpentry labor.

6. Split-ring connectors may be used to join any two or more intersecting members. The resulting joints are much stronger than nailed joints.

7. Nail plates, because of their tremendous holding power, make it possible to mass-produce trusses cheaply.

8. Adhesives of many types are produced which make it possible to use materials in new ways. Because of the large contact area, glued joints possess tremendous strength.

Some of these joints may be substituted for one another; others, because of design restrictions, building codes, and availability of special equipment, are sometimes specifically indicated. The intelligent application of these methods demands a background of engineering design and practical experience.

TAKING THE VERTICAL SECTION

The cutting-plane line must be carefully placed on the floor plan to create the most useful section. Sometimes more than one section must be shown to demonstrate all conditions necessary for proper construction of the building. Large or complex buildings will require many sections. When only one structural section is indicated for a simple project, it is usually called a "typical section." The cutting-plane line may be offset, or "jogged," if necessary to show important features or to avoid tedious detail.

All details cut by the cutting plane must be shown accurately on the section. In the case of cabinets, for example, shown elsewhere in the set of drawings, only the outline is needed in addition to a note of the location of the detail. All objects cut by the cutting plane must be drawn in strong object lines. Lines generated by the outlines of the section, but beyond the section, should be shown as lighter object lines. All lines representing unrelated objects beyond the section should be omitted for clarity. All of these recommendations should be followed in drafting other sectional drawings of the set, such as window, door, and cabinet sections.

STANDARDS OF ACCURACY

In all drafting, accuracy and scale are extremely important. Any mistake in measurement on a large-scale drawing such as a structural section is particularly serious, first, because large-scale drawings take precedence over small-scale drawings; second, because an experienced person will notice the mistake at a glance; and third, because serious problems can arise when closely related drawings are found to conflict; in fact, many drawings are totally dependent on one or more dimensions of other drawings. For these reasons the draftsman must constantly check critical dimensions from one drawing to another, and he must be extremely careful in drawing all materials to accurate size.

The sizes, spacings, clearances, and so on of all manufactured materials and appliances, such as windows and doors, are furnished by their manufacturers and are easily available. Sizes of common construction materials must be learned by the architectural draftsman. Some of these are:

1. *Rough lumber:* Drawn exactly as described.
2. *Finished lumber:* Varies in size from one area to another. Joists, planks, and beams may have either $\frac{1}{2}$ in. or $\frac{3}{8}$ in. milled from the nominal size. Check local suppliers. Nominal 1-in. sheathing is usually $\frac{3}{4}$ in.
3. *Plywood:* The same size as its nominal size.
4. *Concrete block and bricks:* Also vary according to the locality.

In addition, windows, doors, and other objects in the section must be properly placed and installed. These details are available from the manufacturers' brochures. Certain often-used details such as fixed windows are specified in standard architectural reference books.

DRAFTING THE STRUCTURAL SYSTEM

After deciding on the type of foundation, wall, floor, ceiling, and roof to be used in the section, the actual drafting of the section is very easy. The process follows.

1. Compute sizes of all members used in construction.
2. Decide on the scale to be used and the amount of space the drawing will occupy. Draw a full section or sections using the scale $\frac{1}{2}$ in. = 1 ft 0 in. or greater.
3. Establish the grade line, bottom of footing, top of foundation wall, finish-floor level, and top of plate as construction lines (Fig. 23-16).
4. Establish the width of the footing and foundation wall, size of the floor joists or thickness of the slab, thickness of the wall, and thickness and pitch of the roof structure (Fig. 23-16).
5. Darken outlines of all structural parts.
6. Draw in all structural connections.
7. Draw in all sheathing and finish materials.
8. Dimension all important parts above and below finish floor.
9. Profile outline of section if desired.
10. Place all call-outs and notes.
11. Draw large-scale details showing structural connections.

Note: Check illustrations for method of dimensioning and location of notes. Refer to the drawings which

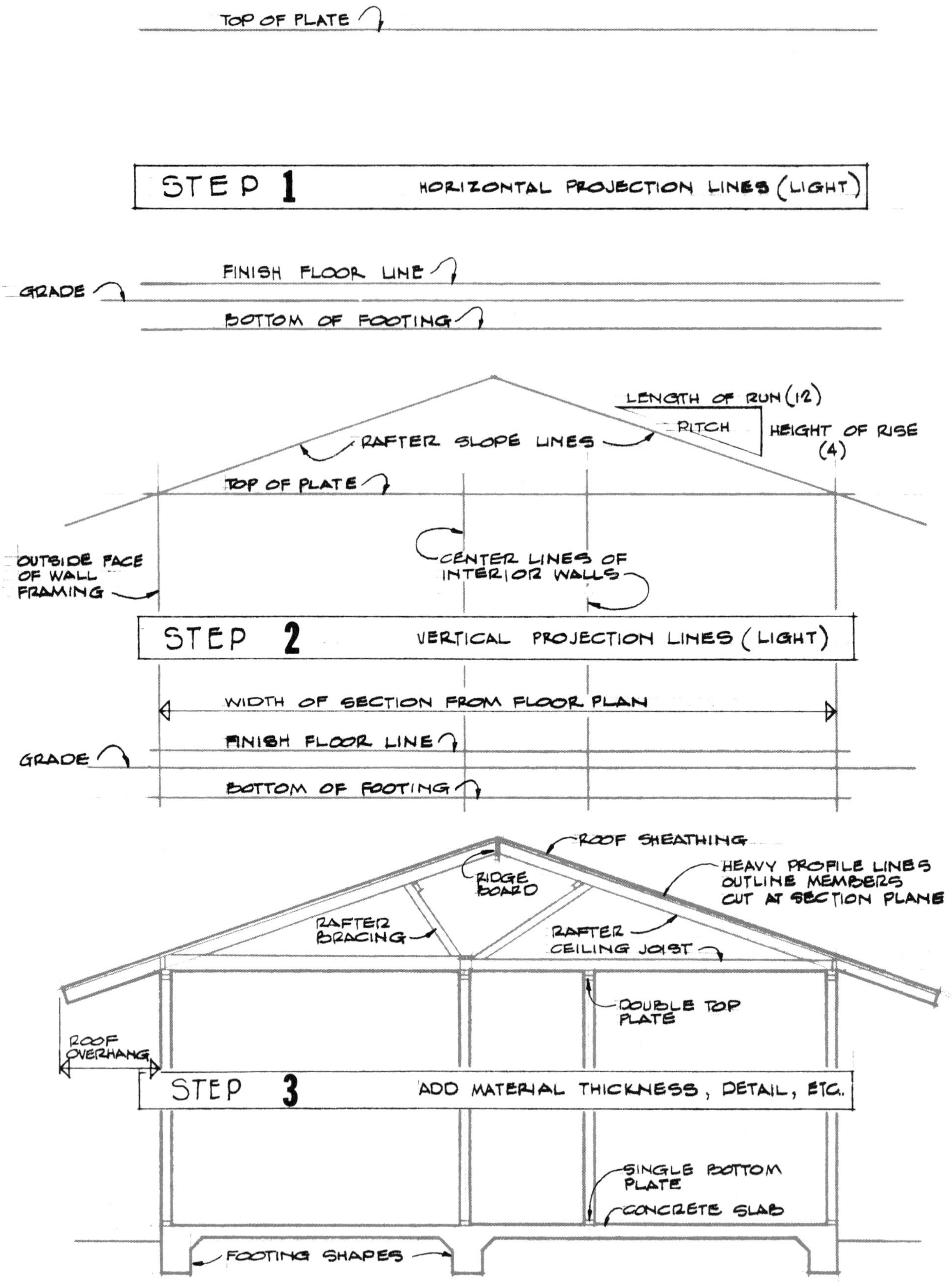

TOP OF PLATE

STEP **1**   HORIZONTAL PROJECTION LINES (LIGHT)

GRADE

FINISH FLOOR LINE

BOTTOM OF FOOTING

LENGTH OF RUN (12)

PITCH

HEIGHT OF RISE (4)

RAFTER SLOPE LINES

TOP OF PLATE

OUTSIDE FACE OF WALL FRAMING

CENTER LINES OF INTERIOR WALLS

STEP **2**   VERTICAL PROJECTION LINES (LIGHT)

WIDTH OF SECTION FROM FLOOR PLAN

GRADE

FINISH FLOOR LINE

BOTTOM OF FOOTING

ROOF SHEATHING

HEAVY PROFILE LINES OUTLINE MEMBERS CUT AT SECTION PLANE

RIDGE BOARD

RAFTER BRACING

RAFTER CEILING JOIST

DOUBLE TOP PLATE

ROOF OVERHANG

STEP **3**   ADD MATERIAL THICKNESS, DETAIL, ETC.

SINGLE BOTTOM PLATE

CONCRETE SLAB

FOOTING SHAPES

220

FIGURE 23-16   Procedures for drafting a structural section

define pictorially the various structural parts of the building.

REVIEW QUESTIONS

1. Look at a picture of a building in a magazine. Can you draw a reasonably accurate cross section of it based on what is visible from the outside? You will have to make a few educated guesses about certain construction features.
2. In a simple gable roof, why do the ceiling joists run in the same direction as the rafters?
3. Does the term *flat roof* always refer to a horizontal roof?
4. Does the building code in your area require that footings for residential construction go deeper than 12 in. below grade? Why?
5. Are concrete floors often used locally in residential construction? Why?
6. Compare brick, wood frame, and hollow concrete-block wall sections. What parts perform similar functions at the top and bottom of the walls?
7. In a simple gable roof, what similar functions do the ceiling joists (flat ceiling) and central beam (open-beam ceiling) perform?
8. Why must shingle roofs be steeper than $4:12$ pitch?
9. *a.* If the total uniformly distributed weight on the perimeter wall of a building is 225,000 lb, the length of the wall is 150 ft, and the bearing capacity of the soil is 2,000 psf, what is the minimum width of continuous running footing which would support the building? (No tables are required.)
   b. Using a bearing capacity of 3,000 psf, what would be the width of the footing?
   c. Under local building codes, what is the minimum width of footing permissible?
10. Assume a 12- by 24-ft rectangular office building with no interior bearing partitions for the following questions. The walls are 8 ft high, and the gable ends are on the 12-ft walls. All joists bear on the 24-ft walls; the roof is $9:12$ pitch with a 2-ft overhang all around. The soil is sandy clay. The building materials are slate roof covering, wood-joist roof structure, wood-joist and acous-

tic-tile ceiling, 2- by 4-in. stud with lath and plaster walls, wood-joist and $\frac{3}{4}$-in. wood floor, and a concrete foundation. Draw a quick perspective sketch of the building for reference, and answer the following questions.
   a. What is the weight of the slate roof material? (Remember that the proportions of the roof-pitch triangle are $3:4:5$.)
   b. What is the weight of the supporting roof structure?
   c. What is the weight of the ceiling structure?
   d. What is the weight of the wall structure on the long walls?
   e. What is the weight of the wall structure on the gable ends?
   f. What is the weight of the floor structure?
   g. What is the weight of the concrete foundation on the long walls? (Assume a cross section close to the size expected—in this case, 6-in. wall, 6 in. above grade; 12- by 6-in. footing, 24 in. below grade. Use 1.5 cu ft per running foot of wall.)
   h. What is the weight of the concrete foundation on the gable-end walls?
11. What are the live loads on the building?
   a. On the roof? (No snow load. Use horizontal distance from eave to eave.)
   b. On the floor?
   c. What is the maximum allowable bearing value of sandy clay?
12. What is the minimum allowable width of the footing on the long walls? (These walls must bear the live and dead loads of the floor and roof, the dead load of the long walls, and the weight of the concrete in the foundations under the long walls.)
13. What is the minimum allowable width of the footing on the gable-end walls? (These walls need only bear the weight of the gable-end wall and the concrete foundation.)
14. What is the minimum width of footing allowed by code?
15. Assume a foundation footing of the following dimensions: $d = 6$ in., $w = 23$ in., $t = 6$ in. Will it be necessary to use reinforcing steel in this footing? (Refer to A-7.) How many No. 4 bars would be needed?
16. What size and spacing of joists are required to span

21 ft under the following conditions: no plaster below (therefore deflection is not critical), 1,450-lb fiber stress, 40-lb live load, 12-in. joist spacing? (Refer to A-8.)

17. What size and spacing of joists are required to span 21 ft under the following conditions: plaster below (therefore deflection must be limited to 1/360 of span), 40-lb live load, 12-in. joist spacing? (Refer to A-8.)

18. What is the maximum span permitted with 3 by 6 sugar-pine decking with a live load of 50 psf? (Refer to A-11.)

19. What is the maximum span permitted using 2 by 6 joists at 16 in. o.c. when there is access to the attic? (Refer to A-9.)

20. What is the maximum span permitted using 2 by 6 joists at 16 in. o.c. when there is no access to the attic? (Refer to A-9.)

21. What size lintel would be required to span 9 ft 0 in. in a single-story frame building? (Refer to A-12a.)

22. *a.* What size wood rafter is required to span 10 ft under the following conditions: 24-in. spacing, 1,200-psi fiber stress, roof slope $2\frac{1}{2}:12$, 20-lb live load + 8-lb dead load? (Refer to A-10.)

    b. What size wood rafter is required to span 10 ft under the above conditions but with a fiber stress of 1,000 psi?

    c. What distance can a wood rafter span under the following conditions: 12-in. spacing, 1,500-psi fiber stress, roof slope $9:12$, 16-lb live load + 8-lb dead load?

23. What is the maximum distance between supports in any direction of an 8-in. reinforced-masonry exterior bearing wall? (Refer to A-13.)

STUDY SUGGESTIONS

1. Compare the drawings of a partially completed building with the actual construction. Try to identify all the structural parts, and describe their functional purposes.
2. Visit the building sites of structures of several different types of construction. Try to determine the practical reasons for the use of each structural system for the particular job.
3. The questions in this section are extremely simple and are based on the use of tables. To get a more comprehensive picture of what is involved, get a textbook on elementary design and study further.

STUDENT PROBLEM

1. Compute the sizes of the foundation elements or use the minimums specified by the building code. Size all structural members using the tables in this book. Check on the sizes of and methods of attaching the finish materials.
2. Draw the structural section based on the above information.

CHAPTER 24
ROOF AND FLOOR FRAMING PLANS

DEFINITION AND PURPOSE

The floor or roof framing plan shows the top view of the floor or roof construction. All structural members are shown in their proper relationships based on the floor plan, structural sections, and elevations. The basic structural analysis and materials selection are made in the preliminary design stage prior to the start of these drawings. The scale of floor and roof framing plans is usually the same as that of the floor plan (Figs. 14-1, and 24-1 to 24-3).

Though all types of construction require framing drawings to complete a set, the problem of describing all systems—wood, metal, and concrete—is too large to be taken up here. A simple wood-frame system is shown complete in the following pages, while portions of other systems will be extracted. Framing systems, however, should be drawn in the order of their construction for logical reasons. Before starting any drawing, the student must learn the functions and symbols for all structural parts used in the plan.

A separate floor framing plan is needed only above the ground floor. In this book, foundation and first-floor framing plans are labeled "Foundation Plan."

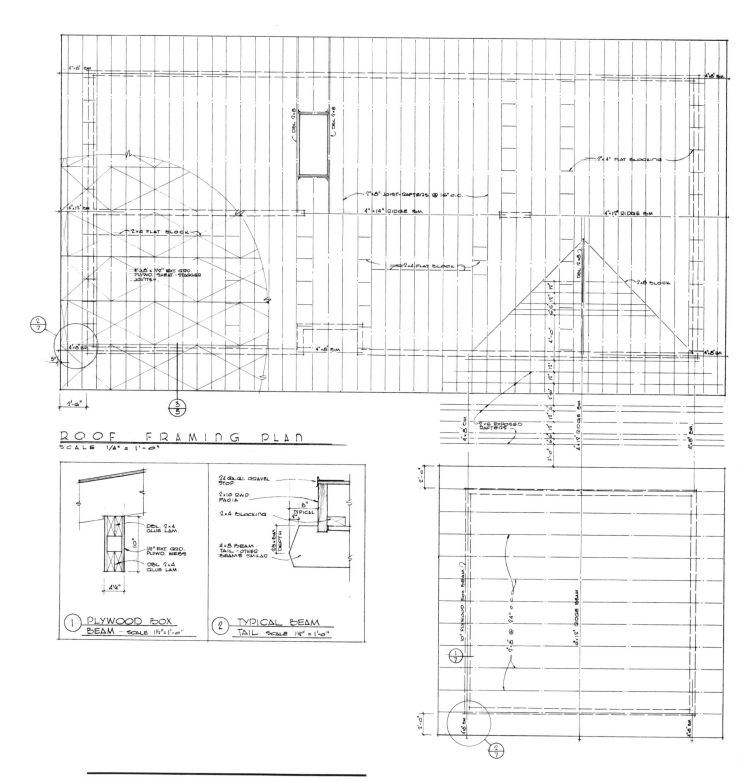

FIGURE 24-1 Roof framing plan of a small residence

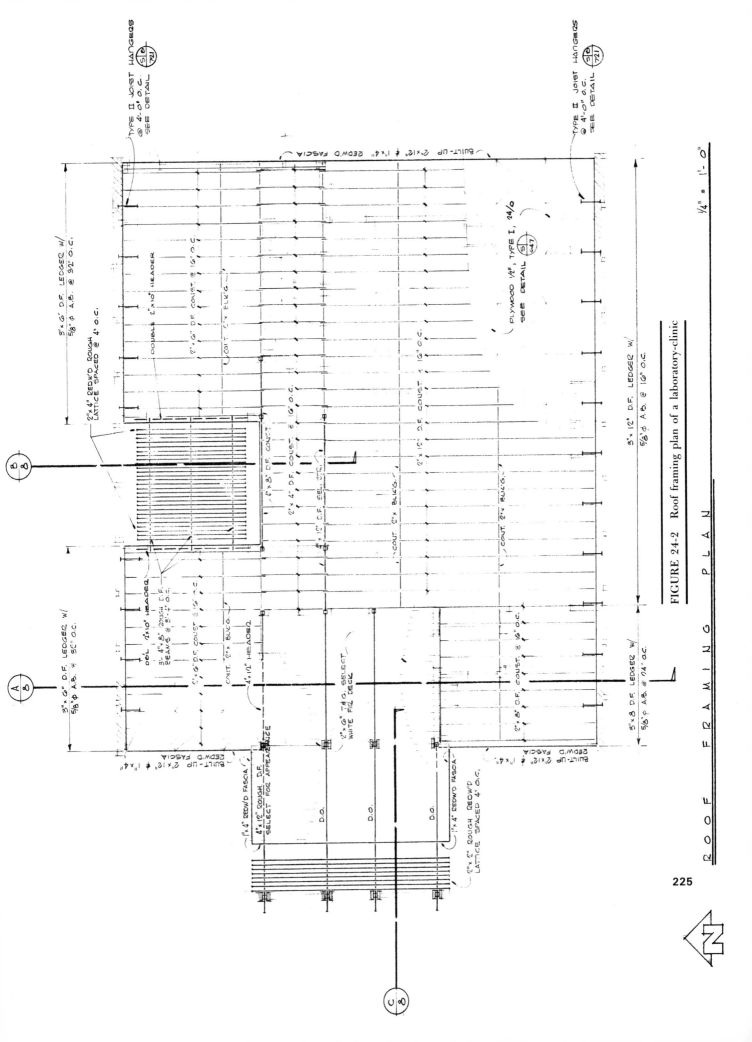

FIGURE 24-2 Roof framing plan of a laboratory-clinic

ROOF FRAMING PLAN

$1/4" = 1'-0"$

225

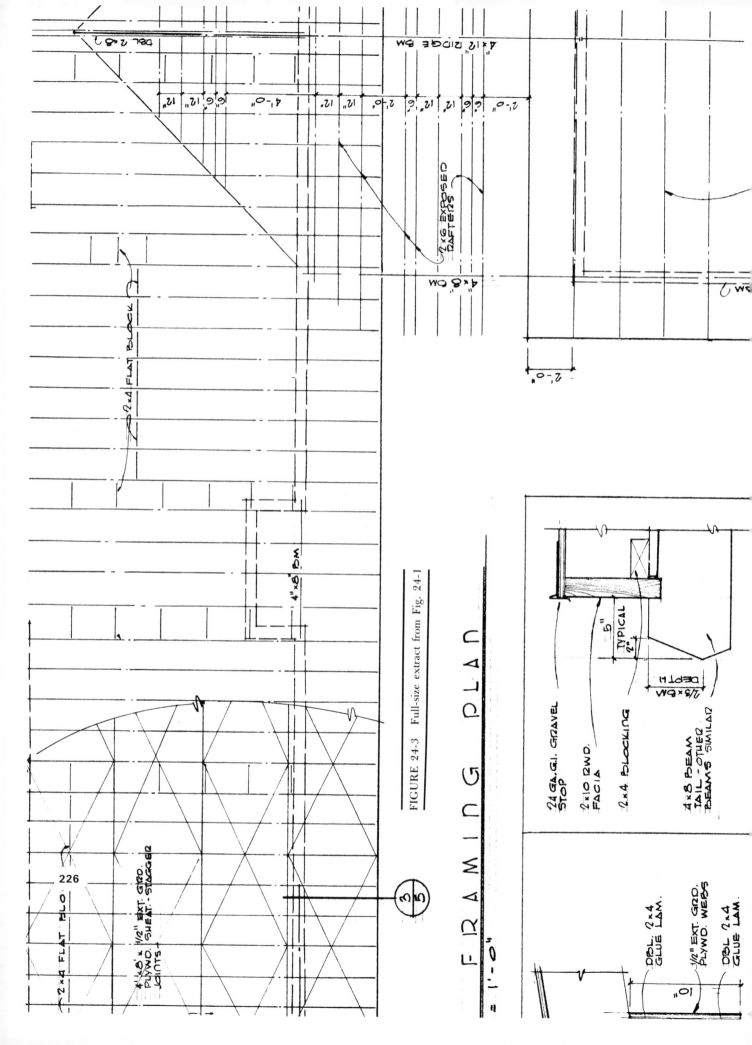

FIGURE 24-3 Full-size extract from Fig. 24-1

F R A M I N G   P L A N
= 1'-0"

226

2×4 FLAT BLO.
4'×8' 1/2" EXT. GRD.
PLYWD. SHEAT. STAGGER
JOINTS

2×4 FLAT BLOCK

DBL. 2×8

4"×12 RIDGE BM

2×6 EXPOSED
RAFTERS

4×8 BM

2'-0" 2'-6" 12" 12" 2'-0" 2'-6" 12" 12" 2'-0" 12" 12" 6'-6" 12" 4'-0" 4'-0"

2'-0"

4"×8" BM

24 GA.G.I. GRAVEL
STOP

2×10 RWD.
FACIA

2×4 BLOCKING

5"
TYPICAL
2"

2/3×BM
DEPTH

4×8 BEAM
TAIL - OTHER
BEAMS SIMILAR

DBL. 2×4
GLUE LAM.

1/2" EXT. GRD.
PLYWD. WEBS

DBL. 2×4
GLUE LAM.

10"

3
5

DRAFTING THE FLOOR FRAMING PLAN

The procedure for drawing a wood-floor framing plan follows (Fig. 22-2):

1. Size all joists, beams, and so on (see A-8).
2. In light lines draw the outline of the structure and the locations of all bearing walls and structures which rest on or pass through the floor.
3. Locate the members which support the floor structure, for example, beams, girders, dwarf walls, as solid lines.
4. Locate all posts or piers which support beams according to their size and shape.
5. Draw in, as solid lines at the proper spacing, the individual joists or beams which support the sub-floor.
6. Where bearing walls are parallel to joists, show doubled joists as center lines; where they are at an angle to joists, show solid blocking as solid lines.
7. Locate with solid lines all headers around stairwells, fireplaces, or other structures which pass through the floor.
8. Dimension where required.
9. Call out all structural members by note. Show size and spacing of all members, use of joist hangers, and so on. Key plan to structural sections.
10. Letter in general notes, title, and scale.

ROOF INTERSECTIONS

Before drawing the roof framing plan it is necessary to locate the important lines of the roof. This information is also needed for the plot plan and the landscape plan.

GENERAL PROCEDURE

1. No matter what type of roof is being shown, the first lines drawn represent the roof overhang.
2. Locate all chimneys or other constructions which pierce the roof. At this point, a flat or one-pitch roof would be complete; it has no ridges, hips, or valleys (Figs. 24-4 and 24-5).

PROCEDURE FOR GABLE ROOFS

1. Same as above.
2. Same as above.
3. Find the center of each span of the building (in the direction of the rafters) and draw a ridge line, assuming that both sides of the roof have the same slope. If there are no intersecting spans, the ridge line completes the construction (Figs. 24-4 and 24-5).
4. If the axis of the building changes, bisect the angle at the eaves and continue this line until it strikes the ridge line of the narrow span; draw a line from this point back to the other eave line of the narrow span. These are valley lines. Usually the spans intersect at 90°, in which case the valley lines are drawn at 45°. This is true also in the construction of valleys on a hip roof (Figs. 24-4 and 24-5).

PROCEDURES FOR HIP ROOFS

1. Same as General Procedure.
2. Same as General Procedure.
3. Hip lines bisect the angles of the eaves at the roof corners. They are drawn until they intersect; the ridge continues from this intersection point as with a gable roof. Most roofs have 90° corners in plan; therefore these hip lines are at 45° (Figs. 24-4 and 24-5).

PROCEDURE FOR BOSTON OR HAWAIIAN GABLES

Boston or Hawaiian gables are merely small gables in the ends of hip roofs, and are constructed accordingly (Figs. 24-4 and 24-5).

VARYING PLATE LINES

In the preceding cases it has been assumed that the plate heights and slopes of all spans were the same.

227

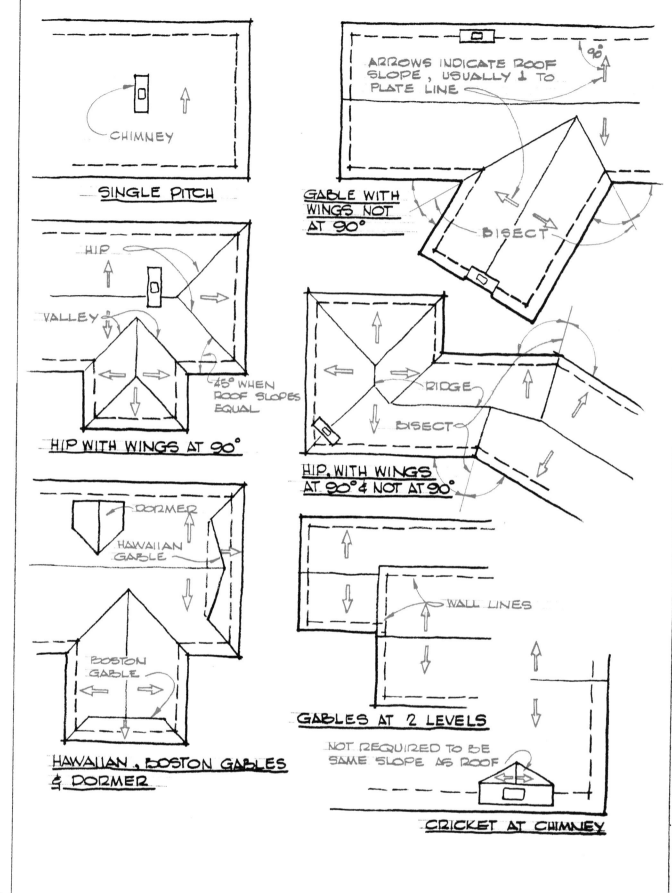

SINGLE PITCH

CHIMNEY

GABLE WITH WINGS NOT AT 90°

ARROWS INDICATE ROOF SLOPE, USUALLY ⊥ TO PLATE LINE

BISECT

HIP WITH WINGS AT 90°

HIP

VALLEY

45° WHEN ROOF SLOPES EQUAL

HIP, WITH WINGS AT 90° & NOT AT 90°

RIDGE

BISECT

HAWAIIAN, BOSTON GABLES & DORMER

DORMER

HAWAIIAN GABLE

BOSTON GABLE

GABLES AT 2 LEVELS

WALL LINES

CRICKET AT CHIMNEY

NOT REQUIRED TO BE SAME SLOPE AS ROOF

228

FIGURE 24-4   Roof intersections of various types of roofs of constant plate height

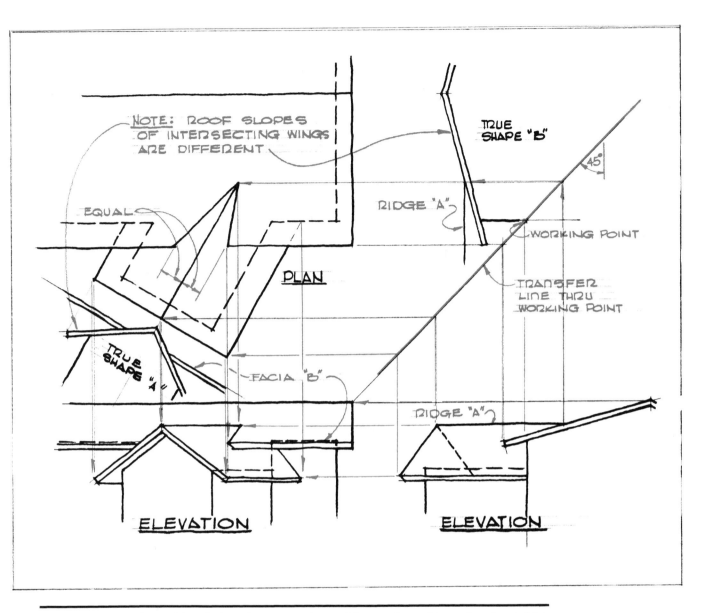

FIGURE 24-5   Orthographic solution of more complex roof intersections with varying plate heights

When plate heights or slopes vary, it is necessary to solve the problem orthographically (Fig. 24-5).

CRICKETS

It is inadvisable in the usual simple structure to have a trough, or horizontal valley, of any length, because such a trough could lead to a leaking roof. When a trough occurs, as at a wide chimney parallel to a ridge or at an intersection between parallel ridges, a *cricket* is constructed. A cricket is merely a small gable with a ridge perpendicular to the trough or chimney. It eliminates the danger spot in the drainage system of the roof (Fig. 24-4).

DRAFTING THE ROOF FRAMING PLAN

The procedure for drawing a wood-frame roof framing plan follows (Fig. 24-1).

229

1. Size all rafters, beams, and so on (see A-9 to A-11).
2. In dashed lines draw the outline of the structure, the location of all bearing walls, structures which pass through the roof, and the extent of the roof overhang.
3. Locate any members, such as beams, which support the roof structure as object or center lines.
4. Draw any posts or columns which support the beams according to their size and shape.
5. Draw in as light lines the breaks of the roof surface, such as ridges, hips, and valleys.
6. Draw in as object lines all ridges, hips, valleys, and so on.
7. Draw in with solid lines the individual rafters at the proper spacing.
8. Locate as object lines all headers around structures which pass through the roof.
9. Draw in the fascia board, if required, as an object line.
10. Dimension where required.
11. Call out the structural members by note; show size and spacing of all members, and use of hangers, clips, plates, rings. Key the plan to the structural sections.
12. Letter in general notes, title, and scale.

REVIEW QUESTIONS

1. Define the terms: joist, rafter, beam, header, solid blocking, column.
2. Draw a plan view of the construction used to frame an opening through a floor.
3. Define the terms: ridge, hip, valley, cricket, fascia, gravel stop, soffit.

STUDY SUGGESTIONS

1. Visit a building under construction, and compare the floor and roof structure with the symbols on the drawing.
2. Compare a trussed-roof system with a joist-rafter system. Consider such things as type of labor used in building, speed of erection, and size of spans.
3. Study the design of simple braced and trussed roof structures in a book on elementary design.

STUDENT PROBLEM

The structural section, floor plan, and plot plan are used when drawing the roof and floor framing plans.

1. Size all of the structural members in the roof.
2. Draft the roof framing plan.
3. The floor framing plan is required only above the first floor. If one is needed, follow the procedure outlined in this chapter.

CHAPTER 25
PLUMBING PLAN

DEFINITION AND PURPOSE

The plumbing plan is a plan view of the building, traced from the floor plan, which shows all plumbing lines and fixtures above and below the ground. Soil and waste lines, gas lines, hot- and cold-water lines, steam, air and gas lines, vents, and all fixtures and appliances (connected or proposed) are described. The sizes and types of all lines and fittings are described by note (Figs. 25-1 to 25-4). Extensions of lines and appliances beyond the lines of the floor plan are often shown on the plot plan.

Dimensioning is used for safety in critical areas, especially in locating fixtures. The lengths of pipelines are seldom given. The plumbing plan is closely coor-dinated with the floor plan, foundation plan, electrical plan, and heating and ventilating plans. In some cases isometric drawings are used to clarify certain details of construction.

When drawing the plumbing plan, refer to the plan views of plumbing symbols and lines (see A-27). Consult the Appendix for pipe, waste, and vent sizes (see A-28 to A-37).

DEFINITIONS

Waste and soil lines are gravity-flow drains which connect to all toilets, tubs, and other fixtures and carry solid and liquid waste matter to the house drain. The

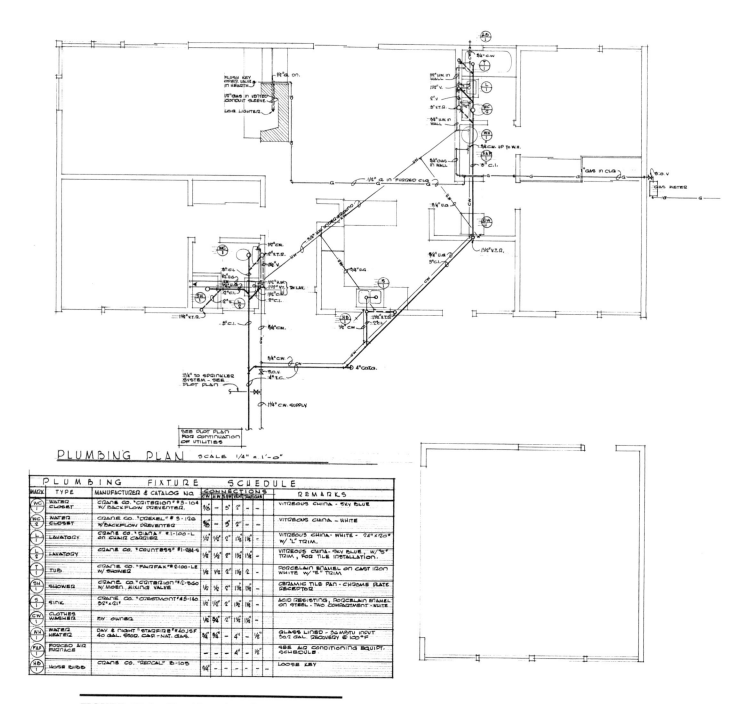

PLUMBING PLAN SCALE 1/4" = 1'-0"

PLUMBING	FIXTURE	SCHEDULE								
MARK	TYPE	MANUFACTURER & CATALOG NO.	CONNECTIONS							REMARKS
			C.W.	H.W.	W.	V.	TRAP	GAS		
WC 1	WATER CLOSET	CRANE CO. "CRITERION" #3-104 W/ BACKFLOW PREVENTER	3/8"	–	5"	2"	–	–		VITREOUS CHINA - SKY BLUE
WC 2	WATER CLOSET	CRANE CO. "DREXEL" #3-126 W/ BACKFLOW PREVENTER	3/8"	–	5"	2"	–	–		VITREOUS CHINA - WHITE
L 1	LAVATORY	CRANE CO. "DIANA" #1-100-L ON CHAIR CARRIER	1/2"	1/2"	2"	1½"	1¼"	–		VITREOUS CHINA- WHITE - 24"x20" W/ "L" TRIM
L 2	LAVATORY	CRANE CO. "COUNTESS" #1-284-S	1/2"	1/2"	2"	1½"	1¼"	–		VITREOUS CHINA- SKY BLUE, W/ "S" TRIM, FOR TILE INSTALLATION
T 1	TUB	CRANE CO. "FAIRFAX" #2-100-LE W/ SHOWER	1/2"	1/2"	2"	1½"	2"	–		PORCELAIN ENAMEL ON CAST IRON WHITE W/ "E" TRIM
SH 1	SHOWER	CRANE CO. "CRITERION" #2-360 W/ MOEN MIXING VALVE	1/2"	1/2"	2"	1½"	1¾"	–		CERAMIC TILE PAN - CHROME PLATE RECEPTOR
S 1	SINK	CRANE CO. "CRESTMONT" #5-180 32"x21"	1/2"	1/2"	2"	1½"	1¼"	–		ACID RESISTING, PORCELAIN ENAMEL ON STEEL - TWO COMPARTMENT - WHITE
CW 1	CLOTHES WASHER	BY OWNER	1/2"	3/4"	2"	1½"	1½"	–		
WH 1	WATER HEATER	DAY & NIGHT "STARFIRE" #40JSF 40 GAL. STOR. CAP.- NAT. GAS	3/4"	3/4"	–	4"	–	1/2"		GLASS LINED - 36 MBTU INPUT 50.2 GAL. RECOVERY @ 100°F
FAF 1	FORCED AIR FURNACE		–	–	–	4"	–	1/2"		SEE AIR CONDITIONING EQUIPT. SCHEDULE
HB 1	HOSE BIBB	CRANE CO. "REDCAL" B-105	3/4"	–	–	–	–	–		LOOSE KEY

FIGURE 25-1   Plumbing plan of a small residence

232

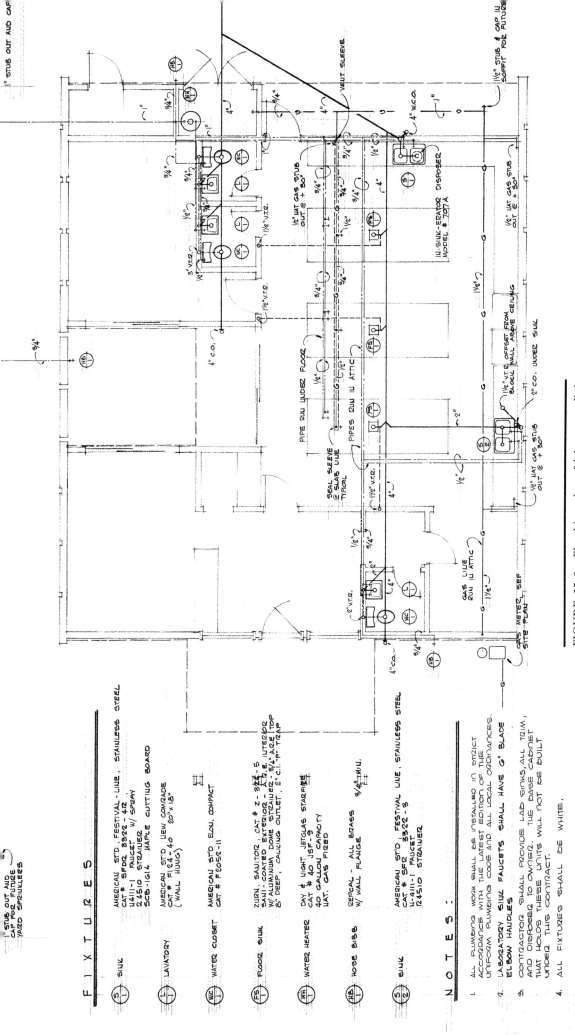

FIGURE 25-2 Plumbing plan of laboratory-clinic

233

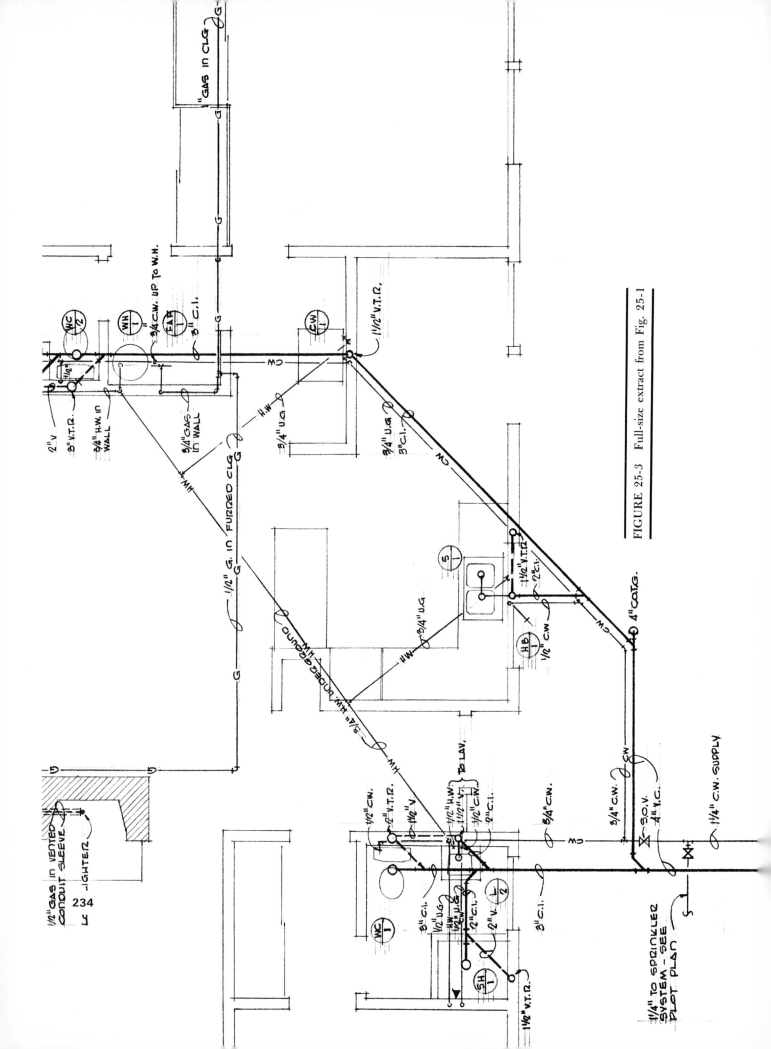

FIGURE 25-3 Full-size extract from Fig. 25-1

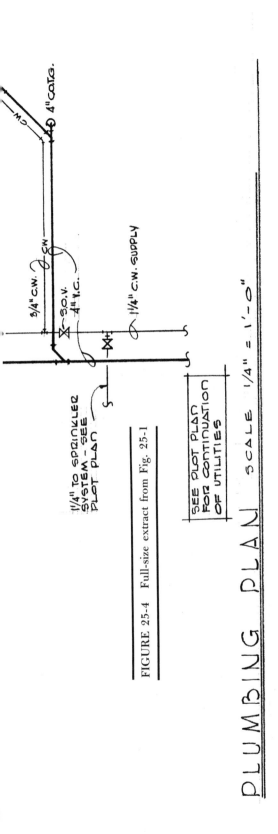

3/4" C.W.

4" C.ôTG.

C.W.

1 1/4" TO SPRINKLER SYSTEM - SEE PLOT PLAN

S.O.V.
4" V.C.

1 1/4" C.W. SUPPLY

SEE PLOT PLAN FOR CONTINUATION OF UTILITIES

FIGURE 25-4 Full-size extract from Fig. 25-1

PLUMBING PLAN SCALE 1/4" = 1'-0"

PLUMBING FIXTURE SCHEDULE

MARK	TYPE	MANUFACTURER & CATALOG NO.	CONNECTIONS						REMARKS
			CW	HW	S&W	VENT	TRAP	GAS	
WC 1	WATER CLOSET	CRANE CO. "CRITERION" #3-104 W/BACKFLOW PREVENTER.	3/8"	-	3"	2"	-	-	VITREOUS CHINA - SKY BLUE
WC 2	WATER CLOSET	CRANE CO. "DREXEL" #3-126 W/BACKFLOW PREVENTER	3/8"	-	3"	2"	-	-	VITREOUS CHINA - WHITE
L 1	LAVATORY	CRANE CO. "DIANA" #1-100-L ON CHAIR CARRIER	1/2"	1/2"	2"	1 1/2"	1 1/2"	-	VITREOUS CHINA - WHITE - 24"x20" W/"L" TRIM.
L 2	LAVATORY	CRANE CO. "COUNTESS" #1-284-S	1/2"	1/2"	2"	1 1/2"	1 1/4"	-	VITREOUS CHINA - SKY BLUE, W/"S" TRIM., FOR TILE INSTALLATION.
T 1	TUB	CRANE CO. "FAIRFAX" #2-100-LE W/SHOWER	1/2"	1/2"	2"	1 1/2"	2	-	PORCELAIN ENAMEL ON CAST IRON WHITE W/"E" TRIM
SH 1	SHOWER	CRANE CO. "CRITERION" #2-360 W/MOEN MIXING VALVE	1/2"	1/2"	2"	1 1/2"	1 1/2"	-	CERAMIC TILE PAN - CHROME PLATE RECEPTOR
S 1	SINK	CRANE CO. "CRESTMONT" #5-140 32"x21"	1/2"	1/2"	2"	1 1/2"	1 1/2"	-	ACID RESISTING, PORCELAIN ENAMEL ON STEEL - TWO COMPARTMENT - WHITE
CW 1	CLOTHES WASHER	BY OWNER	1/2"	3/4"	2"	1 1/2"	1 1/2"	-	
WH 1	WATER HEATER	DAY & NIGHT "STARFIRE" #40JSF 40 GAL. STOR. CAP. - NAT. GAS.	3/4"	3/4"	-	4"	-	1/2"	GLASS LINED - 36 MBTU INPUT 30.2 GAL. RECOVERY @ 100°F
FAF 1	FORCED AIR FURNACE		-	-	-	4"	-	1/2"	SEE AIR CONDITIONING EQUIPT. SCHEDULE
HB 1	HOSE BIBB	CRANE CO. "REDCAL" B-103	3/4"	-	-	-	-	-	LOOSE KEY

235

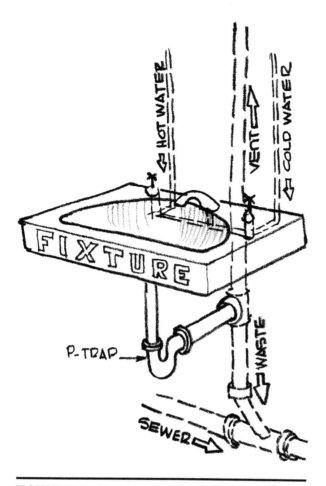

FIGURE 25-5   Typical fixture, showing trap, vent, supply, and waste lines

1. The locations, types, and sizes of all fixtures must be determined. Many of these decisions are based on practical experience.
2. Locate all serving utilities—gas, steam, sewer, water, and so on—and decide how and where they will be connected to the building.
3. Compute the sizes of all lines to all fixtures. This includes the lines which serve heating and refrigeration machinery, elevators, hoists, and so forth. Start computing the load at the most remote fixture, and work toward the serving utility, the meter, the shutoff valve, and so on.
4. Locate all traps, cleanouts, vents, check valves, pressure reducers. These are always called for in the plumbing code or the fixture manufacturer's literature.
5. Locate and size all fittings: tees, ells, wyes, and the like.
6. Prepare a list of fixtures, and list all connections serving each one. For instance, a kitchen sink requires hot-water, cold-water, drain, and convenience-outlet connections. This information should all be placed in the plumbing schedule.

house drain becomes the house sewer or house trap when it passes beyond the foundation line. The house sewer is connected to the sewer main which is located in the street, alley, or sewer easement.

All fixtures require a trap or water seal ahead of the waste line to prevent gases and vermin from entering the house through the drain. In addition, each fixture or group of fixtures must have a vent. The vent permits air to enter the drains as wastes are drained away (Figs. 25-5 and 25-6).

DESIGN

Before the working drawing can be started, many
decisions and computations must be made.

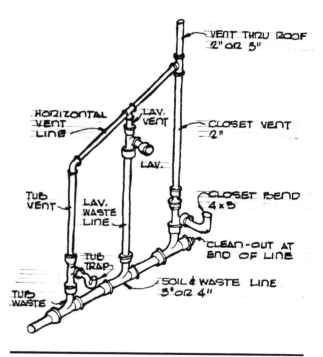

FIGURE 25-6   Isometric drawing of bathroom plumbing, showing types of fittings used

DRAFTING THE SOIL AND WASTE LINES

The procedure for drawing the soil and waste lines follows (Figs. 25-1 and 25-3):

1. Choose the fixtures, toilets, sinks, tubs, showers, and size the lines (see A-28 and A-29).
2. Trace the floor plan on the back of the paper. See Working Drawings (Fig. 13-5).
3. Draw construction lines from each fixture to the house drain. Check the local code for the number of fixtures to each line. Draw the house drain to a point which will be convenient to the sewer main or septic tank. Locate all plumbing vents according to code. Draw in taps and fittings.

4. Darken all lines. The exact location of taps, fittings, and so on is left to the judgment of the plumber.
5. Call out the size and material of all piping.

DRAFTING THE WATER LINES

Hot- and cold-water lines provide water under pressure ($\pm$ 45 psi) to all fixtures. The procedure for drawing the hot- and cold-water lines follows:

1. Choose the fixtures, hot-water tank, water softener, and so on, and size the lines (see A-30 and A-31).
2. Draw construction lines from the main shutoff valve to all fixtures which require cold water. Consult the local building code. Next, run lines to the water heater from all fixtures which require hot water.

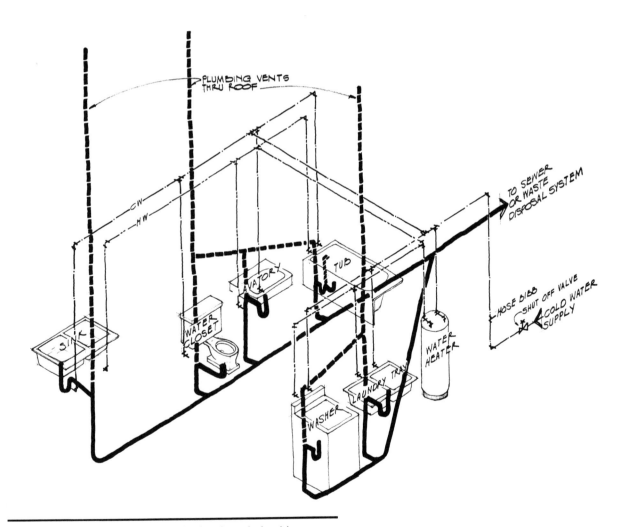

FIGURE 25-7 One-line isometric drawing of plumbing system

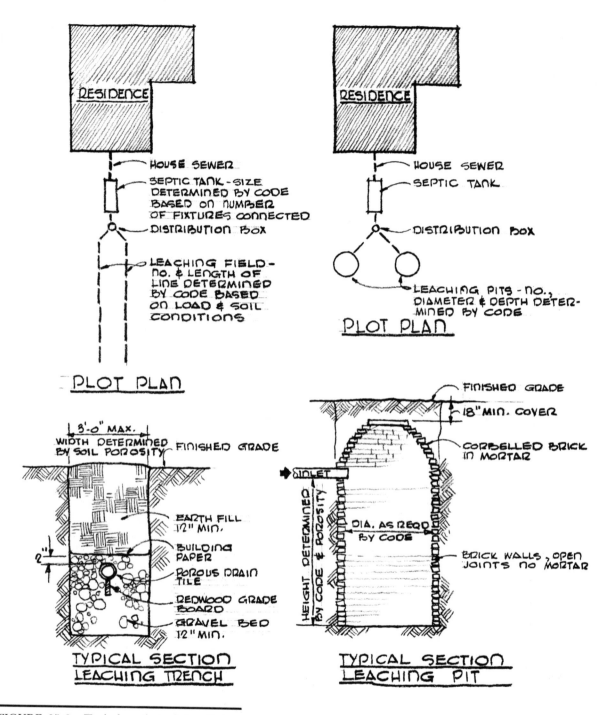

RESIDENCE

HOUSE SEWER

SEPTIC TANK - SIZE
DETERMINED BY CODE
BASED ON NUMBER
OF FIXTURES CONNECTED

DISTRIBUTION BOX

LEACHING FIELD -
NO. & LENGTH OF
LINE DETERMINED
BY CODE BASED
ON LOAD & SOIL
CONDITIONS

PLOT PLAN

RESIDENCE

HOUSE SEWER

SEPTIC TANK

DISTRIBUTION BOX

LEACHING PITS - NO.,
DIAMETER & DEPTH DETER-
MINED BY CODE

PLOT PLAN

3'-0" MAX.
WIDTH DETERMINED
BY SOIL POROSITY   FINISHED GRADE

2"

EARTH FILL
12" MIN.

BUILDING
PAPER

POROUS DRAIN
TILE

REDWOOD GRADE
BOARD

GRAVEL BED
12" MIN.

TYPICAL SECTION
LEACHING TRENCH

FINISHED GRADE

18" MIN. COVER

CORBELLED BRICK
IN MORTAR

INLET

HEIGHT DETERMINED
BY CODE & POROSITY

DIA. AS REQD
BY CODE

BRICK WALLS, OPEN
JOINTS NO MORTAR

TYPICAL SECTION
LEACHING PIT

FIGURE 25-8 Typical septic tank installations

Parallel the hot- and cold-water lines where possible (Figs. 25-1 and 25-2).

3. Darken all lines.
4. Call out the size and material of all pipes. The type of fittings to be used is often left to the plumber.

DRAFTING THE GAS LINES

The gas lines supply natural or bottled gas to all required fixtures. The drawing procedure follows:

1. Size supply lines based on the capacity of heating units. Use the manufacturer's recommendations (see A-32 and A-33).
2. Using construction lines, run lines from all fixtures to the gas meter or point of entrance (Figs. 25-1 and 25-2).
3. Darken all lines.
4. Call out the size and material of all pipes.

Other plumbing lines, which are used mostly in commercial occupancies, are steam lines, air, oxygen, and other gas lines. The procedure for drawing them is identical to that described above.

SCHEDULES

The plumbing plan includes a tabular schedule which has the following headings (Fig. 25-4):

1. *Symbol:* Shape of the fixture as shown on the drawing.
2. *Type:* Name of the fixture.
3. *Location:* Fixture symbol, such as WC 2, sink 3.
4. *Manufacturer and Number:* Taken from the catalog.
5. *Connections:* For instance, a kitchen sink would show HW, hot water; CW, cold water; T, trap; V, vent; S & W, soil and waste; Elec, electrical, if there is a garbage disposal.

In certain situations where a plan drawing might be misinterpreted, isometric drawings of plumbing installations are sometimes made. These are usually one-line drawings using symbolic fittings. The single line represents the center line of the pipe. Sometimes the isometrics are drawn to scale (Fig. 25-7).

SEPTIC TANKS

In areas where sewers are not available, septic tanks are required for the sanitary disposal of waste (Figs. 25-8, 25-9, and 25-10). The size of tank and the length of leaching lines are controlled by local codes. The septic tank and leaching field are not usually drawn on the plumbing plan but are placed on the plot plan. Sizes of septic tanks and leaching fields are based on the number of fixtures, rate of use, and soil conditions (A-34 to A-37).

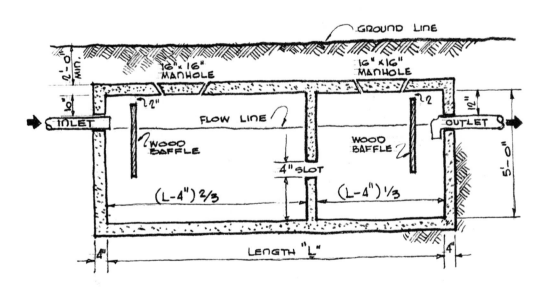

FIGURE 25-9 Section through a typical septic tank

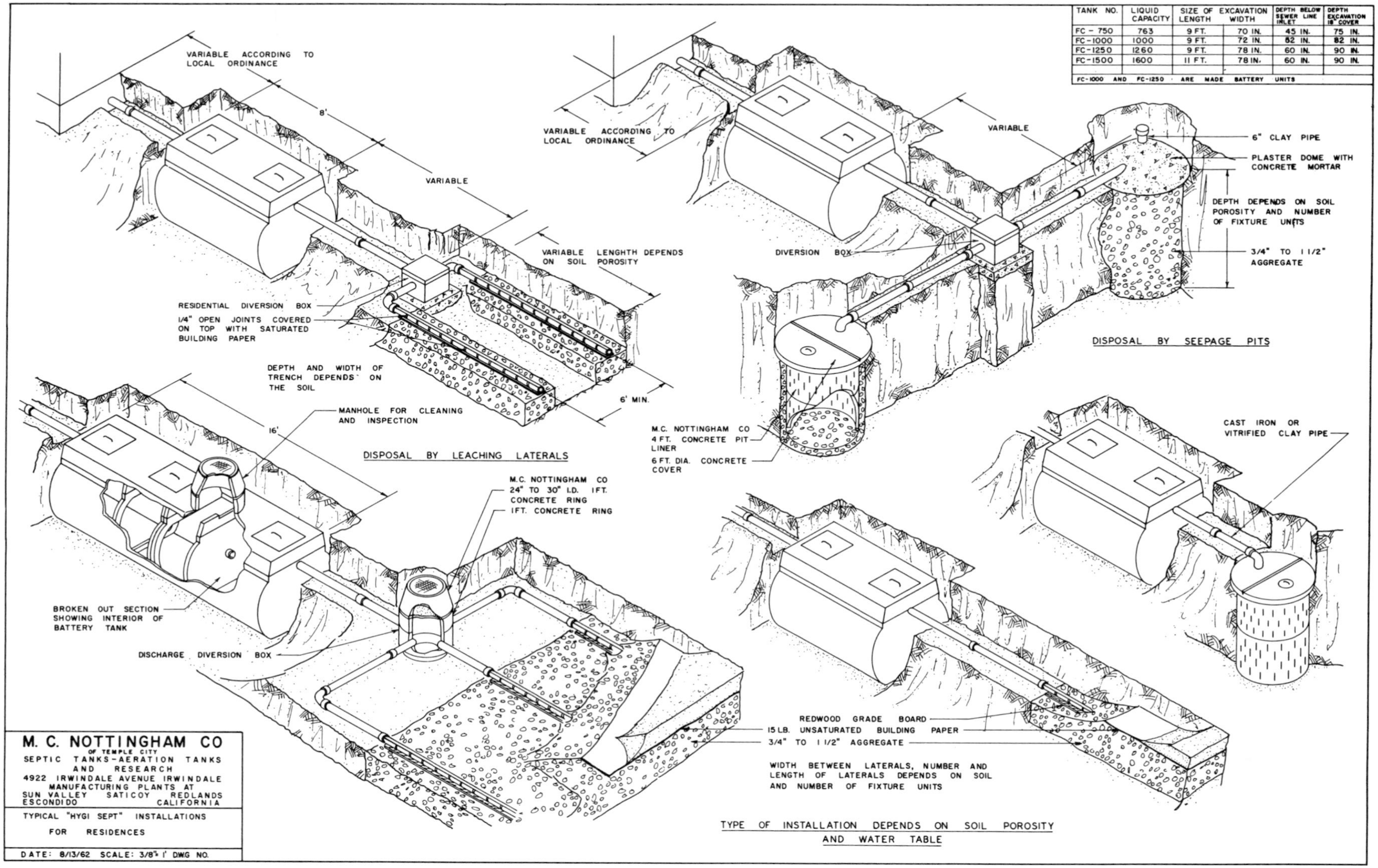

TANK NO.	LIQUID CAPACITY	SIZE OF EXCAVATION LENGTH	WIDTH	DEPTH BELOW SEWER LINE INLET	DEPTH EXCAVATION 18" COVER
FC - 750	763	9 FT.	70 IN.	45 IN.	75 IN.
FC - 1000	1000	9 FT.	72 IN.	62 IN.	82 IN.
FC - 1250	1260	9 FT.	78 IN.	60 IN.	90 IN.
FC - 1500	1600	11 FT.	78 IN.	60 IN.	90 IN.

FC-1000 AND FC-1250 ARE MADE BATTERY UNITS

FIGURE 25-10 Typical septic tank installation (M. C. Nottingham Company)

REVIEW QUESTIONS

1. Why are toilets, sinks, and so on drawn to scale, and convenience outlets, switches, and the like drawn as symbols?
2. What is the function of a trap?
3. What is the function of a vent?
4. Draw a cross section of a sink, its trap, its vent, and the drain. What would happen if the vent were to become stopped up while the sink was draining?
5. Why are vents and traps used on waste and soil lines but not on hot- and cold-water lines?
6. Using the table A-28, determine the following:
   a. What is the trap size for a bathtub?
   b. A toilet is equivalent to how many fixture units?
   c. A toilet, bathtub, floor drain, clothes washer, shower, residential sink, three washbasins, and a drinking fountain together are equivalent to how many fixture units?
7. Using the table A-29, determine the following:
   a. As drainage piping, how many fixture units can a 6-in. pipe carry horizontally?
   b. As drainage piping, how many fixture units can a 4-in. pipe carry vertically?
   c. As drainage piping, how many feet can a 4-in. pipe run vertically?
   d. As vent piping, how many fixture units can a 3-in. pipe carry?
8. Using the table A-30, determine the following:
   a. For public use, a toilet is equivalent to how many fixture units of water demand?
   b. For private use, a hose bibb is equivalent to how many fixture units of water demand?
9. Using the table A-31, determine the following in a flush-tank system at 40 psi:
   a. What is the maximum number of fixture units which can be handled through a 1-in. meter and a 1¼-in. building-supply pipe over a maximum distance of 80 ft?
   b. What size meter would be required to handle 445 fixture units up to a distance of 40 ft?
10. Using the table A-32, determine the following:
    a. What is the demand in cubic feet per hour of a domestic gas range?
    b. What is the total demand of a 50-gal storage water heater plus a clothes dryer and a barbeque?

11. Using the table A-33, determine the following:
    a. In a system with a length of 70 ft, what size pipe would be required to handle the total load in problem 10b?
    b. If the length were 300 ft for the same demand, would a 1-in. pipe be large enough?
12. Using the table A-34, determine the following:
    a. What is the minimum distance from a stream that a cesspool may be located?
    b. What is the minimum distance between two disposal fields using 3-ft-wide trenches?
13. Using the table A-35, determine the following:
    a. How many gallons of water per day are required per machine in a self-service laundry?
    b. How many gallons of water per day are required by a 30-seat restaurant?
14. Using the table A-36, determine the following:
    a. What is the minimum capacity of a septic tank for a four-bedroom single dwelling?
    b. What is the minimum capacity of a septic tank for a six-unit apartment building with one-bedroom apartments?
    c. What is the minimum capacity of a septic tank for any occupancy using 90 fixture units per day?
    d. In a single dwelling, how many bedrooms would be permitted if the septic tank were of 2,000-gal capacity?
15. Using the table A-37, how many square feet of absorption area are needed in fine sand for a septic tank of 1,200-gal capacity?

STUDY SUGGESTIONS

1. Visit a plumbing-supply house; look at the various fixtures, piping, fittings, and so on, and note how they are put together.
2. Go to a building under construction, and compare the plumbing fixtures and fittings with the symbols on the plumbing plan.

STUDENT PROBLEM

Draft the plumbing plan, consulting the rough floor plan and plot plan as you do. The type and number of fixtures may be decided by you or by the client.

CHAPTER 26
HEATING, VENTILATING, AND AIR-CONDITIONING PLAN

DEFINITION AND PURPOSE

The heating, ventilating, and air-conditioning plan is a plan view of the building traced from the floor plan and showing all heating, ventilating, and air-conditioning equipment above and below ground (Figs. 26-1, 26-2, 26-5, and 26-6). Sizes and types of all lines, ducts, and equipment are called out by note. Dimensioning is occasionally required in critical areas, particularly the equipment room.

The heating, ventilating, and air-conditioning plan is most closely coordinated with the structural sections and the floor, foundation, plumbing, and electrical plans. Scale is the same as the floor plan. In some cases, elevations and isometric drawings are used to clarify certain details of construction.

DESIGN

Any complex or unusual heating or air-conditioning system should be designed by an engineer. A simple, conventional system can be developed by a draftsman using tabular data.

The computations involved in the design of a heating or cooling system, regardless of type, are as follows:

1. The heat loss or gain of the structure under the

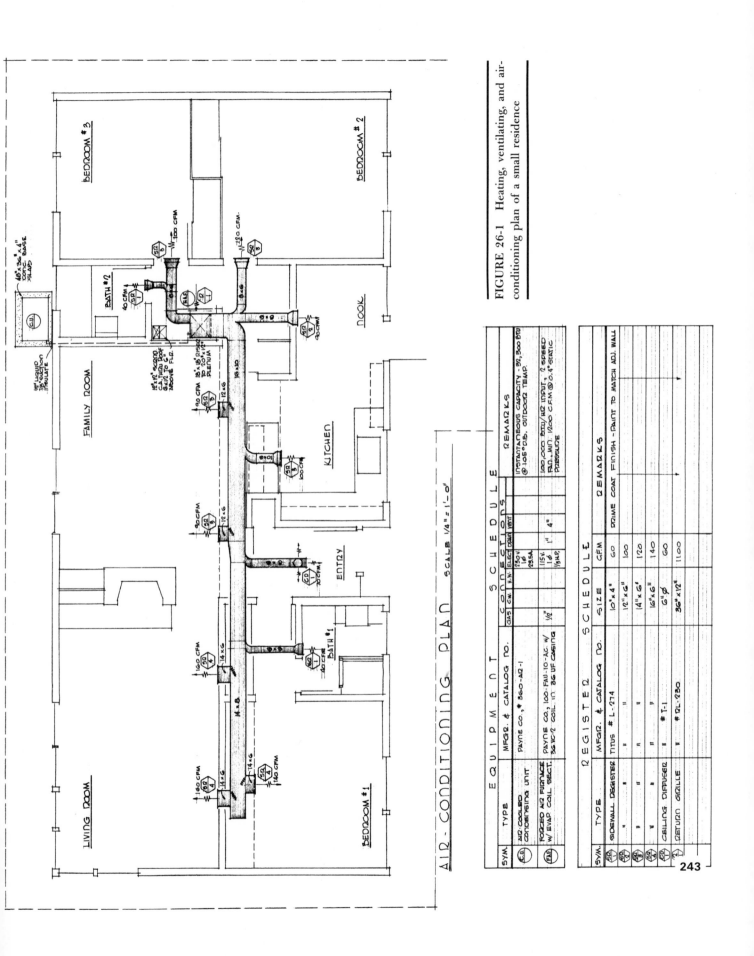

FIGURE 26-1 Heating, ventilating, and air-conditioning plan of a small residence

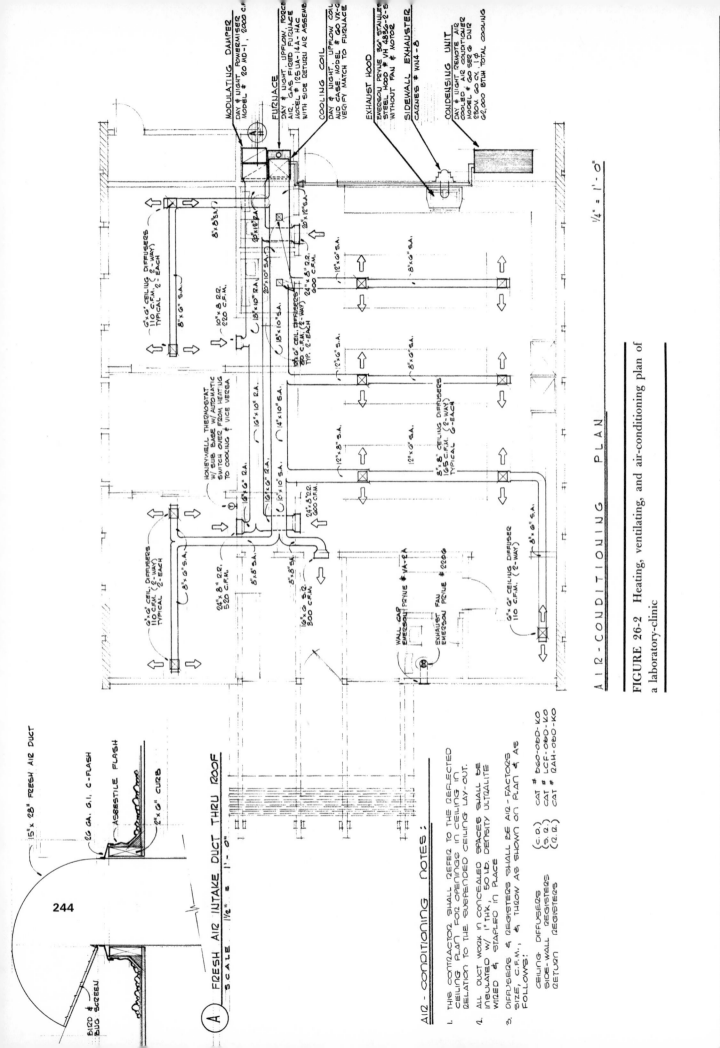

FIGURE 26-2 Heating, ventilating, and air-conditioning plan of a laboratory-clinic

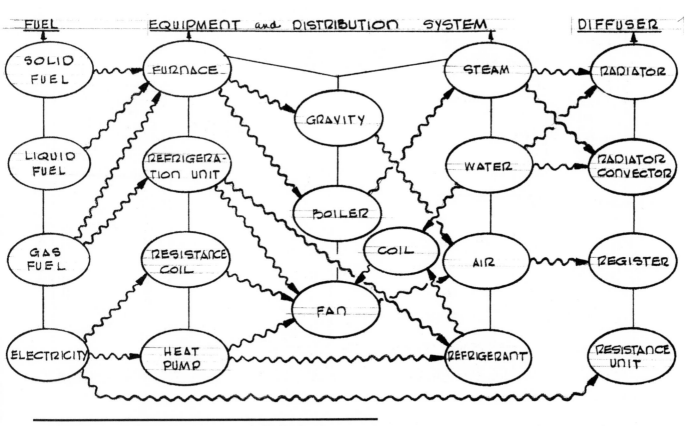

FIGURE 26-3   Methods of producing and distributing heat energy

most severe conditions expected must be determined.

2. The most effective system for producing and distributing the heating or cooling must be chosen. The size of the heating or cooling equipment is based on the above figures.

3. Sizes of all conductors (pipes, ducts, wires, and so on) to each room must be sized to provide the proportional amount of air, water, steam, or electric current required in each room.

4. Heat exchange devices must be located throughout the structure in relation to the demands of each area. These devices may be registers, radiators, coils, resistance elements, or the like. Sizes are based on the volume of air or amount of heat energy needed at each point.

5. Thermostats must be located where they will be exposed to the average temperature of the room in which they are located.

6. Provision must be made for all fuel, electric, water,

steam, and other lines running to the heat machines—furnace, refrigeration equipment, and so on.

7. Essential elements in the operation of the system must be provided, such as fuel storage bins or tanks, condensing coils, water-cooling towers, and dry wells.

The process of determining exactly the heating and cooling requirements of a building, choosing and sizing the equipment, and planning the distribution system involves considerable experience and many computations. The interested student should study one of the references cited in the bibliography. Abbreviated computation forms, or "short forms," which are available shorten and simplify the process. Because these forms are widely used and are reasonably accurate, the heating and cooling loads for the student project will be based on the use of a short form.

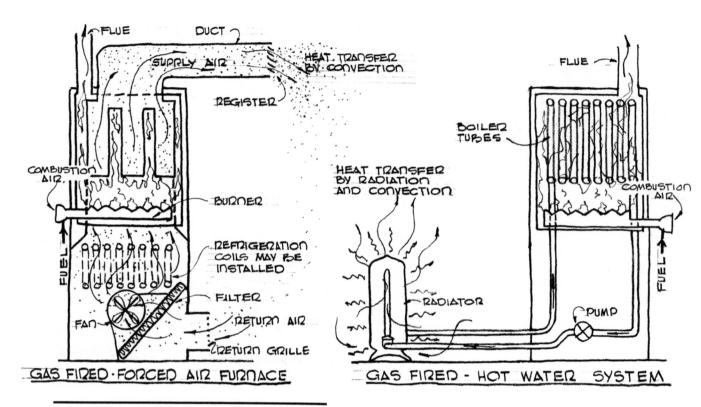

FIGURE 26-4   Cross sections of two typical furnaces

TYPES OF SYSTEMS

Of the many possible combinations of equipment and means of exchanging heat, one system has been chosen to demonstrate the use of the short form (Figs. 26-3 and 26-4). The short form in the Appendix provides heating and cooling load estimates for forced-air heating and cooling (see A-23). Short forms are available for use with other systems and are obtainable from most heating-equipment manufacturers. Evaporative coolers, which have been found to work well only in areas of low humidity, are sized according to local practice.

DRAFTING THE HEATING, VENTILATING, AND AIR-CONDITIONING PLAN

The procedure for drawing the heating and ventilating plan follows (Figs. 26-1 and 26-2):

1. Select and compute the size of the heating and/or cooling unit required; size ducts, pipes, radiators, and so on (see A-19 to A-25).

2. Trace the floor plan on the back of the tracing paper (Fig. 13-5).

3. Place the heating and/or cooling equipment. If the job calls for a simple floor or wall heater, placing of the unit and thermostat completes the drawing. In this case, however, no separate drawing would be needed. All the information could easily be put on the floor plan. Following are the items of equipment required for each type of job:

   a. *Heating alone:* Furnace, boiler, or other heating device

   b. *Heating and evaporative cooling:* Furnace and evaporative cooler

   c. *Heating and refrigerated cooling:* Furnace, cooling coils, compressor, and condenser and/or dry well

   d. *Heat-pump heating and cooling:* Compressor and inside and outside coils

4. Locate the radiators, coils, registers, air returns, or other means of exchanging heat and/or air (Fig. 26-5).

5. Run the water, electric, gas, or oil lines to the heating equipment. Indicate fuel tanks or storage if required.

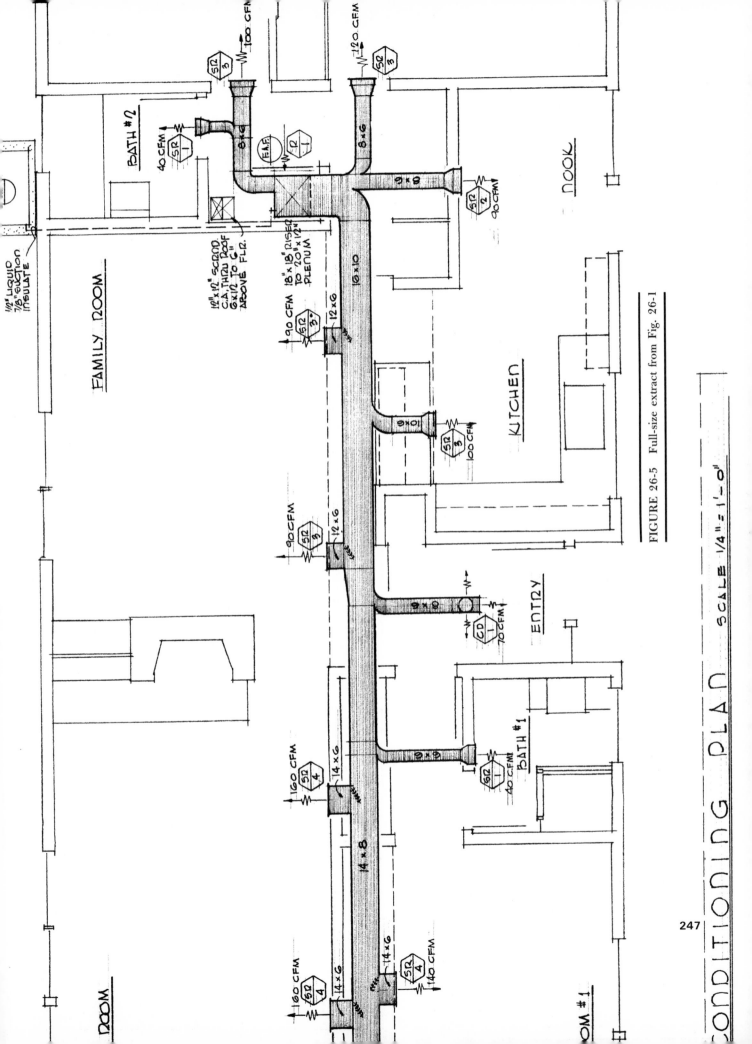

FIGURE 26-5 Full-size extract from Fig. 26-1

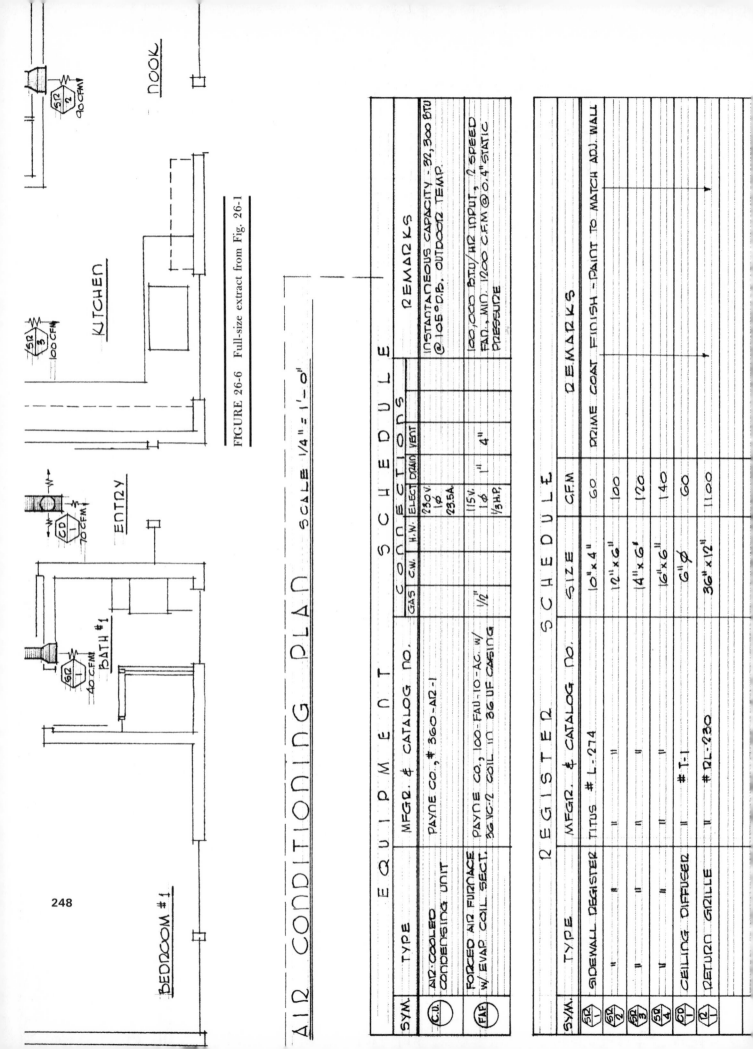

BEDROOM #1

BATH #1

ENTRY

KITCHEN

NOOK

FIGURE 26-6 Full-size extract from Fig. 26-1

248

AIR CONDITIONING PLAN   SCALE 1/4" = 1'-0"

EQUIPMENT SCHEDULE

SYM.	TYPE	MFGR. & CATALOG NO.	CONNECTIONS						REMARKS
			GAS	C.W.	H.W.	ELECT.	DRAIN	VENT	
CU 1	AIR-COOLED CONDENSING UNIT	PAYNE CO., # 360-A2-1				230V 1Ø 23.5A			INSTANTANEOUS CAPACITY - 32,300 BTU @ 105°D.B. OUTDOOR TEMP.
FAF 1	FORCED AIR FURNACE W/ EVAP. COIL SECT.	PAYNE CO., 100-FAU-10-A.C. W/ 36VC-2 COIL IN 36 UF CASING	1/2"			115V 1Ø 1/3 H.P.	1"	4"	100,000 BTU/HR INPUT, 2 SPEED FAN, MIN. 1200 C.F.M @ 0.4" STATIC PRESSURE

REGISTER SCHEDULE

SYM.	TYPE	MFGR. & CATALOG NO.	SIZE	C.F.M	REMARKS
512/1	SIDEWALL REGISTER	TITUS # L-274	10"x4"	60	PRIME COAT FINISH - PAINT TO MATCH ADJ. WALL
512/2	"	"	12"x6"	100	
512/3	"	"	14"x6"	120	
512/4	"	"	16"x6"	140	
CD/1	CEILING DIFFUSER	" #T-1	6"Ø	60	
R/1	RETURN GRILLE	" #RL-230	36"x12"	1100	

6. Run the distribution lines between the heating equipment and the radiators, registers, radiant panels, or returns. Heating ducts are drawn to scale. Steam and water pipes are drawn as single lines, and sizes are called out.
7. Place thermostats and other controls.
8. Draw the equipment schedule.
9. Key the equipment to the equipment schedule.
10. Letter all notes including title and scale.

Further information concerning distribution systems may be found in the Appendix.

SCHEDULES

Schedules are used with heating, ventilating, and air-conditioning plans to identify the symbols used on the drawing. The following headings and items of information should be shown (Fig. 26-6):

1. The indoor and outdoor design conditions for summer and winter are usually placed at the top.
2. *Symbol:* Mark identifying each part, for example, register, diffuser, condenser, furnace, heat pump, and thermostat
3. *Number:* Quantity of each unit required
4. *Manufacturer:* Trade name
5. *Model:* Catalog number
6. *Connections:* Electrical and horsepower rating, vent, drain, suction, liquid, gas, and so on
7. *Output in Btu/hr:* For cooling and heating
8. *Equipment finish*
9. *Remarks:* Any further explanation

Other classifications may be included. These symbols are supplemented by additional notes on the drawing.

REVIEW QUESTIONS

1. Name three heating systems. How and by what medium is heat transferred in each case?
2. Why are certain objects drawn to scale and others drawn as symbols on the air-conditioning plan?
3. Assuming the following data for heating—inside design temp. = 75°F, outside design temp. = 25°F, design temp. diff. = 70°F—and using the short forms shown in A-23, determine the following values:
   a. Heat loss in Btu/hr for 35 sq ft of double-hung window in 40 lin ft of exposed light-masonry wall.
   b. Heat loss through a 15- by 20-ft ceiling with $3\frac{5}{8}$-in. insulation.
   c. Heat loss through slab on grade floor 15 by 20 ft.
   d. Correct the heat-loss figure of 8,000 Btu/hr at 70°F to the design temperature difference of 40°F.
   e. Determine the room cfm for 9,000 Btu/hr and a register temperature of 140°F.
4. Assuming the following data for cooling—outside design temp. = 100°F, daily temp. range = 20°F—and using the short forms shown in A-23, determine the following values:
   a. Solar transmission heat gain through windows and doors with a 24-in. overhang, eastern exposure, and 30 sq ft of sash area.
   b. Heat gain through a sunlit light-masonry wall 20 ft long with no overhang.
   c. Heat gain through a sunlit 2-in. insulated frame wall 20 ft long with a 48-in. overhang.
   d. Heat gain through a pitched roof with 2-in. ceiling insulation, no attic ventilation, and 12 by 30 ft in size.
   e. Using a correction factor of 1.17 and a value of 4,000 Btu/hr before correction, what is the corrected value?
5. With the help of A-24, A-25, and A-26, determine the following:
   a. Using a 20- by 6-in. register with a single deflection damper, what is the throw in feet at 200 cfm?
   b. Using a 40- by 10-in. floor outlet, what is the spread in feet at 120 cfm?
   c. What diameter ceiling outlet should be used for a discharge of 220 cfm?
   d. What size sidewall return grille would be used to handle 900 cfm of return air?
   e. What sizes of rectangular supply ducts will handle 2,500 cfm in a residential application?
   f. What sizes of rectangular supply ducts will handle 2,500 cfm in a commercial application?
6. What is the inside design temperature recommended for a store in summer? (Use A-19.)

STUDY SUGGESTIONS

1. Go to an air-conditioning-supply warehouse; inspect the many types of furnaces, air-conditioning units, registers, radiators, and so on; and note how they are used in a building.
2. Visit a building under construction, and compare the air-conditioning system with the drawings.
3. Compute the heat loss of your own house in winter, using the reference tables and formula. You may have to make an educated guess as to the wall insulation.
4. Study the basic principles of air conditioning in a text such as "Modern Air Conditioning Practice." Compare the results of the computation of heating loads with the results obtained by the use of short forms.

STUDENT PROBLEM

Weather conditions, fuel supplies, and individual preference vary so greatly that it would be pointless to specify a certain type of heating system for the student project. Therefore, it must be the instructor's responsibility to determine the type of heating or air-conditioning system for his students.

The locations and sizes of air-conditioning ducts and piping must usually be carefully checked against the floor, foundation, roof, and floor framing plans and the structural section.

1. Size all components using the tables in the Appendix.
2. Choose the air-conditioning units and locate them.
3. Draw the air-conditioning plan.

CHAPTER 27
ELECTRICAL PLAN

DEFINITION AND PURPOSE

The electrical drawing is a plan view of the building traced from the floor plan showing the service entrance and meter, all the electric outlets and controls in the house, and a description of all the symbols used on the drawing (Figs. 27-1 to 27-3). Electrical design and engineering should be done by someone competent in that field; however, a draftsman can use charts and tables to satisfy simple, standard conditions.

ELECTRICAL SERVICE

The point at which the electric power enters the building from the utility company's lines is called the service entrance. Current may enter the service entrance switchgear from overhead or through an underground conduit. This must be checked with the power company before starting the wiring layout (see A-15).

In most residential and light-commercial construction today, three wires are run in to provide 120/240-volt single-phase 60-cycle alternating current. Sometimes only two wires are run in, but then only 120-volt single-phase 60-cycle alternating current will be available. It is better to specify three-wire service, because 240 volts is much more efficient for heavy loads or long runs of wire.

An electric meter is wired in ahead of everything else; its purpose is to measure the total amount of electric energy used in that building. Next in line is the service entrance switch, or disconnect, which is

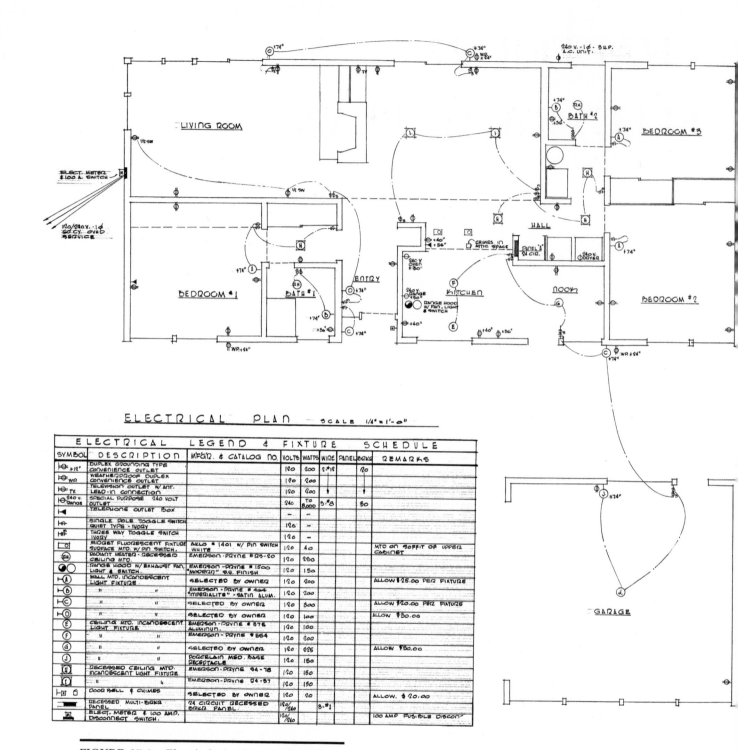

FIGURE 27-1   Electrical plan for a small residence

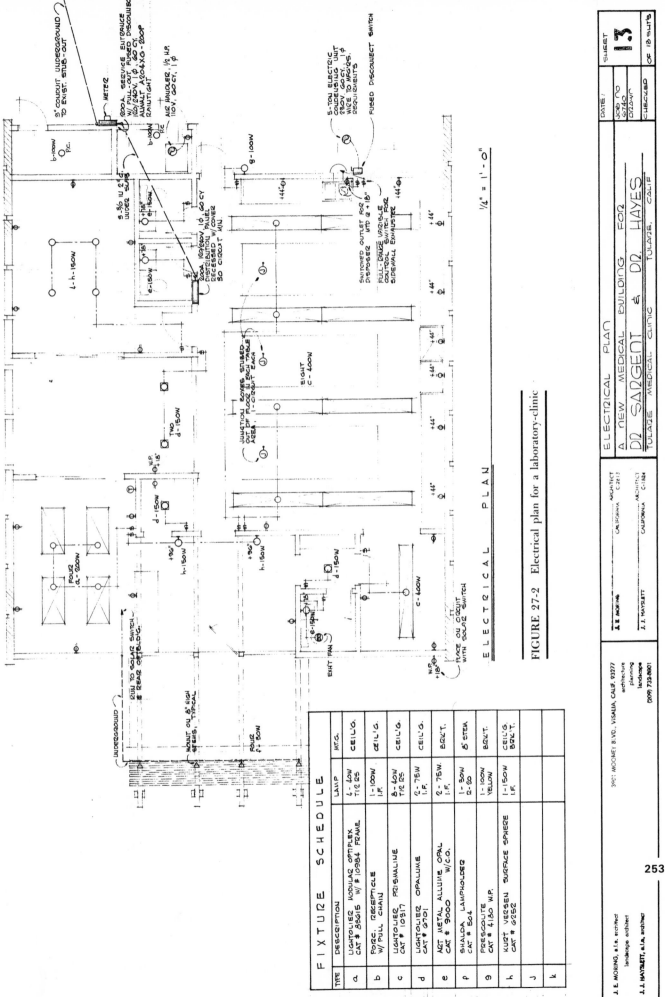

FIGURE 27-2 Electrical plan for a laboratory-clinic

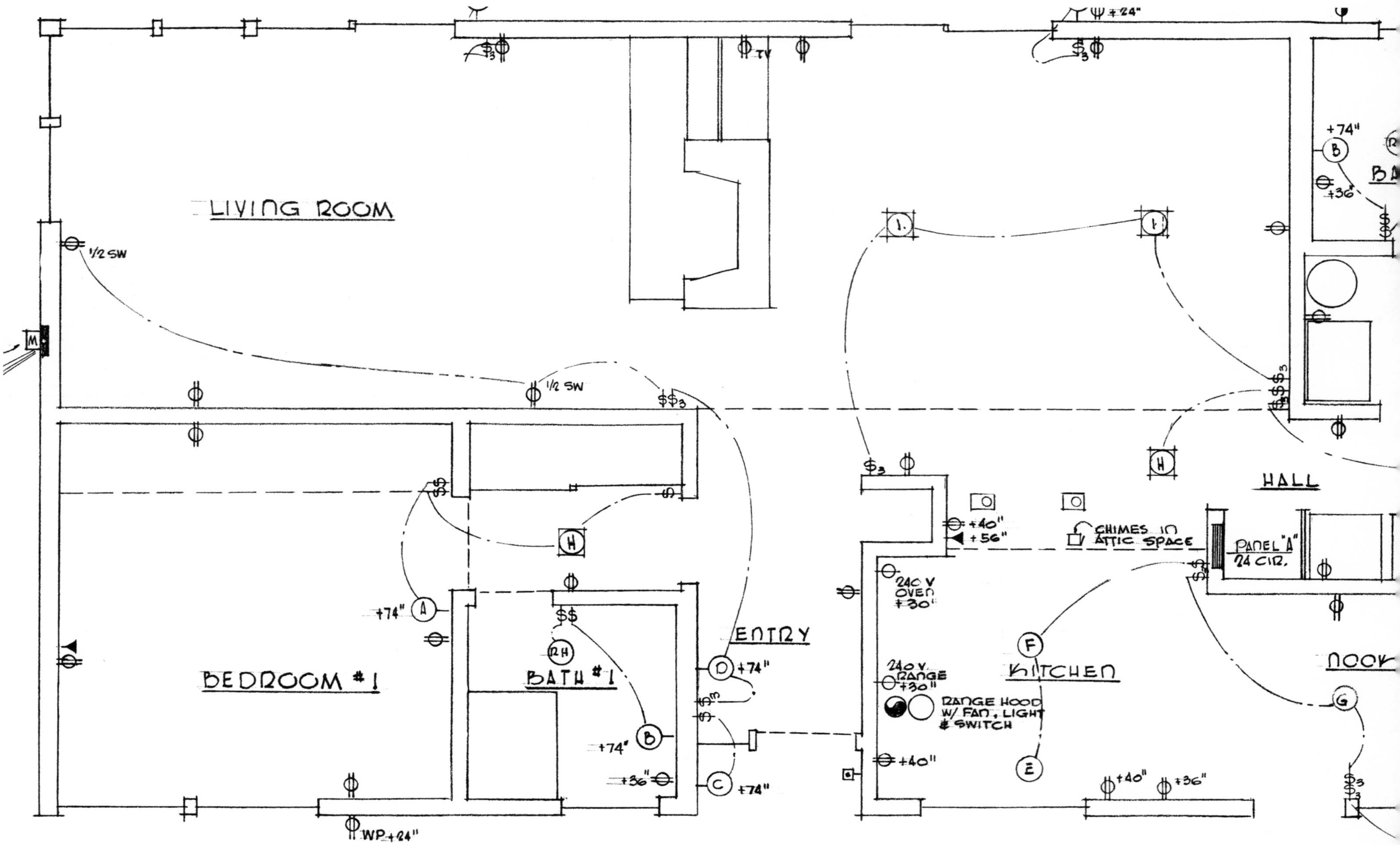

FIGURE 27-3 Full-size extract from Fig. 27-1

used to turn off all power to the building. Behind the disconnect are the branch circuit switches which control the individual power and lighting circuits. Most main and branch circuits at present are protected by circuit breakers rather than fuses (Fig. 27-4), since they are safer and more convenient. When a circuit is broken because of an overload or short circuit, it may be reset after the trouble is corrected merely by pushing the switch to the "reset" position. A residence of about 1,200 sq ft should have a three-wire entrance switch of 100 amp capacity minimum and 12 branch circuits to provide an adequate number of 120- and 240-volt circuits. Commercial buildings vary greatly in electrical requirements, and they often require three-phase power at 220 volts or more.

POSSIBLE SERVICE ARRANGEMENTS

In some buildings the meter, main disconnect, and branch circuit panel are all contained in the same box (Fig. 27-4). Sometimes it is more practical to have the meter and the main disconnect located at the point where the power enters the building, and to place one or more branch circuit panels inside the building. One possible arrangement is to have a power distribution panel at one point and a lighting distribution panel at another (Fig. 27-4). Systems involving transformer vaults, direct current, and electronic controls must be designed by an electrical engineer.

TYPES OF WIRING

Structures are wired in many ways depending on local building codes. Following are descriptions of the most common types:

1. *Line-voltage systems* (120-volt). Switches and outlets handle line voltage.
   a. Conduit and insulated wire is most durable and

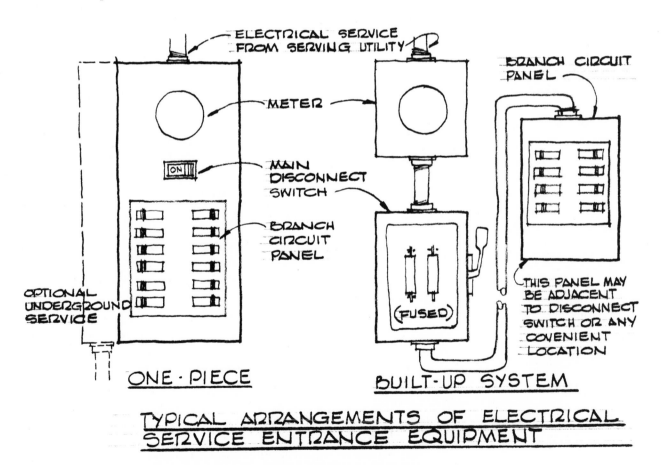

FIGURE 27-4 Typical arrangements of electrical service entrance equipment

most expensive. Wiring can easily be repaired or changed at a later date.

 b. BX or metallic-sheathed cable has a coiled metal covering over insulated wire. It is flexible and can be placed easily in difficult places.

 c. Nonmetallic-sheathed cable has a paper and fiber covering over insulated wire. It is most economical and easy to install.

2. *Low-voltage switching systems* (6 to 24 volts). Only fixture outlets handle line voltage.

 a. Auxiliary-bell system is in limited use in practically every building.

 b. Low-voltage switching through relays can be used in place of any line-voltage system.

ELECTRIC OUTLETS

All systems use the same kinds of line-voltage outlets; the differences lie in the switches and relays. The term *outlet* means floor, wall, and ceiling boxes of any type, including switch boxes, line voltage, or low voltage. Types of outlets and installations requiring outlets are listed below.

1. Duplex convenience outlets are used more often than any other type. They provide two 120-volt receptacles for lights and appliances. They are usually mounted 12 in. above the floor or at any convenient height above work surfaces, but they may be mounted at any place they are needed (ten or less per circuit).

2. Television or radio outlets provide a convenience outlet plus an aerial.

3. Clock outlets are built into a recessed plate so that the clock can mount flush with the wall.

4. Single three-wire 240-volt outlets are used for ranges, ovens, clothes dryers, or other appliances drawing heavy current. Many different types are available.

5. Bracket or wall lights are used in halls, near entrances, and so on.

6. Telephone outlets are wired by the telephone company, but the draftsman locates them.

7. Radio-intercom panels and speakers are often installed in residences and light-commercial buildings.

8. Ceiling-fixture outlets are most often used. They accept any surface-mounted fixture and can use incandescent or fluorescent lamps.

9. Flush-mounted ceiling fixtures do not extend into the room. They require careful planning and must be built into the structure before the ceiling finish is applied. Either incandescent or fluorescent lamps may be used with them.

10. Luminous ceiling systems combine the functions of ceiling and lighting fixtures. Their use demands careful planning. They may employ incandescent or fluorescent lamps.

11. Convenience outlets on the floor are used often in commercial, but seldom in residential, construction.

12. Telephone jacks on the floor are used in offices where desks must be moved around.

13. Electric heaters, radiant or convection, are used for spot heating. They may be on a wall or ceiling.

14. Fans are used in kitchens, laboratories, bathrooms, and so on.

15. Light-fan-heater combinations are used in bathrooms.

16. Range hoods, combining fan and light, are used in kitchens.

17. Floor lights or spotlights are used at entrances and also for decorative illumination.

18. Speakers are connected to the radio or intercom system.

19. Push buttons for doorbells are placed at front and back doors of residences or light-commercial buildings.

20. Chimes or bells are usually placed in a central part of the building.

21. Single-pole switches are used to control any one or a group of 120-volt outlets.

22. Three-way switches are used when it is desired to switch one or a group of outlets from two places.

23. Four-way switches are used to provide the third, fourth, or more position from which to switch one or a group of outlets.

24. Two-pole switches must be used to switch 240-volt outlets or devices.

Switch legs are the wires run from the outlet to the switch box.

The outlets listed are those most often used in the design of a residence or light-commercial structure.

Many others are used for special jobs. Information regarding them is available through various catalogs and manufacturers' publications. Their use is too technical to be described here.

The foregoing information concerns a line-voltage system only. Though the doorbell, chimes, speakers, and telephone are low-voltage devices, they are shown on almost every job and hence were included with the line-voltage devices.

ELECTRICAL SCHEDULES

When many special fixtures are used in a building, an electrical-fixture schedule may be needed. This schedule describes the actual fixtures to be used at the various outlets (Fig. 27-5).

The headings used are:

1. *Symbol:* Identifying mark
2. *Description:* Type of fixture
3. *Watts:* Number and size of lamps
4. *Volts:* Rated voltage
5. *Manufacturer and catalog number*
6. *Wire:* Wire gauge
7. *Panel:* Location of circuit switch
8. *Circuit:* Number of circuit switch
9. *Remarks:* Any further explanation

PLANNING

Before starting the actual electrical plan it is necessary to plan the type, number, and location of outlets. Naturally all decisions in this area are based on lighting requirements and the locations of electric appliances. Tables in the reference section provide a basis for planning which will be adequate for student use (see A-17 and A-18). When placing outlets it is better to put in too many rather than too few. They are fairly inexpensive to install while the building is being constructed, but are very expensive to add to the completed structure. Use only weatherproof outlets out-of-doors.

BUILT-IN LIGHTING

Several effective arrangements for lighting can be built into the structure and require only the simplest and cheapest fixtures. Soffit lights, cornice lights, cove lights, and others are illustrated in Fig. 27-6. Incandescent or fluorescent lamps, white or colored, may be used in special fixtures for very effective results. Weatherproof outdoor-lighting fixtures are available which can be used to advantage in the design of a residence or a commercial building.

DRAFTING THE ELECTRICAL PLAN

The procedure for drawing the electrical plan follows (Figs. 27-1 and 27-2):

1. Select fixture types and locations based on lighting requirements, and locate all fixtures and outlets.
2. Trace the floor plan on the back of the paper (Fig. 13-5).
3. Place the service entrance as required by local codes and the serving utility company.
4. Place all convenience outlets.
5. Place all 240-volt three-wire outlets near the proper equipment—stove, oven, dryer, air conditioner, meat case, or other high-current device.
6. Place all ceiling fixtures and outlets.
7. Place all floor outlets.
8. Place all special outlets and fixtures.
9. Place all switches, and connect switch legs to proper fixtures or outlets.
10. Draw the electrical-outlet schedule and also the electrical-fixture schedule if needed.
11. Letter in all notes, title, and scale.

LOW-VOLTAGE SWITCHING SYSTEMS

A low-voltage switching system differs from a line-voltage system in several respects.

1. Line-voltage wires run to the outlet or main control panel only.
2. All switches operate at low voltage (6 to 24 volts).
3. Each switched outlet is controlled by the switch through a relay. In some systems the relay is mounted on the outlet, while in others it is mounted in a master control panel.
4. Any number of switches can control any number of outlets. There are no three- or four-way switches.

ELECTRICAL PLAN
SCALE 1/4"=1'-0"

ELECTRICAL LEGEND & FIXTURE SCHEDULE

SYMBOL	DESCRIPTION	MFGR. & CATALOG NO.	VOLTS	WATTS	WIRE	PANELBOARD	REMARKS
	DUPLEX GROUNDING TYPE CONVENIENCE OUTLET		120	200	2-#12	no	
WP	WEATHERPROOF DUPLEX CONVENIENCE OUTLET		120	200	→	→	
TV	TELEVISION OUTLET W/ ANT. LEAD-IN CONNECTION		120	200			
240 V. RANGE	SPECIAL PURPOSE 240 VOLT OUTLET		240	TO 8,000	3-#8	30	
	TELEPHONE OUTLET BOX		-	-			
S	SINGLE POLE TOGGLE SWITCH QUIET TYPE - IVORY		120	-			
S3	THREE WAY TOGGLE SWITCH IVORY		120	-			
	MIDGET FLUORESCENT FIXTURE SURFACE MTD. W/ PIN SWITCH	AKLO #1401 W/ PIN SWITCH WHITE	120	40			MTD ON SOFFIT OF UPPER CABINET
RH	RADIANT HEATER - RECESSED CEILING MTD.	EMERSON-PRYNE #R3-20	120	250			
	RANGE HOOD W/ EXHAUST FAN, LIGHT & SWITCH.	EMERSON-PRYNE #1500 "MODERN" S.S. FINISH	120	150			
A	WALL MTD. INCANDESCENT LIGHT FIXTURE	SELECTED BY OWNER	120	200			ALLOW $25.00 PER FIXTURE
B	"	EMERSON-PRYNE #464 "IMPERIALITE"-SATIN ALUM.	120	200			
C	"	SELECTED BY OWNER	120	300			ALLOW $20.00 PER FIXTURE
D	"	SELECTED BY OWNER	120	100			ALLOW $30.00
E	CEILING MTD. INCANDESCENT LIGHT FIXTURE	EMERSON-PRYNE #375 ALUMINUM	120	100			
F	"	EMERSON-PRYNE #554	120	200			
G	"	SELECTED BY OWNER	120	225			ALLOW $50.00
J	"	PORCELAIN MED. BASE RECEPTACLE	120	150			
H	RECESSED CEILING MTD. INCANDESCENT LIGHT FIXTURE	EMERSON-PRYNE 64-78	120	150			
I	"	EMERSON-PRYNE 04-57	120	150			
	DOOR BELL & CHIMES	SELECTED BY OWNER	120	20			ALLOW $20.00
	RECESSED MULTI-BKR PANEL	24 CIRCUIT RECESSED BKR. PANEL	120/240		3-#1		
M	ELECT. METER & 100 AMP. DISCONNECT SWITCH.		120/240				100 AMP FUSIBLE DISCONN.

FIGURE 27-5 Full-size extract from Fig. 27-1

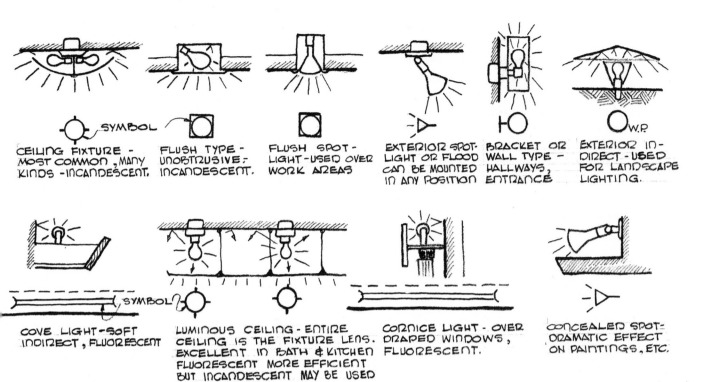

FIGURE 27-6   Examples of different types of lighting

5. Any or all of the switches may easily be controlled by a centrally located master switch.
6. Light bell wire may be used to wire in switch circuits, and the wires can be stapled directly to the structure without protection.
7. There is no danger of electric shock at the switches.

Procedure for drawing a low-voltage switching system is similar to that used for a line-voltage system. Because of differences in the several low-voltage systems, it is necessary to refer to the manufacturer's brochure on the particular system used to get complete information needed for drawing.

Other electrical systems using dc (direct current) large motor controllers, electronic control devices, and so on are designed and drawn by electrical engineering firms and need not be described here.

REVIEW QUESTIONS

1. What type of current is used for most wiring in the United States, alternating or direct?
2. Which is most desirable, a two- or three-wire service? Why?
3. What types of wiring materials are called for by code for your own project?
4. What is the difference between a line-voltage system and a low-voltage switching system?
5. Sketch sections through a surface-mounted and a flush-mounted light fixture to show how they differ.
6. From the standpoint of safety, why is a low-voltage system desirable?
7. For a residence of 1,400 sq ft in area, estimate the following (use A-15 as a reference):
   a. Wire size of the service
   b. Size of main switch in amperes
   c. Size of fuses in main switch
   d. Number of general-purpose circuits
   e. Size of wires to a small electric range
   f. Size of wires to an electric dryer
   g. Minimum number of appliance circuits
   h. Size of wire to carry 40 amp
   i. Wattage of a $\frac{1}{4}$-hp motor.

259

8. What level of illumination in footcandles is required for sewing on dark cloth?
9. State the formula for finding the number of lamp lumens required to light a certain room to a given level of illumination.
10. How many lumens per watt does the average incandescent lamp produce?
11. Compute the number of 100-watt incandescent lamps required to light a 10- by 10-ft room to a level suitable for sewing on dark cloth.
12. How many 48-in. fluorescent lamps would be needed for the conditions in Question 11?

STUDY SUGGESTIONS

1. Visit an electric-supply warehouse, and inspect the different types of boxes, conductors, outlets, and fixtures available.
2. Visit two buildings under construction, one with a line-voltage and the other with a low-voltage switching system. Note the differences in construction. Compare the hardware with the drawing symbols.
3. Many books are available on basic electricity, wiring, and lighting; study these.

STUDENT PROBLEM

Following are the requirements for the electrical plan.

1. *Kitchen:* Two duplex convenience outlets over sink; flush fixtures, one over sink; three-way switches to adjacent rooms; proper outlets for all appliances, installed or NIC
2. *Utility room:* One duplex convenience outlet on empty wall; flush fixture in ceiling; proper outlets for all appliances
3. *Living room:* Six duplex convenience outlets, one of which is switched to entrance; soffit lights (48-in. fluorescent) in window cornices, if used
4. *Dining or family room:* Four duplex convenience outlets; hanging fixture in middle of room or over dining area
5. *Bathrooms:* One duplex convenience outlet near mirror; flush fixture over sink; combination fan light; ceiling heater
6. *Bedrooms:* Four duplex convenience outlets; any type of ceiling fixture; light fixture in wardrobe closet; any type switch
7. *Hall:* One duplex convenience outlet; any type ceiling fixture; three-way switches to fixture
8. *Above scuttle (if used):* One duplex convenience outlet; one pull-chain fixture
9. *Garage:* Four duplex convenience outlets; two ceiling fixtures; three-way switches to both doors
10. *Outside:* One weatherproof convenience outlet near patio or terrace, switched from inside; four weatherproof floodlights under eaves, switched at front and back doors; entrance lights at front and back doors; three-way switches from garage and one other entrance
11. *Other lighting:* As desired
12. *Service entrance:* 200 amp mains; 3-wire 120/240 volt alternating current; 24 branch circuits

Note: Changes may be made from these requirements if they conflict with the client's wishes or with local practice.

CHAPTER 28
SPECIFICATIONS

Specifications are the written instructions required to supplement the drawings for a project. The intent of the specification should always be to clarify or describe in the simplest terms the items necessary to complete the project that are not shown on the drawings. Specifications sometimes become excessively wordy, often duplicating information in the drawings and occasionally confusing the intent of the project.

Most specifications are typewritten on standard 8½-by 11-in. sheets and bound into a single booklet which can be distributed with the drawings. Occasionally in the case of a small project with a minimum amount of specification information, the specifications may be typed or printed on the same reproducible sheets on which the drawings are prepared, and bound in with the drawings. The reproduction process varies with the number of reproductions needed and the availability of reproduction equipment.

The Construction Specifications Institute has made great progress in recent years in its attempt to standardize a specification format and to organize and identify the mass of manufacturers' literature available. Wherever possible the format developed by the C.S.I. should be followed. Both the American Institute of Architects and the Construction Specifications Institute have published excellent specification manuals and are attempting to develop standards for use by the construction industry.

For convenience of organization, specifications are divided into four basic sections. *Bidding requirements* are developed for use in the selection of a contractor; *contract forms,* when executed, become the legal agreement between the owner and contractor assuring completion of the project. *Conditions, general and special,* define the rights and responsibilities of all parties to the construction contract. (Standard forms for contracts and conditions developed by the A.I.A. have received widespread acceptance by the construction industry and are available at nominal cost.) *Technical information* describes the materials and methods of construction, supplementing the graphic descriptions of the drawings.

The outline format shown here is similar to those of both the C.S.I. and the A.I.A. and has been used successfully by many architectural firms.

BIDDING REQUIREMENTS

1. *Invitation to bid* is a brief description which informs prospective bidders of the scope of the project and contains the following information:
    a. Project identification, indicating project name, name of owner, location, and architect's name.
    b. Work to be performed, describing in simple terms the type of structure, function, and size.
    c. Availability of plans and specifications, indicating where the documents are to be obtained and what deposit charges may be required.
    d. Type of proposal required, whether it be segregated, lump-sum, or itemized unit proposals.
    e. Time and place for submitting and opening bids.
    f. Bidders' qualifications required for the project.

The invitation is usually sent directly to prospective bidders or published in daily or weekly trade journals depending on the type of coverage the project owner desires.

2. *Instructions to bidders* describes in more detail all the information covered in the invitation to bid and usually contains further qualification requirements such as:
    a. Anticipated construction schedule, indicating proposed starting and completion dates.
    b. Penalties and bonuses for completion of the work after or before scheduled dates.

    c. Bid securities required and the forms that may be acceptable.
    d. The time period for which bids must be held before award or rejection is made.
    e. Methods of modifying, withdrawing, or disqualifying bids. Wherever possible the owner should reserve the right to reject proposals or waive irregularities in the proposals.

3. *Proposal forms* are furnished each bidder to complete and submit as the formal bid document. The form should contain all information necessary to select the successful bidder, including the following:
    a. Project identification, which should agree with information furnished in the invitation to bidders.
    b. Identification of the documents on which the bid is based, including the list of drawings and specifications and any addenda issued. Addenda are supplementary information or modifications of the documents after their initial issuance.
    c. Specific agreements as outlined in the instructions to the bidders, including a restatement of the time allowance.
    d. Proposed costs, alternate costs, and unit prices. When alternate costs and unit prices are required, they should be *very* carefully defined in the documents.
    e. Signatures and seals of the responsible parties.
    f. Attachments as required by the instructions to bidders, such as bid security, bidder qualifications.

CONTRACT FORMS

1. The *agreement* is a contractual form legally binding the owner and contractor to the completion of a project. It should contain the following information:
    a. Identification of all parties involved: owner, contractor, architect, and so on.
    b. A description of the work included.
    c. The financial remuneration to the contractor, including the method of receiving payment.
    d. Time allowances for the completion of the project, including bonuses and penalties.
    e. Signatures of parties involved.

Outline forms of agreement prepared by the American Institute of Architects are widely accepted. The most commonly used form is A.I.A. document A-101, which is available from the American Institute of Architects, Documents Division, 1735 New York Ave., N.W., Washington, D.C. 20006.

2. *Performance bonds* are used by the owner as a form of insurance for the completion of the project, should the contractor be unable to perform. Standard bond forms available for use include A.I.A. 310, Bid Bond, and A.I.A. 311, Performance Bond and Labor and Material Payment Bond. These forms are also excellent guides for the specification writer who does not wish to use them in their standard form. Such forms should be reviewed by a professional legal advisor to assure the owner that his needs will be met.

GENERAL AND SPECIAL CONDITIONS

1. The general condition format most widely accepted is A.I.A. form A-201. This document is the result of years of construction-industry experience and reflects industry customs most generally followed. It is divided into fourteen articles as follows:
    a. Contract documents
    b. Architect
    c. Owner
    d. Contractor
    e. Subcontractors
    f. Separate contracts
    g. Miscellaneous provisions
    h. Time
    i. Payments and completion
    j. Protection of persons and property
    k. Insurance
    l. Changes in the work
    m. Uncovering and correction of the work
    n. Termination of the contract

Each of the articles describes in detail the conditions most common to a construction project. This document would normally remain constant for any one architectural office, with a minimum of changes. Care should be exercised when making alterations in the A.I.A. general conditions, since they are interlocked with the contract and bond forms.

2. Supplementary general conditions modifying the general conditions should be used to tailor them to the laws in the locality of construction. Care should be exercised in preparing this section, and professional legal advice should be secured. The following articles frequently require modification:
    a. Article 1.3: Copies Furnished and Ownership. The number of copies of the documents that the contractor can expect should be specified clearly.
    b. Article 4.8: Cash Allowances. The cash amount and the description of the work covered should be carefully noted.
    c. Article 4.13: Shop Drawings and Samples. The number of copies of the required drawings should be named, and those items that require samples must be submitted.
    d. Article 5: Subcontractors. Some agencies and political subdivisions prefer to delete any reference to subcontractors; however, legal counsel should advise on such deletions.
    e. Article 6: Separate Contracts. If separate contracts are to be used for the project, the limits of responsibility of each contractor should be indicated.
    f. Article 7.5: Performance Bond. The amount and type of bond should be stipulated.
    g. Article 7.8: Test. All testing required should be indicated and the responsibilities of each party clearly defined.
    h. Article 9: Payments. Because this is an important article to the contractor, it is necessary to make all the conditions for payment clear. It is also helpful to indicate the time schedule for submission of payment requests and receipt of payment.
    i. Article 11: Insurance. Define the limits of both owner's and contractor's required liability insurance. Indicate responsibilities for insurance for fire, vandalism, and malicious mischief.

TECHNICAL INFORMATION

1. Three basic methods of preparing technical information have been adopted by the industry as

standards. The *proprietary method* identifies materials and sets quality standards by using a specific manufacturer's name and catalog number. This is the simplest method and the one most often used on private projects. The *descriptive method* provides a detailed written presentation of the required properties of a product and the workmanship required to complete the installation. Because this method requires a thorough knowledge of materials and is time consuming, it is used mostly on public projects that prohibit use of the proprietary method. The *performance method* establishes the end result desired without limiting the means of achieving that end. This concept permits the contractor to use his ingenuity in meeting the contract requirements.

2. Regardless of the method chosen, the format for the presentation of information is similar. The basic information in each section should describe adequately the work to be performed. It can generally be organized under the following headings:

   a. Scope of work: A brief description of the extent of work to be covered by the section, including any work related to the section which is to be furnished or installed by others.

   b. Products: A detailed description of the materials to be used as a part of the section, including if necessary any preparation or fabrication.

   c. Execution: A description of the methods of installation and the performance desired.

The Construction Specifications Institute has grouped all the technical information into 16 basic divisions as follows:

DIVISION 1: GENERAL REQUIREMENTS
0101 Summary of the Work
0110 Schedules and Reports
0120 Samples and Shop Drawings
0130 Temporary Facilities
0140 Cleaning Up
0150 Project Closeout
0160 Allowances
0170 Alternates

DIVISION 2: SITE WORK
0210 Clearing of Site
0211 Demolition
0212 Structures Moving
0213 Clearing and Grubbing

0220 Earthwork
0221 Site Grading
0222 Excavating and Backfilling
0223 Dewatering
0224 Subdrainage
0225 Soil Poisoning
0226 Soil Compaction Control
0227 Soil Stabilization

0230 Piling

0235 Caissons

0240 Shoring and Bracing
0241 Sheeting
0242 Underpinning

0250 Site Drainage

0255 Site Utilities

0260 Roads and Walks
0261 Paving
0262 Curbs and Gutters
0263 Walks
0264 Road and Parking Appurtenances

0270 Site Improvements
0271 Fences
0272 Playing Fields
0273 Fountains
0274 Irrigation System
0275 Yard Improvements

0280 Lawns and Planting
0281 Soil Preparation
0282 Lawns
0283 Ground Cover and Other Plants
0284 Trees and Shrubs

0290 Railroad Work

0295 Marine Work
0296 Boat Facilities
0297 Protective Marine Structures
0298 Dredging

DIVISION 3: CONCRETE
0310 Concrete Formwork

0320 Concrete Reinforcement

0330 Cast-in-place Concrete
0331 Heavyweight Aggregate Concrete
0332 Lightweight Aggregate Concrete
0333 Post-tensioned Concrete
0334 Nailable Concrete
0335 Specially Finished Concrete
0336 Specially Placed Concrete

0340 Precast Concrete
0341 Precast Concrete Panels
0342 Precast Structural Concrete
0343 Precast Prestressed Concrete

0350 Cementitious Decks
0351 Poured Gypsum Decks
0352 Insulating Concrete Roof Decks
0353 Cementitious Unit Decking

DIVISION 4: MASONRY
0410 Mortar

0420 Unit Masonry
0421 Brick Masonry
0422 Concrete Unit Masonry
0423 Clay Backing Tile
0424 Clay Facing Tile
0425 Ceramic Veneer
0426 Pavers
0427 Glass Unit Masonry
0428 Gypsum Unit Masonry
0429 Reinforced Masonry
0430 Block Masonry
0431 Adobe Masonry

0440 Stone
0441 Rough Stone
0442 Cut Stone
0443 Simulated Stone
0444 Flagstone

0450 Masonry Restoration

DIVISION 5: METALS
0510 Structural Metal

0520 Open-web Joists

0530 Metal Decking

0540 Light Gage Framing

0550 Miscellaneous Metal

0551 Metal Stairs
0552 Floor Gratings
0553 Construction Castings

0570 Ornamental Metal

0580 Special Formed Metal

DIVISION 6: CARPENTRY
0610 Rough Carpentry
0611 Framing and Sheathing
0612 Heavy Timber Work

0620 Finish Carpentry
0621 Wood Trim
0622 Millwork
0623 Wood Siding

0630 Glue-laminated Wood

0640 Custom Woodwork
0641 Custom Cabinetwork
0642 Custom Panelwork

DIVISION 7: MOISTURE CONTROL
0710 Waterproofing
0711 Membrane Waterproofing
0712 Hydrolithic Waterproofing
0713 Liquid Waterproofing
0714 Metallic Oxide Waterproofing
0715 Dampproofing
0716 Bituminous Dampproofing
0717 Silicone Dampproofing
0718 Cementitious Dampproofing
0719 Preformed Vapor Barrier
0720 Building Insulation

0730 Shingles and Roofing Tiles
0731 Asphalt Shingles
0732 Asbestos-cement Shingles
0733 Wood Shingles
0734 Slate Shingles
0735 Clay Roofing Tiles
0736 Concrete Roofing Tiles
0737 Porcelain Enamel Shingles
0738 Metal Shingles

0740 Preformed Roofing and Siding
0741 Preformed Metal Roofing
0742 Preformed Metal Siding
0743 Asbestos-cement Panels

0744 Preformed Plastic Panels
0745 Custom Panel Roofing

0750 Membrane Roofing
0751 Built-up Bituminous Roofing
0752 Prepared Roll Roofing
0753 Elastic Sheet Roofing
0754 Elastic Liquid Roofing

0760 Sheet Metal Work
0761 Sheet Metal Roofing
0762 Metal Roof Flashing and Trim
0763 Gutters and Downspouts
0764 Grilles and Louvers
0765 Decorative Sheet Metal Work

0770 Wall Flashing

0780 Roof Accessories
0781 Plastic Skylights
0782 Metal-framed Skylights
0783 Roof Hatches
0784 Gravity Ventilators

0790 Calking and Sealants

DIVISION 8: DOORS, WINDOWS, AND GLASS
0810 Metal Doors and Frames
0811 Hollow Metal Doors and Frames
0812 Aluminum Doors and Frames
0813 Stainless Steel Doors and Frames
0814 Bronze Doors and Frames
0815 Metal Storm and Screen Doors

0820 Wood Doors

0830 Special Doors
0831 Sliding Metal Firedoors
0832 Metal-covered Doors
0833 Coiling Doors and Grilles
0834 Plastic-faced Doors
0835 Folding Doors
0836 Overhead Doors
0837 Sliding Glass Doors
0838 Tempered Glass Doors
0839 Revolving Doors
0840 Flexible Doors
0841 Hangar Doors

0850 Metal Windows
0851 Steel Windows

0852 Aluminum Windows
0853 Stainless Steel Windows

0855 Bronze Windows

0860 Wood Windows

0870 Finish Hardware

0875 Operators

0880 Weatherstripping

0885 Glass and Glazing

0890 Curtainwall System

0895 Storefront System

DIVISION 9: FINISHES
0910 Lath and Plaster
0911 Metal Furring
0912 Metal Lath
0913 Gypsum Lath
0914 Plaster Partition Systems
0915 Plastering Accessories
0916 Plaster
0917 Stucco
0918 Acoustical Plaster
0919 Plaster Moldings and Ornaments

0925 Gypsum Drywall
0926 Gypsum Drywall System
0927 Gypsum Drywall Finishing

0930 Tile Work
0931 Ceramic Tile
0932 Ceramic Mosaics
0933 Quarry Tile
0934 Glass Mosaics
0935 Conductive Ceramic Tile

0940 Terrazzo
0941 Cast-in-place Terrazzo
0942 Precast Terrazzo
0943 Conductive Terrazzo

0945 Veneer Stone

0950 Acoustical Treatment

0955 Wood Flooring
0956 Wood Strip Flooring
0957 Wood Parquet Flooring

0958 Plywood Block Flooring
0959 Resilient Wood Floor System
0960 Wood Block Industrial Floor

0965 Resilient Flooring
0966 Resilient Tile Flooring
0967 Resilient Sheet Flooring
0968 Conductive Resilient Floors

0970 Special Flooring
0971 Magnesium Oxychloride Floors
0972 Epoxy-marble-chip Flooring
0973 Elastomeric Liquid Flooring
0974 Heavy-duty Concrete Toppings

0980 Special Coatings
0981 Cementitious Coatings
0982 Elastomeric Coatings
0983 Fire-resistant Coatings

0990 Painting

0995 Wall Covering

DIVISION 10: SPECIALTIES
1010 Chalkboard and Tackboard

1013 Chutes

1015 Compartments and Cubicles
1016 Hospital Cubicles
1017 Office Cubicles
1018 Toilet and Shower Compartments

1020 Demountable Partitions

1023 Disappearing Stairs

1025 Firefighting Devices

1030 Fireplace Equipment
1031 Fireplace Accessories
1032 Fireplace Dampers
1033 Prefabricated Fireplace

1035 Flagpoles

1037 Folding Gates

1040 Identifying Devices
1041 Directory and Bulletin Boards
1042 Painted Signs
1043 Plaques
1044 Three-dimensional Signs

1050 Lockers

1053 Mesh Partitions

1055 Postal Specialties

1060 Retractable Partitions
1061 Coiling Partitions
1062 Folding Partitions

1065 Scales

1067 Storage Shelving

1070 Sun Control Devices

1075 Telephone Booths

1080 Toilet and Bath Accessories

1085 Vending Machines

1090 Wardrobe Specialties

1095 Waste Disposal Units
1096 Packaged Incinerators
1097 Waste Compactors

DIVISION 11: EQUIPMENT
1110 Bank Equipment
1111 Depository Units
1112 Outdoor Tellers' Windows
1113 Safes
1114 Tellers' Counters
1115 Commercial Equipment

1118 Darkroom Equipment

1120 Ecclesiastical Equipment
1121 Baptismal Tanks
1122 Bells
1123 Carillons
1124 Chancel Fittings
1125 Organs
1126 Pews

1130 Educational Equipment
1131 Art and Craft Equipment
1132 Audiovisual Aids
1133 Language Laboratories
1134 Prefabricated Astro-observatories
1135 Vocational Shop Equipment

1140 Food Service Equipment

1141 Bar Units
1142 Cooking Equipment
1143 Dishwashing Equipment
1144 Food Preparation Machines
1145 Food Preparation Tables
1146 Food Serving Units
1147 Refrigerated Cases
1148 Sinks and Drainboards
1149 Soda Fountains

1150 Gymnasium Equipment

1155 Industrial Equipment

1160 Laboratory Equipment

1163 Laundry Equipment

1165 Library Equipment
1166 Bookshelving
1167 Bookstacks
1168 Charging Counters

1170 Medical Equipment
1171 Dental Equipment
1172 Examination Room Equipment
1173 Hospital Casework
1174 Incubators
1175 Patient Care Equipment
1176 Radiology Equipment
1177 Sterilizers
1178 Surgery Equipment
1179 Therapy Equipment

1180 Mortuary Equipment

1185 Parking Equipment

1188 Prison Equipment

1190 Residential Equipment
1191 Central Vacuum Cleaner
1192 Kitchen and Lavatory Cabinets
1193 Residential Kitchen Equipment
1194 Residential Laundry Equipment
1195 Unit Kitchens

1197 Stage Equipment

DIVISION 12: FURNISHINGS
1210 Artwork

1220 Blinds and Shades

1230 Cabinets and Fixtures
1231 Classroom Cabinets
1232 Dormitory Units

1240 Carpets and Mats

1250 Drapery and Curtains
1251 Drapery Tracks
1252 Fabrics

1260 Furniture

1270 Seating
1271 Auditorium Seating
1272 Classroom Seating
1273 Stadium Seating

DIVISION 13: SPECIAL CONSTRUCTION
1310 Audiometric Room

1315 Bowling Alleys

1320 Broadcasting Studios

1325 Clean Room

1330 Conservatory

1335 Hyperbaric Rooms

1340 Incinerator

1345 Insulated Room

1350 Integrated Ceiling

1355 Observatory

1360 Pedestal Floor

1365 Prefabricated Structures

1370 Radiation Protection

1375 Special Chimney Construction

1380 Storage Vault

1385 Swimming Pool

1390 Zoo Structures

DIVISION 14: CONVEYING SYSTEMS
1410 Dumbwaiters

1420 Elevators

1430 Hoists and Cranes

APPENDIX

RESIDENTIAL PLANNING CHECK LIST

I Room sizes, relationships
   A. Living room
      Approx. area ___12 X 18___ Faces front or rear ___REAR___

      Walls _WOOD PANEL & PLASTER_ floor _CARPET (OWNER)_ ceiling _SLOPING-ACOUSTIC_

      Special features, fireplace, planters?, describe _FIREPLACE w/RAISED_
      HEARTH (FAMILY ROOM)

   B. Kitchen

      Approx. area _8 X 11_ breakfast nook? ___7 X 9___

      type of cabinets _NATURAL WOOD CABINETS - CERAMIC TILE COUNTER_

      walls _PLASTER - ENAMEL_ floor _VINYL-ASB. TILE_ ceiling _PLASTER_

      list special equipment desired _BUILT-IN ELECT RANGE & OVEN,_
      DISHWASHER - PREFERS G.E.

   C. Bedrooms, including den

	Area	Walls	Floors	Ceilings	Type Closet
BR #1	10 X 15	PLASTER	CARPET (N.I.C)	ACOUSTIC	WARDROBE
BR #2	10 X 13	"	"	"	"
BR #3	10 X 13	"	"	"	"
BR #4					
BR #5					

   D. Bathrooms

	Area	Walls	Floors	Ceilings	List Fixtures
Bath #1		CEM. PLASTER	VINYL-ASB	PLASTER	SHR. W.C. LAV.
Bath #2		"	"	"	TUB W.C. LAV.
Bath #3					

   E. Family Room?
      Approx. area ___12 X 20___ Opens to which room ___KITCHEN___

      walls _WOOD PANEL_ floor _VINYL-ASB TILE_ ceiling _ACOUSTIC_

      Special features, fireplace, planters? describe _RADIO, T.V.,_
      RECORD PLAYER CABINET, BOOKSHELVES

   F. Dining Room or dinette
      Approx. area ___—___ walls ___—___ floor ___—___ ceiling ___—___

      Special features _EATING BAR_

   G. Utility room or porch

      Approx. area _MINIMUM_ walls _PLASTER_ floor _VINYL-ASB. TILE_

      ceiling _PLASTER_ list equipment in room _WASHER, DRYER,_
      WILL IRON IN KITCHEN, FAMILY RM. OR BEDROOM,

272

A-1 Residential planning checklist

H Entry, if required

Approx. area MAKE IT FRIENDLY_ opens to which rooms LIVING, FAMILY,

AND BEDROOM HALL

I Storage, service areas
linear ft. of linen closets NO OPINIONS - USE OWN JUDGEMENT

area of heater space, if used PROVIDE REFRIGERATION

space provided for hot water heater? YES GAS FIRED

J Garage, carport
Approx. area 2 CARS - IF COST CAN BE HELD DOWN, PREFER GAR.

K Approx. total area of house, excluding garage
13 - 1400 S.F.

II Plot Plan
A. Size, shape of lot, describe PIE SHAPED LOT IN HILLCREST.
POSSIBLY LOT 6 OR 7, TRACT 1071

B. Largest window areas face? (N.S.E.W.) NO VIEW AVOID WEST

C. Location of patio OFF FAMILY ROOM

D. Location of utilities, gas STREET_____ electricity REAR EASEMENT
sewer STREET_____ water STREET_____

E. Type of fences WOOD, 6' IN REAR YARD
Swimming pool? NO

III Structure
A. Floor
Concrete or wood?_____

B. Walls
stud, post and beam, brick veneer, concrete block, other NO PREFERENCE
WOULD LIKE SOME STONE IF NOT TOO EXPENSIVE.

C. Roof
flat, one pitch, hip or gable, other_____

clerestory, skylights? NO

IV Elevations
Walls--stucco, brick, wood, other_____

Roof--shingle, shake, rock, other GRAVEL OR SLAG - GOOD 20 YRS.

Windows, casement, awning, double hung, other HORIZ. SLIDING ALUM.

Doors, panel, slab_____

Planters? describe NONE INSIDE

Fascia board? Describe NO PREFERENCE

FINAL DATA SHEET

These drawings and notes have been done this semester by my client and myself.

Signed: _____

_____ Floor plan, single line (1/8" = 1'-0")

_____ Plot plan and landscaping (any scale)

_____ Elevations (2) (1/8" = 1'-0")

_____ Structural section (full size of 8½ x 11)

_____ Elevation and section of fireplace and/or interior planters

_____ Elevation of kitchen and bath cabinets

_____ Elevation of special cabinets, hi-fi, etc.

FIXTURES AND APPLIANCES

NAME	BRAND	CAT. NO.	H	W	D
Furnace					
Bath Heater					
Bath Fan					
Kitchen Fan					
Dishwasher					
Water Heater					
Built-in Stove					
Built-in Oven					
Washer					
Dryer					
Freezer					
Refrigerator					
Other					

NOTE: Catalog number needed only if appliance is installed when house is built.

274   A-2 Final residential data sheet

WINDOW SCHEDULE			
HOW MANY	MARK	TYPE SIZE	BRAND AND CAT. NO.

DOOR SCHEDULE			
HOW MANY	MARK	TYPE SIZE	BRAND AND CAT. NO.

ROOM FINISH SCHEDULE			
ROOM	FLOOR	WALLS	CEILING

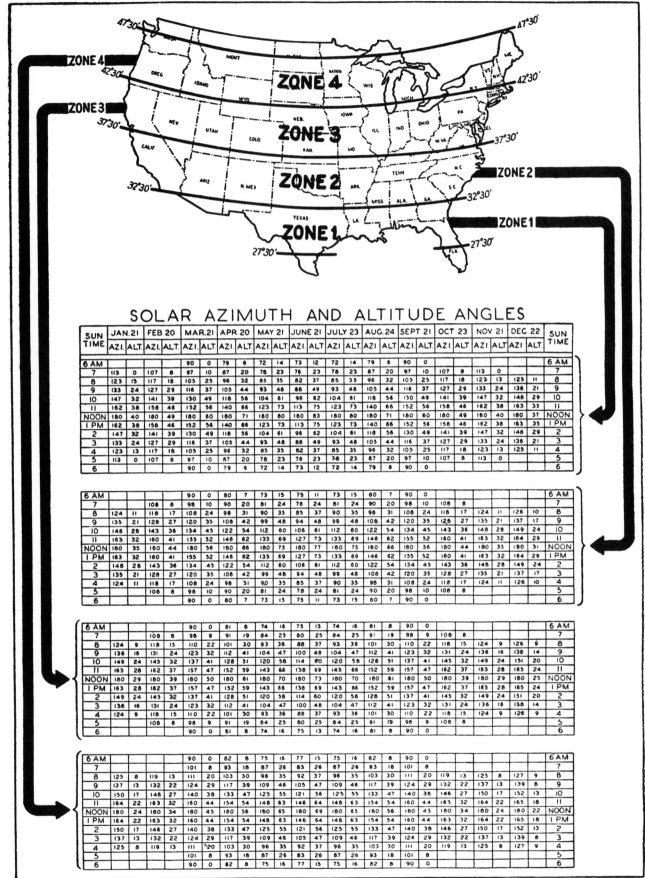

SOLAR AZIMUTH AND ALTITUDE ANGLES

Zone 1

SUN TIME	JAN.21 AZI	ALT	FEB 20 AZI	ALT	MAR.21 AZI	ALT	APR.20 AZI	ALT	MAY 21 AZI	ALT	JUNE 21 AZI	ALT	JULY 23 AZI	ALT	AUG.24 AZI	ALT	SEPT 21 AZI	ALT	OCT 23 AZI	ALT	NOV 21 AZI	ALT	DEC.22 AZI	ALT	SUN TIME
6 AM					90	0	79	6	72	14	73	12	72	14	79	6	90	0							6 AM
7	113	0	107	8	97	10	87	20	78	23	76	23	78	23	87	20	97	10	107	8	113	0			7
8	123	13	117	18	105	25	96	32	85	35	82	37	85	35	96	32	105	25	117	18	123	13	125	11	8
9	133	24	127	29	118	37	105	44	93	48	88	49	93	48	105	44	118	37	127	29	133	24	136	21	9
10	147	32	141	39	130	49	118	56	104	61	96	62	104	61	118	56	130	49	141	39	147	32	148	29	10
11	162	38	158	46	152	56	140	66	123	73	113	75	123	73	140	66	152	56	158	46	162	38	163	35	11
NOON	180	40	180	49	180	60	180	71	180	80	180	83	180	80	180	71	180	60	180	49	180	40	180	37	NOON
1 PM	162	38	158	46	152	56	140	66	123	73	113	75	123	73	140	66	152	56	158	46	162	38	163	35	1 PM
2	147	32	141	39	130	49	118	56	104	61	96	62	104	61	118	56	130	49	141	39	147	32	148	29	2
3	133	24	127	29	118	37	105	44	93	48	88	49	93	48	105	44	118	37	127	29	133	24	136	21	3
4	123	13	117	18	105	25	96	32	85	35	82	37	85	35	96	32	105	25	117	18	123	13	125	11	4
5	113	0	107	8	97	10	87	20	78	23	76	23	78	23	87	20	97	10	107	8	113	0			5
6					90	0	79	6	72	14	73	12	72	14	79	6	90	0							6

Zone 2

SUN TIME	JAN.21 AZI	ALT	FEB 20 AZI	ALT	MAR.21 AZI	ALT	APR.20 AZI	ALT	MAY 21 AZI	ALT	JUNE 21 AZI	ALT	JULY 23 AZI	ALT	AUG.24 AZI	ALT	SEPT 21 AZI	ALT	OCT 23 AZI	ALT	NOV 21 AZI	ALT	DEC.22 AZI	ALT	SUN TIME
6 AM					90	0	80	7	73	15	75	11	73	15	80	7	90	0							6 AM
7			108	8	98	10	90	20	81	24	78	24	81	24	90	20	98	10	108	8					7
8	124	11	118	17	108	24	98	31	90	35	85	37	90	35	98	31	108	24	118	17	124	11	126	10	8
9	135	21	128	27	120	35	108	42	99	48	94	48	99	48	108	42	120	35	128	27	135	21	137	17	9
10	148	28	143	36	134	45	122	54	112	60	106	61	112	60	122	54	134	45	143	36	148	28	149	24	10
11	163	32	160	41	155	52	146	62	133	69	127	73	133	69	146	62	155	52	160	41	163	32	164	29	11
NOON	180	35	180	44	180	56	180	66	180	75	180	77	180	75	180	66	180	56	180	44	180	35	180	31	NOON
1 PM	163	32	160	41	155	52	146	62	133	69	127	73	133	69	146	62	155	52	160	41	163	32	164	29	1 PM
2	148	28	143	36	134	45	122	54	112	60	106	61	112	60	122	54	134	45	143	36	148	28	149	24	2
3	135	21	128	27	120	35	108	42	99	48	94	48	99	48	108	42	120	35	128	27	135	21	137	17	3
4	124	11	118	17	108	24	98	31	90	35	85	37	90	35	98	31	108	24	118	17	124	11	126	10	4
5			108	8	98	10	90	20	81	24	78	24	81	24	90	20	98	10	108	8					5
6					90	0	80	7	73	15	75	11	73	15	80	7	90	0							6

Zone 3

SUN TIME	JAN.21 AZI	ALT	FEB 20 AZI	ALT	MAR.21 AZI	ALT	APR.20 AZI	ALT	MAY 21 AZI	ALT	JUNE 21 AZI	ALT	JULY 23 AZI	ALT	AUG.24 AZI	ALT	SEPT 21 AZI	ALT	OCT 23 AZI	ALT	NOV 21 AZI	ALT	DEC.22 AZI	ALT	SUN TIME
6 AM					90	0	81	8	74	16	75	13	74	16	81	8	90	0							6 AM
7			108	8	98	9	91	19	84	25	80	25	84	25	91	19	98	9	108	8					7
8	124	9	118	15	110	22	101	30	93	36	88	37	93	36	101	30	110	22	118	15	124	9	126	9	8
9	136	16	131	24	123	32	112	41	104	47	100	48	104	47	112	41	123	32	131	24	136	16	138	14	9
10	149	24	145	32	137	41	128	51	120	58	114	60	120	58	128	51	137	41	145	32	149	24	151	20	10
11	163	28	162	37	157	47	152	59	143	66	138	69	143	66	152	59	157	47	162	37	163	28	165	24	11
NOON	180	29	180	39	180	50	180	61	180	70	180	73	180	70	180	61	180	50	180	39	180	29	180	25	NOON
1 PM	163	28	162	37	157	47	152	59	143	66	138	69	143	66	152	59	157	47	162	37	163	28	165	24	1 PM
2	149	24	145	32	137	41	128	51	120	58	114	60	120	58	128	51	137	41	145	32	149	24	151	20	2
3	136	16	131	24	123	32	112	41	104	47	100	48	104	47	112	41	123	32	131	24	136	16	138	14	3
4	124	9	118	15	110	22	101	30	93	36	88	37	93	36	101	30	110	22	118	15	124	9	126	9	4
5			108	8	98	9	91	19	84	25	80	25	84	25	91	19	98	9	108	8					5
6					90	0	81	8	74	16	75	13	74	16	81	8	90	0							6

Zone 4

SUN TIME	JAN.21 AZI	ALT	FEB 20 AZI	ALT	MAR.21 AZI	ALT	APR.20 AZI	ALT	MAY 21 AZI	ALT	JUNE 21 AZI	ALT	JULY 23 AZI	ALT	AUG.24 AZI	ALT	SEPT 21 AZI	ALT	OCT 23 AZI	ALT	NOV 21 AZI	ALT	DEC.22 AZI	ALT	SUN TIME
6 AM					90	0	82	8	75	16	77	15	75	16	82	8	90	0							6 AM
7					101	8	93	18	87	26	83	26	87	26	93	18	101	8							7
8	125	8	119	13	111	20	103	30	96	35	92	37	96	35	103	30	111	20	119	13	125	8	127	9	8
9	137	13	132	22	124	29	117	39	109	46	105	47	109	46	117	39	124	29	132	22	137	13	139	8	9
10	150	17	146	27	140	38	133	47	125	56	121	56	125	56	133	47	140	38	146	27	150	17	152	13	10
11	164	22	163	32	160	44	154	54	148	63	146	64	148	63	154	54	160	44	163	32	164	22	165	18	11
NOON	180	24	180	34	180	45	180	56	180	65	180	68	180	65	180	56	180	45	180	34	180	24	180	22	NOON
1 PM	164	22	163	32	160	44	154	54	148	63	146	64	148	63	154	54	160	44	163	32	164	22	165	18	1 PM
2	150	17	146	27	140	38	133	47	125	55	121	56	125	55	133	47	140	38	146	27	150	17	152	13	2
3	137	13	132	22	124	29	117	39	109	46	105	47	109	46	117	39	124	29	132	22	137	13	139	8	3
4	125	8	119	13	111	20	103	30	96	35	92	37	96	35	103	30	111	20	119	13	125	8	127	9	4
5					101	8	93	18	87	26	83	26	87	26	93	18	101	8							5
6					90	0	82	8	75	16	77	15	75	16	82	8	90	0							6

276

A-3   Sun angle tables (from "Heating and Ventilating's Engineering Databook")

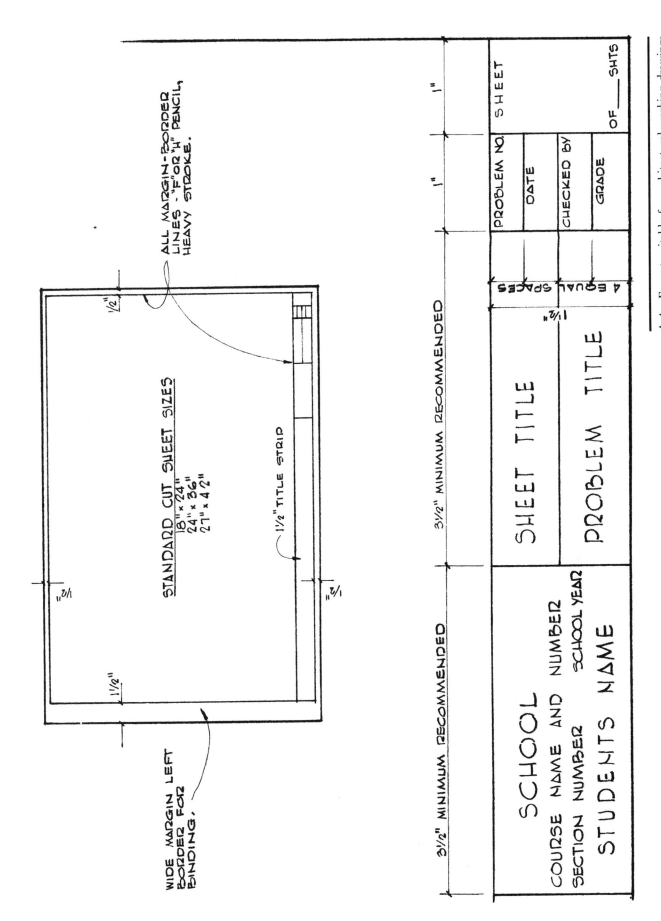

ALL MARGIN-BORDER LINES - "F" OR "H" PENCIL, HEAVY STROKE.

STANDARD CUT SHEET SIZES
18" × 24"
24" × 36"
27" × 42"

1½" TITLE STRIP

WIDE MARGIN LEFT BORDER FOR BINDING.

½"

1½"

1½"

3½" MINIMUM RECOMMENDED

3½" MINIMUM RECOMMENDED

1"

1"

4 EQUAL SPACES

1½"

PROBLEM NO.	SHEET
DATE	
CHECKED BY	
GRADE	OF ____ SHTS

SHEET TITLE

PROBLEM TITLE

SCHOOL

COURSE NAME AND NUMBER

SECTION NUMBER   SCHOOL YEAR

STUDENTS NAME

A-4   Format suitable for architectural working drawings

277

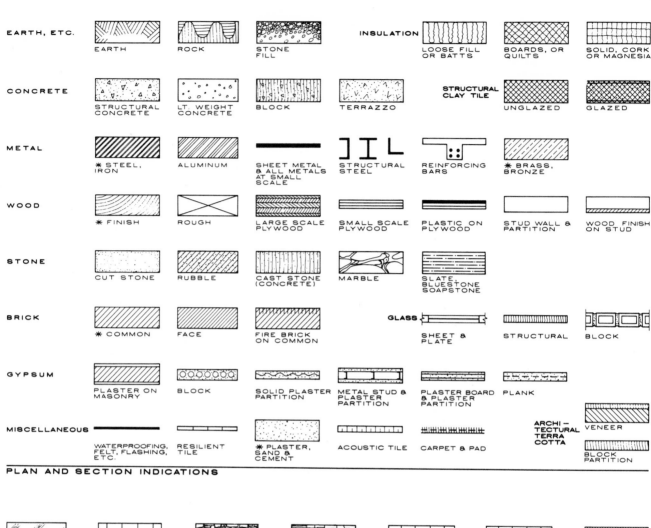

| EARTH, ETC. | EARTH | ROCK | STONE FILL | INSULATION | LOOSE FILL OR BATTS | BOARDS, OR QUILTS | SOLID, CORK OR MAGNESIA |

| CONCRETE | STRUCTURAL CONCRETE | LT. WEIGHT CONCRETE | BLOCK | TERRAZZO | STRUCTURAL CLAY TILE | UNGLAZED | GLAZED |

| METAL | * STEEL, IRON | ALUMINUM | SHEET METAL & ALL METALS AT SMALL SCALE | STRUCTURAL STEEL | REINFORCING BARS | * BRASS, BRONZE |

| WOOD | * FINISH | ROUGH | LARGE SCALE PLYWOOD | SMALL SCALE PLYWOOD | PLASTIC ON PLYWOOD | STUD WALL & PARTITION | WOOD FINISH ON STUD |

| STONE | CUT STONE | RUBBLE | CAST STONE (CONCRETE) | MARBLE | SLATE, BLUESTONE SOAPSTONE |

| BRICK | * COMMON | FACE | FIRE BRICK ON COMMON | GLASS | SHEET & PLATE | STRUCTURAL | BLOCK |

| GYPSUM | PLASTER ON MASONRY | BLOCK | SOLID PLASTER PARTITION | METAL STUD & PLASTER PARTITION | PLASTER BOARD & PLASTER PARTITION | PLANK |

| MISCELLANEOUS | WATERPROOFING, FELT, FLASHING, ETC. | RESILIENT TILE | * PLASTER, SAND & CEMENT | ACOUSTIC TILE | CARPET & PAD | ARCHITECTURAL TERRA COTTA | VENEER / BLOCK PARTITION |

PLAN AND SECTION INDICATIONS

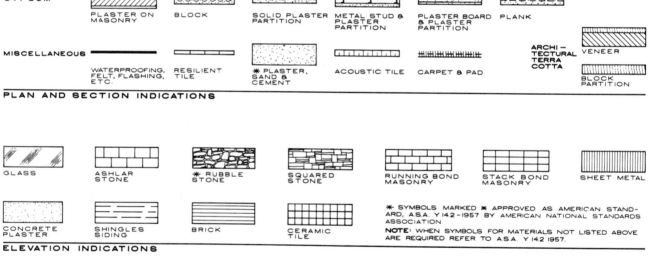

GLASS ASHLAR STONE * RUBBLE STONE SQUARED STONE RUNNING BOND MASONRY STACK BOND MASONRY SHEET METAL

CONCRETE PLASTER SHINGLES SIDING BRICK CERAMIC TILE

* SYMBOLS MARKED * APPROVED AS AMERICAN STANDARD, A.S.A. Y14.2-1957 BY AMERICAN NATIONAL STANDARDS ASSOCIATION.
NOTE: WHEN SYMBOLS FOR MATERIALS NOT LISTED ABOVE ARE REQUIRED REFER TO A.S.A. Y14.2 1957.

ELEVATION INDICATIONS

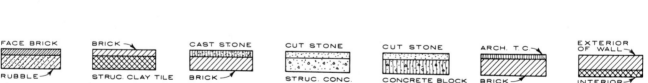

FACE BRICK BRICK CAST STONE CUT STONE CUT STONE ARCH. T.C. EXTERIOR OF WALL
RUBBLE STRUC. CLAY TILE BRICK STRUC. CONC. CONCRETE BLOCK BRICK INTERIOR

PLANS OF EXTERIOR WALLS

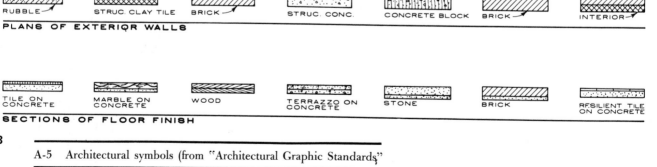

TILE ON CONCRETE MARBLE ON CONCRETE WOOD TERRAZZO ON CONCRETE STONE BRICK RESILIENT TILE ON CONCRETE

SECTIONS OF FLOOR FINISH

A-5 Architectural symbols (from "Architectural Graphic Standards")

A-6 Procedure for designing footings

The size of a footing is generally determined by two factors:

1. The load or weight of the structure it is to support, including the live load (anticipated movable load) as well as the dead weight of the construction.
2. The bearing capacity of the supporting soil.

The first step in the design of footings for residential or light structures is to determine the load-bearing capacity of the soil. This can be done by visual inspection of the site and by the use of the arbitrary tables established by the local building codes. Soil classifications are generally divided into five categories based on the relative size of soil particle and its crushing strength. The following table is shown for reference only, and all loading values should be checked with local codes.

A-6a Bearing values of common soils

Soil classification	Min. depth below undisturbed soil	Bearing value of material, psf
ROCK	0'0"	5,000 or 20% of ultimate crushing value
SAND		
Coarse compact	1'0"	1,500
Fine compact	1'0"	1,000
Fine loose	2'0"	500
CLAY		
Hard	1'0"	3,000
Sandy	1'0"	2,000
Soft	2'0"	1,000
ADOBE	2'0"	1,000
SILT, DRY	2'0"	500

The values given in the right-hand column of the table are the allowable weights that may be supported by each square foot of footing area.

WEIGHTS OF BUILDING MATERIALS

When the soil-bearing values have been determined, the weight of the structure is calculated from A-6b.

A-6b Weights of building construction

Materials	Weight
ROOF COVERINGS	
Wood shingles	3 psf
$\frac{1}{4}$" slate	10 psf
Spanish tile	15 psf
Copper sheet	2 psf
Corrugated iron	2 psf
Corrugated aluminum	1 psf
Asbestos shingle	5 psf
Composition shingle	1 psf
Tar and gravel	6 psf
ROOF STRUCTURES	
Wood joist and sheathing	3 psf
Wood truss and purlin	3 psf
2" plank and beam	5 psf
CEILINGS	
Wood joist and plaster	10 psf
Wood joist and $\frac{1}{2}$" gypsum board	7 psf
Wood joist and acoustic tile	5 psf
Suspended metal lath and plaster	10 psf
WALLS	
2 x 4 stud—gypsum lath and plaster	20 psf
2 x 4 stud—$\frac{1}{2}$" gypsum board	12 psf
Metal stud and plaster	20 psf
4" clay tile and plaster	20 psf
8" brick, reinforced	85 psf
8" concrete block	70 psf
8" concrete, reinforced	100 psf
12" stone	140 psf
FLOORS	
Wood joist—$\frac{3}{4}$" wood floor	6 psf
Wood joist—linoleum	5 psf
Wood joist—ceramic tile	16 psf
4" concrete	50 psf
FOOTINGS	
Concrete	150 pcf

Multiply the weights of the materials by the surface area, total all the dead loads, and add the applicable live loads from A-6c.

Divide the total load (live + dead) of the structure by the allowable soil-bearing value to determine the required footing area. All footings of a structure should be proportioned to provide uniform bearing on the soil. Unbalanced loadings have a tendency to cause settling and cracking of a structure. The footing under the heavy end of a structure must be proportionately wider than that under the lighter end.

Where soil values are 1,500 psf or greater and wood-frame construction is used, arbitrary footing sizes may be used from A-6d.

279

Area under Consideration	Live Load, psf
ROOFS	20 plus snow load
FLOORS	
Residence	40
Apartment	40
Public corridor	100
Balconies	100
Fire escape	100
Garage	50
Hotel	40
Office	50
Restrooms	50
Stores	75

A-6d   Footing sizes for one- and two-story structures

Stories of height	Min. thickness of foundation wall	Min. width of footing	Min. thickness of footing	Min. depth below nat. grade
1	6″	12″	6″	12″
2	8″	15″	7″	18″

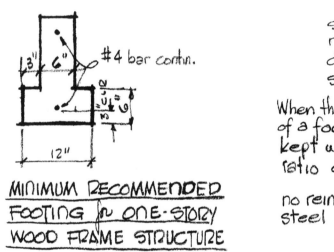

#4 bar contn.

MINIMUM RECOMMENDED FOOTING for ONE-STORY WOOD FRAME STRUCTURE

shaded area not necessary - does not contribute structurally

When the proportions of a footing are kept within this ratio $d = \dfrac{w-t}{1.14}$ no reinforcing steel is required.

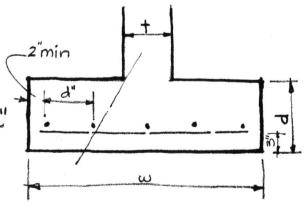

When $d < \dfrac{w-t}{1.14}$ provide ½″ dia (#4) bars at a spacing not to exceed d″ in each direction

A-7   Foundation reinforcing steel table

280

This Table was calculated using fiber-stress of 1,200 lb. per sq. in. This is generally accepted as allowable on good common grades of yellow pine and fir. However, some ultra-conservative ordinances limit these grades to 1,000 lb. For 1,000 lb. fiber-stress, reduce the allowable spans 1/6. For 1,800 lb. "stress-graded" lumber, or for selected joists of clear heart fir or yellow pine, they may be increased over half. Be sure to check your local code for compliance.

A-8   Wood floor and ceiling joist table

Size of Joists	Distance c. to c.	40 # S.F. Total Load	50 ± S.F. Total Load	60 # S.F. Total Load	70 # S.F. Total Load	80 # S.F. Total Load	90 # S.F. Total Load	100 # S.F. Total Load
2 x 4	12″	8′ 5″	7′ 6″	6′ 11″	6′ 4″	6′ 0″	5′ 7″	5′ 4″
2 x 4	16″	7′ 1″	6′ 6″	6′ 0″	5′ 6″	5′ 2″	4′ 10″	4′ 8″
2 x 4	18″	6′ 11″	6′ 2″	5′ 7″	5′ 2″	4′ 11″	4′ 7″	4′ 4″
2 x 4	24″	6′ 0″	5′ 4″	4′ 11″	4′ 6″	4′ 3″	4′ 0″	3′ 9″
2 x 6	12″	13′ 1″	11′ 9″	10′ 8″	9′ 11″	9′ 3″	8′ 9″	8′ 3″
2 x 6	16″	11′ 4″	10′ 1″	9′ 3″	8′ 7″	8′ 0″	7′ 7″	7′ 2″
2 x 6	18″	10′ 8″	9′ 7″	8′ 9″	8′ 1″	7′ 7″	7′ 1″	6′ 9″
2 x 6	24″	9′ 9″	8′ 3″	7′ 7″	7′ 0″	6′ 6″	6′ 2″	5′ 10″
2 x 8	12″	17′ 5″	15′ 7″	14′ 5″	13′ 2″	12′ 4″	11′ 8″	11′ 0″
2 x 8	16″	15′ 2″	13′ 5″	12′ 4″	11′ 5″	10′ 8″	10′ 1″	9′ 7″
2 x 8	18″	14′ 3″	12′ 9″	11′ 8″	10′ 9″	10′ 1″	9′ 6″	9′ 0″
2 x 8	24″	12′ 4″	11′ 0″	10′ 1″	9′ 4″	8′ 9″	8′ 3″	7′ 10″
2 x 10	12″	22′ 1″	19′ 9″	18′ 1″	16′ 9″	15′ 8″	14′ 9″	14′ 0″
2 x 10	16″	19′ 3″	17′ 1″	15′ 8″	14′ 6″	13′ 6″	12′ 9″	12′ 1″
2 x 10	18″	18′ 1″	16′ 2″	14′ 9″	13′ 8″	12′ 9″	12′ 0″	11′ 5″
2 x 10	24″	15′ 8″	14′ 0″	12′ 9″	11′ 10″	11′ 1″	10′ 5″	9′ 11″
2 x 12	12″	26′ 9″	23′ 11″	21′ 10″	20′ 3″	18′ 11″	17′ 11″	16′ 11″
2 x 12	16″	23′ 3″	20′ 2″	18′ 11″	17′ 7″	16′ 4″	15′ 5″	14′ 8″
2 x 12	18″	21′ 10″	19′ 6″	17′ 11″	16′ 6″	15′ 5″	14′ 7″	13′ 10″
2 x 12	24″	18′ 11″	16′ 11″	15′ 5″	14′ 4″	13′ 5″	12′ 7″	12′ 0″

A-9   Wood ceiling joist tables

A 1200 lb. per. sq. in. fiber stress is allowed upon the joists.

The following table of maximum joist spans may be used for ceiling joists where there is access to the attic, with the possibility that the attic may be used for light storage. It includes a plaster on rock lath ceiling under, but no flooring over, and a 20 lb. per sq. ft. live load allowance.

Size of Joists	12″ CC	16″ OC	24″ OC
2″ x 8″	20′ 4″	17′ 10″	14′ 10″
2″ x 6″	15′ 6″	13′ 7″	11′ 3″
2″ x 4″	10′ 2″	8′ 10″	7′ 4″

The following table may be used for ceiling joists where there is no access to the attic. Plaster on rock lath is included, but no live loading. The lengths of spans and spacing given are adequate for practically all kinds of dry-wall ceilings, but the longer spans and wider spacings may give trouble from sagging in time, under the load of a plaster ceiling, though the timbers are theoretically adequate.

Size of Joists	12″ OC	16″ OC	24″ OC
2″ x 6″	28′ 4″	25′ 6″	21′ 9″
2″ x 4″	19′ 4″	17′ 3″	14′ 6″

A-10   Wood-rafter table

Size of member	Spacing of member— center to center	MAXIMUM ALLOWABLE SPAN IN FEET AND INCHES					
		FLAT SLOPES 0 to 4/12			STEEP SLOPES 4/12 and GREATER		
		1,000 psi	1,200 psi	1,500 psi	1,000 psi	1,200 psi	1,500 psi
2 x 4	12″	6′6″	8′0″	9′6″	7′0″	9′0″	10′0″
	16″	5′6″	7′0″	8′0″	6′0″	7′6″	8′6″
	24″	4′6″	6′0″	6′6″	5′0″	6′0″	7′0″
	32″	4′0″	5′0″	5′6″	4′0″	5′6″	6′0″
2 x 6	12″	11′6″	14′0″	16′6″	12′6″	15′0″	17′6″
	16″	10′0″	12′0″	14′0″	11′0″	13′0″	15′6″
	24″	8′0″	10′0″	11′6″	9′0″	10′6″	12′6″
	32″	7′0″	8′6″	10′0″	7′6″	9′6″	11′0″
2 x 8	12″	16′0″	19′0″	22′0″	17′6″	21′0″	23′6″
	16″	14′0″	16′6″	19′0″	15′0″	18′0″	20′6″
	24″	11′6″	13′6″	15′6″	12′6″	14′6″	16′6″
	32″	8′0″	12′0″	13′6″	10′6″	12′6″	14′6″
2 x 10	12″	21′6″	26′0″	27′6″	23′0″	28′0″	30′0″
	16″	18′6″	22′6″	24′0″	20′0″	24′0″	26′0″
	24″	15′0″	18′6″	19′6″	16′0″	19′6″	21′0″
	32″	13′0″	16′0″	17′0″	14′0″	17′0″	18′0″
		20# LL + 8# DL			16# LL + 8# DL		

MAXIMUM SPANS / **SELECTED and COMMERCIAL DECKING** (6″ and wider)

Spans based on uniform live load. Assumed 10psf dead load.
Random length spans. Deflection 1/240 of span.
Spans may be modified for other deflection limitations (.93 for 1/360, 1.10 for 1/180).

Western Pine Association Rules January 1, 1961

SPECIES	Nominal Thick.	Live Load						
		20psf	30psf	40psf	50psf	60psf	70psf	80psf
WHITE FIR	2″	9′1″	8′0″	7′2″	6′8″	6′4″	6′0″	5′8″
	3″	14′8″	12′10″	11′8″	10′9″	10′2″	9′11″	9′4″
	4″	19′7″	17′1″	15′7″	14′5″	13′7″	12′11″	12′4″
PONDEROSA PINE IDAHO WHITE PINE SUGAR PINE LODGEPOLE PINE INCENSE CEDAR RED CEDAR *ENGELMANN SPRUCE	2″	8′10″	7′8″	7′0″	6′6″	6′1″	5′10″	5′6″
	3″	14′2″	12′5″	11′5″	10′6″	9′11″	9′5″	9′0″
	4″	19′0″	16′7″	15′0″	14′0″	13′1″	12′6″	12′0″
DOUGLAS FIR AND/OR LARCH	2″	10′1″	9′0″	8′2″	7′7″	7′1″	6′10″	6′6″
	3″	16′8″	14′6″	13′2″	12′5″	11′6″	10′11″	10′6″
	4″	22′2″	19′5″	17′7″	16′4″	15′5″	14′7″	14′0″
†ENGELMANN SPRUCE	2″	8′10″	7′8″	7′0″	6′6″	6′1″	5′10″	5′6″
	3″	13′7″	11′9″	10′6″	9′8″	9′0″	8′5″	7′10″
	4″	18′1″	15′8″	14′0″	12′9″	11′11″	11′0″	10′5″

*Applies to Selected Decking only.
†Applies to Commercial Decking only.
 For 1-9/16″ thickness reduce nominal 2″ thickness spans 4%.
 For 1½″ thickness reduce nominal 2″ thickness spans 8%.

A-12   Lintel tables (from "Time-Saver Standards")

A-12a   Wood lintel table

Arbitrary table for light frame single-story structures. Supporting roof structures whose span does not exceed 26 ft. Verify with local code requirements.

Spans to 3′6″ = 4 x 4
3′6″ to 5′6″ = 4 x 6
5′6″ to 7′6″ = 4 x 8
7′6″ to 9′6″ = 4 x 10
9′6″ to 11′0″ = 4 x 12

A-13   Maximum span of masonry walls between supports

NONBEARING WALLS					BEARING WALLS
Exterior unreinforced 20t	Exterior reinforced 30t	Interior unreinforced 36t	Interior reinforced 48t	Wall thickness t	Reinforced 25t
6′8″	10′0″	12′0″	16′0″	4″	
10′0″	15′0″	18′0″	24′0″	6″	12′6″
13′4″	20′0″	24′0″	32′0″	8″	16′8″
20′0″	30′0″	36′0″	48′0″	12″	25′0″

A-12b   Reinforced concrete lintels

Clear opening	Total load	Size	Wall thick.	Bars	Cu ft conc per ft	Lb steel per ft
3′	400	6″ x 8″	6″	2—$\frac{1}{4}$″ϕ	.33	.33
	535	8″ x 8″	8″	2—$\frac{1}{4}$″ϕ	.45	.33
	800	12″ x 8″	12″	2—$\frac{1}{4}$″ϕ	.67	.33
4′	625	6″ x 8″	6″	2—$\frac{1}{4}$″ϕ	.33	.33
	835	8″ x 8″	8″	2—$\frac{1}{4}$″ϕ	.45	.33
	1250	12″ x 8″	12″	2—$\frac{1}{4}$″ϕ	.67	.33
6′	1250	6″ x 8″	6″	3—$\frac{1}{4}$″ϕ	.33	.50
	1670	8″ x 8″	8″	3—$\frac{1}{4}$″ϕ	.45	.50
	2500	12″ x 8″	12″	2—$\frac{3}{8}$″ϕ	.67	.75
8′	2000	6″ x 8″	6″	1—$\frac{1}{4}$″ϕ 1—$\frac{3}{8}$″ϕ	.33	1.05
	2670	8″ x 8″	8″	3—$\frac{3}{8}$″ϕ	.45	1.13
	4000	12″ x 8″	12″	2—$\frac{1}{4}$″ϕ 1—$\frac{3}{8}$″ϕ	.67	1.71

All loads calculated on triangular loading at 45°.
No stirrups required.

FIREPLACE DESIGN

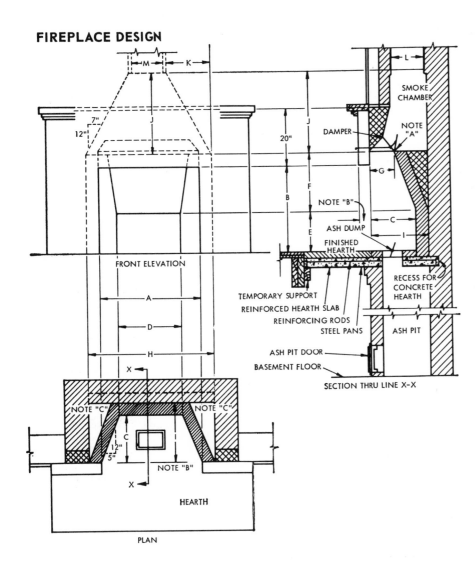

FRONT ELEVATION

SECTION THRU LINE X-X

PLAN

HEARTH

SMOKE CHAMBER

DAMPER

NOTE "A"

NOTE "B"

ASH DUMP

FINISHED HEARTH

RECESS FOR CONCRETE HEARTH

ASH PIT

TEMPORARY SUPPORT

REINFORCED HEARTH SLAB

REINFORCING RODS

STEEL PANS

ASH PIT DOOR

BASEMENT FLOOR

NOTE "C"

NOTE "B"

Fireplaces will give trouble-free service when properly proportioned and built, and when sufficient air for combustion is supplied. Shown on these two pages are basic designs that work — the style is a matter of preference. The drawings, left, and table below are for the usual or conventional fireplace which has one face exposed to the room.

Notes

A.—The back flange of the damper must be protected from intense heat by being fully supported by the back wall masonry. Damper should not be built in solidly at the ends. It should be left free to expand, as shown in the front elevation view.

B.—The drawing indicates thickness of brick fireplace front as 4 in. No definite dimension can be given for this because the various materials, such as marble, stone, tile, etc., have various thicknesses.

C.—These hollow spaces should be filled to form solid backing.

Standard Flue Linings

The custom of using flue linings has become universal, due to the recommendation of the National Fire Underwriters and building code requirements. Flue linings should be tightly cemented together. This is especially important where more than one flue occupies a single stack. Otherwise there may be suction of smoke down one flue while smoke ascends in the other. A minimum of 4 in. of masonry between parallel flues is likewise recommended.

Hearth Shape—Sides should go straight back for about 4 in., then toe-in at an angle of 5 in. to the foot.

Separate Flue—A separate flue should be provided for each fireplace. It should rise from the top center of the smoke chamber, and any change of direction from the vertical should be above this starting point and no slope of the flue should be greater than 7 inches per foot of rise.

Rear Wall—Should be plumb for 14 or 15 in., then slope forward to form smoke shelf and to support rear flange of damper. This shape deflects heat forward into room while smoke and gases pass through damper.

Smoke Chamber—Just above the damper is the smoke chamber. The sides should slope about 7 in. to each foot in height. Smooth, unobstructed walls are important.

APPROX. DIMENSIONS IN INCHES

A	B	C	D	E	F	G	H	I	J	K	L		M	Inside Area	Outside Dimension	Inside Area	Inside Dimension	Inside Area
											Rectangular				Modular		Round	
24	24	16	11	14	15	8¾	32	20	19	11¾	8½ ×	8½		52.56	8 × 12	57	8	50.26
26	24	16	13	14	15	8¾	34	20	21	12¾	8½ ×	8½			8 × 16	74		
28	24	16	15	14	15	8¾	36	20	21	11½	8½ ×	13		80.5	12 × 12	87	10	78.54
30	29	16	17	14	21	8¾	38	20	24	12½	8½ ×	13						
32	29	16	19	14	21	8¾	40	20	24	13½	8½ ×	13			12 × 16	120	12	113
36	29	16	23	14	21	8¾	44	20	27	15½	13 ×	13		126.56				
40	29	16	27	14	21	8¾	48	20	29	17½	13 ×	13						
42	32	16	29	14	23	8¾	50	20	32	18½	13 ×	13			16 × 16	162	15	176
48	32	18	33	14	23	8¾	56	22	37	21½	13 ×	13						
54	37	20	37	16	27	13	68	24	45	25	13 ×	18		182.84	16 × 20	208		
60	37	22	42	16	27	13	72	27	45	27	13 ×	18						
60	40	22	42	16	29	13	72	27	45	27	18 ×	18		248.06	20 × 20	262	18	254
72	40	22	54	16	29	13	84	27	56	33	18 ×	18						
84	40	24	64	20	26	13	96	29	61	36	20 ×	20		298.00	20 × 24	320	20	314.1
96	40	24	76	20	26	13	108	29	75	42	24 ×	24		441.00	24 × 24	385	22	380.13

283

A-14   Fireplace table (continued on next page)

DATA FOR MULTI-OPENING FIREPLACE DESIGN

The trend in contemporary houses toward open planning of rooms has resulted in many fireplaces being designed so they are open on two, three or even four sides, the latter being free-standing.

The chimney flue in a fireplace must be sized for the opening. A fireplace opened on two or more sides will re-quire a larger flue than that for a fireplace of conventional design. *Each face of a fireplace must be included when computing flue size.*

For efficient operation of a corner, two-way or three-way fireplace, use a damper, or damper and smoke chamber designed for the particular fireplace style, and follow the manufacturer's details, including flue sizes.

CORNER FIREPLACE

ASH DUMP

FACE DIMENSION VARIES WITH THE MATERIAL'S THICKNESS I.E. MARBLE, TILE, STONE ETC.

PLAN

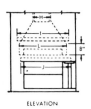

ELEVATION

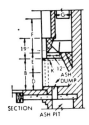

SECTION   ASH PIT

FIREPLACE OPEN TO THREE SIDES

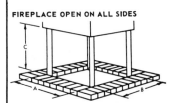

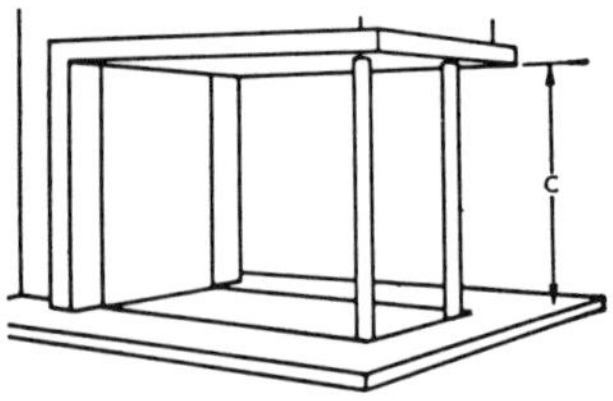

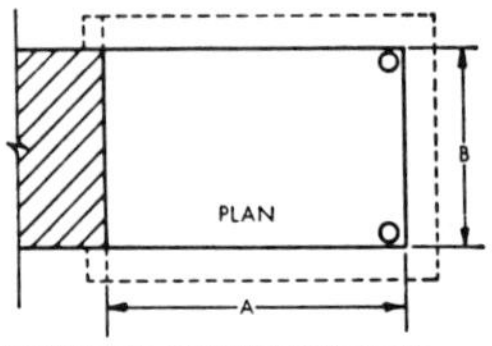

PLAN

MINIMUM AREA OF FLUE (AND DAMPER)
= AREA OF OPEN FRONT + AREA OF OPEN SIDES / 12

A	B	C	D	E	F	Rectangular Flue G	H	Modular Flue G	H	L	Upper Angle I	Lower Angle	Plate Lintel K	Corner Post
32"	29"	16"	14"	20"	32"	13"	13"	12"	16"	40"	42"	42"	11" x 16"	29"
36"	29"	16"	14"	20"	32"	13"	18"	16"	16"	44"	48"	48"	11" x 16"	29"
40"	29"	16"	14"	20"	35"	13"	18"	16"	20"	48"	54"	54"	11" x 16"	29"
48"	32"	20"	14"	24"	40"	13"	18"	16"	20"	56"	60"	60'	11" x 16"	32"

Hearth Size		Maximum Opening Height For Standard Flue Tile (C)				
A	B	13x13	13x18	18x18	18x24	24x24
30	34	21	27	35	38	—
37	41	—	—	21	27	32
34	24	20	26	34	—	—
38	28	—	22	30	36	—
42	28	—	—	29	35	—
46	28	—	—	28	34	40
58	32	—	—	24	30	36

FIREPLACE OPEN TO TWO SIDES

NOT RECOMMENDED AS A MEANS OF HEATING TWO ROOMS, AS THERE IS NO MEANS OF REFLECTING HEAT IN EITHER DIRECTION.

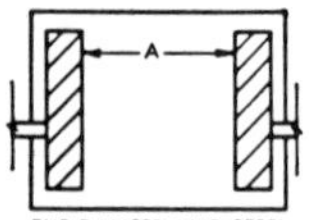

THE DAMPER AND STEEL "T" SHOULD NOT BE BUILT IN SOLID AT THE ENDS, BUT ALLOWED TO EXPAND WITH HEAT.

PLAN

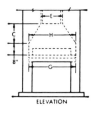

ELEVATION

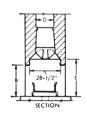

SECTION

FIREPLACE OPEN ON ALL SIDES

A	B	C	Non-Modular Flue D	E	Modular Flue Size D	E	G	H
32"	29"	21"	13"	18"	16"	16"	42"	40"
36"	29"	21"	13"	18"	16"	20"	42"	44"
40"	29"	27"	18"	18"	16"	20"	48"	48"
48"	32"	32"	18"	18"	20"	20"	54"	56"

Hearth Size		Maximum Opening Height For Standard Flue Tile (C)				
A	B	13x18	18x18	20x24	24x24	
34	34	20	28	32	—	
41	41	—	—	28	32	
38	24	22	30	—	—	
42	28	20	28	32	—	
46	28	—	26	31	—	
48	28	—	24	30	35	
58	32	—	21	27	32	

WARM AIR CIRCULATING FIREPLACES

BECAUSE OF THE SCARCITY of skilled masons who know how to build an all-masonry fireplace, and because fireplaces constructed with liners have proved to be more efficient heating units, many builders are constructing the all-masonry type only in cases where unusual shapes may prevent the use of the standard fireplace liner.

Cost difference between the all-masonry and liner type units is nominal; because of this the builders can put more sales appeal into their houses by installing the type of fireplace which will give more heat per fuel consumed.

These circulator liners for fireplaces are constructed of sheet metal shells; with a duct system where circulating air, taken into the air heating chamber, is warmed by coming in contact with the hot sides of the fire box and the fins and baffles placed inside of the chamber, and is discharged back into the room or rooms through ductwork and grilles.

The advantages of the circulating fireplaces are easily recognized. The all-masonry units can provide no amount of circulation through the fire box opening, or mouth; all of the heat delivered to the room must be delivered by radiation.

Construction of the fireplace is greatly simplified by using the liner since it provides a form for the mason to work to, hence journeyman experience is not required. All-masonry units, because of the intricacies of corbelling for the smoke chamber, mounting the damper, building the smoke shelf, laying the firebrick, etc., require men of experience in fireplace construction to do the job, in order to produce a fireplace which will perform properly.

284

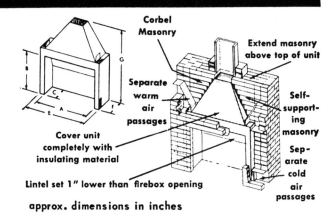

Corbel Masonry

Extend masonry above top of unit

Separate warm air passages

Self-supporting masonry

Separate cold air passages

Cover unit completely with insulating material

Lintel set 1" lower than firebox opening

approx. dimensions in inches

A	B	C	D	E	G	Flue Opening	Size of Flue Liner
33	27½	16	39½	19½	53	10 x 10	12 x 12 or 8½ x 13
37	27½	16	43½	19½	53	10 x 10	12 x 12 or 8½ x 13
41	30	18	47½	23½	58½	10 x 13¾	12 x 16 or 13 x 13
49	30	18	55½	23½	61	10 x 13¾	12 x 16 or 13 x 13

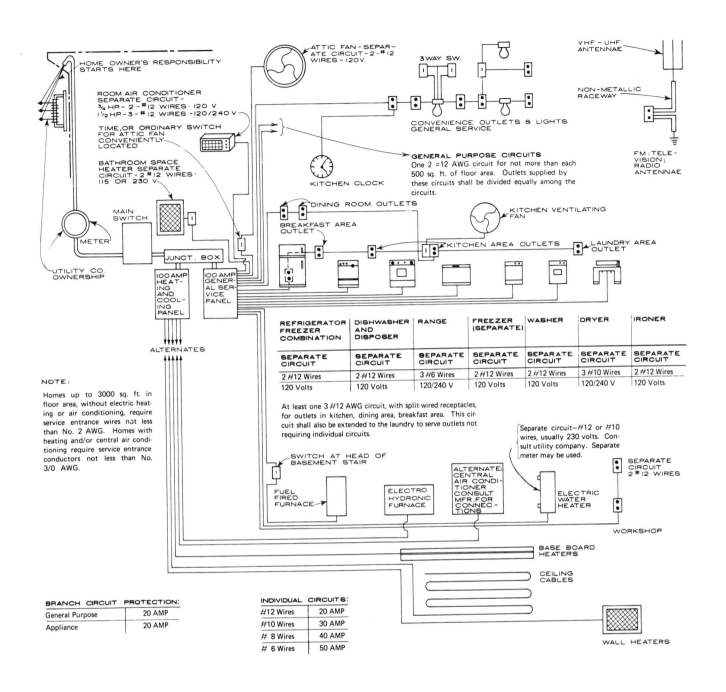

BRANCH CIRCUIT PROTECTION:

General Purpose	20 AMP
Appliance	20 AMP

INDIVIDUAL CIRCUITS:

#12 Wires	20 AMP
#10 Wires	30 AMP
# 8 Wires	40 AMP
# 6 Wires	50 AMP

WATTAGE * OF ELECTRICAL OUTLETS FOR RESIDENTIAL WORK:

(* AVERAGE)

TYPE	WATTS	TYPE	WATTS	TYPE	WATTS
Air Conditioner	850–1200, 3100	Home Freezer	300–670	Refrigerator	200–670
Attic Fan	500–1500	Hot Plate	600–1000	Roaster	1150–1650
Chafing Dish	660	Infra-Red Lamp	500	Sewing Machine	75
Clothes Dryer	Up to 4500	Iron, Hand	660–1000	Shaver	11
Dishwasher	530–1000	Ironer, Home	1275–1620	Sunlamp	250
Disposer	380–530	Juice Extractor	60–100	Television	200–400
Egg Cooker	660	Mixer	125–150	Toaster	600–1350
Electric Fan	50–300	Motor, 1/4 H.P.	530	Vacuum Cleaner	300
Furnace Blower	380–670	Oil Burner	300–550	Waffle Iron	660–1000
Grill	1000	Percolator	400–600	Washing Machines:	
Hair Dryer	250	Power Tools	Up to 1000	Automatic	350–900
Heater	1000–1650	Radio	50–200	Wringer Type	375–400
Heating Pad	65	Range	7000–14000	Water Heater	750–3000

285

A-15　Residential electrical wiring (from "Architectural Graphic Standards," page 633)

Graphic symbols shown on this page have been extracted from American Standard Y32.9–1943, with the permission of the publisher, The American Institute of Electrical Engineers. These symbols have been made as simple as possible and are not intended to depict the structure of the electrical devices shown. The symbols should be drawn to a size commensurate with the particular drawing being made. Additional symbols, or those not yet commonly accepted, should be included in a legend.

ELECTRICAL SYMBOLS FOR ARCHITECTURAL PLANS
Prepared by American Standards Association and published by Industry Committee on Interior Wiring Design

Description	Ceiling	Wall	Description	Symbol	Description	Symbol
GENERAL OUTLETS			**SWITCHES**		**PANELS, CIRCUITS, MISC.**	
Outlet			Single Pole Switch	S	Generator	
Blanket Outlet			Double Pole Switch	S_2	Motor	
Clock Outlet			Three Way Switch	S_3	Instrument	
Drop Cord			Four Way Switch	S_4	Transformer	
Electrical Outlet: *use when plain circle may be confused with column or other symbols*			Automatic Door Switch	S_D	Controller	
			Electrolier Switch	S_E	Isolating Switch	
Fan Outlet			Key Operated Switch	S_K	**AUXILIARY or Low Voltage SYSTEMS**	
Junction Box			Switch and Pilot Lamp	S_P	Push Button	
Lamp Holder			Circuit Breaker	S_{CB}	Buzzer	
Lamp Holder with Pull Switch			Weatherproof Circuit Breaker	S_{WCB}	Bell	
Pull Switch			Momentary Contact Switch	S_{MC}	Annunciator	
Outlet for Vapor Discharge Lamp			Remote Control Switch	S_{RC}	Telephone	
Exit Light Outlet			Weatherproof Switch	S_{WP}	Interconnecting Telephone	
CONVENIENCE OUTLETS			**SPECIAL OUTLETS**		Telephone Switchboard	
Duplex Convenience Outlet			*Any standard symbol, with a lower case subscript added, may be used for special indications. When so used, a legend on each drawing and description in specifications are strongly recommended*	a,b,c etc.	Electric Door Opener	
Convenience Outlet other than Duplex 1 = Single, 3 = Triplex, etc.				a,b,c etc.	Fire Alarm Bell	
				S a,b,c etc.	Fire Alarm Station	
Weatherproof Conv. Outlet			**PANELS, CIRCUITS, MISC.**		City Fire Alarm Station	
Range Outlet			Lighting Panel		Fire Alarm Central Station	
Switch and Convenience Outlet			Power Panel		Automatic Fire Alarm Device	
Radio and Convenience Outlet			*Branch Circuit — Ceiling or Wall		Watchman's Station	
Special Purpose Outlet (desc. in Spec.)			*Branch Circuit — Floor		Watchman's Central Station	
Floor Outlet			*without other designation indicates 2-wire circuit. For 3 wires, use For 4 wires		Horn	
			Feeders: use heavy lines and designate by number for quick reference		Nurse's Signal Plug	
			Underfloor Duct & Junction Box - Triple System: *for double or single systems use two lines or one. Symbol also adaptable to Auxiliary or Low Voltage systems*		Maid's Signal Plug	
					Radio Outlet	
					Signal Central Station	
					Interconnection Box	
					Battery	
					Auxiliary System Circuits: *without other designation indicates 2-wire circuit. For others, use numbers, as:* — —12 - #18 W - ¾" C. or *designate by number for quick reference*	
					Special Auxiliary Outlets: *subscripts refer to notes in plans, schedules or specifications*	a,b,c

A-16   Electrical symbols (from "Time-Saver Standards")

COMPUTING WATTAGE

The table (A-17) is designed to compute the wattage required to light a certain room to a given level of illumination. Because of the great number of variables involved in lighting problems, the information presented represents only average conditions for a few selected situations. When used with the formula shown, this data will yield approximate answers which will serve as useful guides.

The formula for finding the number of lumens required to produce a given general illumination level expressed as footcandles is

$$LL = \frac{FC \times A}{CU \times MF}$$

where LL = lamp lumens

FC = footcandles in service

A = room area, sq ft

CU = coefficient of utilization—depends upon room proportions, absorption of light by the fixtures, and absorption of light by the room surfaces. For the purposes of this discussion, an average factor of .35 will be used.

MF = maintenance factor—depends upon the type, accessibility, and maintenance of the fixture. An average factor of .6 should be used here.

Only two light sources will be considered, namely, incandescent and the ordinary, widely used cool-white fluorescent. Most incandescent lamps produce about 15 lumens per watt; a 48-in. fluorescent produces 2,650 lumens; a 24-in. fluorescent produces 1,450 lumens.

The procedure in sizing the lamps to produce the required general light level in a room follows:

1. Select the light level from A-17.
2. Compute the floor area of the room.
3. Substitute these values in the equation. Use the values given for CU and MF.
4. Divide this value in lumens by the number of lumens produced by the light sources you choose.

A-17 Lighting requirements

Area of activity	Footcandles on task
Benchwork	50–100
Drafting	200
Entrance hall	10
Reading and writing	
Large type	30
Small type	70
Sales area	50
Sewing	
Dark cloth	200
Light cloth	50
Shaving	50
Show windows, general	200
Show windows, feature	1,000
Storage	10
Toilet room	30

A-18 Recommended spacing of convenience outlets

Any habitable room	1 per 12′ of wall plus 1 in each 4′ wall segment—at least 3.
Kitchens	1 each side of sink plus 1 for each fixed appliance.
Hall	At least 1.
Office space	1 per 12′ of wall plus 1 for each desk.
Garage	At least 2.
Bathroom	At least 1 near sink.
Outside of residence	At least 2 near points of greatest use. Must be weatherproof.

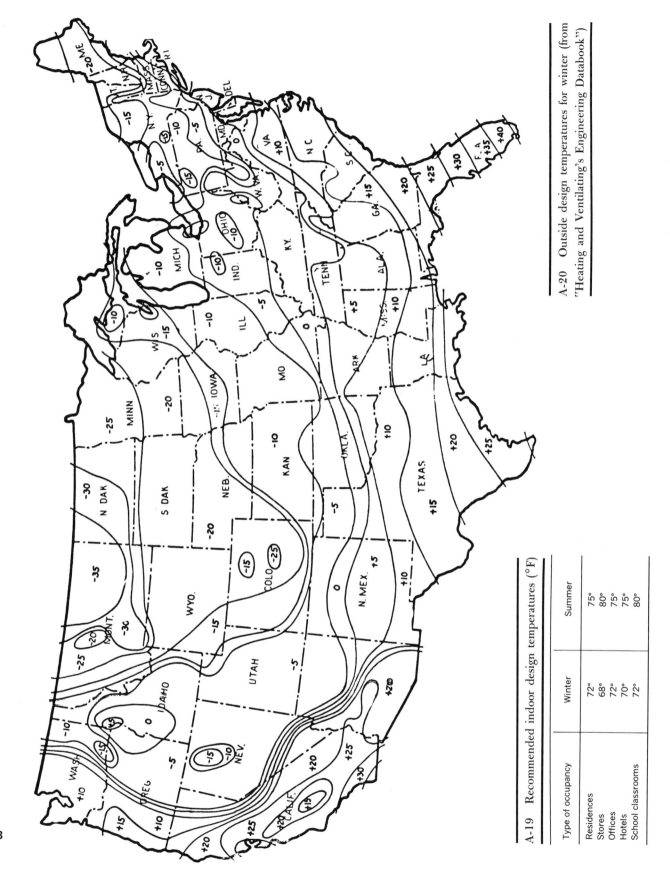

A-20 Outside design temperatures for winter (from "Heating and Ventilating's Engineering Databook")

A-19 Recommended indoor design temperatures (°F)

Type of occupancy	Winter	Summer
Residences	72°	75°
Stores	68°	80°
Offices	72°	75°
Hotels	70°	75°
School classrooms	72°	80°

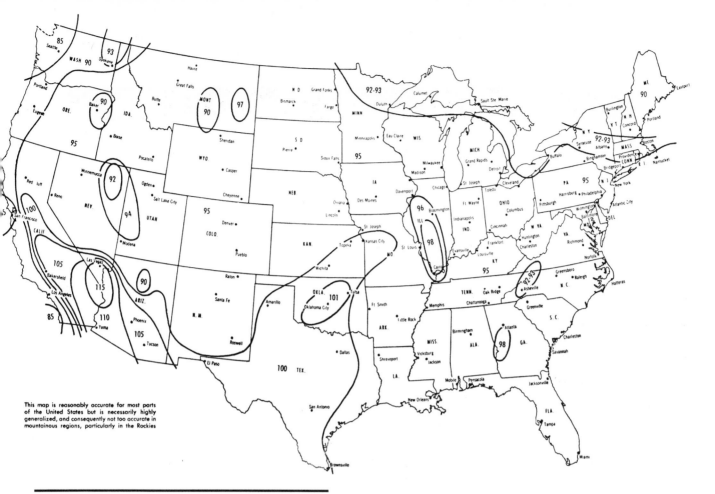

This map is reasonably accurate for most parts of the United States but is necessarily highly generalized, and consequently not too accurate in mountainous regions, particularly in the Rockies

A-21   Summer outside dry bulb design temperature (°F)

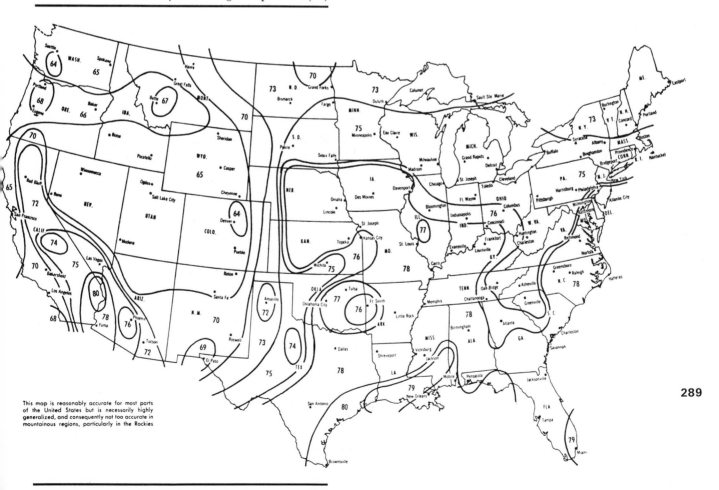

This map is reasonably accurate for most parts of the United States but is necessarily highly generalized, and consequently not too accurate in mountainous regions, particularly in the Rockies

A-22   Summer outside wet bulb design temperature (°F)

RESIDENTIAL HEATING SURVEY

Name __JAMES SMITH RES.__   Date _____

Contractor __ALTA CONSTRUCTORS__   Estimator _____

Address __1343 PARNEL__   Salesman _____

City __BAKERSFIELD, CALIF.__

INSIDE DESIGN TEMPERATURE __75__ °F.

OUTSIDE DESIGN TEMPERATURE __25__ °F.

DESIGN TEMPERATURE DIFFERENCE __50__ °F.

HOUSE ☑ NEW ☐ EXISTING

TYPE PAYNE FURNACE __UPFLOW__   SIZE _____   MODEL _____

BLOWER: ☐ DIRECT DRIVE ☑ BELT DRIVE _____ H.P. MOTOR _____ SPEED

GAS: ☑ NATURAL; ☐ L.P.G.; ☐ _____; SERVICE PRESSURE _____ ″ W.C. __1100__ BTU/CU. FT.

UNIT LOCATION: ☑ CLOSET ☐ BASEMENT ☐ ATTIC ☐ _____

ELECTRIC: __120/240__ VOLTS __1∅__ PHASE __60__ CYCLES

WALLS: ☑ FRAME
    ☐ HEAVY MASONRY
    ☐ LIGHT MASONRY
    Insulated
    ☑ YES   ☐ 1″   ☐ 2″   4″
    ☐ NO

ROOF OR CEILING: ☐ PITCHED
    ☑ FLAT
    Insulated
    ☑ YES   ☐ 1″   ☐ 2″   ☑ 3⅝″
    ☐ NO

FLOOR: ☐ WOOD
    ☑ SLAB ON GRADE
    ☐ OVER CRAWL SPACE
    ☐ OVER BASEMENT
    ☐ OPEN
    ☐ INSULATED

WINDOWS: ☐ DOUBLE HUNG
    ☐ CASEMENT
    ☐ DOUBLE GLAZED
    ☑ WEATHERSTRIPPED
    ☐ STORM SASH
    ☑ SLIDING DOOR

290

A-23   Residential heating survey (continued on pages 291 to 301)

RESIDENTIAL HEATING ESTIMATE

ROOM	SASH AND DOORS Type	Sq. Ft.	WALLS Constr.	Lin. Ft.	BTU/HR (1000)	CEILING (3¾" INSUL.) & FLOOR LENGTH	WIDTH	BTU/HR (1000)	ROOM HEAT LOSS CALCUL. (70° T.D.)	CORRECTED HEAT LOSS	ROOM C.F.M.	SUPPLY REGISTER AND PIPE SIZE	RETURN GRILLE AND PIPE SIZE
ENTRY	F.G.	14	L.F.	5	2.0	10 / 4x52	5	.4	2000 / 400 / 230	(1800)	12		
LIVING	F.&S.	144		30	18.0	20 / 30x58	12	1.7	18,000 / 1,700	(14,700)	124		
FAMILY	S	42		20	5.7	18 / 20x58	14	1.6	5,700 / 1,800 / 1,200	(6,400)	87		
KITCHEN	S	35		16	5.1	18 / 18x58 / 12	9 / 3	1.2 / .3	5,100 / 1,200 / 1,000 / 300	(5,000)	87		
HALL									200	(200)	6		
BATH 1	S	9		8	1.7	6 / 8x58	6	.3	1,200 / 300 / 500	(1430)	25		
BATH 2	S	9		5	1.4	7 / 5x58	5	.3	1,400 / 300 / 300	(1430)	18		
B.R.1	F.G.	56		24	7.1	16 / 24x58	12	1.4	7,100 / 1,400 / 1,400	(7100)	96		
B.R.2	F.G.	56		25	7.1	13 / 25x58	11	1.1	7,100 / 1,100 / 1,400	(7000)	90		
B.R.3	F.G.	56		23	6.9	11 / 23x58	11	1.0	6,900 / 1,000 / 1,400	(6900)	90		

SUM OF ROOM HEAT LOSSES . . . . 51,860 BTU/HR
(OUTPUT OF FURNACE)
SUM OF ROOM C.F.M. . . . . . . 635 C.F.M.

CHECK FIGURES

BTU/SQ. FT. = 3.7

EQUIPMENT SELECTION

TYPE PAYNE FURNACE __80 FAU-14-AC__ MODEL _____

SIZE _____ INPUT __80,000__ OUTPUT __64,000__

_____ INPUT _____ OUTPUT _____

Less Correction for Altitude
(4% per 1000' above Sea Level)

291

RESIDENTIAL HEATING LOAD ESTIMATE

INSTRUCTIONS

1. **SURVEY:** Complete survey by checking items and filling blanks pertaining to the house to be estimated.

2. **WINDOWS:** List type of windows, i.e. Weatherstripped, Double Hung (Plain), Metal Casement, Storm Sash, etc. List square feet of glass under "Sq. Ft." columns for each room opposite the type you indicated.

3. **WALLS:** List type of construction, i.e. Light Masonry, Frame, Heavy Masonry, 1" insulated or 2" insulated Frame. List linear ft. of exposed walls under "Lin. Ft." columns for each room opposite the type you indicated. See TABLE 1 and select the combined heat loss for the amount of glass and wall you indicated for each room and list in "Btu/Hr" columns for each room.

4. **CEILING & FLOORS:** List the amount of insulation. List room dimensions under "Length & Width" columns for each room. Be sure to include dimensions of closets and halls adjacent to proper rooms. From TABLE 2, select the heat loss for ceilings and floors and list in "Btu/Hr" columns for each room, opposite the amount of insulation you listed. Slab floors should be listed separately from ceiling.

5. **ROOM HEAT LOSS (70° F. difference):** Total the heat losses for each room and list in this space for each room.

6. **ROOM HEAT LOSS (for Design difference):** See SURVEY for *your* DESIGN TEMPERATURE DIFFERENCE (Room Temperature — Outside Temperature). From TABLE 3 correct each ROOM HEAT LOSS based on *your* DESIGN TEMPERATURE DIFFERENCE.

7. **20% RESERVE FOR SPECIAL ROOMS:** For Baths, Sun Porches, Basement Rooms, Rooms over Garages and Isolated Rooms; increase Heat Loss 20%.
   Total the final losses and enter for each room.

8. **ROOM C.F.M.:** See TABLE 4. Select the desired REGISTER TEMPERATURE for *your* installation. 135° REGISTER TEMPERATURE is usually considered the optimum. Others are listed here for your convenience or customer's specifications. Notes under TABLE 4 explain its use. Record ROOM C.F.M. under each ROOM to be conditioned. Space is provided to list NUMBER AND SIZE of SUPPLY REGISTERS AND RETURN GRILLES.

9. **SUM OF ROOM HEAT LOSSES:** Add the TOTAL ROOM HEAT LOSSES and enter here.

   Note: If outside air is to be used the above HEAT LOSS must be adjusted.

   Example: a. Calculated Load before outside air = 76,000 (Includes duct loss).
         b. C.F.M. for 135° Register Temperature = 940 C.F.M.
         c. Room Temperature 70° F.
         d. Outside Temperature 20° F.
         e. 20% outside air desired.

   Find: a. New TOTAL HEAT LOSS.

   Solution: a. C.F.M. Outside Air = .20 x 940 = 188 C.F.M.
         b. Outside Air HEAT LOSS = 188 x 1.08 (70° - 20°) = 10,200 Btu/Hr.
         c. Outside Air HEAT LOSS = 76,000 + 10,200 = 86,200 Btu/Hr.

10. **SUM OF ROOM C.F.M.:** Add the ROOM CFM and enter here.

11. **EQUIPMENT SELECTION:** Space is provided to list (1) Type of Furnace; (2) Model Number; (3) Btu/Hr. Input and Output; and correction for altitude, if any. Make sure the furnace you select fills the requirements you have calculated.

12. See APPLICATION SECTION under LOAD CALCULATION for more information.

TABLE 1

COMBINED HEAT LOSSES IN 1000 BTU/HOUR THROUGH WALLS, WINDOWS AND INFILTRATION

Linear Ft. Exposed Wall

Sub-columns under each Linear Ft. value, left→right: **LM** = Light Masonry, **FM** = Frame or Hev. Mas., **1″F** = 1″ Ins. Frame, **2″F** = 2″ Ins. Frame.

SQ.FT. SASH AREA	TYPE	5 LM	5 FM	5 1″F	5 2″F	10 LM	10 FM	10 1″F	10 2″F	15 LM	15 FM	15 1″F	15 2″F	20 LM	20 FM	20 1″F	20 2″F	25 LM	25 FM	25 1″F	25 2″F	30 LM	30 FM	30 1″F	30 2″F	35 LM	35 FM	35 1″F	35 2″F	40 LM	40 FM	40 1″F	40 2″F
0		1.5	.9	.5	.3	3.0	1.7	.9	.6	4.4	2.6	1.4	.9	5.9	3.5	1.8	1.2	7.4	4.3	2.3	1.6	8.9	5.2	2.7	1.9	10.4	6.1	3.2	2.2	11.8	7.0	3.6	2.5
5	Weatherst'pd	1.9	1.4	1.0	.8	3.4	2.2	1.5	1.1	4.9	3.1	1.9	1.1	6.4	4.0	2.4	1.8	7.9	4.8	2.8	2.1	9.3	5.7	3.3	2.4	10.8	6.6	3.7	2.7	12.3	7.4	4.2	3.0
5	Double Hung	2.0	1.4	1.1	.9	3.5	2.3	1.5	1.3	5.0	3.2	2.0	1.3	6.5	4.0	2.4	1.9	7.9	4.8	2.9	2.2	9.4	5.8	3.3	2.5	10.9	6.6	3.8	2.8	12.4	7.5	4.2	3.1
5	Casement	2.1	1.5	1.2	1.0	3.6	2.4	1.6	1.4	5.1	3.3	2.1	1.4	6.6	4.1	2.5	2.0	8.0	5.0	3.0	2.3	9.5	5.9	3.4	2.6	11.0	6.8	3.9	2.9	12.5	7.6	4.3	3.2
10	Weatherst'pd	2.4	1.8	1.6	1.4	3.9	2.7	2.0	1.7	5.4	3.6	2.5	1.7	6.8	4.4	2.9	2.4	8.3	5.3	3.4	2.7	9.8	6.2	3.8	3.0	11.3	7.0	4.3	3.3	12.8	7.9	4.7	3.6
10	Double Hung	2.6	2.0	1.7	1.6	4.0	2.9	2.2	1.9	5.5	3.7	2.6	1.9	7.0	4.6	3.1	2.5	8.5	5.5	3.5	2.8	10.0	6.3	4.0	3.1	11.4	7.2	4.4	3.4	12.9	8.1	4.9	3.8
10	Casement	2.8	2.2	1.9	1.8	4.3	3.1	2.4	2.1	5.7	3.9	2.8	2.1	7.2	4.8	3.3	2.8	8.7	5.7	3.7	3.0	10.2	6.5	4.2	3.3	11.7	7.4	4.6	3.7	13.1	8.3	5.1	4.0
15	Weatherst'pd	2.8	2.3	2.1	2.0	4.3	3.2	2.6	2.3	5.8	4.1	3.0	2.3	7.3	4.9	3.5	2.9	8.8	5.8	3.9	3.2	10.2	6.7	4.4	3.5	11.7	7.5	4.8	3.8	13.2	8.4	5.3	4.1
15	Double Hung	3.1	2.5	2.3	2.2	4.6	3.4	2.8	2.5	6.0	4.3	3.2	2.5	7.5	5.1	3.7	3.1	9.0	6.0	4.1	3.4	10.5	6.9	4.6	3.7	12.0	7.8	5.0	4.1	13.5	8.6	5.5	4.4
15	Casement	3.4	2.9	2.7	2.5	4.9	3.7	3.1	2.8	6.4	4.5	3.6	2.8	7.9	5.5	4.0	3.5	9.3	6.3	4.5	3.8	10.8	7.2	4.9	3.8	12.3	8.1	5.4	4.4	13.8	9.0	5.8	4.7
20	Weatherst'pd	3.3	2.8	2.7	2.5	4.8	3.7	3.1	2.8	6.3	4.5	3.6	2.8	7.7	5.4	4.0	3.5	9.2	6.3	4.4	3.8	10.7	7.1	4.9	4.1	12.2	8.0	5.4	4.4	13.7	8.9	5.8	4.7
20	Double Hung	3.6	3.1	3.0	2.8	5.1	4.0	3.4	3.1	6.6	4.8	3.9	3.1	8.1	5.7	4.3	3.8	9.5	6.6	4.8	4.1	11.0	7.4	5.2	4.4	12.5	8.3	5.7	4.7	14.0	9.2	6.1	5.0
20	Casement	4.1	3.5	3.4	3.3	5.5	4.4	3.8	3.6	7.0	5.3	4.3	3.6	8.5	6.1	4.7	4.2	10.0	7.0	5.2	4.5	11.5	7.9	5.7	4.8	12.9	8.8	6.1	5.1	14.4	9.6	6.6	5.4
25	Weatherst'pd	3.8	3.3	3.2	3.1	5.2	4.2	3.7	3.4	6.7	5.0	4.1	3.4	8.2	5.9	4.6	3.9	9.7	6.8	5.0	4.3	11.6	7.6	5.5	4.6	12.6	8.5	5.9	4.9	14.5	9.7	6.7	5.3
25	Double Hung	4.2	3.7	3.6	3.4	5.6	4.5	4.0	3.7	7.1	5.4	4.5	3.8	8.6	6.3	4.9	4.3	10.1	7.1	5.4	4.7	11.6	8.0	5.8	5.0	13.0	8.9	6.3	5.3	15.1	9.7	7.3	5.6
25	Casement	4.7	4.2	4.1	4.0	6.2	5.1	4.6	4.3	7.7	5.9	5.0	4.3	9.1	6.8	5.4	4.9	10.6	7.7	5.9	5.2	12.1	8.5	6.4	5.6	13.6	9.4	6.8	5.9	15.1	10.3	7.3	6.2
30	Weatherst'pd	4.2	3.8	3.8	3.6	5.7	4.6	4.2	3.9	7.2	5.5	4.8	3.9	8.7	6.4	5.1	4.6	10.1	7.2	5.6	4.9	11.6	8.1	6.0	5.2	13.1	9.0	6.5	5.5	14.6	9.9	6.9	5.8
30	Double Hung	4.7	4.2	4.2	4.0	6.2	5.1	4.7	4.4	7.7	6.0	5.3	4.4	9.1	6.8	5.6	5.0	10.6	7.7	6.0	5.3	12.1	8.6	6.5	5.6	13.6	9.4	6.9	5.9	15.7	10.3	8.0	6.3
30	Casement	5.3	4.9	4.9	4.7	6.8	5.7	5.3	5.0	8.3	6.6	5.8	5.0	9.8	7.5	6.2	5.7	11.3	8.3	6.7	6.0	12.8	9.2	7.1	6.3	14.2	10.1	7.6	6.6	15.7	11.0	8.0	6.9
35	Weatherst'pd	4.7	4.3	4.3	4.2	6.1	5.1	4.8	4.5	7.6	6.0	5.2	4.5	9.1	6.9	5.7	5.1	10.6	7.7	6.1	5.4	12.1	8.6	6.6	5.7	13.5	9.5	7.0	6.0	15.0	10.3	7.5	6.4
35	Double Hung	5.2	4.8	4.8	4.7	6.7	5.6	5.3	5.0	8.2	6.5	5.8	5.0	9.7	7.4	6.2	5.6	11.1	8.2	6.6	5.9	12.6	9.1	7.1	6.3	14.1	10.0	7.5	6.6	15.6	10.9	8.0	6.9
35	Casement	6.0	5.5	5.5	5.5	7.5	6.4	6.1	5.8	9.0	7.3	6.5	5.8	10.4	8.1	6.9	6.3	11.9	9.0	7.4	6.6	13.4	9.9	7.9	6.9	14.9	10.8	8.3	7.3	16.4	11.7	8.8	7.6
40	Weatherst'pd					8.1	7.1	6.8	6.5	8.7	7.1	6.4	6.3	9.6	7.8	6.8	6.3	11.1	8.7	7.2	6.8	12.6	9.6	7.7	7.1	14.0	10.5	8.2	7.2	15.5	11.4	8.6	6.9
40	Double Hung					8.8	7.7	7.5	7.2	9.6	7.9	7.6	7.2	10.2	7.8	7.8	7.1	12.6	9.7	7.9	8.1	14.0	13.0	8.6	7.8	15.5	11.4	9.0	7.5	16.1	12.3	9.5	7.5
40	Casement					9.4	8.4	8.3	8.0	10.2	8.6	8.0	8.0	11.1	8.8	8.8	8.1	12.8	11.4	8.9	8.4	14.0	13.2	9.1	9.0	15.5	14.6	9.9	9.0	17.0	12.3	9.5	8.4
45	Weatherst'pd									9.3	7.6	7.0	6.3	10.0	7.8	7.9	6.9	11.5	8.7	7.9	6.8	13.0	9.6	8.4	7.2	14.5	10.4	8.8	7.8	15.9	11.3	9.2	7.8
45	Double Hung									10.2	8.6	8.0	7.2	10.7	8.5	7.9	7.5	12.2	9.4	7.9	7.8	13.7	10.2	8.6	8.5	15.2	11.1	8.8	7.8	16.7	12.0	10.2	8.1
45	Casement									11.7	9.3	8.8	8.3	11.7	9.5	9.5	8.5	13.2	10.3	9.6	8.8	14.7	11.2	10.2	9.1	16.2	12.1	10.9	9.4	17.6	13.0	11.3	9.1
50	Weatherst'pd									9.0	7.4	6.9	6.1	10.5	8.3	7.8	6.8	11.9	9.0	7.8	6.9	13.4	10.0	8.2	7.4	14.9	10.9	8.7	8.0	16.4	11.8	9.1	8.0
50	Double Hung									9.8	8.2	7.6	6.9	11.3	9.1	8.5	7.6	12.8	9.9	8.5	7.6	14.2	10.8	9.0	8.1	15.7	11.7	9.4	8.5	17.2	12.5	9.9	8.8
50	Casement									10.9	9.3	8.7	8.0	12.4	10.1	9.6	8.3	13.8	11.0	9.6	8.3	15.3	11.9	10.1	9.2	16.8	12.8	10.5	9.2	18.3	13.6	11.0	9.5
6 Ft. High Picture Window Wall		3.5	3.4	3.3	3.3	7.1	6.8	6.6	6.5	10.6	10.2	9.9	9.8	14.2	13.6	13.2	13.0	17.7	17.0	16.4	16.3	21.3	20.4	19.7	19.5	24.8	23.8	23.0	22.8	28.4	27.2	26.3	26.0

293

NOTES

1. Light Masonry .... U = .46
   Frame or Heavy Masonry .... U = .27
   Insulated Frame (1″ Ins.) .... U = .14
   Insulated Frame (2″ Ins.) .... U = .097
2. Based on 8 ft. wall height and 70° temperature difference between inside and out.
3. For partition: joining unheated space, figure ½ linear feet of length.
4. Consider wall adjoining garage as outside wall.
5. Consider wall adjoining attic spaces as ceiling.
6. For basement walls under ground, use 25% of value for heavy masonry wall.
7. Consider outside doors as double hung plain glass.
8. For storm sash or door; or double panel glass, use ½ actual glass area.
9. Table includes 15% for duct heat loss.

EXAMPLE

Room has 33 linear ft. of exposed frame wall and 13 sq. ft. of weatherstripped glass. Find the HEAT LOSS for 70° F. temperature difference.

1. Round glass area and linear ft. of wall off to nearest 5.
   i.e., 13 sq. ft. glass = 15 sq. ft. glass
   i.e., 33 linear ft. wall = 35 linear ft. wall
2. Reading in TABLE 1 opposite 15 sq. ft. weatherstripped glass and below 35 linear ft. of frame wall—
   Heat Loss = 7.5 × 1000 = 7,500 Btu/Hr for 70° F. temperature difference.

TABLE 2
HEAT LOSSES IN 1000 BTU/HOUR THROUGH FLOORS AND CEILINGS

Length or Width of Room			LENGTH OR WIDTH OF ROOM 3	4	5	6	7	8	9	10	11	12	13	14	15	16	17	18	19	20	21	22	23	24	25	26	27	28	29	30
4	Floor	No Insulation	0.3	0.4	0.5	0.6	0.7	0.8	0.9	1.0	1.1	1.2	1.3	1.4	1.5	1.6	1.7	1.8	1.9	2.0	2.1	2.2	2.3	2.4	2.5	2.6	2.7	2.8	2.9	3.0
	Ceiling	No Insulation	0.3	0.4	0.5	0.6	0.7	0.8	0.9	1.0	1.1	1.2	1.3	1.4	1.5	1.6	1.8	1.9	2.0	2.1	2.2	2.3	2.4	2.5	2.6	2.7	2.8	2.9	3.0	3.1
		2" Insulation	0.1	0.2	0.2	0.2	0.3	0.3	0.3	0.4	0.4	0.5	0.5	0.5	0.6	0.6	0.7	0.7	0.7	0.8	0.8	0.9	0.9	0.9	1.0	1.0	1.0	1.1	1.1	1.2
		3⅝" Insulation	0.1	0.1	0.1	0.2	0.2	0.2	0.3	0.3	0.3	0.3	0.4	0.4	0.4	0.5	0.5	0.5	0.6	0.6	0.6	0.6	0.7	0.7	0.7	0.8	0.8	0.8	0.8	0.9
6	Floor	No Insulation	0.4	0.6	0.8	0.9	1.1	1.2	1.4	1.5	1.7	1.8	2.0	2.1	2.3	2.4	2.6	2.7	2.9	3.0	3.2	3.3	3.5	3.6	3.8	3.9	4.1	4.3	4.4	4.6
	Ceiling	No Insulation	0.5	0.6	0.8	0.9	1.1	1.2	1.4	1.5	1.7	1.9	2.0	2.2	2.3	2.5	2.6	2.8	2.9	3.1	3.2	3.4	3.6	3.7	3.9	4.0	4.2	4.3	4.5	4.6
		2" Insulation	0.2	0.2	0.3	0.3	0.4	0.5	0.5	0.6	0.6	0.7	0.8	0.8	0.9	0.9	1.0	1.0	1.1	1.2	1.2	1.3	1.3	1.4	1.4	1.5	1.6	1.6	1.7	1.7
		3⅝" Insulation	0.1	0.2	0.2	0.3	0.3	0.3	0.4	0.4	0.5	0.5	0.6	0.6	0.7	0.7	0.7	0.8	0.8	0.9	0.9	1.0	1.0	1.0	1.1	1.1	1.2	1.2	1.3	1.3
8	Floor	No Insulation	0.6	0.8	1.0	1.2	1.4	1.6	1.8	2.0	2.2	2.4	2.6	2.8	3.0	3.2	3.4	3.6	3.8	4.0	4.3	4.5	4.7	4.9	5.1	5.3	5.5	5.7	5.9	6.1
	Ceiling	No Insulation	0.6	0.8	1.0	1.2	1.4	1.6	1.9	2.1	2.3	2.5	2.7	2.9	3.1	3.3	3.5	3.7	3.9	4.1	4.3	4.5	4.7	5.0	5.2	5.4	5.6	5.8	6.0	6.2
		2" Insulation	0.2	0.3	0.4	0.5	0.5	0.6	0.7	0.8	0.9	0.9	1.0	1.1	1.2	1.2	1.3	1.4	1.5	1.5	1.6	1.7	1.8	1.9	1.9	2.0	2.1	2.2	2.2	2.3
		3⅝" Insulation	0.2	0.2	0.3	0.3	0.4	0.5	0.5	0.6	0.6	0.7	0.8	0.8	0.9	0.9	1.0	1.0	1.1	1.2	1.2	1.3	1.3	1.4	1.5	1.5	1.6	1.6	1.7	1.7
10	Floor	No Insulation	0.8	1.0	1.3	1.5	1.8	2.0	2.3	2.5	2.8	3.0	3.3	3.5	3.8	4.0	4.3	4.6	4.8	5.1	5.3	5.6	5.8	6.1	6.3	6.6	6.8	7.1	7.3	7.6
	Ceiling	No Insulation	0.8	1.0	1.3	1.5	1.8	2.1	2.3	2.6	2.8	3.1	3.3	3.6	3.9	4.1	4.4	4.6	4.9	5.2	5.4	5.7	5.9	6.2	6.4	6.7	7.0	7.2	7.5	7.7
		2" Insulation	0.3	0.4	0.5	0.6	0.7	0.8	0.9	1.0	1.1	1.2	1.3	1.4	1.4	1.5	1.6	1.7	1.8	1.9	2.0	2.1	2.2	2.3	2.4	2.5	2.6	2.7	2.8	2.9
		3⅝" Insulation	0.2	0.3	0.4	0.4	0.5	0.6	0.7	0.7	0.8	0.9	0.9	1.0	1.1	1.2	1.2	1.3	1.4	1.5	1.5	1.6	1.7	1.7	1.8	1.9	2.0	2.0	2.1	2.2
12	Floor	No Insulation	0.9	1.2	1.5	1.8	2.1	2.4	2.7	3.0	3.3	3.6	3.9	4.3	4.6	4.9	5.2	5.5	5.8	6.1	6.4	6.7	7.0	7.3	7.6	7.9	8.2	8.5	8.8	9.1
	Ceiling	No Insulation	0.9	1.2	1.5	1.9	2.2	2.5	2.8	3.0	3.4	3.7	4.0	4.3	4.6	5.0	5.3	5.6	5.9	6.2	6.5	6.8	7.1	7.4	7.7	8.0	8.3	8.7	9.0	9.3
		2" Insulation	0.3	0.5	0.6	0.7	0.8	0.9	1.0	1.2	1.3	1.4	1.5	1.6	1.7	1.9	2.0	2.1	2.2	2.3	2.4	2.6	2.7	2.8	2.9	3.0	3.1	3.2	3.4	3.5
		3⅝" Insulation	0.3	0.3	0.4	0.5	0.6	0.7	0.8	0.9	1.0	1.0	1.1	1.2	1.3	1.4	1.5	1.6	1.7	1.7	1.8	1.9	2.0	2.1	2.2	2.3	2.3	2.4	2.5	2.6
14	Floor	No Insulation	1.1	1.4	1.8	2.1	2.5	2.8	3.2	3.5	3.9	4.3	4.6	5.0	5.3	5.7	6.0	6.4	6.7	7.1	7.4	7.8	8.1	8.5	8.9	9.2	9.6	9.9	10.3	10.6
	Ceiling	No Insulation	1.1	1.4	1.8	2.2	2.5	2.9	3.2	3.6	4.0	4.3	4.7	5.0	5.4	5.8	6.1	6.5	6.9	7.2	7.6	7.9	8.3	8.7	9.0	9.4	9.7	10.1	10.5	10.8
		2" Insulation	0.4	0.5	0.7	0.8	0.9	1.1	1.2	1.4	1.5	1.6	1.8	1.9	2.0	2.2	2.3	2.4	2.6	2.7	2.8	3.0	3.1	3.2	3.4	3.5	3.7	3.8	3.9	4.1
		3⅝" Insulation	0.3	0.4	0.5	0.6	0.7	0.8	0.9	1.0	1.1	1.2	1.3	1.4	1.5	1.6	1.7	1.8	1.9	2.0	2.1	2.2	2.3	2.4	2.5	2.6	2.7	2.8	2.9	3.0
16	Floor	No Insulation	1.2	1.6	2.0	2.4	2.8	3.2	3.6	4.0	4.5	4.9	5.3	5.7	6.1	6.5	6.9	7.3	7.7	8.1	8.5	8.9	9.3	9.7	10.1	10.5	10.9	11.3	11.7	12.1
	Ceiling	No Insulation	1.2	1.6	2.1	2.5	2.9	3.3	3.7	4.1	4.5	5.0	5.4	5.8	6.2	6.6	7.0	7.4	7.8	8.2	8.7	9.1	9.5	9.9	10.3	10.7	11.1	11.5	12.0	12.4
		2" Insulation	0.4	0.6	0.8	0.9	1.1	1.2	1.4	1.5	1.7	1.9	2.0	2.2	2.3	2.5	2.6	2.8	2.9	3.1	3.2	3.4	3.6	3.7	3.9	4.0	4.2	4.3	4.5	4.6
		3⅝" Insulation	0.3	0.5	0.6	0.7	0.8	0.9	1.0	1.2	1.3	1.4	1.5	1.6	1.7	1.9	2.0	2.1	2.2	2.3	2.4	2.6	2.7	2.8	2.9	3.0	3.1	3.2	3.4	3.5
18	Floor	No Insulation	1.4	1.8	2.3	2.7	3.2	3.6	4.1	4.6	5.0	5.5	5.9	6.4	6.8	7.3	7.7	8.2	8.7	9.1	9.6	10.0	10.5	10.9	11.4	11.8	12.3	12.8	13.2	13.7
	Ceiling	No Insulation	1.4	1.9	2.3	2.8	3.2	3.7	4.2	4.6	5.1	5.6	6.0	6.5	7.0	7.4	7.9	8.3	8.8	9.3	9.7	10.2	10.7	11.1	11:6	12.1	12.5	13.0	13.4	13.9
		2" Insulation	0.5	0.7	0.9	1.0	1.2	1.4	1.6	1.7	1.9	2.1	2.3	2.4	2.6	2.8	3.0	3.1	3.3	3.5	3.7	3.8	4.0	4.2	4.3	4.5	4.7	4.9	5.0	5.2
		3⅝" Insulation	0.4	0.5	0.7	0.8	0.9	1.0	1.2	1.3	1.4	1.6	1.7	1.8	2.0	2.1	2.2	2.3	2.5	2.6	2.7	2.9	3.0	3.1	3.3	3.4	3.5	3.7	3.8	3.9
20	Floor	No Insulation	1.5	2.0	2.5	3.0	3.5	4.0	4.6	5.1	5.6	6.1	6.6	7.1	7.6	8.1	8.6	9.1	9.6	10.1	10.6	11.1	11.6	12.1	12.7	13.2	13.7	14.2	14.7	15.2
	Ceiling	No Insulation	1.5	2.1	2.6	3.1	3.6	4.1	4.6	5.2	5.7	6.2	6.7	7.2	7.7	8.2	8.8	9.3	9.8	10.3	10.8	11.3	11.9	12.4	12.9	13.4	13.9	14.4	14.9	15.5
		2" Insulation	0.6	0.8	1.0	1.2	1.4	1.5	1.7	1.9	2.1	2.3	2.5	2.7	2.9	3.1	3.3	3.5	3.7	3.9	4.1	4.3	4.4	4.6	4.8	5.0	5.2	5.4	5.6	5.8
		3⅝" Insulation	0.4	0.6	0.7	0.9	1.0	1.2	1.3	1.5	1.6	1.7	1.9	2.0	2.2	2.3	2.5	2.6	2.8	2.9	3.0	3.2	3.3	3.5	3.6	3.8	3.9	4.1	4.2	4.4
22	Floor	No Insulation	1.7	2.2	2.8	3.3	3.9	4.5	5.0	5.6	6.1	6.7	7.2	7.8	8.3	8.9	9.5	10.0	10.6	11.1	11.7	12.2	12.8	13.4	13.9	14.5	15.0	15.6	16.1	16.7
	Ceiling	No Insulation	1.7	2.3	2.8	3.4	4.0	4.5	5.1	5.7	6.2	6.8	7.4	7.9	8.5	9.1	9.6	10.2	10.8	11.3	11.9	12.5	13.0	13.6	14.2	14.7	15.3	15.9	16.4	17.0
		2" Insulation	0.6	0.9	1.1	1.3	1.5	1.7	1.9	2.1	2.3	2.6	2.8	3.0	3.2	3.4	3.6	3.8	4.0	4.3	4.5	4.7	4.9	5.1	5.3	5.5	5.7	6.0	6.2	6.4
		3⅝" Insulation	0.5	0.6	0.8	1.0	1.1	1.3	1.4	1.6	1.8	1.9	2.1	2.2	2.4	2.6	2.7	2.9	3.0	3.2	3.4	3.5	3.7	3.8	4.0	4.1	4.3	4.5	4.6	4.8
24	Floor	No Insulation	1.8	2.4	3.0	3.6	4.3	4.9	5.5	6.1	6.7	7.3	7.9	8.5	9.1	9.7	10.3	10.9	11.5	12.1	12.8	13.4	14.0	14.6	15.2	15.8	16.4	17.0	17.6	18.2
	Ceiling	No Insulation	1.9	2.5	3.1	3.7	4.3	5.0	5.6	6.2	6.8	7.4	8.0	8.7	9.3	9.9	10.5	11.1	11.7	12.4	13.0	13.6	14.2	14.8	15.5	16.1	16.7	17.3	17.9	18.5
		2" Insulation	0.7	0.9	1.2	1.4	1.6	1.9	2.1	2.3	2.6	2.8	3.0	3.2	3.5	3.7	3.9	4.2	4.4	4.6	4.9	5.1	5.3	5.6	5.8	6.0	6.3	6.5	6.7	7.0
		3⅝" Insulation	0.5	0.7	0.9	1.0	1.2	1.4	1.6	1.7	1.9	2.1	2.3	2.4	2.6	2.8	3.0	3.1	3.3	3.5	3.7	3.8	4.0	4.2	4.4	4.5	4.7	4.9	5.0	5.2
26	Floor	No Insulation	2.0	2.6	3.3	3.9	4.6	5.3	5.9	6.6	7.2	7.9	8.6	9.2	9.9	10.5	11.2	11.8	12.5	13.2	13.8	14.5	15.1	15.8	16.4	17.1	17.8	18.4	19.1	19.7
	Ceiling	No Insulation	2.0	2.7	3.4	4.0	4.7	5.4	6.0	6.7	7.4	8.0	8.7	9.4	10.0	10.7	11.4	12.1	12.7	13.4	14.1	14.7	15.4	16.1	16.7	17.4	18.1	18.8	19.4	20.1
		2" Insulation	0.8	1.0	1.3	1.5	1.8	2.0	2.3	2.5	2.8	3.0	3.3	3.5	3.8	4.0	4.3	4.5	4.8	5.0	5.3	5.5	5.8	6.0	6.3	6.5	6.8	7.0	7.3	7.5
		3⅝" Insulation	0.6	0.8	0.9	1.1	1.3	1.5	1.7	1.9	2.1	2.3	2.5	2.6	2.8	3.0	3.2	3.4	3.6	3.8	4.0	4.1	4.3	4.5	4.7	4.9	5.1	5.3	5.5	5.7
28	Floor	No Insulation	2.1	2.8	3.5	4.3	5.0	5.7	6.4	7.1	7.8	8.5	9.0	9.9	10.6	11.3	12.0	12.8	13.5	14.2	14.9	15.6	16.3	17.0	17.7	18.4	19.1	19.8	20.5	21.3
	Ceiling	No Insulation	2.2	2.9	3.6	4.3	5.0	5.8	6.5	7.2	7.9	8.7	9.4	10.1	10.8	11.5	12.3	13.0	13.7	14.4	15.1	15.9	16.6	17.3	18.0	18.8	19.5	20.2	20.9	21.6
		2" Insulation	0.8	1.1	1.4	1.6	1.9	2.2	2.4	2.7	3.0	3.2	3.5	3.8	4.1	4.3	4.6	4.9	5.1	5.4	5.7	6.0	6.2	6.5	6.8	7.0	7.3	7.6	7.8	8.1
		3⅝" Insulation	0.6	0.8	1.0	1.2	1.4	1.6	1.8	2.0	2.2	2.4	2.6	2.8	3.0	3.2	3.4	3.7	3.9	4.1	4.3	4.5	4.7	4.9	5.1	5.3	5.5	5.7	5.9	6.1
30	Floor	No Insulation	2.3	3.0	3.8	4.6	5.3	6.1	6.8	7.6	8.3	9.1	9.9	10.6	11.4	12.1	12.9	13.7	14.4	15.2	15.9	16.7	17.5	18.2	19.0	19.7	20.5	21.3	22.0	22.8
	Ceiling	No Insulation	2.3	3.1	3.9	4.6	5.4	6.2	7.0	7.7	8.5	9.3	10.0	10.8	11.6	12.4	13.1	13.9	14.7	15.5	16.2	17.0	17.8	18.5	19.3	20.1	20.9	21.6	22.4	23.2
		2" Insulation	0.9	1.2	1.4	1.7	2.0	2.3	2.6	2.9	3.2	3.5	3.8	4.1	4.3	4.6	4.9	5.2	5.5	5.8	6.1	6.4	6.7	7.0	7.2	7.5	7.8	8.1	8.4	8.7
		3⅝" Insulation	0.7	0.9	1.1	1.3	1.5	1.7	2.0	2.2	2.4	2.6	2.8	3.0	3.3	3.5	3.7	3.9	4.1	4.4	4.6	4.8	5.0	5.2	5.4	5.7	5.9	6.1	6.3	6.5

NOTES

1. Floor (No Insulation) .... U = .34
   Ceiling (No Insulation) .... U = .32
   Ceiling (2" Insulation) .... U = .10
   Ceiling (3⅝" Insulation) .... U = .0726
2. Based on 70° F. temperature difference between outside and inside.
3. For slab on grade heat loss is equal to linear ft. wall perimeter x 58 Btu/Hr.
4. No heat loss is to be figured through floor over heated basement or ceiling of first floor of two story house when second floor is heated.
5. For wood floors over unheated spaces that are enclosed, multiply floor loss by 0.46.
6. Table includes 15% for duct heat loss.

EXAMPLE

Room has dimensions of 18 ft. x 27 ft. Ceiling has 2" insulation and floor has no insulation. Find the HEAT LOSS for ceiling and floor for 70° F. temperature difference.
Opposite 18 ft. ceiling with 2" insulation and below 27 ft.
HEAT LOSS = 4.7 x 1000 = 4,700 Btu/Hr. for 70°F. temperature difference.
Opposite 18 ft. floor and below 27 ft.
HEAT LOSS = 12.3 x 1000 = 12,300 Btu/Hr. for 70°F. temperature difference.

TABLE 3

CORRECTION TABLE FOR ADJUSTING CALCULATED HEAT LOSSES TO DESIGN TEMPERATURE DIFFERENCE

TEMPERATURE DIFFERENCE	HEAT LOSSES AT 70° TEMPERATURE DIFFERENCE										
	500	1000	2000	3000	4000	5000	6000	7000	8000	9000	10,000
30	210	430	860	1290	1720	2150	2570	3000	3430	3860	4290
35	250	500	1000	1500	2000	2500	3000	3500	4000	4500	5000
40	290	570	1140	1710	2280	2860	3430	4000	4570	5140	5710
45	320	640	1290	1930	2570	3220	3860	4500	5140	5790	6430
50	360	710	1430	2140	2860	3570	4280	5000	5710	6430	7140
55	390	790	1570	2360	3140	3930	4720	5500	6290	7070	7860
60	430	860	1710	2570	3430	4290	5140	6000	6860	7710	8570
65	460	930	1860	2790	3720	4650	5570	6500	7430	8360	9290
70	500	1000	2000	3000	4000	5000	6000	7000	8000	9000	10,000
75	540	1070	2140	3210	4280	5350	6420	7500	8560	9630	10,700
80	570	1140	2290	3430	4570	5720	6860	8000	9140	10,290	11,430
85	610	1210	2430	3640	4860	6070	7280	8500	9710	10,930	12,140
90	640	1290	2570	3860	5140	6430	7720	9000	10,290	11,570	12,860
95	680	1360	2710	4070	5430	6790	8140	9500	10,860	12,210	13,570
100	720	1430	2860	4290	5720	7150	8570	10,000	11,430	12,860	14,290
105	750	1500	3000	4500	6000	7500	9000	10,500	12,000	13,500	15,000
110	790	1570	3140	4710	6280	7860	9430	11,000	12,570	14,140	15,710

NOTES

1. Round HEAT LOSS off to nearest 500 Btu/Hr, i.e. 27,650 = 27,500 or 27,670 = 28,000 Btu/Hr.

2. *Example:* ROOM HEAT LOSS from Heating Estimate = 27,350 Btu/Hr. DESIGN TEMPERATURE DIFFERENCE from SURVEY is 55.

So
```
10,000 = 7,860
10,000 = 7,860
 7,000 = 5,500
  350 say 500 = 390
              _____
Corrected = 21,610 Btu/Hr
```

TABLE 4

ROOM CFM FOR VARYING BTU/HOUR HEAT LOSSES AND REGISTER TEMPERATURES

BTU/HR. HEAT ‡ LOSS	REGISTER TEMPERATURE °F. *					
	130°	135°	140°	145°	150°	155°
500	7	6	6	5	5	5
1,000	14	12	12	11	10	10
2,000	27	25	23	21	20	19
3,000	41	37	35	32	30	29
4,000	54	50	46	43	40	38
5,000	68	62	58	54	51	48
6,000	81	74	69	64	61	57
7,000	95	87	81	75	71	67
8,000	108	99	92	86	80	76
9,000	122	112	104	96	90	86
10,000	135	124	115	107	101	95

ROOM CFM FOR VARYING BTU/HOUR HEAT LOSSES AND REGISTER TEMPERATURES

1. Round ROOM HEAT LOSS off to nearest 500 Btu/Hr.
   Example: TOTAL ROOM HEAT LOSS = 21,610 Btu/Hr, ROOM TEMPERATURE desired is 70° and 135° REGISTER TEMPERATURE is selected.

```
10,000 Btu/Hr = 124 C.F.M.
10,000        = 124
 1,000        = 12
  610 Say 500 = 6
              ____
So C.F.M. for 21,600 Btu/Hr = 266 C.F.M.
```

* Room temperature 70° F.
‡ 15% duct loss included.
  CFM in table is based on air at standard conditions.

RESIDENTIAL 24-HOUR COOLING LOAD SURVEY

Name _JAMES SMITH RES._

Date_____

Contractor _ALTA CONSTRUCTORS_

Estimator_____

Address _1343 PARNEL_

Salesman_____

City _BAKERSFIELD, CAL._

OUTSIDE DESIGN TEMPERATURE _105_ °F.

DAILY TEMPERATURE RANGE _25_ °F.

HOUSE ☑ NEW   ☐ EXISTING

HOUSE FACES   ☐ N   ☐ NE   ☐ E   ☐ SE   ☑ S   ☐ SW   ☐ W   ☐ NW

UNIT LOCATION: ☑ CLOSET   ☐ BASEMENT   ☐ ATTIC — OTHER_____

TYPE EVAPORATOR COIL: ☑ UP FLOW   ☐ DOWN FLOW   ☐ HORIZONTAL FLOW   ☐ FAN COIL

CONDENSER OR TOWER LOCATION: _NORTH SIDE_

ELECTRICAL VOLTS _240_   PHASE _1 Ø_   CYCLE _60_

FURNACE: TYPE _UP-FLOW_   SIZE_____   MODEL _80-FAU-14-AC_

BLOWER: ☐ DIRECT DRIVE   ☑ BELT DRIVE _____H.P. MOTOR _____SPEED

GAS: ☐ NATURAL;   ☐ L.P.G.   ☐ _____; SERVICE PRESSURE_____" W.C. _1100_ BTU/CU. FT.

UNIT LOCATION: ☐ CLOSET   ☐ BASEMENT   ☐ ATTIC   ☐ _____

ELECTRIC: _120/240_ VOLTS _1 Ø_   PHASE _60_ CYCLES

WALLS: ☑ FRAME
        ☐ HEAVY MASONRY
        ☐ LIGHT MASONRY

Insulated
☑ YES   ☐ 1"   ☐ 2"   4"
☐ NO

Color
☐ DARK   ☐ LIGHT
_40_ INCH ROOF OVERHANG

FLOOR: ☐ WOOD
        ☑ SLAB ON GRADE
        ☐ OVER CRAWL SPACE
        ☐ OVER BASEMENT
        ☐ OPEN
296   ☐ INSULATED

ROOF OR CEILING: ☐ PITCHED
        ☑ FLAT

Insulated
☐ YES   ☐ 1"   ☐ 2"   ☑ 3⅝"
☐ NO

Color
☐ DARK   ☑ LIGHT

WINDOWS: ☑ SLIDING DOOR
          ☐ DOUBLE HUNG
          ☐ CASEMENT
          ☐ DOUBLE GLAZED
          ☐ VENETIAN BLINDS
          ☐ KOOLSHADE
          ☐ AWNINGS
          _40_ INCH ROOF OVERHANG

RESIDENTIAL 24-HOUR COOLING LOAD ESTIMATE

Room	Windows 1,3 Overhang	Exposure	Sq. Ft.	Btu/Hr	Sunlit Walls (U = .097) 1,4 Overhang	Length	Btu/Hr	Shaded Wall (U = .097) 1,4 Length	Btu/Hr	Roof (4" Insul.) 1,3 .0126 Length	Width	Btu/Hr	Floor Area	Btu/Hr	People Cooking	Room Total	C.F.M.	Register	Return
ENTRY	36	S	35	1,200						10	5	210	50		0	1,410	5% 60	10x4	
LIVING	36 / 24	N / S	84 / 49	4,680 / 3,500 → 6,680	24	6	155 → 155	8	120	20	12	1,000	240		1800	9,135	27% (2) 320	16x6	
FAMILY	36	N	42	1,300 → 1,300				18	320 / 320	18	14	1,050	250		1,800	4,150	15% 180	20x6	
KITCHEN	36	S	40	1,350 → 1,350	36	10	240 → 240			18	9	680	160		1,840 / 920	5,030	15% 180	12x6	
HALL										12	3	160	40			160	2% 20	6"ø	
BATH 1	36	S	9	310 → 310	36	6	140 → 140			6	6	160	40			610	4% 40	10x4	
BATH 2	36	N	9	290 → 290				5	85	5	7	180	35			470	4% 40	10x4	
B.R. 1	36 / 24	S	56 / 56	1,850 / 1,850	36 / 24	4 / 12	100 / 320 → 420			16	12	800	190		800	3,070	12% 140	16x6	
B.R. 2	36 / 24	E	56 / 56	1,850 / 1,850	36 / 24	4 / 12	700 / 320 → 120			13	11	650	140			2,920	10% 120	14x6	
B.R. 3	36 / 24	N	56	1,800 → 1,800	24	11	300 → 300	4	70	11	11	550	130			3,650	10% 100	14x6	

CHECK FIGURES

Over-all Size: 25' × 56' = 1,400 Total Sq. Ft.

Sq. Ft. floor area per ton = 560

% Glass area per V Area = _____   Sq. Ft. Glass = _____ %

Sq. Ft. Wall = _____

EQUIPMENT SELECTION

MODEL NO. COND. UNIT: 360-AR-1

MODEL NO. EVAP. COIL: 36-VC-2, 1200 CFM

TOTAL CFM = _____   H.T.H. = 30   = 1,000

MINIMUM C.F.M. = _____   HOUSE VOLUME CU. FT. = 880 / 15

SUMMARY

HOUSE TOTAL HEAT GAIN = 29,615

HOUSE TOTAL HEAT GAIN = ... Btu/Hr

For ducts in Slab, closed crawl space or basement; or in attic with 2" mineral wool insulation, multiply HOUSE TOTAL HEAT GAIN by 0.96

RESIDENTIAL 24-HOUR COOLING LOAD ESTIMATE

INSTRUCTIONS

1. **SURVEY:** Complete survey by checking items and filling blanks pertaining to the house to be estimated.

2. **WINDOWS:** Under "Overhang" column, indicate for each window facing the amount of roof overhang. Under "Exposure", indicate each window facing. Under "Sq. Ft." columns for each room, indicate the sq. ft. of glass area. From Table 1, find the proper Btu/Hr from appropriate roof overhang and window facing. Under Table 1, find the correction factor for YOUR "Outside Design Temperature" and "Daily Temperature Range" and see Table 4 for adjusting "Window Sub-Total" for each room.

3. **WALLS:** Under "Overhang" column, indicate for each wall facing the amount of roof overhang. Under "Length" columns for each room, indicate the linear ft. of exposed wall opposite its overhang. From Table 2, find the proper Btu/Hr from appropriate roof overhang and construction. When all wall Btu/Hr have been found, add each room. Under Table 2, find the correction factor for YOUR "Outside Design Temperature" and "Daily Temperature Range" and see Table 4 for adjusting totals for each room. If exterior walls are *light colored*, apply the 0.75 color correction factor.

4. **ROOF:** Enter room dimensions under "Length & Width" column for each room. Be sure to include closets and hall adjacent to proper rooms. From Table 3, find the proper Btu/Hr from appropriate construction. Under Table 3, find the correction factor for YOUR "Outside Design Temperature" and "Daily Temperature Range" and see Table 4 for adjusting the roof values for each room. If roof color is *white, light* or *white marble chip*, apply the 0.75 color correction factor.

5. **FLOOR:** If floors are over unconditioned space or with underside exposed to outside, enter area of room under "Area" for each room and multiply times appropriate factor found under Table 3 *Floor* Notes to get the Btu/Hr.

6. **PEOPLE:** The Total Heat Gain from people is estimated at 460 Btu/Hr each. The number of people is generally known. For a speculative house where the number of people is unknown, the recommendation is one per bedroom plus one. Include People load with Living Room load.

7. **COOKING:** The average Total Heat Gain from cooking is estimated at 1840 Btu/Hr and is added to the Kitchen Load.

8. **ROOM TOTAL HEAT:** Total the figures in each Room Btu/Hr column. Add these figures horizontally to get the "ROOM TOTAL HEAT GAIN" and enter the results in the column. House Total Heat Gain is sum of room totals. If duct is to be installed in the slab, closed crawl space or basement, or in attic with 2" mineral wool insulation, multiply "HOUSE TOTAL HEAT GAIN" by 0.96. All ducts except those in slab must be insulated with 1" mineral wool with a vapor barrier covering.

9. **EQUIPMENT SELECTION:** Selection is made on the "HOUSE TOTAL HEAT GAIN." Enter the size of the air conditioning unit in the proper spaces. The "TOTAL C.F.M." is obtained by dividing the "HOUSE TOTAL HEAT GAIN" by 30. The "TOTAL C.F.M." should *always* equal or exceed the "MINIMUM C.F.M." which is obtained by dividing the "HOUSE VOLUME CU. FT." by 15, which is equal to 4 air changes per hour.

10. **ROOM C.F.M.:** Divide ROOM TOTAL HEAT by 30 to arrive at ROOM C.F.M. — Space is provided to record the above C.F.M. as well as number and sizes of supply registers and return grilles.

11. See APPLICATION SECTION under LOAD CALCULATION for information, concerning register and grille sizing, and duct-work sizing.

TABLE 1
SOLAR AND TRANSMISSION HEAT GAIN THROUGH WINDOWS OR GLASS DOORS
(GRAND TOTAL HEAT — BTU/HR PER SQ. FT. SASH AREA)

0" OVERHANG

SQ. FT. SASH AREA	1	2	3	4	5	6	7	8	9	10	20	30	40	50	60	70	80	90	100
N	30	50	80	100	130	160	180	210	230	260	520	780	1040	1300	1560	1820	2080	2350	2610
NE - NW	40	90	130	180	220	270	310	360	400	440	890	1330	1780	2220	2670	3110	3560	4000	4450
E - W	60	120	180	240	300	360	420	480	540	600	1200	1790	2390	2990	3590	4190	4780	5380	5980
SE - SW	50	110	160	210	270	320	380	430	480	540	1070	1610	2150	2680	3220	3760	4290	4830	5370
S	40	70	110	140	180	210	250	280	320	350	710	1060	1410	1760	2120	2470	2820	3170	3530

12" OVERHANG

SQ. FT. SASH AREA	1	2	3	4	5	6	7	8	9	10	20	30	40	50	60	70	80	90	100
N	30	50	80	100	130	160	180	210	230	260	520	780	1040	1300	1560	1820	2080	2350	2610
NE - NW	40	90	130	170	210	260	300	340	390	430	860	1290	1720	2150	2580	3000	3430	3870	4290
E - W	60	120	170	230	290	350	410	470	520	580	1170	1750	2330	2910	3500	4080	4660	5240	5830
SE - SW	50	100	150	200	250	300	350	400	460	510	1010	1520	2020	2530	3040	3540	4050	4550	5060
S	30	60	90	120	150	180	210	250	280	310	610	920	1230	1530	1840	2150	2450	2760	3070

24" OVERHANG

SQ. FT. SASH AREA	1	2	3	4	5	6	7	8	9	10	20	30	40	50	60	70	80	90	100
N	20	50	70	100	120	150	170	200	220	250	490	740	980	1230	1470	1720	1960	2210	2450
NE - NW	40	80	120	160	200	240	280	320	360	400	800	1200	1600	2000	2390	2790	3190	3590	3990
E - W	50	110	160	210	270	320	380	430	480	540	1070	1610	2150	2680	3220	3760	4290	4830	5370
SE - SW	40	90	130	170	210	260	300	340	390	430	860	1290	1720	2150	2580	3000	3430	3870	4290
S	30	50	80	100	130	160	180	210	230	260	520	780	1040	1300	1560	1820	2080	2350	2610

36" OVERHANG

SQ. FT. SASH AREA	1	2	3	4	5	6	7	8	9	10	20	30	40	50	60	70	80	90	100
N	20	50	70	100	120	150	170	200	220	250	490	740	980	1230	1470	1720	1960	2210	2450
NE - NW	40	70	120	150	180	220	260	290	330	370	740	1100	1470	1840	2210	2580	2940	3310	3680
E - W	50	100	150	200	250	290	340	390	440	490	980	1470	1960	2450	2940	3430	3920	4420	4910
SE - SW	40	80	110	150	190	230	270	310	340	380	770	1150	1530	1910	2300	2700	3060	3450	3830
S	30	50	80	100	130	160	180	210	230	260	520	780	1040	1300	1560	1820	2080	2350	2610

48" OVERHANG

SQ. FT. SASH AREA	1	2	3	4	5	6	7	8	9	10	20	30	40	50	60	70	80	90	100
N	20	50	70	100	120	150	170	200	220	250	490	740	980	1230	1470	1720	1960	2210	2450
NE - NW	40	70	110	140	180	210	250	280	320	350	710	1060	1410	1760	2120	2470	2820	3170	3530
E - W	40	90	130	180	220	270	310	360	400	440	890	1330	1780	2220	2670	3110	3560	4000	4450
SE - SW	30	70	100	130	170	200	240	270	300	340	670	1010	1350	1690	2020	2360	2700	3030	3370
S	30	50	80	100	130	160	180	210	230	260	520	780	1040	1300	1560	1820	2080	2350	2610

CORRECTION FACTORS

	90°	95°	100°	105°
15° D.R.	.90	1.10	1.30	1.50
20°	.80	1.00	1.20	1.40
25°	.70	.90	1.10	1.30

NOTES

a. Based on drapes, venetian blinds or roll shades full drawn.
b. For omission of above—increase values 17%.
c. For awnings use values under 48" overhang.
d. For double glazing use 0.80 Table values.
e. Overhangs greater than 48", use North values.
f. Roof overhang shading applies to single story house or second floor of two story house.
g. Windows with KOOLSHADE, use North values.
h. Windows shaded all day, by trees or buildings, use North values.
i. Outside solid doors considered as outside walls.

EXAMPLE

46 sq. ft. east glass with 24" roof overhang:
- 40 sq. ft. = 2150
- 6 sq. ft. = 320
- 46 sq. ft. = 2470 Btu/Hr

TABLE 2
HEAT GAIN THROUGH SUNLIT AND SHADED WALLS
(GRAND TOTAL HEAT — BTU/HR PER LINEAR FT. OF EXPOSED PERIMETER)

0" ROOF OVERHANG — SUNLIT WALLS

Linear Ft. Exposed Wall	U	1	2	3	4	5	6	7	8	9	10	20	30	40
Light Masonry	.46	110	210	320	430	540	640	750	860	970	1070	2150	3220	4290
Frame or Heavy Masonry	.27	60	130	190	250	310	380	440	500	570	630	1260	1890	2520
Insulated Frame (1" Ins.)	.14	30	60	100	130	160	190	230	260	290	320	640	970	1290
Insulated Frame (2" Ins.)	.097	20	50	70	90	120	140	160	180	210	230	460	690	920

12" ROOF OVERHANG — SUNLIT WALLS

Linear Ft. Exposed Wall	U	1	2	3	4	5	6	7	8	9	10	20	30	40
Light Masonry	.46	100	190	290	390	480	580	680	770	870	970	1930	2900	3860
Frame or Heavy Masonry	.27	60	110	170	230	280	340	400	450	510	570	1130	1700	2260
Insulated Frame (1" Ins.)	.14	30	60	90	120	150	170	200	230	260	290	580	870	1160
Insulated Frame (2" Ins.)	.097	20	40	60	80	100	120	140	170	190	210	410	620	830

24" ROOF OVERHANG — SUNLIT WALLS

Linear Ft. Exposed Wall	U	1	2	3	4	5	6	7	8	9	10	20	30	40
Light Masonry	.46	90	170	260	350	430	520	610	700	780	870	1740	2610	3480
Frame or Heavy Masonry	.27	50	100	150	200	250	310	360	410	460	510	1020	1530	2040
Insulated Frame (1" Ins.)	.14	30	50	80	100	130	160	180	210	230	260	520	780	1040
Insulated Frame (2" Ins.)	.097	20	40	60	70	90	110	130	150	170	190	370	560	740

36" ROOF OVERHANG — SUNLIT WALLS

Linear Ft. Exposed Wall	U	1	2	3	4	5	6	7	8	9	10	20	30	40
Light Masonry	.46	80	150	230	310	390	460	540	620	700	770	1550	2320	3090
Frame or Heavy Masonry	.27	50	90	140	180	230	270	320	360	410	450	910	1360	1810
Insulated Frame (1" Ins.)	.14	20	50	70	90	120	140	160	190	210	230	460	700	930
Insulated Frame (2" Ins.)	.097	20	30	50	70	80	100	120	130	150	170	330	500	660

48" ROOF OVERHANG — SUNLIT WALLS

Linear Ft. Exposed Wall	U	1	2	3	4	5	6	7	8	9	10	20	30	40
Light Masonry	.46	70	150	220	290	370	440	510	580	660	730	1460	2190	2920
Frame or Heavy Masonry	.27	40	90	130	170	210	260	300	340	380	430	850	1280	1710
Insulated Frame (1" Ins.)	.14	20	40	70	90	110	130	150	180	200	220	440	660	880
Insulated Frame (2" Ins.)	.097	20	30	50	60	80	90	110	120	140	160	310	470	620

NORTH OR SHADED WALLS — ALL OVERHANGS

Linear Ft. Exposed Wall	U	1	2	3	4	5	6	7	8	9	10	20	30	40
Light Masonry	.46	50	110	160	210	270	320	380	430	480	540	1070	1610	2150
Frame or Heavy Masonry	.27	30	60	90	130	160	190	220	250	280	310	630	940	1260
Insulated Frame (1" Ins.)	.14	20	30	50	60	80	100	110	130	140	160	320	480	640
Insulated Frame (2" Ins.)	.097	10	20	30	50	60	70	80	90	100	110	230	350	460

CORRECTION FACTORS

	90°	95°	100°	105°
15° D.R.	.90	1.2	1.5	1.8
20°	.70	1.0	1.3	1.6
25°	.50	.80	1.1	1.4

NOTES

a. Based on 8 ft. wall height.
b. Wall adjoining unconditioning space—use North values.
c. Wall adjoining attic space—use roof values.
d. Roof overhang shading applies to single story house or second floor of two story house.
e. Listed construction are common to most residences. For others, heat gain values are proportional to U factor.
g. For picture window walls, use glass values only.
h. For light walls, use 0.75 times Table values.
i. Overhangs greater than 48", use North or Shade values.

EXAMPLE

36 linear ft. sunlit frame wall with 24" roof overhang:
- 30 ft. = 1530
- 6 ft. = 310
- 36 ft. = 1840 Btu/Hr

TABLE 3
HEAT GAIN THROUGH SUNLIT PITCHED AND FLAT ROOFS (GRAND TOTAL HEAT — BTU/HR PER SQ. FT.)

Width of Ceiling Ft.	Ceiling Insulation	3	4	5	6	7	8	9	10	11	12	13	14	15	16	17	18	19	20	21	22	23	24	25	26	27	28	29	30
4	0"	170	230	290	350	400	460	520	580	630	690	750	810	860	920	980	1040	1090	1150	1210	1270	1320	1380	1440	1500	1560	1610	1670	1730
4	2"	50	70	90	110	130	140	160	180	200	220	230	250	270	290	310	320	340	360	390	400	410	430	450	470	490	500	520	540
4	3⅝"	40	50	60	80	90	100	120	130	140	160	170	180	190	210	220	230	250	260	270	280	300	310	320	340	350	360	370	390
6	0"	260	350	430	520	600	690	780	860	950	1040	1120	1210	1300	1380	1470	1560	1640	1730	1810	1900	1990	2070	2160	2250	2330	2420	2510	2590
6	2"	80	110	140	160	190	220	240	270	300	320	350	380	410	430	460	490	510	540	570	590	620	650	680	700	730	760	780	810
6	3⅝"	60	80	100	120	140	160	170	190	210	230	250	270	290	310	330	350	370	390	410	430	450	460	480	500	520	540	560	580
8	0"	350	460	580	690	810	920	1040	1150	1270	1380	1500	1610	1730	1840	1960	2070	2190	2300	2420	2530	2650	2760	2880	3000	3110	3230	3340	3460
8	2"	110	140	180	220	250	290	320	360	400	430	470	500	540	580	610	650	680	720	760	790	830	860	900	940	970	1010	1040	1080
8	3⅝"	80	100	130	160	180	210	230	260	280	310	340	360	390	410	440	470	490	520	540	570	590	620	650	670	700	720	750	780
10	0"	430	580	720	860	1010	1150	1300	1440	1580	1730	1870	2020	2160	2300	2450	2590	2740	2880	3020	3170	3310	3460	3600	3740	3890	4030	4180	4320
10	2"	140	180	230	270	320	360	410	450	500	540	590	630	680	720	770	810	860	900	950	990	1040	1080	1130	1170	1220	1260	1310	1350
10	3⅝"	100	130	160	190	230	260	290	320	360	390	420	450	480	520	550	580	610	650	680	710	740	780	810	840	870	900	940	970
12	0"	520	690	860	1040	1210	1380	1560	1730	1900	2070	2250	2420	2590	2760	2940	3110	3280	3460	3630	3800	3970	4150	4320	4490	4670	4840	5010	5180
12	2"	160	220	270	320	380	430	490	540	590	650	700	760	810	860	920	970	1030	1080	1130	1190	1240	1300	1350	1400	1460	1510	1570	1620
12	3⅝"	120	160	190	230	270	310	350	390	430	460	500	540	580	620	660	700	740	780	810	850	890	930	970	1010	1050	1090	1120	1160
14	0"	600	810	1010	1210	1410	1610	1810	2020	2220	2420	2620	2820	3020	3230	3430	3630	3830	4030	4230	4440	4640	4840	5040	5240	5440	5640	5850	6050
14	2"	190	250	320	380	450	500	570	630	690	760	820	880	950	1010	1070	1130	1200	1260	1320	1390	1450	1510	1580	1640	1700	1760	1830	1890
14	3⅝"	140	180	230	270	320	360	410	450	500	540	590	630	680	720	770	810	860	900	950	990	1040	1090	1130	1180	1220	1270	1310	1360
16	0"	690	920	1150	1380	1610	1840	2070	2300	2530	2760	3000	3230	3460	3690	3920	4150	4380	4610	4840	5070	5300	5530	5760	5990	6220	6450	6680	6910
16	2"	220	290	360	430	500	580	650	720	790	860	940	1010	1080	1150	1220	1300	1370	1440	1510	1580	1660	1730	1800	1870	1940	2020	2090	2160
16	3⅝"	160	210	260	310	360	410	470	520	570	620	670	720	780	830	880	930	980	1030	1090	1140	1190	1240	1290	1340	1400	1450	1500	1550
18	0"	780	1040	1300	1560	1810	2070	2330	2590	2850	3110	3370	3630	3890	4150	4410	4670	4920	5180	5440	5700	5960	6220	6480	6740	7000	7260	7520	7780
18	2"	240	320	410	490	570	650	730	810	890	970	1050	1130	1220	1300	1380	1460	1540	1620	1700	1780	1860	1940	2030	2110	2190	2270	2350	2430
18	3⅝"	170	230	290	350	410	470	520	580	640	700	760	810	870	930	990	1050	1100	1160	1220	1280	1340	1400	1450	1510	1570	1630	1690	1740
20	0"	860	1150	1440	1730	2020	2300	2590	2880	3170	3460	3740	4030	4320	4610	4900	5180	5470	5760	6050	6340	6620	6910	7200	7490	7780	8060	8350	8640
20	2"	270	360	450	540	630	720	810	900	990	1080	1170	1260	1350	1440	1530	1620	1710	1800	1890	1980	2070	2160	2250	2340	2430	2520	2610	2700
20	3⅝"	190	260	320	390	450	520	580	650	710	780	840	900	970	1030	1100	1160	1230	1290	1360	1420	1490	1550	1620	1680	1740	1810	1870	1940
22	0"	950	1270	1580	1900	2220	2530	2850	3170	3480	3800	4120	4440	4750	5070	5390	5700	6020	6340	6650	6970	7290	7600	7920	8240	8550	8870	9190	9500
22	2"	300	400	500	590	690	790	890	990	1090	1190	1290	1390	1490	1580	1680	1780	1880	1980	2080	2180	2280	2380	2480	2570	2670	2770	2870	2970
22	3⅝"	210	280	360	430	500	570	640	710	780	850	920	990	1070	1140	1210	1280	1350	1420	1490	1560	1630	1710	1780	1850	1920	1990	2060	2130
24	0"	1040	1380	1730	2070	2420	2760	3110	3460	3800	4150	4490	4840	5180	5530	5880	6220	6570	6910	7260	7600	7950	8290	8640	8990	9330	9680	10020	10370
24	2"	320	430	540	650	760	860	970	1080	1190	1300	1400	1510	1620	1730	1840	1940	2050	2160	2270	2380	2480	2590	2700	2810	2920	3020	3130	3240
24	3⅝"	230	310	390	460	540	620	700	780	850	930	1010	1090	1160	1240	1320	1400	1470	1550	1630	1710	1780	1860	1940	2020	2090	2170	2250	2330
26	0"	1120	1500	1870	2250	2620	3000	3370	3740	4120	4490	4870	5240	5620	5990	6360	6740	7110	7490	7860	8240	8610	8990	9360	9730	10110	10480	10860	11230
26	2"	350	470	590	700	820	940	1050	1170	1290	1400	1520	1640	1760	1870	1990	2110	2220	2340	2460	2570	2690	2810	2930	3040	3160	3280	3390	3510
26	3⅝"	250	340	420	500	590	670	760	840	920	1010	1090	1180	1260	1340	1430	1510	1600	1680	1760	1850	1930	2020	2100	2180	2270	2350	2440	2520
28	0"	1210	1610	2020	2420	2820	3230	3630	4030	4440	4840	5240	5640	6050	6450	6850	7260	7660	8060	8470	8870	9270	9680	10080	10480	10890	11290	11690	12100
28	2"	380	500	630	760	880	1010	1130	1260	1390	1510	1640	1760	1890	2020	2140	2270	2390	2520	2650	2770	2900	3020	3150	3280	3400	3530	3650	3780
28	3⅝"	270	360	450	540	630	720	810	900	990	1090	1180	1270	1360	1450	1540	1630	1720	1810	1900	1990	2080	2170	2260	2350	2440	2530	2620	2710
30	0"	1300	1730	2160	2590	3020	3460	3890	4320	4750	5180	5620	6050	6480	6910	7340	7780	8210	8640	9070	9500	9910	10370	10800	11230	11660	12100	12380	12820
30	2"	410	540	680	810	950	1080	1220	1350	1490	1620	1760	1890	2030	2160	2300	2430	2570	2700	2840	2970	3110	3240	3380	3510	3650	3780	3920	4050
30	3⅝"	290	390	480	580	680	780	870	970	1070	1160	1260	1360	1450	1550	1650	1740	1840	1940	2030	2130	2230	2330	2420	2520	2620	2710	2810	2910
		3	4	5	6	7	8	9	10	11	12	13	14	15	16	17	18	19	20	21	22	23	24	25	26	27	28	29	30

Length of Ceiling (Ft.)

0" Insulation U = .32
2" Insulation U = .10
3⅝" Insulation U = .0726

ROOF CORRECTION FACTORS

	90°	95°	100°	105°
15° D.R.	.90	1.1	1.3	1.5
20°	.80	1.0	1.2	1.4
25°	.70	.90	1.1	1.3

NOTES:
a. Use floor area for roof area.
b. No positive ventilation in attic. (With positive attic ventilation and ceiling insulation, use 0.75 Table values.)
c. For white marble chip, white or aluminum color roofs, use 0.75 Table values.
d. Listed construction are common to most residences. For others, heat gain values are proportional to U factor.

EXAMPLE
Room has dimensions of 18 ft. x 27 ft. Ceiling has 2" insulation. Opposite 18 ft. with 2" insulation and below 27 ft. ROOF HEAT GAIN = 2190 BTU/HR.

FLOOR
a. No floor heat gain for floors over cool basements, crawl space or concrete slab on ground.
b. For floor over unconditioned space such as apartment over non-conditioned store, floor heat gain equals 3 Btu/Hr. per sq. ft.
c. For floor with underside exposed to outside air such as car port, floor heat gain equals 6 Btu/Hr. per sq. ft.

TABLE 4

CORRECTION FACTOR TABLE
(BTU/HR BEFORE CORRECTION)

Correction Factor	BTU/HR BEFORE CORRECTION																	
	50	100	200	300	400	500	600	700	800	900	1000	2000	3000	4000	5000	6000	7000	8000
0.50	25	50	100	150	200	250	300	350	400	450	500	1000	1500	2000	2500	3000	3500	4000
0.70	40	70	140	210	280	350	420	490	560	630	700	1400	2100	2800	3500	4200	4900	5600
0.75	40	80	150	230	300	380	450	530	600	680	750	1500	2250	3000	3750	4500	5250	6000
0.80	40	80	160	240	320	400	480	560	640	720	800	1600	2400	3200	4000	4800	5600	6400
0.90	45	90	180	270	360	450	540	630	720	810	900	1800	2700	3600	4500	5400	6300	7200
0.96	50	100	190	290	380	480	580	670	770	860	960	1920	2880	3840	4800	5760	6720	7680
1.10	60	110	220	330	440	550	660	770	880	990	1100	2200	3300	4400	5500	6600	7700	8800
1.17	60	120	230	350	470	590	700	820	940	1050	1170	2340	3510	4680	5850	7020	8190	9360
1.20	60	120	240	360	480	600	720	840	960	1080	1200	2400	3600	4800	6000	7200	8400	9600
1.30	70	130	260	390	520	650	780	910	1040	1170	1300	2600	3900	5200	6500	7800	9100	10,400
1.40	70	140	280	420	560	700	840	980	1120	1260	1400	2800	4200	5600	7000	8400	9800	11,200
1.50	80	150	300	450	600	750	900	1050	1200	1350	1500	3000	4500	6000	7500	9000	10,500	12,000
1.60	80	160	320	480	640	800	960	1120	1280	1440	1600	3200	4800	6400	8000	9600	11,200	12,800
1.80	90	180	360	540	720	900	1080	1260	1440	1620	1800	3600	5400	7200	9000	10,800	12,600	14,400

NOTES

a. This Table has been prepared to eliminate correction factor multiplications.

EXAMPLE

A room has a "Window Sub-Total" heat of 9,640 Btu/Hr. The house is located in an area of 100° "Outside Design Temperature" and 25° "Daily Range Temperature." Under Table 1 we find a correction factor of 1.10. Reading across Table 4 opposite the 1.10 correction factor line we find that the correction for

```
8000 Btu/Hr  =  8,800 Btu/Hr
1000         =  1,100
 600         =    660
  40 (Use 50) =    60
                _____
Corrected figure = 10,620
```

HIGH SIDE WALL REGISTERS FOR RESIDENTIAL

CFM	SINGLE DEFLECTION MULTI-SHUTTER VOLUME DAMPER		DOUBLE DEFLECTION OPPOSED BLADE VOLUME DAMPER	
	Size	Throw-Feet	Size	Throw-Feet
60	10x4	10	8x4	5-10
80	10x6	12	8x4	7-12
100	14x6	14	12x4	7-12
120	14x6	16	12x4	8-14
140	16x6	16	10x6	8-16
160	16x6	18	10x6	10-17
180	20x6	14	14x6	10-17
200	20x6	16	14x6	10-19
220	20x6	18	14x6	11-20
240	20x6	20	20x6	11-19
260	24x6	20	20x6	11-20
280	30x6	18	20x6	12-22
300	30x6	20	20x6	13-23

NOTES:

1. Sizes are based on the recommended velocities for residential applications.
2. The sizes shown for the single deflection, multi-shutter volume damper are minimum sizes.
3. Double-deflection, opposed blade volume damper sizes are on registers set to the maximum (55°) deflections. For a straight flow, select the next smaller size and the throw will be doubled.
4. The throw should equal ¾ of the distance to the wall opposite the register.
5. For further information, reference should be made to the manufacturer's catalogs.

PERIMETER OUTLETS

CFM	LOW SIDE WALL		FLOOR		CONTINUOUS BASEBOARD	
	Size	Spread	Size	Spread	Length	Spread
60	10x6	10 ft.	2¼x10	7 ft.	4 ft.	12 ft.
80	10x6	11 ft.	2¼x12	11 ft.	4 ft.	14 ft.
100	10x6	13 ft.	2¼x14	11 ft.	6 ft.	16.5 ft.
120	12x6	13 ft.	4x10	11 ft.	6 ft.	18 ft.
140	14x6	13 ft.	4x10	13 ft.	8 ft.	19.5 ft.
160	14x6	14 ft.	4x12	13 ft.	10 ft.	22 ft.

NOTE: The "spread" figure represents the horizontal length that will be effectively blanketed with air.

CEILING OUTLETS

CFM	SIZE
100	6"
120	8"
140	8"
160	8"
180	8"
200	10"
220	10"
240	10"

NOTES:

1. Diffusers should be located in the center of the ceiling of each room.
2. In cases where the room is rectangular and the long side is more than one and one-half times the length of the shorter side, two diffusers should be used.

RETURN AIR GRILLES FOR RESIDENTIAL

CFM	SQ. IN. FREE AREA	SIDE WALL RETURN GRILLES	FLOOR GRILLES		
60- 140	40	10x 6	4x14		
140- 170	48	12x 6	4x18	6x10	
170- 190	55	10x 8	4x18	6x12	
190- 235	67	12x 8		6x14	
235- 260	74	18x 6		6x16	8x14
260- 370	106	12x12			8x20
370- 560	162	18x12			8x30
560- 760	218	24x12	10x30	12x24	
760- 870	252	18x18		12x30	
870- 960	276	30x12		12x30	
960-1,170	340	24x18			14x30
1,170-1,470	423	30x18	18x30		
1,470-1,580	455	24x24		20x30	
1,580-1,770	510	36x18			22x30
1,770-1,990	572	30x24	24x30		
1,990-2,400	690	36x24	24x36		
2,400-3,020	870	36x30		30x36	

A-24   Table for sizing registers, outlets, and grilles in an air-distribution system (from Day and Night Manufacturing Company)

MINIMUM SUPPLY AND RETURN DUCT SIZES FOR RESIDENTIAL APPLICATION

CFM	Supply Ducts				Return Ducts			
	Round	Rectangular		Riser	Round	Rectangular		Riser
50	5″	8x 6		10x3¼	6″	8x 6		10x3¼
75	6″	8x 6		10x3¼	7″	8x 6		12x3¼
100	6″	8x 6		10x3¼	8″	8x 6		14x3¼
125	7″	8x 6		12x3¼	8″		8x 8	
150	7″	8x 6		14x3¼	9″		8x 8	
175	8″	8x 6			9″		10x 8	
200	8″		8x 8		10″	8x10	10x 8	
250	9″		8x 8		12″	10x10	12x 8	
300	10″	8x10	10x 8		12″	10x10	14x 8	
350	10″	8x10	10x 8		12″	12x10	16x 8	
400	10″	10x10	12x 8		12″	14x10	16x 8	
500	12″	10x10	14x 8		14″	16x10	20x 8	
600	12″	12x10	14x 8		16″	18x10	24x 8	
700	12″	14x10	16x 8		16″	20x10	26x 8	
800	14″	16x10	20x 8		16″	22x10	30x 8	
900	14″	16x10	22x 8		18″	24x10	32x 8	
1,000	16″	18x10	24x 8		18″	26x10	22x12	
1,200	16″	22x10	28x 8		20″	30x10	24x12	
1,400	18″	26x10	22x12		20″	36x10	28x12	
1,600	18″	28x10	24x12		22″	40x10	32x12	
1,800	20″	32x10	24x12		22″	28x14	36x12	
2,000	20″	34x10	26x12		24″	32x14	38x12	
2,500	22″	40x10	32x12		26″	38x14	46x12	
3,000	24″	32x14	38x12		26″	44x14	38x16	
3,500	24″	36x14	44x12		28″	50x14	42x16	
4,000	26″	40x14	48x12		30″	56x14	48x16	

A-25 Table for sizing supply and return ducts in a residential air-distribution system (from Day and Night Manufacturing Company)

MINIMUM AIR DISTRIBUTION SIZES FOR COMMERCIAL APPLICATION

CFM	Round	Supply or Return Sizes — Rectangular			High Side Wall Registers — Size	High Side Wall Registers — Throw Feet	Ceiling Diffuser Inches	Return Grille
50	5″	8x 6			8x 4	5- 8	6″	10x 6
75	5″	8x 6			8x 4	6-12	6″	10x 6
100	6″	8x 6			8x 4	9-16	6″	10x 6
125	6″	8x 6			10x 6	8-14	6″	10x 6
150	7″	8x 6			10x 6	9-16	6″	10x 6
175	7″	8x 6			10x 6	11-20	8″	10x 6
200	7″	8x 6			10x 6	12-22	8″	10x 6
250	8″	6x10	8x 8	6x12	14x 6	13-23	8″	10x 8
300	9″	6x10	8x 8	6x12	14x 6	15-28	10″	12x 8
350	9″	8x10	8x 8	6x12	14x 6	18-32	10″	18x 6
400	9″	8x10	10x 8	6x12	20x 6	17-30	10″	12x12
500	10″	10x10	12x 8	8x12	20x 6	21-38	12″	12x12
600	12″	10x10	12x 8	8x12	20x 8	22-40	12″	18x12
700	12″	12x10	14x 8	10x12	20x 8	26-45	15″	18x12
800	12″	12x10	16x 8	10x12	30x 8	24-43	15″	24x12
900	14″	14x10	18x 8	12x12	30x 8	27-47	15″	24x12
1,000	14″	14x10	18x 8	12x12	30x 8	30-52	15″	24x12
1,200	14″	16x10	22x 8	14x12				18x18
1,400	16″	18x10	24x 8	16x12				24x18
1,600	16″	20x10	28x 8	18x12				24x18
1,800	16″	24x10	30x 8	20x12				30x18
2,000	18″	26x10	32x 8	20x12				30x18
2,500	18″	30x10	20x14	24x12				30x24
3,000	20″	36x10	24x14	28x12				36x24
3,500	22″	40x10	28x14	32x12				36x30
4,000	24″	26x16	32x14	38x12				36x30

NOTES:

1. Shorter throws indicated for the high sidewall registers refer to 55° deflection settings, while the longer throws indicated are for straight deflection.

2. The figures for high sidewall registers refer to those of the double deflectional type.

A-26   Table for sizing supply and return ducts in a commercial air-distribution system (from Day and Night Manufacturing Company)

AIR CONDITIONING

Brine Return

Brine Supply

Circulating Chilled or
Hot-Water Flow

Circulating Chilled or
Hot-Water Return

Condenser Water Flow

Condenser Water Return

Drain

Humidification Line

Make-Up Water

Refrigerant Discharge

Refrigerant Liquid

Refrigerant Suction

HEATING

Air-Relief Line

Boiler Blow Off

Compressed Air

Condensate or Vacuum
Pump Discharge

Feedwater Pump Discharge

Fuel-Oil Flow

Fuel-Oil Return

Fuel-Oil Tank Vent

High-Pressure Return

High-Pressure Steam

Hot-Water Heating Return

Hot-Water Heating Supply

Low-Pressure Return

Low-Pressure Steam

Make-Up Water

Medium-Pressure Return

Medium-Pressure Steam

PLUMBING

Acid Waste

Cold Water

Compressed Air

Drinking-Water Flow

Drinking-Water Return

Fire Line

Gas

Hot Water

Hot-Water Return

Soil, Waste or Leader
(Above Grade)

Soil, Waste or Leader
(Below Grade)

Vacuum Cleaning

Vent

PNEUMATIC TUBES

Tube Runs

SPRINKLERS

Branch and Head

Drain

Main Supplies

A-27   Plumbing symbols continued on pages 306 to 308

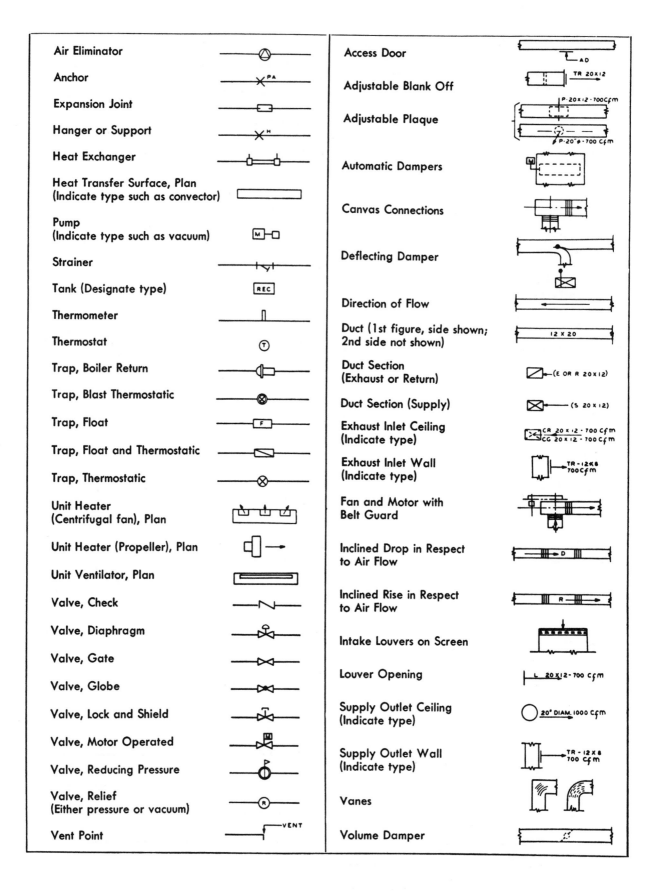

Air Eliminator		Access Door
Anchor		Adjustable Blank Off
Expansion Joint		Adjustable Plaque
Hanger or Support		
Heat Exchanger		Automatic Dampers
Heat Transfer Surface, Plan (Indicate type such as convector)		Canvas Connections
Pump (Indicate type such as vacuum)		Deflecting Damper
Strainer		
Tank (Designate type)		Direction of Flow
Thermometer		Duct (1st figure, side shown; 2nd side not shown)
Thermostat		Duct Section (Exhaust or Return)
Trap, Boiler Return		Duct Section (Supply)
Trap, Blast Thermostatic		Exhaust Inlet Ceiling (Indicate type)
Trap, Float		Exhaust Inlet Wall (Indicate type)
Trap, Float and Thermostatic		Fan and Motor with Belt Guard
Trap, Thermostatic		
Unit Heater (Centrifugal fan), Plan		Inclined Drop in Respect to Air Flow
Unit Heater (Propeller), Plan		Inclined Rise in Respect to Air Flow
Unit Ventilator, Plan		Intake Louvers on Screen
Valve, Check		Louver Opening
Valve, Diaphragm		Supply Outlet Ceiling (Indicate type)
Valve, Gate		
Valve, Globe		Supply Outlet Wall (Indicate type)
Valve, Lock and Shield		
Valve, Motor Operated		Vanes
Valve, Reducing Pressure		
Valve, Relief (Either pressure or vacuum)		Volume Damper
Vent Point		

Capillary Tube	
Compressor	
Compressor, Enclosed, Crank-case, Rotary, Belted	
Compressor, Open Crankcase, Reciprocating, Belted	
Compressor, Open Crankcase, Reciprocating, Direct Drive	
Condenser, Air Cooled, Finned, Forced Air	
Condenser, Air Cooled, Finned, Static	
Condenser, Water Cooled, Concentric Tube in a Tube	
Condenser, Water Cooled, Shell and Coil	
Condenser, Water Cooled, Shell and Tube	
Condensing Unit, Air Cooled	
Condensing Unit, Water Cooled	
Cooling Tower	
Dryer	
Evaporative Condenser	
Evaporator, Circular, Ceiling Type, Finned	
Evaporator, Manifolded, Bare Tube, Gravity Air	
Evaporator, Manifolded, Finned, Forced Air	
Evaporator, Manifolded, Finned, Gravity Air	
Evaporator, Plate Coils, Headered or Manifold	
Filter, Line	
Filter & Strainer, Line	
Finned Type Cooling Unit, Natural Convection	
Forced Convection Cooling Unit	
Gauge	
High Side Float	
Immersion Cooling Unit	
Low Side Float	
Motor-Compressor, Enclosed Crankcase, Reciprocating, Direct Connected	

Motor-Compressor, Enclosed Crankcase, Rotary, Direct Connected	
Motor-Compressor, Sealed Crankcase, Reciprocating	
Motor-Compressor, Sealed Crankcase, Rotary	
Pressurestat	
Pressure Switch	
Pressure Switch With High Pressure Cut-Out	
Receiver, Horizontal	
Receiver, Vertical	
Scale Trap	
Spray Pond	
Thermal Bulb	
Thermostat (Remote bulb)	
Valve, Automatic Expansion	
Valve, Compressor Suction Pressure Limiting, Throt-tling Type (Compressor Side)	
Valve, Constant Pressure, Suction	
Valve, Evaporator Pressure Regulating, Snap Action	
Valve, Evaporator Pressure Regulating, Thermostatic Throttling Type	
Valve, Evaporator Pressure Regulating, Throttling Type (Evaporator side)	
Valve, Hand Expansion	
Valve, Magnetic Stop	
Valve, Snap Action	
Valve, Suction Vapor Regulating	
Valve, Thermo Suction	
Valve, Thermostatic Expansion	
Valve, Water	
Vibration Absorber, Line	

307

HEATING SYMBOLS

Unless otherwise noted, these are A.S.A. Standards (Z 14.2, 1935), as recommended by A.S.H.V.E. . Symbols starred (*) are assembled from other sources. When possibility of misinterpretation exists, incorporate symbols in a key or legend. See also T.S.S. A 1.3.1

PIPING

General

Air - *Pressure Flow*

*Air - *Return*

Gas

Oil

Refrigerant

Steam - *Supply*

Steam - *Return (Condensate)*

Vacuum

Water - *Cold*

Water - *Hot, Flow*

*Water - *Hot, Return*

PIPE FITTINGS

Screwed type shown; for other types & fittings see T.S.S. A 1.3.1

Bushing

Expansion Joint, *Flanged*

*Sleeve

Stop Cock

Trap - *Radiator (Elev.)*

Trap - *Radiator (Plan)*

Union

Valves (*see also "Controls"*)

Check

Float Operated

Gate

Globe

Lock and Shield

Quick Opening

Safety

RADIATION

Indirect Radiator - *Plan*

Indirect Radiator - *Elev.*

Pipe Coil - *Plan*

Pipe Coil - *Elev.*

Tube Radiator - *Plan*

Tube Radiator - *Elev.*

Wall Radiator - *Plan*

Wall Radiator - *Elev.*

AIR DUCTS and FITTINGS

Ducts

Supply - *Section*

*Supply - *Plan*

Exhaust - *Section*

*Exhaust - *Plan*

Dampers

Butterfly - *Plan*

Butterfly - *Elev.*

Deflecting

Vanes

Supply Outlet

Exhaust Inlet

CONTROLS

*Aquastat

*Damper Motor - *General*

*Damper Motor - *Modulating*

*Damper Motor - *2 Position*

*Diaphragm Damper Motor

*Ductstat - *Extended Tube*

*Ductstat - *Rigid Tube*

*Humidistat - *Room Type*

*Relay

*Stop and Waste Cock

*Switch

Thermostat - *Room Type*

Valves

*Air Reducing

Diaphragm

Gate - *Motor Operated*

*Globe - *Motor Operated*

Reducing - *Steam*

*Self-contained Thermostatic

INSULATION SYMBOLS

Symbols shown here have been proposed to the Research Committee on Insulation, A.S.H.V.E., for use on working drawings to assist in calculating heating and cooling loads. In scale details, show type, location and amount of insulation by any clear graphic indication.

Any insulation type not determined

Any fill type batt or loose

Rigid board as sheathing

Rigid board on interior

Any flexible blanket or curtain

Reflective curtain 2 sides or multiple

Reflective metal one side only

To show transmittance "*u*"

$u = .09$

A-28 Fixture unit and trap table (from Uniform Plumbing Code)

Kind of Fixture	Minimum Trap Size	Units
Bathtubs	1½"	2
Bidets	1½"	2
Dental Units or Cuspidors	1½"	1
Drinking Fountains	1¼"	1
Floor Drains	2"	2
Interceptors for grease, oil, solids, etc.	2"	3
Interceptors for sand, auto wash, etc.	3"	6
Laundry tubs or clotheswashers (residential) ...	1½"	2
Laundry tubs or clotheswashers (self-service laundry—2 units each)	1½"	2
Receptors (floor sinks) indirect waste receptors for refrigerators, coffee urn, water station, etc.	1½"	1
Receptors, indirect waste receptors for commercial sinks, dishwashers, airwashers, etc.	2"	3
Showers, single stalls	2"	2
Showers, gang, (one unit per head)	2"	
Sinks, bar, residential (1½ min. waste)	1½"	1
Sinks, bar, commercial (2" min. waste)	1½"	2
Sinks, commercial or industrial, schools, etc. including dishwashers, wash up sinks and wash fountains (2" min. waste)	1½"	3
Sinks, flushing rim, clinic	3"	6
Sinks, and/or dishwashers (residential) (2" min. waste)	1½"	2
Sinks, service	2"	3
Trailer park traps (one for each trailer)	3"	6
Urinals, pedestal	3"	6
Urinals, stall	2"	2
Urinals, wall (2" min. waste)	1½"	2
Urinals, wall trough (2" min. waste)	1½"	3
Wash basins (lavatories) single	1½"	1
Wash basins, in sets	1½"	2
Water closets	3"	6

A-29 Waste and vent sizing table (from Uniform Plumbing Code)

Lists Maximum Unit Loading and Maximum Length of Drainage and Vent Piping

Size of Pipe (Inches)	1¼"	1½"	2"	2½"	3"	4"	5"	6"	8"	10"	12"
Max. Units											
Drainage Piping											
Vertical	0	†2	**16	**32	***48	256	600	1380	3600		
Horizontal	0	1	**8	**14	***27	180	256	600	2200	3900	6912
Max. Length (Feet)											
Drainage Piping											
Vertical	0	65	85	148	212	300	390	510	750		
Horizontal Unlimited											
Vent Piping											
Horizontal and Vertical											
Max. Units	*1	**8	24	48	84	256	600	1380	3600		
Max. Length	*45	60	120	180	212	300	390	510	750		
(See note)											

†Except Sinks and Urinals

*Vertical Only

**Except Six-Unit Traps or Fixtures

***Only two 6-unit traps or fixtures allowed on any horizontal branch or drain and four 6-unit fixtures allowed on any vertical pipe or stack, provided that not more than two 6-unit fixtures are connected to the stack in any one story and that water closets are limited to flush tank type.

NOTE: The diameter of an individual vent shall be not less than one and one quarter (1¼) inches, nor less than one half (½) the diameter of the drain to which it is connected. Not to exceed one third (⅓) of the total permitted length of any vent may be installed in a horizontal position.

A-30   Fixture units for hot and cold water (from Uniform Plumbing Code)

Equivalent Fixture Units

(Includes Combined Hot and Cold Water Demand)

Fixture	Number of Fixture Units Private Use	Public Use
Bar sink	1	2
Bathtub (with or without shower over)	2	4
Dental unit or cuspidor	—	1
Drinking fountain (each head)	—	1
Hose bibb or sill cock (standard type)	3	5
House trailer (each)	6	6
Laundry tub or clotheswasher (each pair of faucets)	2	4
Lavatory	1	2
Lavatory (dental)	1	1
Lawn sprinklers (standard type, each head)	1	1
Shower (each head)	2	4
Sink (bar)	1	2
Sink or dishwasher	2	4
Sink (flushing rim, clinic)	—	10
Sink (washup, each set of faucets)	—	2
Sink (washup, circular spray)	—	4
Urinal (pedestal or similar type)	—	10
Urinal (stall)	—	5
Urinal (wall)	—	5
Urinal (flush tank)	—	3
Water closet (flush tank)	3	5
Water closet (flushometer valve)	6	10

Water supply outlets for items not listed above shall be computed at their maximum demand, but in no case less than:

⅜ inch	1	2
½ inch	2	4
¾ inch	3	6
1 inch	6	10

A-31   Pipe sizes based on hot and cold water (from Uniform Plumbing Code)

FIXTURE UNIT TABLE FOR DETERMINING WATER PIPE AND METER SIZES FOR FLUSH TANK SYSTEMS PRESSURE RANGE—30 to 45 psi

Meter and Street Service	Building Supply & Branches	40	60	80	100	150	200
			Maximum Allowable Length in Feet				
¾″	½″	6	5	4	4	3	2
¾″	¾″	18	16	14	12	9	6
¾″	1″	29	25	23	21	17	15
1″	1″	36	31	27	25	20	17
1″	1¼″	54	47	42	38	32	28
1½″	1¼″	90	68	57	48	38	32
1½″	1½″	151	124	105	91	70	57
2″	1½″	210	162	132	110	80	64
1½″	2″	220	205	190	176	155	138
2″	2″	372	329	292	265	217	185
2″	2½″	445	418	390	370	330	300

A-32   Minimum demands of typical gas appliances (from Uniform Plumbing Code)

MINIMUM DEMAND OF TYPICAL GAS APPLIANCES IN CUBIC FEET PER HOUR (CFH)

(Based on Natural Gas of 1100 B.T.U. per cubic foot)

Appliance	Demand
Domestic Gas Range	75
Domestic Recessed top burner section	50
Domestic Recessed oven section	25
Storage Water Heater—up to 30 gal. tank	30
Storage Water Heater—40 to 50 gal. tank	45
Domestic Clothes Drier	20
Fireplace Log Lighter	25
Barbecue (Residential)	50
Gas Refrigerator	3
Bunsen Burner	3
House Trailers (each)	*
Gas Engines (per horsepower)	10
Steam Boilers (per horsepower)	50

*Branches and mains serving house trailer sites shall be sized using the following values beginning with the most remote outlet on each branch or main:

For the first outlet on any branch or main .... 125 CFH
For the second outlet on any branch or main ...... 100 CFH
For the third outlet on any branch or main .... 75 CFH

After the third outlet, subsequent main line loadings may be computed using a value of fifty (50) cubic feet per outlet.

310

Maximum delivery capacity in cubic feet of gas per hour (CFH) of I.P.S. pipe carrying natural gas of 0.65 specific gravity

LENGTH IN FEET

A-33 Pipe sizes based on gas demand (from Uniform Plumbing Code)

Pipe Size	10'	20'	30'	40'	50'	60'	70'	80'	90'	100'	125'
½	170	118	95	80	71	64	60	55	52	49	44
¾	360	245	198	169	150	135	123	115	108	102	92
1	670	430	370	318	282	255	235	220	205	192	172
1¼	1,320	930	740	640	565	510	470	440	410	390	345
1½	1,990	1,370	1,100	950	830	760	700	650	610	570	510
2	3,880	2,680	2,150	1,840	1,610	1,480	1,350	1,250	1,180	1,100	1,000
2½	6,200	4,120	3,420	2,950	2,600	2,360	2,180	2,000	1,900	1,800	1,600
3	10,900	7,500	6,000	5,150	4,600	4,150	3,820	3,550	3,300	3,120	2,810
3½	16,000	11,000	8,900	7,600	6,750	6,200	5,650	5,250	4,950	4,650	4,150
4	22,500	15,500	12,400	10,600	9,300	8,500	7,900	7,300	6,800	6,400	5,700

Pipe Size	150'	200'	250'	300'	350'	400'	450'	500'	550'	600'
½	40	34	30	27	25	23	22	21	20	19
¾	83	71	63	57	52	48	45	43	41	39
1	158	132	118	108	100	92	86	81	77	74
1¼	315	270	238	215	200	185	172	162	155	150
1½	460	400	350	320	295	275	255	240	230	220
2	910	780	690	625	570	535	500	470	450	430
2½	1,450	1,230	1,100	1,000	920	850	800	760	720	690
3	2,550	2,180	1,930	1,750	1,600	1,500	1,400	1,320	1,250	1,200
3½	3,800	3,200	2,860	2,600	2,400	2,200	2,100	2,000	1,900	1,800
4	5,200	4,400	3,950	3,600	3,250	3,050	2,850	2,700	2,570	2,450

A-34 Location of sewage-disposal system (from Uniform Plumbing Code)

Minimum Horizontal Distance In Clear Required From:	Building Sewer	Septic Tank	Disposal Field	Seepage pit or Cesspool
Buildings or Structures*	2 feet	5 feet	8 feet	8 feet
Property line adjoining private property	Clear	5 feet	5 feet	8 feet
Water supply wells	50 feet	50 feet	50 feet	100 feet
Streams	50 feet	50 feet	50 feet	100 feet
Large trees	—	10 feet	10 feet	10 feet
Seepage pits or cesspools	—	5 feet	5 feet	12 feet
Disposal field	—	5 feet	4 feet**	5 feet
Domestic water line	1 foot	5 feet	5 feet	5 feet
Distribution box	—	—	5 feet	5 feet

NOTE:

When disposal fields and/or seepage pits are installed in sloping ground the minimum horizontal distance between any part of the leaching system and ground surface shall be fifteen (15) feet.

All non-metallic drainage piping shall clear domestic water supply wells by at least fifty (50') feet. This distance may be reduced to not less than twenty-five (25) feet when approved type metallic piping is installed.

Where special hazards are involved the distance required shall be increased, as may be directed by the Health Officer or the Administrative Authority.

All non-metallic drainage piping shall clear domestic water supply wells by at least fifty (50)
*Including porches and steps whether covered or uncovered, breezeways, roofed porte-cocheres, roofed patios, car ports, covered walks, covered doorways and similar structures or appurtenances.
**Two (2) times width of trench for trenches wider than two (2) feet (See also Section 1116).

A-35 Fixture demand for commercial usage (from Uniform Plumbing Code)

TYPE OF BUILDING	DAILY PER CAPITA	BASIC FACTOR
Grammar School	15 gallons	
Grammar School with Cafeteria	20 gallons	35 students per class room
High School with Cafeteria and shower baths	25 gallons	
Factories	20 gallons (without showers)	Each 8-hour shift
	25 gallons (with showers)	Each 8-hour shift
Restaurants	50 gallons	Per seat
Trailer Parks—Community Baths	50 gallons	3 persons per trailer
Trailer Parks—Private Baths or independent trailers	60 gallons	3 persons per trailer
Motels—Baths and Toilets	50 gallons	3 persons per unit
Motels—Bath, Toilet & Kitchen	60 gallons	3 persons per unit
Self-Service Laundry	300 gallons per machine per day	
Drive-in Theaters	5 gallons per car per day	

*NOTE: In order to provide sludge retention capacity, when computing septic tank sizes for occupancies listed in this table, multiply the total daily sewage production by two (2) to obtain the septic tank size.

A-36 Sizes of septic tanks based on fixture demand (from Uniform Plumbing Code)

Single family dwellings—number of bedrooms	Multiple dwelling units or apartments— one bedroom each	Other uses; maximum fixture units served	Minimum septic tank capacity in gallons
1 or 2		15	750
3		20	1000
4	2 units	25	1200
5 or 6	3	33	1500
	4	45	2000
	5	55	2250
	6	60	2500
	7	70	2750
	8	80	3000
	9	90	3250
	10	100	3500

Extra bedroom, 150 gallons each
Extra dwelling units over 10, 250 gallons each
Extra fixture units over 100, 25 gallons per fixture unit

NOTE:
Septic tank sizes in this table include sludge storage capacity and the connection of domestic food waste disposal units without further volume increase.

A-37 Required absorption areas for leaching systems (from Uniform Plumbing Code)

Required absorption area in square feet per one hundred (100) gallons of septic tank liquid capacity for five (5) types of soil.

Type of Soil	Square feet per 100 gallons
(1) Coarse sand or gravel	20
(2) Fine sand	25
(3) Sandy loam or sandy clay	40
(4) Clay with considerable sand or gravel	60
(5) Clay with small amount of sand or gravel	90

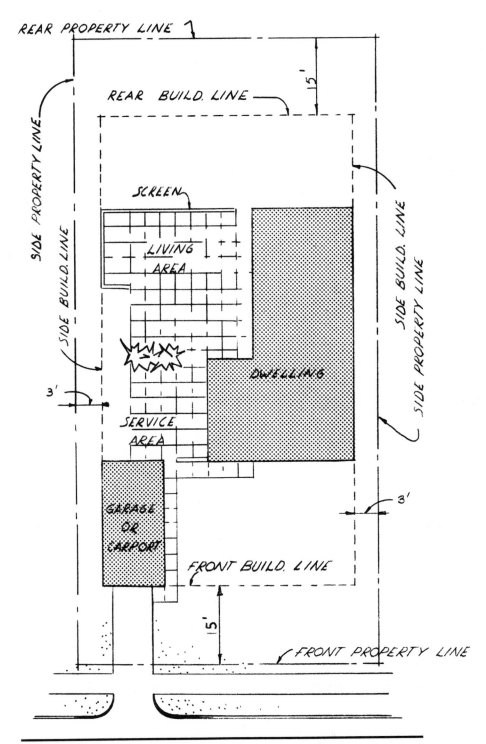

REAR PROPERTY LINE

SIDE PROPERTY LINE

REAR BUILD. LINE

15'

SCREEN

SIDE BUILD. LINE

SIDE BUILD. LINE

SIDE PROPERTY LINE

LIVING AREA

DWELLING

3'

SERVICE AREA

3'

GARAGE OR CARPORT

FRONT BUILD. LINE

5'

FRONT PROPERTY LINE

A-38 Typical residential yard requirements for a rectangular interior lot (from Federal Housing Administration, "Minimum Property Standards")

313

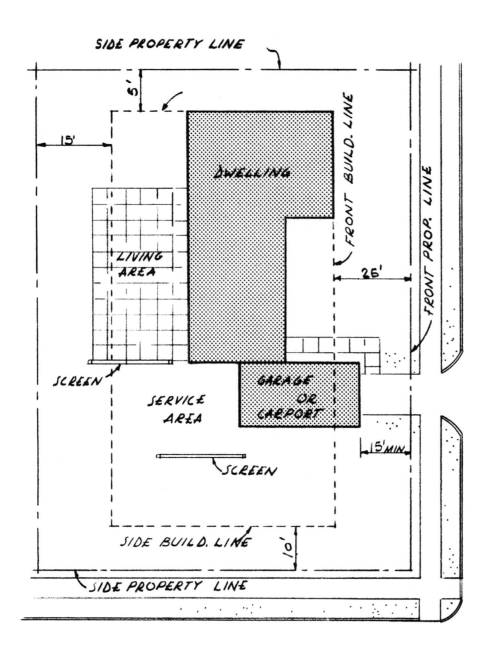

SIDE PROPERTY LINE

5'

15'

DWELLING

FRONT BUILD. LINE

FRONT PROP. LINE

LIVING AREA

25'

SCREEN

SERVICE AREA

GARAGE OR CARPORT

15' MIN

SCREEN

SIDE BUILD. LINE

10'

SIDE PROPERTY LINE

NOTE: ON A CORNER LOT, EITHER YARD FACING STREET MAY BE CONSIDERED *FRONT*. YARD OPPOSITE SELECTED FRONT IS REAR YARD.

A-39 Typical residential yard requirements for a corner lot (from Federal Housing Administration, "Minimum Property Standards")

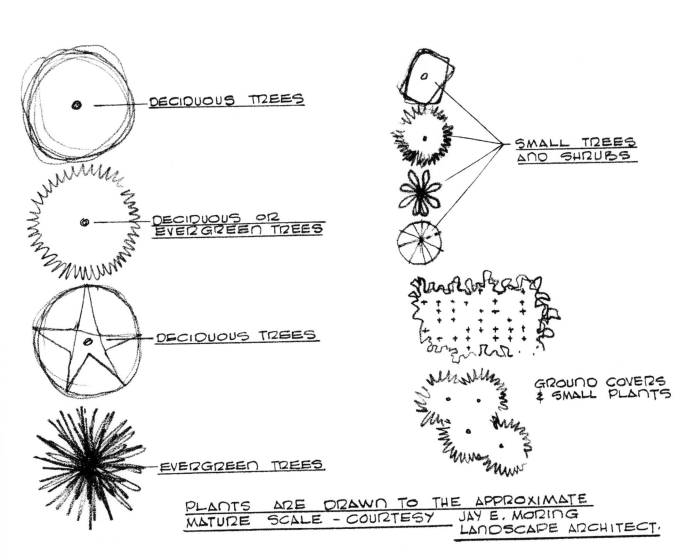

DECIDUOUS TREES

DECIDUOUS OR EVERGREEN TREES

DECIDUOUS TREES

EVERGREEN TREES

SMALL TREES AND SHRUBS

GROUND COVERS & SMALL PLANTS

PLANTS ARE DRAWN TO THE APPROXIMATE MATURE SCALE - COURTESY JAY E. MORING LANDSCAPE ARCHITECT.

A-40   Landscape symbols

315

BIBLIOGRAPHY

BOOKS

AEC Architectural Catalog File, Times Mirror Company, Times Mirror Square, Los Angeles. Published annually.

Architectural Catalog File, Sweet's Division, McGraw-Hill Information Systems Company, New York. Published annually.

Aronin, Jeffrey E.: "Climate and Architecture," Reinhold Publishing Corporation, New York, 1953.

Atkin, W. W., et al.: "Pencil Techniques in Modern Design," Reinhold Publishing Corporation, New York, 1963.

Callender, J. H. (ed.): "Time-Saver Standards: A Handbook of Architectural Design," 4th ed., McGraw-Hill Book Company, New York, 1966.

Capelle, F. W.: "Professional Perspective Drawing for Architects and Engineers," McGraw-Hill Book Company, New York, 1969.

Choate, C.: "Architectural Presentation in Opaque Water Colors," Reinhold Publishing Corporation, New York, 1962.

"Concrete Masonry Design Manual," Concrete Masonry Association, 3250 W. 6th Street, Los Angeles, 1970.

"Concrete Masonry Handbook," Portland Cement Association, 33 W. Grand Avenue, Chicago, 1970.

Cowgill, Clinton H., and Ben John Small: "Architectural Practice," Reinhold Publishing Corporation, New York, 1959.

Croft, Terrell, Clifford C. Carr, and John H. Watt (eds.): "American Electricians' Handbook," 9th ed., McGraw-Hill Book Company, New York, 1970.

Eckbo, Garret: "The Art of Home Landscaping," McGraw-Hill Book Company, New York, 1956.

French, Thomas E., and Charles J. Vierck: "Fundamentals of Engineering Drawing," 2d ed., McGraw-Hill Book Company, New York, 1966.

Halse, Albert O.: "Architectural Rendering," McGraw-Hill Book Company, New York, 1960.

"Handbook of Residential Wiring Design," Industry Committee on Interior Wiring Design, Room 2650, 420 Lexington Avenue, New York.

Harris, Norman C.: "Modern Air Conditioning Practice," McGraw-Hill Book Company, New York, 1959.

Kautzky, Theodore: "Pencil Broadsides," Reinhold Publishing Corporation, New York, 1960.

Kennedy, Robert Woods: "The House and the Art of Its Design," Progressive Architecture Library, Reinhold Publishing Corporation, New York, 1959.

"Manual of Millwork," Woodwork Institute of California, 1833 Broadway, Fresno, Calif., 1962.

McPartland, J. F., and the Editors of *Electrical Construction and Maintenance:* "How to Design Electrical Systems," McGraw-Hill Book Company, New York, 1968.

Merritt, Frederick S. (ed.): "Building Construction Handbook," 2d ed., McGraw-Hill Book Company, New York, 1965.

"National Electric Code," National Fire Protection Association, 60 Batterymarch Street, Boston, 1968.

Newman, M.: "Standard Structural Details for Building Construction," McGraw-Hill Book Company, New York, 1968.

Olgyay, Aladar: "Solar Control and Shading Devices," Princeton University Press, Princeton, N.J., 1957.

Parker, Harry E.: "Simplified Engineering for Architects and Builders," 3d ed., John Wiley & Sons, Inc., New York, 1967.

"Practical Builder Data and Specification Files," Industrial Publications Inc., 55 Wabash Avenue, Chicago, 1955.

Ramsey, Charles G., and Harold R. Sleeper: "Architectural Graphic Standards," 6th ed., John Wiley & Sons, Inc., New York, 1970.

Schroeder, Francis D.: "Anatomy for Interior Designers," Whitney Library of Design, New York, 1951.

Simonds, John O.: "Landscape Architecture," McGraw-Hill Book Company, New York, 1961.

Strock, Clifford: "Heating and Ventilating's Engineering Databook," The Industrial Press, New York, 1948.

Sunset Magazine, "How to Plan and Build Your Fireplace," Lane Magazine & Book Company, Menlo Park, Calif., 1951.

"Uniform Building Code, Vol. I," International Conference of Building Officials, 610 S. Broadway, New York, 1970.

"Uniform Plumbing Code," Western Plumbing Officials Association, P. O. Box 752711, Los Angeles, 1969.

MAGAZINES

Architectural Forum, Time Inc., Rockefeller Center, New York.

Architectural Record, McGraw-Hill, Inc., New York.

Arts and Architecture, 3305 Wilshire Blvd., Los Angeles.

House and Home, McGraw-Hill, Inc., New York.

Progressive Architecture, Reinhold Publishing Corporation, New York.

INDEX